A Guide to Bird Finding in New Jersey

American Goldfinch, New Jersey's State Bird

·A· ·G·U·I·D·E· ·T·O·
Bird Finding
in New Jersey

William J. Boyle, Jr.

RUTGERS UNIVERSITY PRESS

New Brunswick, New Jersey

Fourth paperback printing, 1994

Maps by William J. Boyle, Jr.
Drawings by David A. Sibley

Library of Congress Cataloging-in-Publication Data

Boyle, William J.
  A Guide to bird finding in New Jersey.

  Bibliography: p.
  Includes index.
  1. Bird watching—New Jersey—Guide-books. I. Title.
QL684.N5B68   1986   598'.07'234759   85–26192
ISBN 0–8135–1145–3

To Tom Halliwell, Joe Burgiel,
and the late Bill Lecington,
birding companions of countless hours,
who shared many of the experiences
that led to this book.

Contents

Contents • vii

Maps

Illustrations

Preface

The idea for this book developed from the *New Jersey Field Trip Guide* that I revised and rewrote for the Summit Nature Club in 1978. The original *Field Trip Guide*, published by the club in 1964, was a brief compilation of 22 birding spots around the state. It was assembled by Dick Lindner, the club's field trip chairman, and contained short descriptions of the locales with schematic maps and directions from Summit. In 1971, the *Field Trip Guide* was revised by Harold Crandall, who made some additions and deletions to reflect the changing birding scene.

Because of the success of the *Field Trip Guide*, the 1971 edition was out of print by 1978. I undertook to revise and greatly expand the guide for a third edition (renamed the *New Jersey Field Trip Guide*), which covers 38 birding spots and is now in its fourth printing. The guide, however, provides only a limited amount of information on each birding spot and omits many good birding areas. In fact, the lack of a good bird-finding book covering the entire state of New Jersey led me to think of writing such a book. I discussed the idea with the Executive Board of the Summit Nature Club in early 1983; the board was enthusiastic and agreed to help try to publish it.

When Rutgers University Press asked me in the spring of 1983 if I would be interested in writing a book about bird finding in New Jersey, I had already formulated ideas about the structure of such a book. After the Press had reviewed my proposal and sample entries, the Summit Nature Club agreed that the Press would be a more appropriate vehicle for publishing the book, and graciously relieved me of any obligation to the club.

This book does not aim to be all inclusive. Many good birding areas in New Jersey are not mentioned, but I think you will find that all of the best areas are included. The spots covered are entirely of my own choosing and necessarily reflect my own opinions about what constitutes a good birding spot. Except for a few of the sites mentioned as "Additional Birding Spots," I have birded in all the places covered in the book, visiting most of them many times.

Although the information given about each selection is largely based on my own experience, I have benefited greatly from the comments of my fellow birders who have read and commented on these entries. Most of the entries have been reviewed by one or more local experts more knowledgeable about the given area than I; the book was enormously improved by the generous assistance of these birders, whose names will be found in the Acknowledgments. However, I remain responsible for any errors of commission or omission. As I hope that the book will be sufficiently popular to warrant a revised edition in the future, I would appreciate readers bringing any errors to my attention through the publisher.

Certain matters of style are worth mentioning. I have chosen to capitalize the complete names of all bird and plant species; this is the practice adhered to in *American Birds*, *Birding*, *The Auk*, and most other birding journals. Furthermore, in lists of species with the same last name, as in Chipping, Field, Swamp, and Song Sparrow, I have chosen to capitalize the last name. Although books and journals are about evenly divided on this practice, I find the capitalized name easier to read.

Most of the distances in the directions are given in the form "*about* (so many) miles," because of inevitable differences in odometer readings among cars. Distance figures "from the exit ramp" of limited-access highways are measured from the *end* of the ramp. Wording of highway exit signs is enclosed in parentheses, e.g., "Follow I-287 north to Exit 18B (US 206 North, Bedminster, Netcong)." In most cases, road names and landmarks are given, and the maps should usually help you locate your position.

Acknowledgments

The writing of a book such as this, even for a state as small as New Jersey, involves the accumulation and presentation of much more information than one person can hope to know. During the 12 years that I have birded New Jersey intensively, I have learned much about many different parts of the state. Wherever I go, however, there are usually birders who are more knowledgeable about that particular area. I am fortunate to have been able to draw on the expertise of many fellow birders in writing this book, and I express my deep gratitude to all of them.

My special thanks go to my long-time friend and recent big-day companion Peter Bacinski, who made available all the material he had gathered for a similar, but unrealized, endeavor at writing a bird-finding guide to the state. Peter accumulated much of this information by soliciting accounts from New Jersey birders of their favorite local birding areas; these contributions are acknowledged below. Additional sources of information have been John and Justin Harding's *Birding the Delaware Valley*, James Akers' *All Year Birding in Southern New Jersey*, and numerous "Birdfinder's Guides" published by the New Jersey Audubon Society in *Records of New Jersey Birds*.

I am especially indebted to Tom Halliwell and Rich Kane, who read many of the individual entries and provided numerous helpful comments; and to Paul Buckley, who read the entire manuscript, field tested many of the entries, and made many valuable suggestions. Other birders who examined entries and added their knowledge are Peter Bacinski, Ray Blicharz, Joe Burgiel, Peter Dunne, Jerry Haag, Greg Hanisek, David Harrison, Brian Moscatello, Jim Meritt, Ted Proctor, Rick Radis, Bill Smith, Fred Tetlow, and Wade Wander. The time and effort that each of them put into reviewing these selections is reflected in the thorough and thoughtful comments and suggestions that they provided. This book is much better because of their efforts, and I am sincerely grateful to each of them. Others who provided information, directly or indirectly, are the late

Art Barber, Peggy Bayer, Philip Conroy, John Danzenbaker, Mike Hannisian, Charlie Leck, Len Little, John McNeil, John Moffet, Ken Prytherch, Richard Ryan, Joseph Schmeltz, John Serrao, Cathy Smith, Len Soucy, Tom Southerland, Ken Tischner, Blanche Waddington, Floyd Wolfarth, Carl Woodward, Jr., and Steve Zipko.

Finally, I owe a special debt of gratitude to Gail Boyle, who read the first draft of every selection in the manuscript and provided innumerable suggestions for improving the clarity and consistency of the text.

A Guide to
Bird Finding in
New Jersey

Birding New Jersey

Introduction

New Jersey is one of the smallest states, with only 7,836 square miles, and it has the greatest population density of any state. Nevertheless, the remarkable diversity of its birdlife surpasses that of many much larger states. The wealth of New Jersey's birdlife has recently been surveyed by Charles F. Leck (1984) in his book *The Status and Distribution of New Jersey's Birds*.

Well over 400 species of birds have been recorded in New Jersey (about 420 species are well documented, and there are unsubstantiated reports of numerous others), and an active birder can hope to see more than 300 species in a year. A big-day team in May 1984 broke the previous record by finding 202 species in New Jersey in one day, this record was broken in 1987 with 205 species, and in 1990 the record hit 210. Only seven other states have big-day records of 200 or more species by teams following the rules of the American Birding Association. About 190 species nest in New Jersey in any given year; more than 200 species have nested here at least once.

The enormous variety of New Jersey's birdlife stems from a favorable geographical situation and a wide diversity of habitats. As a coastal state, New Jersey attracts an abundance of ducks, geese, shorebirds, gulls, terns, and other water-associated species. It lies on a major flyway for the migration of many of these birds, and serves as a nesting area or wintering ground for many others. In addition, the nearby offshore waters harbor a wide variety of pelagic birds. New Jersey's location on the mid-Atlantic coast results in an interesting mixture of northern and southern species. Many northern birds seen here are near the southern limit of their normal range in the East, such as Common Eider, King Eider, Harlequin

Duck, Barrow's Goldeneye, Gyrfalcon, Iceland Gull, Glaucous Gull, Thick-billed Murre, Razorbill, Snowy Owl, Boreal Chickadee, Northern Shrike, Lapland Longspur, and Pine Grosbeak. Similarly, many southern species that are numerous or regular in New Jersey are rare or uncommon farther north along the East Coast; for example, Tricolored Heron, Yellow-crowned Night-Heron, White Ibis, Black Vulture, Mississippi Kite, American Avocet, Sandwich Tern, Carolina Chickadee, White-eyed Vireo, Yellow-throated Warbler, Prothonotary Warbler, Kentucky Warbler, Summer Tanager, Blue Grosbeak, Boat-tailed Grackle, and Orchard Oriole.

The meeting of north and south is reflected in the varied habitats to be found in New Jersey, from the salt marshes and hardwood swamps of the Delaware Bayshore to the hemlock glens and dry ridgetops of the Highlands and the Kittatinny Mountains. In between are the vast Pine Barrens of the coastal plain, with its cedar swamps and pine-oak woodlands, as well as the farm fields, lakes, rivers, swamps, and upland deciduous forest of the central and northern parts of the state. At Dividing Creek, Cumberland County, during the breeding season you'll find such typical southern birds as Chuck-will's-widow, Yellow-throated Warbler, Prothonotary Warbler, Kentucky Warbler, Summer Tanager, and Blue Grosbeak. Only 150 miles north in the Pequannock Watershed, the breeding birds include northern species such as Alder Flycatcher, Red-breasted Nuthatch, Winter Wren, Golden-crowned Kinglet, Solitary Vireo, Blackburnian Warbler, and occasionally White-throated Sparrow and Dark-eyed Junco.

Because of New Jersey's large population, its inclusion in two large metropolitan areas (New York City and Philadelphia), and the tourist attractions of its coastal beaches, much of the state has been urbanized, suburbanized, condominiumized, industrialized, or otherwise built upon. Even in the rural areas, the practices of agriculture are not usually beneficial to birdlife. Fortunately for the birder, a significant portion of the state has been preserved in the form of federal public lands; state, county, and local parks; state forests; wildlife management areas; private wildlife preserves; or other protected areas. The state parks and forests system includes almost 250,000 acres, while the Wildlife Management Areas (WMAs) administered by the New Jersey Division of Fish, Game and Wildlife contain another 160,000 acres. Thus, although much additional wildlife habitat is lost to development every year, many places remain for birders to pursue their hobby.

Birding by Season

As a coastal state with a diversity of inland habitats, New Jersey offers something for the birder at any season. The coast, predictably, has the greatest variety of birdlife most of the year, especially in the winter, but there are usually interesting species to be found elsewhere. The following suggestions are not meant to be comprehensive, but only to give ideas for places to visit at the various seasons. The locations mentioned are included in the regional maps, and directions are given in each individual chapter.

Many non-birders think of winter as the time when all the birds have gone south; to the birder in New Jersey, however, winter is a time to look for rarities and uncommon winter visitors. This is the time to visit Barnegat Light in search of Harlequin Duck, eiders, Purple Sandpiper, rare gulls, and possibly a Snowy Owl. The North Shore harbors many grebes, geese, ducks, gulls (including rarer ones like Black-headed, Little, Glaucous, Iceland, and Lesser Black-backed), occasional alcids, and other water-associated species. Brigantine National Wildlife Refuge, too, has numbers of waterfowl plus numerous wintering raptors, including Rough-legged Hawk, Bald Eagle, an occasional Golden Eagle, and (rarely) Gyrfalcon. Cape May offers the greatest variety of birdlife at this season, because of the many wintering landbirds and waterbirds.

In the north, Sandy Hook is a good spot for Red-necked Grebe and winter rarities. Liberty State Park is favored by Short-eared Owl, Snowy Owl, and Common Black-headed Gull, and has attracted both Red-necked and Eared Grebes, as well as many ducks and gulls. The nearby Kearny Marsh and Hackensack Meadowlands are famous for their huge concentrations of gulls, including rarities, that gather around the garbage dumps in winter; raptors are also common.

Winter is the time to check Ringwood State Park, Pequannock Watershed, Wawayanda State Park, High Point State Park, Stokes

State Forest, Worthington State Forest, and Washington Crossing State Park for winter finches or other northern species. Alpha frequently has Short-eared Owl, Snow Bunting, and Lapland Longspur. Princeton and the Stony Brook–Millstone Reserve are worth checking for owls, while nearby Rosedale Park usually has Loggerhead Shrike and Eastern Bluebird. Trenton Marsh is a great spot for wintering Common Snipe. In the southwestern part of the state, Fish House, Flood Gates, and Mannington Marsh are all excellent for wintering waterfowl, while the Delaware Bayshore of Salem and Cumberland counties (see Dividing Creek and Heislerville) has large numbers of wintering raptors.

With the arrival of spring, many of the wintering species depart and early migrants arrive. Late March brings the first Ospreys, Eastern Phoebes, swallows, and Pine Warblers. April is the month when many birders visit Pedricktown and Salem County in search of Black Vulture, Lesser Golden Plover, Ruff, and Upland Sandpiper. March and April are also good for migrant waterfowl at Assunpink WMA, Brigantine, Salem County, Spruce Run State Recreation Area, and many other spots. By the end of April most of the herons and egrets have returned to the coastal marshes, along with terns and early shorebirds. At Cape May, Sandy Hook, Trenton Marsh, and Princeton the songbird migration has begun in earnest, while at Parvin State Park, many of the local specialties such as Prothonotary Warbler and Louisiana Waterthrush are in full song.

May is the month when you want to be everywhere. The songbird and shorebird migrations reach their peak for number of species during the first three weeks of the month. Birders flock to Princeton, Trenton Marsh, Bull's Island, and Waterloo to see warblers and other passerines, then head for the coast at Tuckerton, Brigantine, Stone Harbor, and Cape May to look for shorebirds. By the end of the month, the variety has diminished, but it is the best time to visit the Delaware Bayshore at Reeds Beach, Moores Beach, Thompsons Beach, and East Point to see the spectacle of hundreds of thousands of Sanderlings, Semipalmated Sandpipers, Ruddy Turnstones, and Red Knots feeding on the eggs of horseshoe crabs.

By the beginning of June, the birding pace has slowed. This is the time to visit Parvin State Park, Glassboro Woods, Lebanon State Forest, and Dividing Creek in the southwest, and High Point State

Park, Pequannock Watershed, Wawayanda State Park, and other places in the northwest in search of interesting breeding birds. June is also a good month for Mississippi Kite and other vagrants at Cape May and other coastal points. July is a slow month inland, because birdsong has diminished, but the higher parts of the northwest can provide enjoyable birding and hiking. Only the hardy brave the heat and insects of the Pine Barrens at this season! By midmonth, however, the fall shorebird migration is in full swing along the coast. Although the main shorebird migration lasts into October, the greatest numbers of birds are present in late July.

August brings the beginning of the fall songbird migration. This is a good time to visit Cape May, Sandy Hook, Lincoln Park Gravel Pits, Princeton Avenue Woods, Princeton, and Rancocas for warblers and local specialties such as Yellow-bellied Flycatcher, Olive-sided Flycatcher, and Philadelphia Vireo, especially toward the end of the month. August is the best month to walk down Holgate to see the massing flocks of Willets, American Oystercatchers, and other shorebirds, and to search through the flocks of Common and Royal Terns for Sandwich and Roseate Terns.

September is the peak month for fall migration, and birders tend to concentrate on hot spots for migrants, including Brigantine, Island Beach State Park, and all the places mentioned in the preceding paragraph, especially Cape May. The hawk migration begins in earnest during September, as raptor enthusiasts head for Cape May, Montclair, Raccoon Ridge, and Sunrise Mountain. October brings the greatest variety to the hawk watches, and sees the last migrant songbirds pass through. These include sparrows (some much sought after, such as Lincoln's, Lark, Clay-colored, and the rare Henslow's), as well as Orange-crowned Warbler and other rarities. Along the coast, hundreds of loons, cormorants, and scoters pass by.

November is a good time to visit Island Beach and other spots along the coast for Red-throated Loon, Northern Gannet, Black-legged Kittiwake, and migrant sea ducks. At the hawk watches, the season is winding down, but November is the best month for Golden Eagle, Northern Goshawk, Rough-legged Hawk, and Northern Raven (rare). Waterfowl gather at many coastal and inland locations, while most of the wintering songbirds have arrived. November is also a good month for rarities, so be sure to consult the Rare Bird Alerts (listed in the following section). December is a good time to scout for rarities or late-lingering species, in preparation for the Christmas Bird Counts that occupy most birders during the latter half of the month. With the new year, many birders retreat indoors, but winter can be an exciting season, as I noted at the beginning of this section.

Rare Bird Alerts

New Jersey birders are fortunate in having access to four Rare Bird Alerts, which cover the state and adjacent areas of New York, Pennsylvania, and Delaware. These tape-recorded telephone messages run about five minutes and are changed at least once a week, usually on Wednesday or Thursday; they are often updated when a real rarity is discovered. The oldest of the RBAs is the New York Rare Bird Alert, sponsored by the National Audubon Society and the Linnaean Society of New York; phone (212) 832-6523. With the advent of the other RBAs, this alert now concentrates on Long Island and southern New York State. The Voice of New Jersey Audubon, sponsored by the New Jersey Audubon Society, covers bird sightings for the entire state, and is the most comprehensive for the New Jersey birder; phone (908) 766-2661. The Cape May Birding Hotline is run by the Cape May Bird Observatory, and focuses mainly on Atlantic, Cape May, and Cumberland counties in the southern part of the state; phone (609) 884-CMBO. The Delaware Valley Birding Hotline, sponsored by the Delaware Valley Ornithological Club and the Philadelphia Academy of Natural Sciences, covers southern New Jersey, southeastern Pennsylvania, and most of Delaware; phone (215) 567-BIRD. Although their emphasis is on rarities, all these alerts provide much useful information on commoner breeding and migrant birds as well.

Birding Ethics

In an increasingly crowded and urbanized state, it is important that birders be constantly aware of the need to respect the rights of property owners and of other birders and to avoid jeopardizing the welfare of the birds. Most of the places discussed in this book, such as state parks and forests, national wildlife refuges, etc., are in public ownership. These public areas usually have rules and regulations governing the hours of access and the types of activities allowed; certain sections are frequently off limits. The failure of individual birders to adhere to such rules has occasionally led to restrictions on the activities of all birders. A few of the areas covered are privately owned, with birders allowed access by the courtesy of the owners. When visiting them, be sure to leave things as you find them.

The most important aspect of birding ethics is attention to the welfare of the birds. Many species, especially those considered threatened and endangered, are easily disturbed on their nesting grounds; such disturbance can be harmful to such species' nesting success. Colonially nesting birds such as herons, egrets, gulls, and terns (including the state-endangered Least Tern and Black Skimmer), are especially sensitive to the presence of humans (or their pets) around the colonies. Piping Plover, another endangered species in New Jersey, nests in very loose colonies along certain of the outer beaches. Although it may be difficult to avoid disturbing the plovers as you walk along the beach, don't linger in an area with an obviously agitated adult. Raptors are also especially sensitive to disturbance around the nest, and will occasionally desert. If you know of or discover the nest of a hawk or owl, avoid approaching it closely and be circumspect about revealing its presence to others. Nest locations for rare or endangered species, such as Northern Goshawk, Cooper's Hawk, Northern Harrier, Bald Eagle, and Short-eared Owl should be reported to the Nongame and Endangered Species Project of the New Jersey Division of Fish, Game and Wildlife, but should otherwise be kept secret. Wintering owls also present a problem in birding ethics. Searching for and finding owls in winter can be challenging and fun, provided you use common sense. Don't break twigs or branches trying to obtain a better view; don't shake the tree or otherwise harass the owl and cause it to flush; don't go owling in large groups or make a lot of noise; and don't reveal the bird's location to people you don't know.

Finally, avoid overusing tape recorders. Tape recordings can be invaluable tools in locating and seeing many nocturnal or secretive species, such as rails, owls, and nightjars (Whip-poor-will and Chuck-will's-widow), plus certain wrens, warblers and sparrows. Playing these tapes too long, too loud, or too frequently, however, may intimidate a bird on its nesting territory and cause it to desert. These actions also make it more difficult for other birders to find and locate the bird. Playing a tape recording of a Screech Owl will frequently attract all the small songbirds in the area, eager to scold the intruding owl. Overuse of this technique is also undesirable for the birds and can be very annoying to other birders. Just as effective is to learn to whistle an imitation of the owl; this is more satisfying, in that you are not relying on a mechanical device, and is not as intrusive as the infernal machine. If you can't manage the owl whistle, vocalizations such as squeaking and "pishing" will often serve just as well.

How to Use This Book

The main body of the text describes birding areas in New Jersey. In order to help the reader locate sites within a particular part of the state, I have divided the state into six regions. Generally, major highways were chosen as the boundaries of the different regions, because these roads are easy to find on a map and usually convey a greater sense of location than some vague county line or other division. Map No. 1 shows the six regions and their boundaries. At the beginning of each regional section, you will find a map showing the locations of the various birding areas within that region with respect to some of the main roads; within the regional section, the areas are organized in geographical order, proceeding roughly from north to south. The road boundaries shown on Map No. 1 are not rigid, so you will find several examples of an area that lies just outside a particular regional boundary, but is included with it because such a grouping is more appropriate. Because of the method of organization, each region does not cover a single, homogeneous habitat type; you will find some sites in the Northeast Region very similar to some in the Northwest Region, and some in the Southwest Region resembling others in the Central Region. However, I think you will find that each region as a whole has a distinctive character of its own.

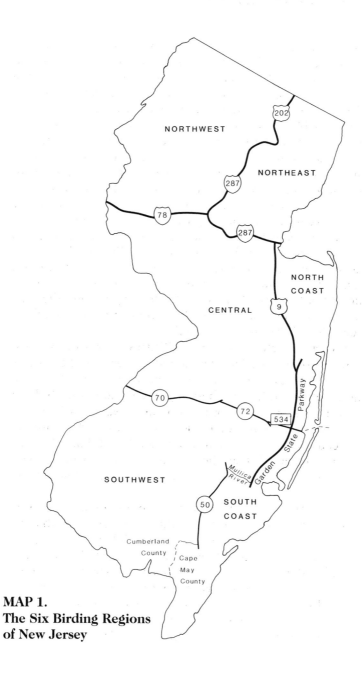

NORTHWEST

NORTHEAST

202

287

NORTH
COAST

78

287

9

CENTRAL

70

72

534

Parkway

State

SOUTHWEST

Garden

Mullica
River

50

SOUTH
COAST

Cumberland
County

Cape
May
County

MAP 1.
The Six Birding Regions
of New Jersey

Each of the 77 detailed entries begins with a description of the birding area and some of its highlights, followed by directions on how to reach the site. Although you should be able to find all the areas in this book using only my directions, it is advisable to keep a good roadmap handy for locating the various highways. The maps of New Jersey available at Exxon gas stations, drawn by General Drafting Corp., are the best that I have seen and are invaluable in finding your way around the state. In addition, good county maps are available for most of the state's counties. Official county maps can be obtained by writing to the Board of Chosen Freeholders at the county seat; there is usually a small fee. Commercially produced maps are available at bookstores and many grocery stores. For more remote areas such as Lebanon State Forest, Pequannock Watershed, and Wharton State Forest, United States Geological Survey (USGS) topographic maps are useful. These can be obtained from certain bookstores; outdoor equipment stores; by writing the Survey at 1200 South Eads St., Arlington, VA 22202; or by writing the New Jersey Department of Environmental Protection, Maps and Publications Office, CN 402, Trenton, NJ 08625.

The main part of each entry, labeled BIRDING, provides suggestions on how to bird a particular area and on some of the species that you might expect to find there. For some areas I have gone into considerable detail, while for others my description is fairly brief and refers you to sections on other, similar, areas for a listing of many of the species that you should look for. Many of the common and widespread species are normally not mentioned, but reference to the annotated checklist at the end of the book will tell you whether a particular bird is to be expected in the area or habitat you are birding.

Following each of the six sections on the birding regions of New Jersey is a brief description of several other birding sites in that region that are worth knowing about, but for which I lacked the space to provide more details. Still other birding areas in the state are known to local birders, but not mentioned in this book. For the most part, they are similar to areas covered, but I'm sure that there are always new and worthwhile areas waiting to be discovered, so don't limit your horizons to the sites I have listed.

After the main body of the text, chapters on pelagic trips and on hawk-watching suggest how and where to pursue these activities. These are followed by a bibliography of books and other publications useful to birders in New Jersey and a list of many of the nature and bird clubs in the state. An annotated checklist of New Jersey's birds that tells you briefly about the abundance and frequency of occurrence of each species, then suggests some places to look for it, is followed by the index. I have tried to make the index as comprehensive and useful as possible: Here you should find every reference to a species of interest or a location that you want to visit.

Some General Precautions

Carry a compass when visiting some of the more remote areas or when hiking the trails of any of the larger parks, forests, refuges, or WMAs. Many of the trails at places like Black River WMA, Scherman-Hoffman Sanctuaries, Higbee Beach (Cape May), and other spots are very wet in the morning after a heavy dew, so rubber boots or other waterproof footgear can make your outing more comfortable.

During the warmer months, insect pests can be a nuisance. Watch out for wood ticks, especially in shrubby, overgrown fields; they are most abundant in May and June, but can be found into the autumn. Any outing into a tick-infested area should be followed by a careful tick inspection. A few wood ticks in New Jersey carry Rocky Mountain spotted fever, but many of the tiny deer ticks carry Lyme disease, so try to remove ticks before they have a chance to burrow into your skin. Insect repellent supposedly helps to deter ticks; although they are a nuisance, they can be coped with and should not be allowed to discourage you from exploring places where they occur.

Mosquitoes are present from spring through fall in the coastal marshes, and from about May to September in inland woodlands. Repellent works for them, except where they are especially abundant; in those places a headnet and long-sleeved clothing can provide some relief. Greenhead flies are exasperating pests at Brigantine NWR and other coastal marshes in July and August, while deer flies are persistent nuisances, especially in deciduous woodlands, during the summer months. A hat is a must when walking in deer-fly country, as they insist on getting into your hair. Unfortunately, insect repellent seems to have little effect on the flies.

Common and Widespread Species

The species in the following lists are so frequently encountered that they are not normally mentioned in the text as occurring at a particular location. Permanent residents can be assumed to be present all year, while nesting or wintering species will be found during the appropriate seasons. Refer to the annotated checklist for more information.

Deciduous woodland

Downy and Hairy Woodpeckers, Northern Flicker, Eastern Wood-Pewee, Great Crested Flycatcher, Blue Jay, American Crow, Black-capped (north) and Carolina (central and southern) Chickadees, Tufted Titmouse, White-breasted Nuthatch, Blue-gray Gnatcatcher, Veery (north), Wood Thrush, American Robin, European Starling, Red-eyed Vireo, Ovenbird, Scarlet Tanager, Common Grackle, Brown-headed Cowbird, and Northern Oriole.

Woodland edge, shrubby fields, suburbs, etc.

Many of the above, plus Mourning Dove, House Wren, Gray Catbird, Northern Mockingbird, Yellow Warbler, Common Yellowthroat, Indigo Bunting, Northern Cardinal, Rufous-sided Towhee, Chipping Sparrow, Song Sparrow, White-throated Sparrow (winter), Dark-eyed Junco (winter), Red-winged Blackbird, House Finch, American Goldfinch, and House Sparrow.

Pine Barrens

Downy and Hairy Woodpeckers, Northern Flicker, Eastern Wood-Pewee, Great Crested Flycatcher, Blue Jay, American Crow, House

Wren, Wood Thrush, American Robin, Gray Catbird, Brown Thrasher, Red-eyed Vireo, Pine Warbler, Prairie Warbler, Ovenbird, Common Yellowthroat, Scarlet Tanager, Rufous-sided Towhee, Song Sparrow, Common Grackle, Brown-headed Cowbird, and Northern Oriole.

Good Birding!

Ruffed Grouse

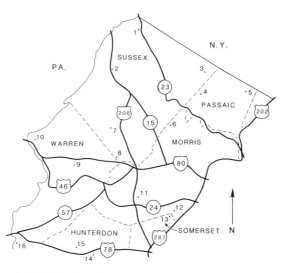

1   High Point State Park
2   Stokes State Forest
3   Wawayanda State Park
4   Pequannock Watershed
5   Ringwood State Park
6   Mahlon Dickerson Reservation
7   Whittingham WMA
8   Waterloo

9   Jenny Jump State Forest
10 Worthington State Forest
11 Black River WMA
12 Jockey Hollow
13 Scherman-Hoffman Sanctuaries
14 Round Valley Recreation Area
15 Spruce Run Recreation Area
16 Alpha

MAP 2. Northwest Region

Northwest

High Point State Park

High Point State Park occupies 13,400 acres of the Kittatinny Mountains in the extreme northwestern corner of the state. Bounded by Stokes State Forest on the south and by New York State on the north, it encompasses the highest elevation in New Jersey. Sitting atop High Point at 1,803 feet is a 220-foot tall obelisk that dominates the landscape for miles around.

Most of the land in the state park was given in 1923 to the people of New Jersey by Col. Anthony Kuser, for whose ancestor the large Natural Area in the northern part of the park is named. This beautiful section of Sussex County contains several lakes, a few streams, numerous beaver swamps, two large bogs, and many hundreds of acres of ridges and valleys. The habitat and the birdlife are very similar to those in neighboring Stokes State Forest, so refer to that chapter for a list of the typical resident birds. High Point has some special places of its own, however, and these are covered in detail below. Noteworthy among the harder-to-find breeding birds are Hermit Thrush, Solitary Vireo, Nashville and Blackburnian Warblers, and, occasionally, Dark-eyed Junco.

At the headquarters a Visitor Center features displays on the history and geology of the state park; there are also rest rooms. Ask for a copy of the park map, which shows the various trails and tells how they are marked. There is also a nature center in the northern part of the park, where the Raccoon Ridge Bird Observatory operates a hawk watch in the fall. This hawk watch is accessible to the handicapped (see Hawk Watching).

Directions

The headquarters and information office at High Point State Park is on Rt. 23 at the crest of the Kittatinny Ridge. To reach this point:

From northeastern New Jersey, take Interstate 80 west to Rt. 23

MAP 3. High Point State Park

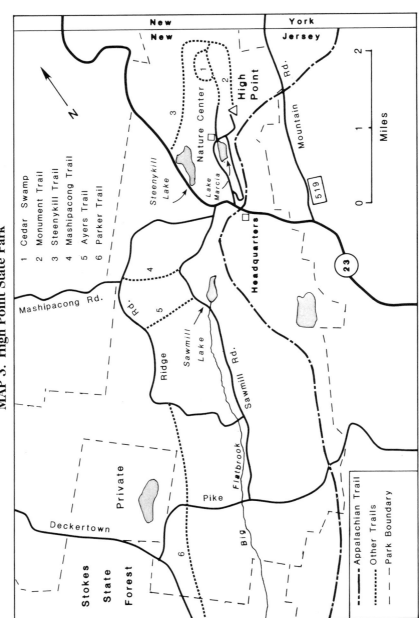

New New York Jersey

1 Cedar Swamp
2 Monument Trail
3 Steenykill Trail
4 Mashipacong Trail
5 Ayers Trail
6 Parker Trail

High Point

Nature Center

Mountain Rd.

Steenykill Lake

Lake Marcia

519

Headquarters

Mashipacong Rd.

23

Ridge Rd.

Sawmill Lake

Sawmill Rd.

Private

Flatbrook

Pike

Big

Deckertown

Stokes State Forest

Miles
2   1   0

N

— · — Appalachian Trail
· · · · · Other Trails
— — — Park Boundary

in Wayne, then follow Rt. 23 north for about 42 miles to the head-quarters, which is on the left.

From southern New Jersey, take the Garden State Parkway north to Exit 153 (Route 3, Clifton). Take Rt. 3 west for 1.5 miles until it merges with US 46, then follow Rt. 46 west for 4 miles to Rt. 23. Go north on Rt. 23 for about 42 miles to the headquarters.

From central New Jersey, the fastest of several routes is to take US 206, I-287, and Rt. 511 to the junction with Rt. 23 in Butler, from where it is about 32 miles to the headquarters. Or take US 206 north through Newton to Rts. 15 and 565. Continue straight ahead on Rt. 565 for 8 miles to Rt. 639, then straight on Rt. 639 for one mile to Rt. 23 in Sussex. The headquarters is about 8 miles north on Rt. 23.

Birding

This chapter will cover only a few of the birding spots, but you should explore some of the other trails if you have time.

Monument Trail

Across Rt. 23 from the headquarters is the entrance road to the northern part of High Point State Park. A fee is charged to enter this area in summer (unless you get there before 8 A.M.), but it is free at other seasons. Take this road for about 0.8 miles, past Lake Marcia on the right and the Lodge on the left. Just beyond the Lodge is a sign for the Nature Center on the left; the drive to the Center is about 200 yards. Another 0.2 miles along the main road you will come to a fork, at which the left fork leads to the cedar swamp (Kuser Natural Area). Follow the right fork for about 0.5 miles to the parking lot at High Point Monument.

During the summer you can climb to the top of the monument, but the view from the parking lot is nearly as impressive. To the west beyond the Delaware River are the Pocono Mountains of Pennsylvania, to the north are the Shawangunk and Catskill Mountains of New York, and to the east lie the hills and valleys of the Highlands of New Jersey. Southwest along the Kittatinny Ridge the Delaware Water Gap is visible almost 40 miles away, while Sunrise Mountain, a favorite hawkwatching spot, is about 10 miles distant.

Monument Trail leads northeast along the ridge for about a mile to the New York State line; it starts at the far (northeast) end of the parking lot. The vegetation along the trail, dominated by Chestnut Oak, is typical of the dry ridgetops of the Kittatinnies. Birdlife is not abundant, but Hermit Thrush, Nashville Warbler, and (occasionally) Dark-eyed Junco have been found nesting here. The trail eventually reaches a gravel road that leads left to the cedar swamp. You can continue your hike to the swamp, which is covered in the next section, or retrace your steps to the parking lot.

Cedar Swamp

This, the centerpiece of the John Dryden Kuser Natural Area, is a legacy of the last ice age. It is a bog that has become densely overgrown with Atlantic White-Cedar and rhododendron, interspersed with Eastern Hemlock and Black Spruce. You might expect to encounter such a spot much further north, in the Adirondacks or the backwoods of Maine.

To reach the cedar swamp from the monument, drive back down the road about 0.5 miles, bear right at the fork, and continue about 0.3 miles to the Kuser Natural Area parking lot. The trail to the swamp is a continuation of the road, which is closed to traffic by a gate. After about 0.4 miles you will come to a fork. Go either way, since the trail makes a loop a little over one mile in length. A side trail from this loop goes north along the edge of the swamp and connects with the Monument Trail.

Northern Waterthrush is a common breeder in the cedar swamp, and several pairs of Nashville Warblers have nested here in recent years. Compare this dense boggy habitat with the dry second-growth deciduous woods along the Monument Trail where Nashville Warbler also nests; this dual habitat preference is typical of Nashville Warbler. Black-throated Green, Blackburnian, and Canada Warblers also nest in the cedar swamp. In winter, you may find Pine Siskin and Common Redpoll.

Sawmill Road

Drive back to the entrance at Rt. 23 and turn right. Go one-third of a mile and turn left onto Sawmill Rd. After 200 yards bear left at a fork and continue through a stretch of scrubby deciduous woods, where you may encounter Golden-winged Warbler. The road then enters a more mature deciduous woods and passes Sawmill Lake and its campground. The tall trees around the Sawmill Lake dam are good for Cerulean Warbler in summer. About 2.5 miles from Rt. 23, just before the road crosses a small bridge, park your car on the shoulder. There is a large beaver swamp on the right. Cross the road and walk east a few hundred yards through a dark hemlock glen to a boggy area. Breeding birds of this glen and bog include Acadian Flycatcher; Solitary Vireo; Black-throated Green, Blackburnian, and Canada Warblers; and Northern and Louisiana Waterthrushes. On the east side of the bog you can follow a stream uphill (a climb of 400 feet) to the top of the ridge, where you will intersect the Appalachian Trail. Hermit Thrush and Worm-eating Warbler are two of the nesting birds here.

After returning to your car, continue across the bridge along Sawmill Rd. After 0.8 miles Ridge Rd. comes in on the right; in another 1.1 miles Sawmill Rd. ends at the Deckertown Pike. There are two beaver swamps along this section of the road, one before and one after Ridge Rd. Here you might find migrant Olive-sided Flycatcher and nesting Wood Duck, Eastern Kingbird, Tree Swallow, Brown Creeper, and Eastern Bluebird. You might even be lucky enough to see a Barred Owl roosting in a tree alongside the road.

Turn right onto the Deckertown Pike and park on the shoulder. The large marsh here has been one of the most reliable places in New Jersey for nesting Alder Flycatcher during the past 10 years. Before beavers flooded the area, Alder and Willow Flycatchers were here every year; with the higher water levels Alder has become less dependable. Willow Flycatcher is always here, however, along with Eastern Kingbird, Yellow Warbler, Common Yellowthroat, and Swamp Sparrow. Orchard Oriole has nested nearby, and Golden-winged Warbler usually nests in the scrubby growth on the south side of the road or to the north of the marsh. Check out every Blue-winged or Golden-winged Warbler song to see if you can find a Brewster's or Lawrence's hybrid, both of which have been seen here.

Ridge Road

At this point, you can continue on into Stokes State Forest or turn around and explore more of High Point State Park. To reach Stokes, continue west on the Deckertown Pike for 1.8 miles, then left on

Crigger Rd. The junction with Grau Rd. is 1 mile ahead, and Steam Mill Campground another 0.4 miles beyond that. To explore Ridge Rd., turn around on Deckertown Pike and left back onto Sawmill Rd. Go 1.1 miles to the junction with Ridge Rd. and turn left.

Ridge Rd. makes a five-mile loop through a variety of habitats before returning to Sawmill Rd., just 200 yards south of Rt. 23. There are several trail junctions along Ridge Rd. and one paved road, Mashipacong Rd., joins Ridge Rd. on the left after about 3.5 miles. Just before Mashipacong Rd. is a large swampy area on the right. Within this is a bog with an impenetrable understory of shrubs, trees such as Tamarack and Black Spruce, and many other plants typical of more northerly climes.

Continue along Ridge Rd. until it rejoins Sawmill Rd., then turn left and go 0.1 miles to Rt. 23. A left turn will take you by Steenykill Lake, out of the park, and down into the Delaware Valley at Port Jervis, New York. A right turn will head you back toward the rest of New Jersey.

Stokes State Forest

This beautiful section of the Kittatinny Mountains covers more than 15,000 acres of Sussex County in the northwest corner of the state. The forest ridges, valleys, streams, and ravines harbor a wide variety of resident and migrant birds. Elevation varies from about 460 feet just below Tillman Ravine to 1,653 feet on Sunrise Mountain. Stokes offers something for the birder at every season. In spring, it is an excellent place for migrants, while in summer you can find a diverse array of breeding birds, including some species that, in New Jersey, nest only in the extreme northwestern part of the state. Late summer and fall bring migrant songbirds heading south, but it is mainly the hawk migration at Sunrise Mountain that draws birders at this season (see section on Hawk-Watching). Late fall and winter are quiet at Stokes, but this is the time to search for winter finches in the birches and the hemlocks; it is also a good season to look for the elusive, but rapidly increasing, Wild Turkey.

During spring migration you can expect to find here almost all the passerines that move through or nest in New Jersey. Some of the more interesting breeding birds are Cooper's Hawk and Northern Goshawk (both rare); Red-shouldered Hawk; Ruffed Grouse; Wild Turkey; Barred Owl; Red-headed (uncommon) and Pileated Woodpeckers; Acadian Flycatcher; Brown Creeper; Golden-crowned Kinglet (rare); Eastern Bluebird; Hermit Thrush; Solitary Vireo; Golden-winged, Nashville (uncommon), Black-throated Blue, Black-throated Green, Blackburnian, Cerulean, Worm-eating, Hooded, and Canada Warblers; Northern and Louisiana Waterthrushes; Dark-eyed Junco (rare); and Purple Finch (uncommon). Rarities that have been found in Stokes Forest include Gyrfalcon, Band-tailed Pigeon, Black-backed Woodpecker, Common Raven, Boreal Chickadee, Townsend's Solitaire, and Varied Thrush.

MAP 4. Stokes State Forest

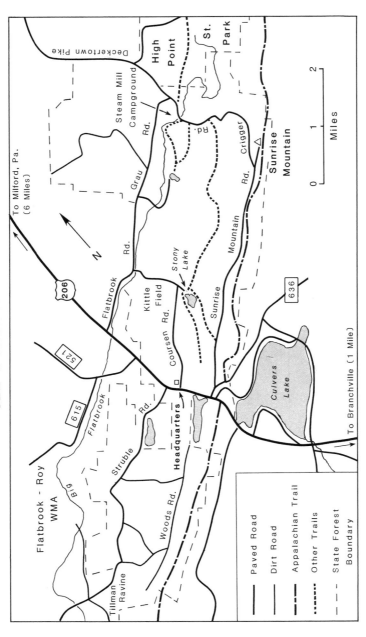

Directions

From Exit 34 on Interstate 80 (Rt. 15 North), follow Rt. 15 for 18 miles to its end at US 206. Continue straight ahead on Rt. 206 for about 7 miles to the Kittatinny Ridge through Culvers Gap, just past Culvers Lake on the right; the Appalachian Trail crosses the road just beyond the crest of the hill. Drive past the turnoff to Sunrise Mountain on the right, then past the turnoff to Kittatinny Lake on the left, until you come to Coursen Rd. and the headquarters building on the right (0.6 miles beyond the Sunrise Mountain turnoff). Stop at the headquarters to obtain a map of the forest.

From Hunterdon, Warren, or Somerset counties take US 206 north through Newton to the junction with Rt. 15, and proceed as described above.

Birding

There are many good birding areas within Stokes State Forest. The following list includes only a few of the better spots; additional exploration on your own might turn up equally good ones. A Sussex County map is useful for exploring the many back roads.

Kittle Field and Stony Lake

From the headquarters, continue north on Coursen Rd. From April through July, pause at a bridge a couple of hundred yards past the headquarters to listen for Louisiana Waterthrush. The birding is good along the road, which passes through mixed deciduous woods and Eastern Hemlock stands. After about 2 miles, you will come to a junction with Kittle Rd. on the left and the road to Stony Lake on the right. Turn left and immediately park on the left. The area around Kittle Field attracts migrants in the spring, and Blue-gray Gnatcatchers are always here. The hemlock grove around the nearby picnic area has nesting Acadian Flycatcher and Black-throated Green Warbler. Several good hiking trails begin at Stony Lake. The road to the lake is frequently closed and there is a fee for parking in summer, but you can leave your car at Kittle Field and walk the one-quarter mile to the lake. Lackner Trail runs south along the west side of the lake, while Swenson Trail begins at the large parking lot at the end of the road into Stony Lake. Coursen Trail branches off on the right from Swenson Trail after about 100 yards. Pine Warbler nests in the spruce and pine groves a little further along Swenson Trail. Coursen Trail is especially good, as it runs south through mature deciduous woods, beaver swamp, and hemlock groves, and connects with Sunrise Mountain Rd. after about 1.2 miles (you can also park on Sunrise Mountain Rd. and hike the trail from the other direction). Red-headed Woodpecker (in the beaver swamp), and Black-throated Blue Warbler (hemlocks) are two of the specialties on this trail.

Some of the typical breeding birds of Stokes State Forest (in addition to those already noted) which can be found along Lackner, Coursen, and Swenson trails, as well as elsewhere in the forest, are Green-backed Heron; Wood Duck (beaver swamps); Broad-winged Hawk; Spotted Sandpiper; American Woodcock; Black-billed and Yellow-billed Cuckoos; Eastern Screech and Great Horned Owls; Red-bellied Woodpecker; Eastern Phoebe (near water); Tree Swallow (beaver swamps); Cedar Waxwing; Yellow-throated Vireo; Blue-winged (scrubby second-growth), Yellow (wet, open areas), Chestnut-sided (in grown up clear-cuts), and Black-and-white Warblers; American Redstart; and Rose-breasted Grosbeak; plus all of the common species noted on p. 12.

Steam Mill Campground (see note 1, page 30)

From Kittle Field, continue along Kittle Rd. After about 0.6 miles, the road makes a right-angle turn, where another road leads left to a group campground; the area around the turn has Golden-winged Warbler and Indigo Bunting. Continuing, the road crosses two bridges (check for Eastern Phoebe and Barn Swallow); the second bridge crosses the Big Flatbrook, where Louisiana Waterthrushes nest. A few hundred feet past this bridge, turn right on Flatbrook Rd.

Follow this road for about 3.3 miles until it ends at Crigger Rd. Along the way, you will pass the Lake Oquittunk Cabin and Camping Area, and the entrance to the New Jersey State School of Conservation. The spruce groves along the school's entrance road have nesting Golden-crowned Kinglet. Beyond Lake Oquittunk, Flatbrook Rd. becomes Grau Rd. (no signs, though), and you drive through an area where Worm-eating Warblers sing from the hillsides and Barred Owls hoot from deep in the woods.

Turn right onto Crigger Rd. (except in winter, when the road is open only to snowmobiles as far as Rt. 636 near Culvers Gap), and go about one-third of a mile to a parking area on the right, just beyond the entrance to Steam Mill Campground. A male Ruby-throated Hummingbird frequently displays around the parking area or down at the nearby Big Flatbrook. Cerulean, and occasionally Hooded, Warblers nest in these woods. Walk to the bridge across the Big Flatbrook. To your left is a beaver pond; a short trail leads away from the road on the far (east) side of the pond. Least Flycatcher nests along the trail, and the flooded areas at its end are good for nesting Eastern Kingbird and Eastern Bluebird and for migrant Olive-sided Flycatchers. Another, longer trail leads west (downstream) along the Big Flatbrook into a dense grove of hemlocks. Barred Owl, Acadian Flycatcher, Solitary Vireo, and Black-throated Green and Blackburnian Warblers nest along the first few hundred yards. The trail eventually intersects with an old road, which leads back to Crigger Rd. a few hundred yards from the Big Flatbrook (round trip about 1.5 miles).

Sunrise Mountain (see note 2, page 30)

Returning to your car, you can turn left onto Crigger Rd. and head into High Point State Park (covered in a separate chapter), or turn right and continue your exploration of Stokes State Forest. If you turn right, drive about 0.8 miles to where the road curves sharply to the right at a Red Pine grove on the right. A small beaver pond on the left attracts migrant warblers in late August–early September. Park on the left, just before the beaver swamp, and follow the trail that leads along the edge of this swampy area. About 100 yards in you can see an open meadow through the trees to your right; Golden-winged Warbler and Least Flycatcher nest here, along with many other songbirds. The woods, swamp, and meadow in this area provide excellent habitat diversity. Check the conifer groves along the next 100 yards or so of trail for interesting breeding birds such as Golden-crowned Kinglet.

About one-quarter mile further along Crigger Rd., where the road curves left and starts uphill, park on the right and walk 100 yards into another beaver swamp. Least Flycatcher breeds here, also, along with other typical birds of this habitat. The surrounding woods have a rich diversity of woodland breeding birds. A female Hooded Merganser was seen here in June 1982.

Another 1.4 miles will bring you to Sunrise Mountain Rd. Hooded Warbler and Black-throated Blue Warbler nest in the Mountain Laurel thickets near this intersection, and you will also find here an excellent stand of Paper Birch, a rare species in New Jersey. A sharp left turn takes you three-quarters of a mile to the Sunrise Mountain parking area, where there are primitive toilets. The Appalachian Trail passes by the parking lot, and a hike along the trail might turn up Hermit Thrush, in addition to the usual birds of the dry ridgetops. (See the chapter on Hawk-watching for more on Sunrise Mountain.)

Drive back to the previous junction and continue left on Sunrise Mountain Rd. This road leads back to Rt. 636 (Upper North Shore Rd. or, on some maps, Matison School Rd.) after about 4 miles. Along the way are several trail junctions where you can park and explore the woods. Look for Chestnut-sided Warbler at the overlook on the right, about one-quarter mile from the Paper Birches, and at the clear-cut in another one-half mile. Turn right at Rt. 636 and go 0.2 miles to US 206.

Tillman Ravine

Turn right onto Rt. 206, go about 0.9 miles to Struble Rd., the first road past the headquarters, and turn left.

Follow this road for 4 miles (the main road becomes Dimon Rd. when Struble turns right as a dirt road) to Brink Rd. Turn right and go about 0.3 miles to the upper parking lot for Tillman Ravine on the left. A display board here describes some of the features of the ravine. There are also primitive toilets here.

Tillman Ravine is a dark and beautiful place. Tillman Brook cascades downhill through a narrow gorge lined with hemlock and rhododendron. The trail from the parking lot leads first through a grove of Eastern White Pines, where Pine Warbler nests, and then into the hemlocks. At the bottom of the ravine, another trail leads back to a second parking lot a few hundred yards downhill from the first. Some of the breeding birds here are Hermit Thrush, Solitary Vireo, and Black-throated Green and Blackburnian Warblers (Dark-eyed Junco has nested here regularly). Birds are not plentiful in the ravine, but it is worth a visit purely for its natural beauty.

Farther down Brink Rd., Prairie Warbler nests in the cedars near the intersection with Mountain Rd. You can turn left onto Mountain Rd. and drive (or walk—the road is abandoned and deteriorating rapidly) a couple of miles to Buttermilk Falls. Wild Turkey is often seen in winter along this road, which is in Delaware Water Gap National Recreation Area.

Head back up Brink Rd., but instead of turning left at Dimon Rd., continue straight ahead on what is now a dirt road. Go about a mile, past the junction with Shay Rd. on the left, to the intersection with Woods Rd. Brink Rd. continues straight ahead (it is not driveable), across Mecca Gap to the other side of the Kittatinny Mountains, crossing the Appalachian Trail along the way. Woods Rd. can be driven or explored on foot for a mile to the right (southwest) and can be walked or driven for almost 1.5 miles to the left (northeast), to where it intersects with Coss Rd. on the left. Coss Rd. leads back to Struble Rd. after about 1.2 miles. This southwestern section of Stokes State Forest has received little attention from birders in recent years. The discovery of three pairs of Nashville Warblers and numerous Solitary Vireos in 1984, however, suggests that the area could benefit from better coverage. Hooded and Black-throated Blue Warblers have also been found in this area.

Culvers Lake

A trip to Stokes State Forest or Sunrise Mountain in late fall or early spring is not complete without a stop at Culvers Lake. This is best done on your way to the forest. From the junction of Rt. 15 and US 206, go north on Rt. 206 for about 4.6 miles to the junction with East Shore Rd. on the right, opposite a Dairy Queen. Turn right and go about 1 mile to the Culvers Lake Association Clubhouse, on the left; the driveway of the clubhouse provides a good vantage point for scanning the lake. Most of the diving ducks have been seen here, including Oldsquaw and all three scoters. A Red Phalarope was found here in November 1983. A half mile further, you will cross the Culvers Lake Causeway. Mute Swan and Ring-necked Duck favor the shallower water on the right. Many Wood Ducks breed here, and

Green-backed Herons feed along the edges. On the left, the northeast section of Culvers Lake attracts loons, grebes, various diving ducks, and many gulls. Pomarine Jaeger was once found on the lake. If you continue around the lake for another 2 miles, you will rejoin US 206 just 200 yards from the turnoff for Sunrise Mountain.

Culvers Lake Outlet

Another good birding spot in May is the outflow of Culvers Lake. To reach this spot, turn left just past the Dairy Queen on US 206. Go about 100 yards, then turn left again and park. Ahead is Culvers Creek, the outlet of Culvers Lake. When a hatch of black flies coincides with the warbler migration in mid-May, the birding here can be incredible. I have seen as many as 20 species of warblers in a few minutes, many of them as close as 15 feet. Thrushes, vireos and other songbirds stop here as well.

NOTE 1: Kittle Road is now closed at the bridge over the Big Flatbrook. In order to reach Steam Mill Campground via Flatbrook Rd. and Grau Rd., you must return to US 206 via the headquarters and Coursen Rd. Turn right on US 206 and go about 1.7 miles to Flatbrook Rd., on the right. The junction of Flatbrook Rd. and Kittle Rd. is about 1.2 miles; from there continue as described.

NOTE 2: As of March 15, 1991, Sunrise Mountain Rd. will become one-way northbound from its junction with Rt. 636 (Upper North Shore Rd.) to Steam Mill Campground. In order to bird the spots described under the section on Sunrise Mountain, you will have to retrace the route in the reverse direction from that given on pages 27–28. To get to the junction of Sunrise Mountain Rd. and Rt. 636, see Map 4, or follow the directions on page 441 in the Hawk-Watching chapter. To reach Tillman Ravine from Steam Mill, return to US 206 via Grau Rd. and Flatbrook Rd., turn left and go about 1.5 miles to Struble Rd., on the right.

Wawayanda State Park

Wawayanda State Park is the second largest state park in New Jersey, covering more than 10,500 acres in northeastern Sussex and northwestern Passaic counties. Most of the park lies on the Wawayanda Plateau, a broad, relatively flat section of the New Jersey Highlands at an elevation of about 1,200 feet, situated between Bearfort Mountain on the southeast and Wawayanda Mountain on the west. To the south, the plateau continues into the Pequannock Watershed (covered in a separate chapter); to the north and west, the terrain drops off sharply to Vernon Valley and Wawayanda Creek.

The birdlife of Wawayanda State Park is similar to that of the neighboring Pequannock Watershed, though not quite as diverse. A wide variety of habitats and the moderately high elevation combine to give the area a long list of interesting nesting species. Birders seldom visit the park outside the breeding season, because most of the species are more readily found elsewhere. Ospreys visit the lake in spring and fall, but few waterfowl stop here in migration. The southeastern section of the park, including Bearfort Waters and Terrace Pond, is covered in the Pequannock Watershed chapter.

Among the more noteworthy species that nest in the park are Red-shouldered Hawk; Barred Owl; Pileated Woodpecker; Acadian Flycatcher; Brown Creeper; Winter Wren; Hermit Thrush; Solitary Vireo; Golden-winged, Black-throated Blue, Black-throated Green, Blackburnian, Cerulean, Worm-eating, Hooded, and Canada Warblers; Northern and Louisiana Waterthrushes; Dark-eyed Junco (rarely); and Purple Finch. These and many other species make Wawayanda a delightful place to spend a morning in late spring or in summer.

Directions

To reach the entrance to Wawayanda State Park, take Rt. 23 north from Interstate 80 for about 17 miles to Rt. 513 (Union Valley Rd.).

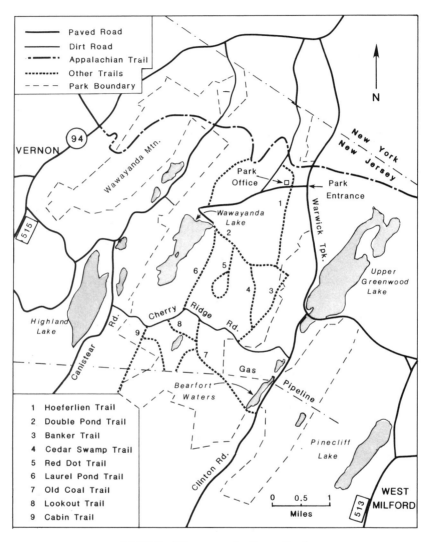

MAP 5. Wawayanda State Park

Go north on Rt. 513 for about 7.3 miles to a fork; bear left on Union Valley Rd. and go about 1.3 miles to another fork. Take the left fork, White Rd., for 0.3 miles to the Warwick Turnpike. Turn left onto the Warwick Pike and go about 4.4 miles to the park entrance, on the left.

Birding

The entrance road reaches the park headquarters after about 0.3 miles; an entrance fee is charged here in summer. The gate opens one-half hour before sunrise and closes one-half hour after sunset, although the collection booth is usually not manned before 8 A.M. If you arrive when the office is open, stop and get a trail map; one is also posted in the display case at the parking lot.

Birding at Wawayanda is done on foot, using the numerous—but not always well marked—trails. These lead through a variety of interesting habitats that harbor many species of birds and some uncommon mammals. Black Bear, Bobcat, Beaver and Porcupine occur within the park, but as they are mainly nocturnal, you are unlikely to encounter them; except for Beaver, they are also rare. Because of its unique plant and animal life, a large portion of the eastern section of the park has been designated a Natural Area under the New Jersey Natural Systems Act.

There are two parking areas from which to start your hike—the one at the headquarters and another, where I usually go, at the boat rental concession. To reach it, follow the main park road to the parking lot at Wawayanda Lake, and continue through that parking area to the next one at the boat rental site. The trails are best covered with the aid of the trail map; several different routes for hikes are suggested.

Walk east from the parking lot for about one-quarter mile, past the dam and past an old iron furnace that was the focus of the small town of Double Pond that flourished here in the mid-1800s. Stay left at the dam on the dirt road that eventually becomes Laurel Pond Trail. After about 250 yards, just across a wooden bridge, is a sign for Double Pond Trail on the left. Follow Double Pond Trail through the group campground and into a mature second-growth deciduous forest.

Some of the birds of the deciduous woods frequently encountered along this trail (and elsewhere in the park) during the nesting season are Broad-winged Hawk; Ruffed Grouse; Black-billed (uncommon) and Yellow-billed Cuckoos; Eastern Screech and Great Horned Owls, Pileated Woodpecker (uncommon); Least Flycatcher; Eastern Kingbird; Brown Creeper; Cedar Waxwing; Chestnut-sided, Black-and-white, Hooded, and Canada Warblers; American Redstart; and Rose-breasted Grosbeak.

After about 0.4 miles, near a wooden bridge across Wawayanda Creek and its open marshy edges, you will find Eastern Kingbird, Eastern Phoebe, Tree Swallow, Yellow Warbler, Louisiana Waterthrush, Common Yellowthroat, Song and Swamp Sparrows, and Red-winged Blackbird. Continue past the junction with Red Dot Trail, through more deciduous woods and some hemlock groves, to the junction with Cedar Swamp Trail on the right, about one mile from the beginning of Double Pond Trail. At this point you can go either way, but I suggest you try Cedar Swamp Trail.

Cedar Swamp Trail leads to a swampy area where the dominant tree is the Atlantic White Cedar, the same species that grows in the cedar swamps of the New Jersey Pine Barrens. Northern and Louisiana Waterthrushes are here; with luck you might find something unusual like a Nashville Warbler, a species that prefers this type of habitat further north, but is an irregular nester in New Jersey. The trail emerges from the swamp into some rhododendron thickets and hemlock groves.

The hemlocks have a few species not found in the deciduous forest, including Acadian Flycatcher (uncommon); Winter Wren (rare); Hermit Thrush (uncommon); Solitary Vireo; Black-throated Blue (rare), Black-throated Green (common) and Blackburnian Warblers; and Dark-eyed Junco (very rare breeder). After about 1.1 miles on the Cedar Swamp Trail, you will come to a T-intersection. At this point you can turn left and return via Banker Trail and Double Pond Trail, or turn right and return via Cherry Ridge Rd. and Laurel Pond Trail.

If you choose the left fork, go about 200 yards and take the left turn onto Banker Trail, which traverses a variety of habitats. It becomes hard to follow towards its north end, but keep to your left when you come to a small pond. After about 1.1 miles the trail ends and a paved road begins; at this point you are no longer in the park.

Go left onto a dirt road for about 0.2 miles, and then re-enter the park where the trail passes between two white posts. This is the eastern end of Double Pond Trail, which leads back to the parking lot, a distance of about 1.8 miles.

If you turn right at the T-intersection, go about 0.3 miles until the trail ends at Cherry Ridge Rd., a one-lane dirt road, and turn right. The first stretch passes through some open deciduous woods with a dense Mountain Laurel understory, where Hooded and Canada Warblers are common. Further along are several hemlock glens where I have found Acadian Flycatcher, Solitary Vireo, and Black-throated Blue Warbler in summer.

After about a mile, on your left, you will pass the junction with Old Coal Rd., which leads through more deciduous woods and hemlock glens down to Bearfort Waters on Clinton Rd. Hooded and Canada Warblers are common along the upper parts of Old Coal Rd. and Hermit Thrush is often in the hemlocks. About 0.3 miles along the Old Coal Rd., Lookout Trail leads to the right. This trail passes by Lake Lookout and rejoins Cherry Ridge Rd. in about three-quarters of a mile.

If you remain on Cherry Ridge Rd., after about 1.4 miles you'll reach the junction with Laurel Pond Trail on your right. (If you come to Lookout Trail on the left, you have missed Laurel Pond Trail. Go back one-third of a mile to the first trail on the left.) There is a marker at the beginning of Laurel Pond Trail, but vandals occasionally destroy the signs in this remote section of the park. From the junction of Cherry Ridge Rd. and Laurel Pond Trail, it is about 1.7 miles back to the parking lot.

Another interesting hike, covering about six miles, leads along Double Pond Trail, the William Hoeferlien Trail, a short section of the Appalachian Trail, and Iron Mountain Rd. Use the trail map for this hike. You can start at either the day-use area or the headquarters parking lot. The habitat covered is similar to that on the hikes described above, except that there are more deciduous and less coniferous woods. The trails pass through some open areas where you will find Blue-winged and possibly Golden-winged Warbler, Chipping Sparrow, and Indigo Bunting.

Cherry Ridge Rd., which was discussed briefly above, is one of the most interesting areas in the park. The road has been abandoned and you can no longer drive the length of it. The parts that are open are very rough and rocky, however, and may do severe damage to a low clearance vehicle. The best idea is to park in one of the parking areas at either end and walk the road.

To reach the east end of Cherry Ridge from the park entrance, turn right onto the Warwick Turnpike and go about 2.2 miles to Clinton Rd., on the right. Take Clinton Rd. south for about 0.8 miles to Cherry Ridge Rd., on the right. Follow Cherry Ridge uphill for about one mile to the entrance to Wawayanda State Park, marked by a sign. You can park here, if you do not want to drive. Hooded Warbler is plentiful at this spot, which is about 0.2 miles from the junction with Banker Trail noted above.

The west end of Cherry Ridge Rd. is much harder to find. From the park, it is most easily reached via the service gate on Wawayanda Rd., just west of the day-use area. This gate is open after 8 A.M., in summer only. From the service gate, follow Wawayanda Rd. for about 1.5 miles to the junction with Breakneck Rd. and Canistear Rd. Turn left onto Canistear and go about 1.2 miles to where the main road turns right and an unmarked road goes straight ahead down a hill. Take this unmarked road, which is Cherry Ridge Rd., past a lake on the right. Ignore the first right turn, but stay right at the next intersection and follow this road around a curve through a residential area until it takes off straight ahead into the woods. At this point you enter Wawayanda State Park; the distance from Canistear Rd. to the park is about 0.3 miles. Cherry Ridge Rd. can also be reached by driving north on Canistear Rd. from Route 23 for about 6.7 miles.

After you have entered the park the road gets rough, but there is a parking lot on the left in about one-quarter mile. Park here and continue on foot. In about 300 yards, Cabin Trail comes in on the right, while Cherry Ridge Rd. continues left. The old road called Cabin Trail on the park map is also shown as Cherry Trail on some maps and is known to birders as part of Cherry Ridge Rd.; this is the trail referred to as Cherry Ridge Trail in the Pequannock Watershed chapter. You can hike south on Cabin/Cherry Ridge Trail for about two miles until you come to gun club property.

About three-quarters of a mile from the start, Cabin Trail passes through a scrubby second-growth deciduous woodland with many birches. A short distance farther, you'll come upon a gas pipeline right-of-way. You can turn left and hike along the pipeline for about one-half mile to a beaver swamp, where Eastern Bluebirds nest. This swamp may be difficult to cross, but if you can, you'll come to a junction with Turkey Ridge Trail on the left after about 0.2 miles. Turkey Ridge Trail leads back to Cabin Trail.

If you continue on Cherry Ridge Trail, across the pipeline, you will soon come to rhododendron and laurel thickets where Hooded and Canada Warblers abound and Black-throated Blue Warbler is an annual breeder. A trail on the left, after about 1.5 miles, leads down to a hemlock glen where Winter Wren, Hermit Thrush, Solitary Vireo, and Northern Waterthrush may be found.

The Appalachian Trail traverses the northern part of Wawayanda State Park. In the eastern section of the park, the trail follows a portion of Iron Mountain Rd. and passes within 0.4 miles of the park headquarters. The trail in the western section of the park crosses a relatively inaccessible area that is infrequently visited by birders. To reach the trail from the park, go out to the entrance, turn left, and follow Warwick Turnpike north into New York for three miles to its end at Route 94, New Milford Rd. Turn left onto Rt. 94 and go about 5.1 miles. Just before the junction with Maple Grange Rd. on the right is a parking area on the left. Park here and walk a short distance farther to the beginning of the Appalachian Trail, marked by white blazes.

The Appalachian Trail follows a gentle slope along the edge of some fields for about 0.4 miles, then starts a steep ascent of Wawayanda Mountain, climbing more than 700 feet in one-half mile. Along the way it passes through mature deciduous woods and a few hemlock groves, where you'll find a variety of birds. On top of the mountain the habitat is the open oak woodland with scattered Pitch Pines typical of the dry ridgetops of the Highlands and the Kittatinny Mountains. Here you will find Hermit Thrush, Veery, Worm-eating and Hooded Warblers, and Ovenbird, but little else.

A rock outcropping along the trail provides outstanding views of Vernon Valley below and the Kittatinny Mountains, with High Point Monument 13 miles to the northwest. It is also a good place to watch hawks in the fall, if you are up to the long climb. About one-half mile farther north along the talus of Wawayanda Mountain is the only stand of Red Pine in New Jersey believed to be native.

Pequannock Watershed

Newark's Pequannock Watershed has the greatest diversity of breeding birds in the state. It is a large and varied area, comprising more than 34,000 acres in Morris, Passaic, and Sussex counties, and lying entirely within the Highlands. The City of Newark owns the land, including five reservoirs which provide water to most of Newark and to several other municipalities. Except for the reservoirs and several ponds, the area is largely covered by second-growth woodland of varying degrees of maturity. A few overgrown fields remain along some of the major roads. Elevation ranges from 600 feet in the southeast to just over 1,400 feet on some of the ridgetops.

As in other parts of the Highlands, the mixture of plateaus, ridges, and valleys supports a variety of vegetation and birdlife. Many of the birds nesting here, such as Winter Wren, Solitary Vireo, and Black-throated Blue and Blackburnian Warblers, are typical of more northern climes, and are near the southern limit of their range east of the Appalachians. Conversely, a number of species of southern affinities, such as Acadian Flycatcher, Yellow-throated Vireo, Louisiana Waterthrush, and Hooded Warbler, also are found here, the last being especially common.

Almost 120 species have been found nesting in the watershed since 1970, when the Urner Ornithological Club began conducting periodic breeding-bird surveys. Birding this area in the summer, you can always hope to find a species new to the state's list of breeding birds, as occurred in 1979 when a pair of Yellow-rumped Warblers was found nesting along Clinton Road. The watershed should not be neglected in winter, however, as the hemlock groves and spruce plantings are good for winter finches and other northern species during flight years.

Directions

You will need a hiking permit to park or wander off the main roads in the watershed. Although you can find many of the sought-after spe-

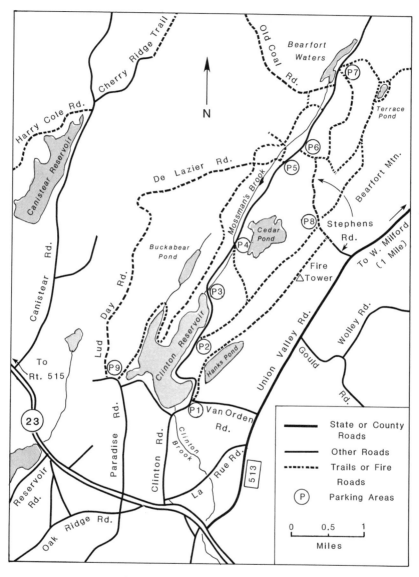

MAP 6. Pequannock Watershed

cies by birding from the roadsides, you'll achieve a much greater appreciation of the birdlife of the area by hiking some of the many trails and roads open to permit holders. Hiking permits, which are $5 for nonresidents of Newark, can be obtained only by appearing in person at one of the offices of the Newark Watershed Conservation and Development Corporation. To reach the office in the watershed: From the intersection of Rts. 23 and 511 in Butler, go west on Rt. 23 for 5.4 miles to the Echo Lake Rd. exit. From the exit ramp, turn right onto Echo Lake Rd. and go one mile to the headquarters, on the left. With your permit (one for each person is required), you will be given a sticker for your car and a trail map for the watershed. At present, this office is only open on weekdays, and the hours are subject to change. Call them at (201) 697-2850 before going there.

Birding

Return to Rt. 23 and continue straight ahead on a rough road that leads to an old house. The road to the left of the house (as you are facing it) goes to some of the areas around the Charlottesburg dam. Here you may find several species that are uncommon elsewhere in the watershed. Among the birds that have been found here during the breeding season, although not necessarily nesting, are Black-crowned Night-Heron, Turkey Vulture, Red-tailed Hawk, Killdeer, Cliff Swallow (nested in the early 1970s), Northern Parula, Bobolink, and Eastern Meadowlark.

Go back to Rt. 23 and turn left (west); after 2.2 miles take the exit for Clinton Rd. The exit is onto LaRue Rd., which ends at Clinton Rd. in about 100 feet. Turn right and go 1.2 miles to the Schoolhouse Rd. on the left, where a bridge crosses Clinton Brook. A small grove of old Norway Spruce here is a favored location of Pine Grosbeak and Pine Siskin in flight years. The dam for Clinton Reservoir is up the hill behind the grove, and the ruins of Clinton Furnace are just downstream from the bridge. Indigo Bunting and occasionally Golden-winged Warbler nest below the dam, and Louisiana Waterthrush nests along the brook. Continuing along Clinton Rd., you will follow the edge of the reservoir for the next 2.5 miles (look for Common Loon in early spring), passing through a mixed hardwood forest dominated by oaks and also including ash, beech, Black Birch, hickories, and maples. In places where the trees are not too large, Mountain Laurel forms a dense understory. During the nesting season look for Broad-winged Hawk, Yellow-billed and Black-billed Cuckoos (numbers fluctuate), Pileated Woodpecker (uncommon), Eastern Wood-Pewee, Great Crested Flycatcher and Veery (both abundant), Wood Thrush, Yellow-throated Vireo (scarce), Chestnut-sided and Black-and-white Warblers, American Redstart, Worm-eating Warbler, Ovenbird (abundant), Hooded and Canada Warblers (in Mountain Laurel), Scarlet Tanager, Rose-breasted Grosbeak, Rufous-sided Towhee, Chipping Sparrow, and Northern Oriole.

At 0.4 miles beyond the dam are Van Orden Rd. and a parking area marked P1. This is the starting point for two long trails, Hanks East and Hanks West, that skirt Hanks Pond and follow the eastern side of Bearfort Mountain for three miles; shorter loops are indicated on the trail map. Another 1.2 miles along Clinton Rd. is parking area P2, the origin of another long trail that goes to the Bearfort Fire Tower and intersects with several other trails. One mile further on is a bridge at the northern end of the reservoir and a right angle turn, where parking area P3 is located. Louisiana Waterthrush and Eastern Phoebe usually nest here, and Winter Wren has nested along the hillside just west of the road.

The next several miles of Clinton Rd. traverse some of the most interesting parts of the watershed, as the road parallels Mossman's Brook through hemlock glens, mature deciduous stands, and younger oak-laurel habitat; the first 1.5 miles is especially productive. Be sure to stop at the hemlock grove 0.4 miles above P3, and at parking area P4, where Mossman's Brook passes under the road. Two trails leading off from either side of the road allow you to explore this habitat more thoroughly. Species nesting here regularly are Red-shouldered Hawk; Great Horned and Barred Owls; Ruby-throated Hummingbird; Least Flycatcher; Solitary Vireo (hemlocks); Blue-winged, Black-and-white, Black-throated Green (hemlocks), Blackburnian (mixed deciduous-hemlocks), Chestnut-sided (younger deciduous), Hooded, and Canada Warblers (both laurel); Northern (wet areas near the brook) and Louisiana (along the brook) Waterthrushes; Common Yellowthroat; American Redstart; Rose-breasted Grosbeak; Chipping Sparrow; and Purple Finch (mainly deciduous). Winter Wren and Hermit Thrush are found in small numbers in the hemlock areas during most years. Other noteworthy species which nest in this area irregularly are Acadian Flycatcher, Red-breasted Nuthatch, Magnolia Warbler (rare), Yellow-rumped Warbler (once), and Pine Siskin (after a big winter flight). During the winter of 1981–82, several Boreal Chickadees, hundreds of White-winged Crossbills and Pine Siskins, and a few Common Redpolls and Red Crossbills could be found along this stretch of road.

Continue along Clinton Rd. to parking area P5, 1.3 miles beyond P4, stopping occasionally to listen for new species. There is an interesting 1.5-mile loop trail starting at P5. Park on the left, where the road is widest, and walk down the abandoned road just ahead on your left, where an old iron gate is usually open. After about 100 yards, turn left onto another road; this is De Lazier Rd. on the maps. In 1980, White-throated Sparrow nested in the open woods on your left. The road crosses Mossman's Brook, with a swampy area where Swamp Sparrow is common, then climbs through hemlocks and some mature deciduous stands for one-half mile. Watch for the white blazes on the trees that mark the intersection with the Bearfort Waters–Clinton Trail; if you come to an open grassy area you have gone about 100 feet too far. Near this intersection you may find Blue-winged and Cerulean Warblers and Solitary Vireo. Turn right onto the trail; you will soon pass the open pit of an old iron mine, then continue through a variety of habitats from dry deciduous woods to dark hemlock glens for 0.7 miles. At the intersection with an old road, turn right; after crossing the brook again, bear right and after about 0.2 miles you will be back at the intersection with De Lazier Rd. Continue straight ahead for 100 yards to Clinton Rd. Other birds to be looked for along this loop are Northern Goshawk; Red-shouldered Hawk; Brown Creeper; Hermit Thrush; Black-throated Blue, Black-throated Green, Blackburnian, Hooded, and Canada Warblers; and both waterthrushes. For the more adventurous, an interesting 10-mile hike covering a variety of terrain can be made via De Lazier Rd. and Lud Day Rd. to the southwest corner of Clinton Reservoir, returning via Clinton West and the Bearfort Waters–Clinton Trail.

One-half mile beyond P5 is the junction with Stephens Rd., on the right. Unfortunately, this area is an in-holding in the watershed and is slated for development. Stephens can be hiked all the way to the top of Bearfort Mountain, through areas that are especially good for Ruffed Grouse and Hermit Thrush, in addition to many species previously mentioned. The area to the south of the road includes Uttertown Bog, one of the few quaking bogs remaining in New Jersey and an area of outstanding botanical interest. Because of the environmental sensitivity of this area, it is closed except by special use permit. At the top of Bearfort Mountain is parking area P8, which can be reached only from Union Valley Rd. on the east. From here, the Fire Tower Trail goes south; after 0.5 miles you come to the fire tower and an exposed outcropping of rocks on the west side, which make a good hawk-watching location in the fall. From P8, another trail leads north into Wawayanda State Park, toward Terrace Pond.

From Stephens Rd., Clinton Rd. continues north into a small section of Wawayanda State Park that is isolated from the main body of the park. After 1.3 miles, you will reach a parking area on the left marked P7. Here a short trail leads to an elongated lake known as Bearfort Waters; this is a good spot for Red-shouldered Hawk, Least Flycatcher, Tree Swallow, and Eastern Bluebird. Across the road from the parking area, the Bearfort Waters–Clinton Trail, marked with yellow blazes, goes south into the watershed. To reach the trail to Terrace Pond, walk north along Clinton Rd. for 0.4 miles to where a gas pipeline right-of-way provides a path up the side of Bearfort Mountain. About three-fourths of the way up, the trail to Terrace Pond, marked with blue blazes, leads off to the right. In about 0.5 miles, you will come to the pond, a delightful spot surrounded by cliffs and rhododendron thickets. Along the trail you may encounter Ruffed Grouse, Hermit Thrush, Veery, Ovenbird, and Hooded Warbler, but birdlife is not abundant on the dry ridgetops of the Highlands. The trail circles the pond and connects with three other trails going off to the south, all of which eventually intersect Stephens Rd. These trails are not well marked, however, so they should be used with caution.

To visit some other areas in the watershed, return to the junction of Clinton Rd. and LaRue Rd., and turn left onto LaRue. Follow this for 0.7 miles and park on the roadside just before the bridge over Clinton Brook. The large grove of Norway Spruce on the west side of the road has nesting Golden-crowned Kinglet and Red-breasted Nuthatch; in winter there may be crossbills or a Boreal Chickadee. To reach Stephens Rd., continue 0.7 miles to Union Valley Rd. Turn left and go 3.2 miles to Stephens Rd., on the left. This road climbs for 0.7 miles to P8 on the ridge of Bearfort Mountain; the road is very rough, so proceed with caution in an ordinary car. Dark-eyed Junco has nested along the upper parts of Stephens Rd.

Another outstanding breeding-bird area is Cherry Ridge Trail, which lies partly in the watershed and partly in Wawayanda State Park. To reach the part in the watershed, return to the junction of Clinton Rd. and Rt. 23. Take Rt. 23 west for 3.2 miles to Canistear Rd., then take Canistear north for 4.2 miles to a point where an un-named paved road leads off to the right. Park on the right just beyond this road and walk up the paved road, which leads to a gun club shooting range. After about 0.3 miles there is a trail on the right, which leads off into an interesting area with Purple Finch, Golden-winged Warbler, Cerulean Warbler, and possibly Nashville Warbler, among others. You can continue on the paved road to the gun club and ask permission to cross the property to hike up Cherry Ridge Trail. If permission is granted, follow the dirt road, which continues for about three miles with a side trail or two worth exploring. The first mile is the most interesting and is the best area in the water-shed for nesting Black-throated Blue Warbler; White-throated Spar-row also has nested here on occasion. Most of the other noteworthy species breeding in the watershed can be found here as well. (If you don't get permission to cross through the gun club, you can reach this section of Cherry Ridge Trail through Wawayanda State Park [see that chapter], although it is a longer walk.) Note that after 8:00 A.M. shooting begins at the gun club and birding in this area is rather difficult.

Returning to Canistear Rd. and starting south, you will come to Harry Cole Rd. in just 0.2 miles. A short walk along this road, which follows the northwest side of Canistear Reservoir for some distance, may produce Golden-winged Warbler and Blue-gray Gnatcatcher (the latter still an uncommon bird in the watershed). Upon reaching Rt. 23, turn right and go 1.1 miles to the exit for Rt. 515. There are three spruce groves and a marsh along this road which are worth investigating. The first spruce grove is on the left, 2.3 miles north of Rt. 23. The second is reached by parking where an old road leads off to the right, another 0.4 miles along. Walk up this dirt road for about 0.3 miles to the grove, on the left. The third grove is an additional 2.6 miles north on Rt. 515. All these groves should be checked for nesting Red-breasted Nuthatch and Golden-crowned Kinglet; in winter they may have northern finches. The marsh is 3.8 miles north of Rt. 23 on the right. Here, look for Golden-winged Warbler, American Kestrel, and Alder Flycatcher. These areas are best checked early in the morning, as they are right on Rt. 515 (except for the second spruce grove), and the traffic noise later in the day can make birding difficult.

Another spot that has had nesting Red-breasted Nuthatch and Golden-crowned Kinglet can be reached by returning to Rt. 23 and going east for 2.3 miles to the exit for Reservoir Rd. Follow this road for 1.1 miles to a spruce grove and listen for the two species. Another grove is a mile further on the right, just before Reservoir Rd. ends at Oak Ridge Rd. To return to Rt. 23, it is safest to make a U-turn and retrace your path, as the left turn onto Oak Ridge Rd. is very hazardous owing to limited visibility.

A good spot for Blue-winged Warbler, Golden-winged Warbler, and hybrids of these two species is a power line cut on Paradise Rd. Go east on Rt. 23 from Reservoir Rd. for about 1.2 miles to the jughandle left turn for Paradise Rd. Drive north on Paradise for about one mile to the power line cut and park. Walk west along the power line to search for the warblers. Red-shouldered Hawk also nests in this area. About a quarter-mile further along Paradise Rd. a dirt road on the left leads to a small pond where Hooded Merganser and Rusty Blackbird have been seen in spring.

Many other places can be explored in the watershed with the help of the trails map, but the areas covered here are the principal ones for the northern-nesting species that are hard to find elsewhere in the state.

The section of the Bearfort Waters–Clinton Trail north of De Lazier Road, described on page 42, has been abandoned because it passed through an in-holding that now has a house on it. De Lazier Road is still good for birding, however.

Ringwood State Park

This little-known state park, which borders on New York State, contains more than 2,600 acres in the Highlands of northern Passaic and Bergen counties. Most of the park is centered around two large estates, Ringwood Manor on the west and Skylands Manor on the east, which have mansions built in the nineteenth (Ringwood) or early twentieth (Skylands) centuries. A third section, Shepherd Lake, lies to the north. The park's wide variety of habitats includes shrubby fields, meadows, lakes, orchards, and gardens around the manor houses plus the extensive deciduous forest of the surrounding hillsides. There are numerous conifer plantings around both mansions and a large stand of Eastern Hemlocks on the southwest corner of Shepherd Lake.

Ringwood is an excellent spot for migrants in spring and fall and supports a diversity of breeding birds. The Bear Swamp Lake area of the park (part of the Skylands Section) includes many of the characteristic breeding birds of the Ramapo Mountains, but it is remote, hard to get to, and seldom birded. The park is best known, however, as a good place to search for winter finches, especially Pine Grosbeak, in invasion years, and for the Bohemian Waxwing that stayed for a month in February–March 1977.

Directions

From the intersection of Interstate 80 and Route 23 in Wayne, Passaic County, go north on Rt. 23 for about 6.8 miles to a traffic circle, where Alternate Rt. 511 intersects Rt. 23. Take the exit for Alt. Rt. 511 North, the Newark-Pompton Turnpike, and go 0.9 miles to the junction with the Paterson-Hamburg Turnpike. Turn right, continue on Alt. Rt. 511 for 0.6 miles to Ringwood Ave., and turn left, staying on Alt. Rt. 511. Follow Ringwood Ave. north for about 8.5 miles (Rt. 511 joins from the left after 1.3 miles) to the junction with

MAP 7. Ringwood State Park

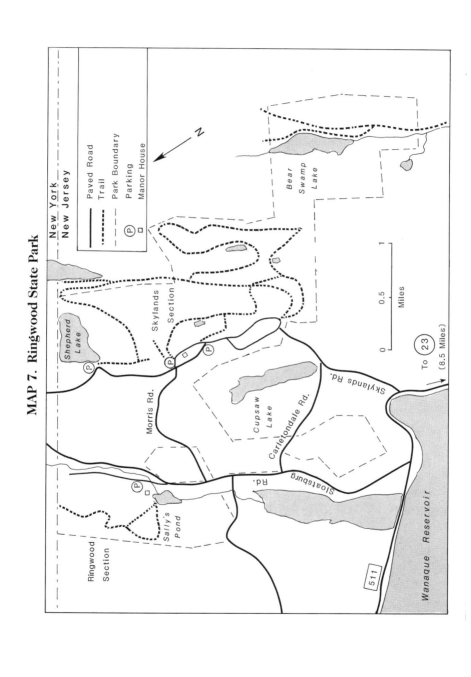

New York
New Jersey

Paved Road
Trail
Park Boundary
Ⓟ Parking
▫ Manor House

N

Shepherd Lake

Skylands Section

Morris Rd.

Cupsaw Lake

Carletondale Rd.

Skylands Rd.

To ㉓
(8.5 Miles)

0   0.5   1
Miles

Bear Swamp Lake

Ringwood Section

Sally's Pond

Sloatsburg Rd.

511

Wanaque Reservoir

Sloatsburg Rd. Turn right, following the signs for Ringwood Manor, onto Sloatsburg and drive about 2.5 miles to the entrance to the Ringwood Manor section of Ringwood State Park, on the left. Follow the entrance road for a few hundred yards to the parking lot.

Birding

The hemlock and spruce plantings around the houses and parking lot at Ringwood Manor are good for northern finches during those winters in which these species come south (invasion years). Purple Finch and Evening Grosbeak are annual migrants in spring and fall, and are often present in winter, as well. Pine Grosbeak, Red Crossbill (rare), White-winged Crossbill (rare), and Pine Siskin (most years) may all occur. In years when Pine Grosbeak is reported in northern New Jersey (listen to the Rare Bird Alert), there are almost always some here. A hiking trail follows the Ringwood River (really just a stream) north into New York. Another, longer, trail departs from the west side of Sally's Pond (on the far side of the manor house from the parking lot), and explores some of the remote areas of the Ringwood Section to the north and west.

To reach the Skylands section of Ringwood State Park, follow the entrance road back to Sloatsburg Rd. and turn right. Go about one-third of a mile and turn left onto Morris Rd., following the sign for Skylands Manor. After about a mile, continue through the intersection with Shepherd Lake Rd. for about a hundred yards and turn left into a parking lot.

Just beyond the parking lot, a paved road (park vehicles only) bears left off the main road. Walk this side road, which leads past a couple of houses and other buildings. It is lined with evergreens and various other plantings and is a good spot in migration and in winter. The pavement ends after several hundred yards, just beyond a house on the left. Continue straight ahead on a path through some shrubbery, until you come to a trail on the left. Here you will see some large spruces, which have had Pine Grosbeak and White-winged Crossbill. Across the path from the spruces is an area of birches and other scrubby trees surrounding a small pond. Follow the trail that leads through the birches to check for Common Redpoll in winter and for warblers in migration. Beyond the birches is a grove of pines, where you might find Red-breasted Nuthatch in winter.

To the east of the road and trail just described is an extensive deciduous woods, with a couple of trails traversing it. Here you should find Pileated Woodpecker and other forest birds. To the west is a large open field lined with two rows of crabapples, where American Robins and Cedar Waxwings feed. Beyond the field is the main park road and the manor house, which is surrounded by numerous tree and shrub plantings that usually harbor a few birds, including Yellow-bellied Sapsucker, in winter.

South of the manor house, the main park road makes a mile-long loop (which you can walk or drive). Just after the road divides into the one-way loop, there is a hill on the left with numerous crabapples and wild roses. This is another favorite feeding area for robins and waxwings in winter, and it was here that a Bohemian Waxwing was found in February 1977. This cooperative bird was seen and photographed by hundreds of birders during its month-long stay.

Near the south end of the loop is the South (Cupsaw Lake) Entrance to Skylands; this gate is open only during the summer, when there is an admission charge to all sections of Ringwood State Park. About 200 yards past the South Entrance is an old road on the right that provides access to a maze of trails that traverse the southeastern half of the Skylands Section. You will need a trail map and a compass to explore these trails, but your efforts will be rewarded with some excellent birding. To the southeast of these trails, on the eastern slope of the Ramapo Mountains, is the Bear Swamp Lake Section of the state park. To bird the Bear Swamp area, you should use a USGS topographic map (Ramsey quadrangle) and a compass, as there are no maintained trails that connect with the main body of Ringwood State Park.

To reach the Shepherd Lake Section of the state park from the first parking lot at Skylands Manor, turn right out of the parking lot onto the main road and go about 100 yards to Shepherd Lake Rd. Turn right and drive about one-half mile to the parking lot for Shepherd Lake. This road is closed in summer, when there is a fee for the Shepherd Lake section; the entrance is off Sloatsburg Rd., about 1.5 miles north of Ringwood Manor. In migration, you may find a small number of diving ducks on the lake, including Ring-necked, Lesser Scaup, Common Goldeneye, Bufflehead, and Hooded and Common Mergansers. A good birding trail follows the south shore of Shepherd Lake, through a grove of hemlocks, for more than half a mile.

There are modern rest rooms at Shepherd Lake, Ringwood Manor, and Skylands Manor. To return to Sloatsburg Rd. from the Shepherd Lake parking lot, continue north on Shepherd Lake Rd. for a little over a mile until you come to the stop sign at Sloatsburg Rd. (at this point, you have been in New York State for about a half-mile). Turn left and you will re-enter New Jersey along the eastern border of the Ringwood Manor Section of the state park in about 0.7 miles.

Mahlon Dickerson Reservation

This preserve is on a plateau in the New Jersey Highlands, near the northwestern corner of Morris County. Comprising almost 1,300 acres, Mahlon Dickerson Reservation is the largest unit in the Morris County Park System. Owing to its moderately high elevation of 1,100 to 1,300 feet, and its combination of mature deciduous forest, hemlock groves, and bog, the park supports an interesting diversity of breeding birds. These include Ruffed Grouse, Wild Turkey, Hermit Thrush, Solitary Vireo, and a long list of warblers. The reservation is an out-of-the-way spot, and receives little attention from birders. It is very attractive, however, and is well worth a morning visit in May, June, or July.

Directions

Take Interstate 80 West to Exit 34 (Rt. 15 North)—Exit 33 eastbound—just north of Dover. Go north on Rt. 15 for about 5 miles to Weldon Rd., following the signs for Milton. Follow Weldon Rd. northeast for about 4.5 miles, past a trailer site on the left and a campground on the right, to the entrance road to a family picnic area, on the left. Follow this road for about 100 yards to a parking area.

Birding

At the parking area, there are primitive toilets and a directory showing the trails traversing Mahlon Dickerson Reservation. The park is divided into two nearly equal sections by Weldon Rd., and best birding is in the northern half. The far northern border of the park, along the Sussex–Morris County line, crosses part of the Great Pine Swamp, an excellent birding area.

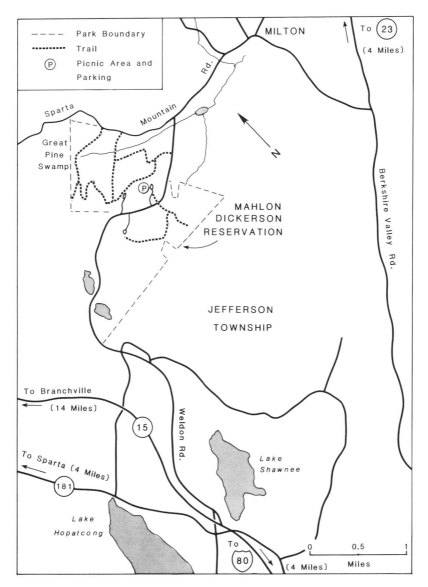

MAP 8. Mahlon Dickerson Reservation

The reservation is of interest mainly because of its diversity of breeding birds. Hike some of the trails in the northern part of the park (with the help of a compass), and you should find many of the following species: Red-shouldered and Broad-winged Hawks; Ruffed Grouse; Wild Turkey; American Woodcock; Black-billed and Yellow-billed Cuckoos; Eastern Screech, Barred, and Great Horned Owls; Pileated Woodpecker; Acadian Flycatcher; Brown Creeper; Winter Wren (rare); Hermit Thrush (uncommon); Solitary (hemlocks) and Yellow-throated Vireos; Blue-winged, Chestnut-sided, Black-throated Green (hemlocks), Blackburnian, Black-and-white, Worm-eating, Hooded, and Canada Warblers; American Redstart; Ovenbird; Northern and Louisiana Waterthrushes; Rose-breasted Grosbeak; and Purple Finch; plus other, more common, species. Worm-eating, Hooded, and Canada Warblers usually sing from the woods around the parking lot.

Another point of access to the northern part of Mahlon Dickerson Reservation is along Sparta Mountain Rd. Drive out the entrance road to Weldon Rd. and turn left. Go about 1.1 miles, past some school buildings, to the first road on the left, which is Sparta Mountain Rd. Follow this winding road, which soon becomes dirt, for about 0.8 miles to where there is a trail (actually an abandoned road) on the left. Park on the side of Sparta Mountain Rd. and hike the trail, which after about a quarter-mile passes along the edge of the Great Pine Swamp (actually a rhododendron–Black Spruce bog).

The shortest route back to I-80 is to return the way you came.

A copy of the trail map for Mahlon Dickerson Reservation can be obtained from the Morris County Park Commission, 53 East Hanover Ave., P.O. Box 1295R, Morristown, NJ 07960.

Whittingham Wildlife Management Area

Whittingham Wildlife Management Area (known to birders as Whittingham Swamp), containing 1,514 acres of fields, hedgerows, wooded limestone ridges, and a large, spring-fed swamp, is located near Newton, Sussex County, in northwestern New Jersey. The Whittingham tract is better known for the abundance and variety of its ferns, including the bizarre Walking Fern, than for its birdlife, but it supports an interesting diversity of breeding birds and attracts migrant songbirds in spring and fall. A 400-acre portion of the WMA is designated a Natural Area, where no hunting is allowed.

The most unusual nesting species at Whittingham is Prothonotary Warbler, here near the northern limit of its range east of the Appalachians. Other summer or year-round residents include Wood Duck, Ruffed Grouse, Wild Turkey, Pileated Woodpecker, and a variety of warblers. Among the mammals that inhabit the swamp and its surroundings are Beaver, River Otter, and Red Fox, but all three are very shy and hard to see.

Note: The Whittingham WMA is open to hunters during the hunting season (roughly October through December) every day but Sunday. On other days at that season, do not venture into the WMA.

Directions

From Interstate 80, Exit 25 (US 206 North, Newton), take Rt. 206 6.0 miles to the only traffic light in Andover. Continue straight through this light for about 2.9 miles to the Fredon-Springdale Rd. (Rt. 618) on the left. The only street sign is a small, obscure one that reads "Fredon Road." Just before the left turn, there is a large old barn on the left with a sign for a flea market. On the northwest corner of the intersection is a small restaurant, which will be on your

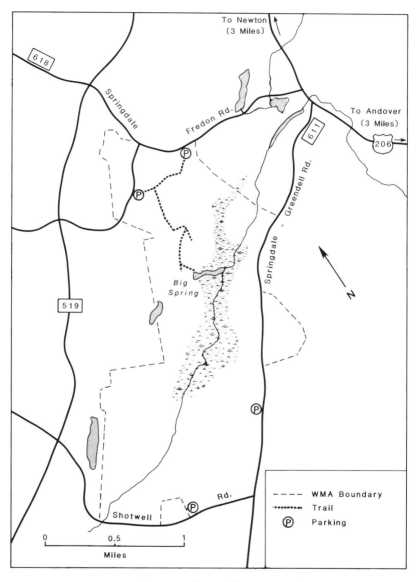

MAP 9. Whittingham WMA

right after you turn left onto Fredon-Springdale Rd. About 1.1 miles along Fredon-Springdale Rd. is a parking lot for the WMA on the left. A better place to park, however, is reached by continuing for another 0.3 miles to a junction, where you turn left. Go 0.4 miles to a small parking area on the left, where there is a gate across an old road.

Birding

Walk around the gate and down the road across a field lined with hedgerows. In a few hundred yards, you will pass around a wooden gate. Just beyond the gate, the road forks; the left fork leads to the first parking area, so take the right fork. In about 0.3 miles, an old fence and gate mark the beginning of the Natural Area. The road soon enters a dense deciduous woodland with numerous rocky outcroppings of limestone. Here you should spend some time examining the variety of ferns and looking for the unique Walking Fern, which grows on moss-covered boulders. The single long, triangular frond of this fern looks much like a leaf from a flowering plant; the fern propagates by taking root wherever the long, pointed end of the frond touches the moss. Whittingham is probably the best place in New Jersey to find this unusual plant easily.

When the road emerges from the woods into an open field, continue straight ahead. After a few hundred yards, you will approach some more woods and will see open water down the hill to the left. Take a path down to the water, where you should be able to see Big Spring as it emerges from under some rocks; this is a principal source of the stream that runs through the Whittingham tract. In summer, Big Spring is home to one or two pairs of Prothonotary Warblers. Several mowed trails connect with the trail to Big Spring; by following them, you can explore most of the northeastern half of the WMA (a compass is helpful).

In May and in August–September, most of the regular migrant songbirds that pass through New Jersey stop off at Whittingham. These include some of the more sought-after species such as Olive-sided and Yellow-bellied (mainly fall) Flycatchers, Gray-cheeked Thrush (mainly fall), Philadelphia Vireo (fall only), and Mourning

Warbler (spring). Breeding birds include Pied-billed Grebe (rare); Green-backed Heron; Wood Duck; Broad-winged and Red-tailed Hawks; Ruffed Grouse; Wild Turkey; Virginia Rail; Sora; Common Moorhen; Spotted Sandpiper; American Woodcock; Belted Kingfisher; Red-bellied and Pileated Woodpecker; Willow Flycatcher; Northern Rough-winged Swallow; Yellow-throated Vireo; Blue-winged, Golden-winged, Cerulean, and Canada Warblers; Northern and Louisiana Waterthrushes; Rose-breasted Grosbeak; Field and Swamp Sparrows; and many of the other common species of northern New Jersey.

To reach several other points of access to the Whittingham WMA, return to the junction of Fredon-Springdale Rd. with US 206. Turn right and go 0.1 miles to the junction with Springdale-Greendell Rd. (Rt. 611). Bear right and go 2.3 miles to another WMA parking lot, on the right. After the first mile of Rt. 611, all the land to your right is part of the Whittingham tract, and there are no No Parking signs, so you can presumably park anywhere and explore the woods, fields, and swamp to the west.

To reach the next parking area, continue on Rt. 611 for 0.6 miles, then turn right onto Shotwell Rd. (Rt. 608). Drive 0.4 miles to a parking area on the right. The final point of access is another parking lot on the right, 0.6 miles farther along Shotwell Rd.

All six eastern swallows nest at nearby Paulins Kill Lake, which has also provided occasional rarities. To reach the best spot, return to US 206, turn left, and follow it into Newton. Just past the center of town, turn left onto Rt. 519, go about 0.8 miles, and turn left onto Plotts Rd., the first left after Don Bosco College. After about 0.8 miles, there is a large marsh on the right which occasionally has Alder Flycatcher. Willow Flycatcher is abundant here, so listen carefully to the songs.

It is 1.2 miles farther to Junction Rd. Turn left, then immediately right onto Parson Rd., which goes under a railroad trestle. In about 0.3 miles, the road becomes a causeway across a marsh at the upper end of Paulins Kill Lake; White Ibis and Purple Gallinule appeared here in the summer of 1975. Hooded Merganser has nested here at least once. Virginia Rail and Sora call from the marsh in spring and summer, and Eastern Phoebe nests under the bridge. Cliff Swallow and Barn Swallow nest in the nearby farm buildings; Purple Martin,

Tree Swallow, Northern Rough-winged Swallow, and Bank Swallow also nest nearby, and all can be seen hawking insects over the lake and marsh from May through the summer.

Another good local birding spot is Swartswood Lake, noted for a variety of ducks in migration. To reach Swartswood Lake from Newton, turn left off US 206 onto Rt. 519 just north of the center of town. Go 0.4 miles and turn left onto Swartswood Rd. (Rt. 622), following the signs to Swartswood Lake State Park. Drive west on Rt. 622 for about 4.5 miles, then turn left onto Swartswood East Side Rd. Go about 0.6 miles, then turn right into Swartswood Lake State Park (there is an entrance fee in summer). During the waterfowl migration in March–April and October–November, a good selection of both dabbling ducks and diving ducks visit the lake. Scaup, Bufflehead, and Common Goldeneye are regular visitors, while rarer species such as Oldsquaw and scoters have also occurred.

Waterloo

The area around Waterloo Village, a restored historic community along the Musconetcong River in extreme southern Sussex County, is a favorite birding location in spring. Other seasons can be rewarding also—especially summer, when there are a variety of breeding species. Most of the best birding spots are within Allamuchy Mountain State Park, an undeveloped preserve covering 6,000 acres in Morris, Sussex, and Warren counties. The main part of the park is accessible from Rt. 517; directions are given on p. 103.

The Waterloo area is famous as supporting one of the first regular breeding colonies of Cerulean Warblers in New Jersey. First discovered here in 1949, these warblers are now widespread as nesting birds in the northern part of the state; however, the Waterloo colony is a continuing attraction. Golden-winged Warbler and Worm-eating Warbler also bring birders to this site.

Directions

From Interstate 80, Exit 25 (Rt. 206 North, Stanhope), follow Rt. 206 for four miles to the traffic light at Waterloo Rd. (watch for the sign to Waterloo Village). Turn left, go about 0.8 miles, and take a dirt road angling off to the left. After a couple of hundred yards turn left on another dirt road (Kay's Rd.), and park at the dead end by the Musconetcong River.

Birding

Walk back along the road to your left, and follow the dirt road back to Waterloo Rd. Turn left and walk a short distance on Waterloo Rd. to an old railroad crossing, where the tracks have been removed. In spring, the area around the old railroad bed for a half-mile in either

59

MAP 10. Waterloo

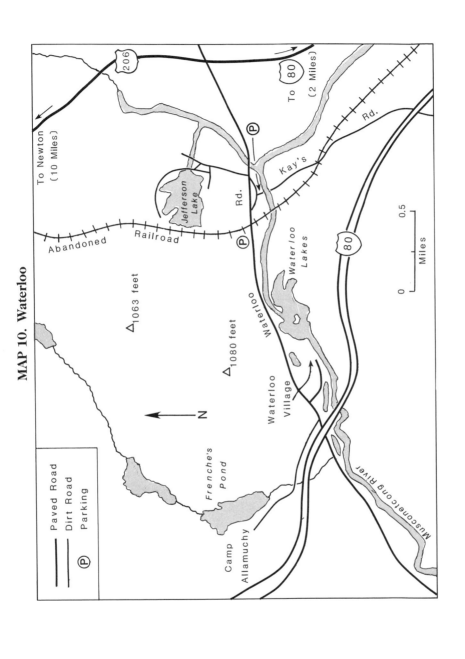

direction is excellent for migrant and nesting passerines. In early 1987, the railroad bed south of Waterloo Rd. was paved to create a new access road to Waterloo Village. The road can still be walked, but the birding is much more difficult because of the traffic, although the birds are still there.

Walk south toward the bridge that spans the Musconetcong River. The woods on your right and those farther down the tracks can be teeming with migrants on a good day in mid-May. Watch for cuckoos, any of the eastern flycatchers (Olive-sided is regular in May), both kinglets, Blue-gray Gnatcatcher, thrushes (all except Gray-cheeked are common), vireos (all but Philadelphia in spring), warblers (more than 30 species are possible in spring), Scarlet Tanager, Rose-breasted Grosbeak, Indigo Bunting, sparrows, Bobolink, blackbirds, Northern Oriole, and Purple Finch, among others. Early in the morning, Wood Ducks and Great Blue Herons often can be seen flying overhead—they feed in a large marshy area a quarter-mile downstream.

As you cross the bridge, listen for Warbling Vireo and Northern Waterthrush, which nest along the river. A short distance ahead on the right, Golden-winged Warbler usually nests around the edges of a field. Blue-winged Warbler is present as well, giving you a chance to compare their two-part song (*bee-buzz*) with the four-part song of the Golden-wing (*bee-bz-bz-bz*). Here, as in other places where the breeding ranges of these two species overlap, the Blue-wing seems to be gradually displacing the Golden-wing, and it may not be many more years before the Golden-wings are gone. Both the Brewster's- and Lawrence's-type hybrids are possible here.

A few pairs of American Woodcock also nest around the edges of the fields. The males can be seen performing their interesting courtship flight most evenings in March and April. To see them, plan to arrive about sunset and stand on the edge of the road facing the field. You should shortly hear the *peent* call of the male. This call is given only from the ground, however, and it will be almost dark before they begin to take flight. When they do, the whistling of their wings gives them away, but they are hard to spot as they circle high in the sky giving a constant twittering call. Finally, after a flight that lasts about a minute, they utter a few chirps and plummet to earth in an erratic zig-zag path.

Beyond the field, the woods on both sides of the road provide varied wooded habitat that is especially attractive to migrants. When you come to a dirt road (Kays Rd.), you can either retrace your path or turn left and follow the road back to the parking area. The road has little traffic and is excellent for migrants.

The first hundred yards along the railroad bed north of Waterloo Rd. also has been a favorite nesting area for Golden-winged Warbler. Worm-eating Warbler is sometimes on the hillside on the right, while Louisiana Waterthrush is usually on territory along the little stream on the left side of the path. Listen for the loud, slow drumming of Pileated Woodpecker, which is frequently heard and occasionally seen flying overhead. This section of the path is good for migrants to at least the north end of Jefferson Lake (about one-half mile); the state park lands include the railroad bed for an additional 1.5 miles. Jefferson Lake may have all the swallows in migration. Pied-billed Grebe, Wood Duck, and Osprey are regular in spring.

Return to Waterloo Rd. and walk west about 200 feet to a path on the right. In the woods along this path you may encounter Ruffed Grouse, which nest commonly, Worm-eating Warbler, and a variety of other nesting and migrant songbirds.

In the fall this area receives less attention, as many birders head for coastal spots. Nevertheless, in August and September the entire stretch along the railroad bed can produce all the regular spring migrants, plus a few of the more sought-after autumn specialties: Yellow-bellied Flycatcher and Philadelphia Vireo are frequent; Gray-cheeked Thrush is more common at this season than in spring, and Connecticut Warbler is a possibility.

Go back to your car and drive west along Waterloo Rd. In about one-half mile you will see on the left Waterloo Lakes, a marshy impoundment of the Musconetcong River that has nesting Mute Swans, Wood Ducks, Marsh Wrens, and Swamp Sparrows. It is easier to park here, on the left side of the road, on your return trip. Yellow-throated Vireo and Cerulean Warbler nest in the tall trees on the right, and Hooded Warbler and Worm-eating Warbler on the steep slopes, but after early morning the traffic on this busy road makes birding difficult.

You will soon come to Waterloo Village on the left. This restored historic village along the Morris Canal is open from the Tuesday after Easter through December, Tuesday to Sunday, from 10:00 A.M.

to 6:00 P.M. Admission is charged. The town re-creates a little of the history of the area 150 years ago, when it was a thriving way station along the Morris Canal, used to transport coal from Pennsylvania to the many iron forges and furnaces in the New Jersey Highlands from 1831 to 1900.

Continuing on Waterloo Rd. for about one-half mile (1.3 miles from the railroad bed), you will find a sign for the Allamuchy Mountain Boy Scout Camp on the right. Turn right and follow this road for about 0.6 miles to the camp entrance. Ask at the ranger's residence (the first building on the left) for permission to bird, then continue about 50 yards to a large parking lot on the left. Cerulean Warblers can usually be seen and heard in the tall trees nearby.

Walk along the road that goes past the parking lot, where there may be many migrants in spring. A wet area on the left has nesting Brown Creeper and Northern Waterthrush. Large rectangular holes in many of the trees are evidence of Pileated Woodpecker, and you may see one if you are lucky. If there are no scouts around, you can explore the camp at leisure. To the north (right) of the road is Frenche's Pond, which teems with swallows during migration.

After returning to your car and driving back to Waterloo Rd., you may want to stop and scan the Waterloo Lakes mentioned earlier. The more adventurous can explore a large section of Allamuchy Mountain State Park, lying to the north and west of Waterloo Rd. between the railroad bed and the Boy Scout Camp, that has no marked trails. This area, which is best birded with a topographical map (Stanhope and Tranquility quadrangles) and a compass, ascends to more than 1,200 feet. Several northern species, including Winter Wren, have been found nesting here.

Jenny Jump
State Forest

Jenny Jump State Forest and the adjacent areas along Shades of Death Rd. (now called Shades Rd.) in Warren County are known for their interesting diversity of breeding birds and for the excellent passage of migrant songbirds in May. The forest consists of several unconnected parcels totaling more than 1,100 acres. The largest unit, and the only one readily accessible to the public, runs for about 2 miles along Jenny Jump Mountain near Hope. Nearby, but outside the state forest, Shades Rd. follows the base of the mountain for several miles above the Pequest River Valley, and takes in a variety of habitats ranging from sod farms, swampy areas, and overgrown fields to dense, mature deciduous woods on steep hillsides.

Along Shades Rd. you can expect to find most of the flycatchers, swallows, thrushes, vireos, warblers, and sparrows that pass through northwestern New Jersey in May, including such hard-to-find species as Olive-sided Flycatcher, Yellow-bellied Flycatcher, Gray-cheeked Thrush (uncommon), and Golden-winged Warbler. Some of the interesting breeding birds at Jenny Jump and Shades Road include Ruffed Grouse, Brown Creeper, Alder Flycatcher (1983), Winter Wren (1984), Hermit Thrush (1984), Golden-winged Warbler, Northern Parula (2 pairs in 1984), Cerulean Warbler (common), and Worm-eating Warbler (common).

Directions

From northeastern New Jersey, take Interstate 80 west to Exit 12 (Rt. 521, Hope, and Blairstown). From the exit ramp, turn left onto Rt. 521. Go about one mile, into Hope, and turn left onto Rt. 519. Drive about 1 mile, then turn right onto Shiloh Rd., where there is a

MAP 11. Jenny Jump State Forest

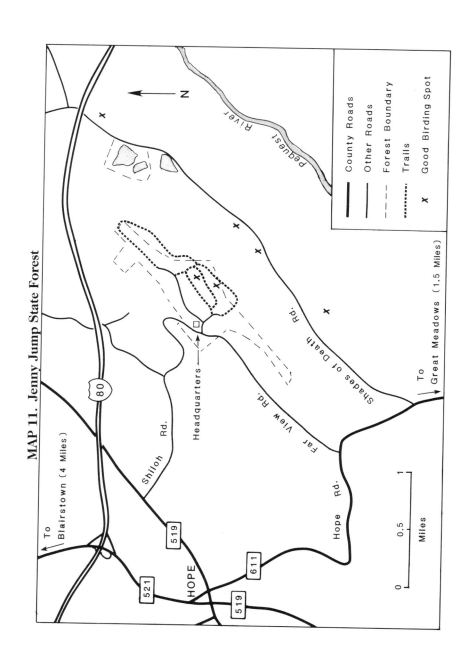

Legend:

———	County Roads
——	Other Roads
– – –	Forest Boundary
········	Trails
X	Good Birding Spot

N

To Blairstown (4 Miles)

HOPE

Shiloh Rd.

Headquarters

Far View Rd.

Shades of Death Rd.

Hope Rd.

Pequest River

521

519

519

611

80

To Great Meadows (1.5 Miles)

Miles
0   0.5   1

sign for Jenny Jump State Forest. Follow this for almost 3 miles, bearing left at the first junction and right at the second, to the entrance to the state forest, on the left.

From southern New Jersey, take the Garden State Parkway or the New Jersey Turnpike, Interstate 287, and US 206 north to the intersection with I-80. Go west on I-80 for 15 miles to exit (Rt. 521), and proceed as described above.

From the Philadelphia or Trenton areas, an alternative is to take Interstate 95 and Rt. 31 north to the intersection with Rt. 519 in Bridgeville, Warren County. Turn right and go 7 miles to Hope, then proceed as described above.

Shades Rd. can also be reached from Exit 19 (Allamuchy-Hackettstown) of I-80 at Rt. 517. Follow Rt. 517 south for about 5 miles into Hackettstown, then turn right (west) onto US 46. Continue for about 5 miles to Great Meadows, then turn right onto Rt. 611 at the sign for Hope. Shades Rd. is 1.7 miles ahead, on the right.

Birding

Enter Jenny Jump State Forest, drive about 200 yards, then turn left onto the oval drive that leads to the headquarters; stop at the office for a map of the forest. Continue up the hill on the entrance road to the parking lot for the Notch Picnic Area, where the trails begin. The Summit Trail begins at the north end of the parking lot, near the modern rest rooms. Follow this trail for about 0.4 miles to a vista, at almost 1,100 feet elevation, that overlooks the scenic Pequest Valley to the east.

The Summit Trail continues for another 300 yards to a trail junction where you have three choices: (1) You can turn right onto the Spring Trail, which makes a steep descent to about 900 feet elevation, then loops around to the south and west and returns to the parking lot. (2) You can turn left and return to the parking lot via the Swamp Trail. (3) The final option, if you are prepared for a longer hike, is to continue straight ahead on the Summit Trail, which eventually reaches Group Campsite "B" at the extreme northern end of the forest after about 0.7 miles. You can then return to the parking lot by the old road that leads south from the group campsite, through the main camping area. Turn left onto the Swamp Trail near the south end of the camping area, and proceed another one-half mile back to your car.

Jenny Jump is seldom visited during migration, when Shades Rd. and other places are more productive, but an interesting variety of nesting birds can be found here from May through July. These include Turkey Vulture; Broad-winged and Red-tailed Hawks; Ruffed Grouse; Wild Turkey; Black-billed and Yellow-billed Cuckoos; Eastern Screech and Great Horned Owls; Pileated Woodpecker (fairly common); Brown Creeper (in hemlock glens); Winter Wren (rare on rocky slopes); Eastern Bluebird; Cedar Waxwing; Blue-winged, Chestnut-sided (common), Black-throated Green (in hemlocks), Prairie, Cerulean (common in tall deciduous trees), Black-and-white, Worm-eating (common on wooded slopes), Hooded, and Canada Warblers; American Redstart; Rose-breasted Grosbeak; Indigo Bunting; Chipping and Field Sparrows; and many other summer and year-round residents.

To reach Shades Rd., return to the state forest entrance and turn left onto Far View Rd. Go about 1.6 miles to Rt. 611, then turn left. Drive 0.7 miles and turn onto the first paved road on the left, which is Shades Rd.

The Pequest Valley, on your right, is a large, flat expanse of truck farms and sod farms. The sod farms attract a variety of grassland shorebirds in August and September. About 0.7 miles along Shades Rd. is the headquarters of Liberty Sod Farms, on the right. The management usually permits birders to park at the headquarters and walk along the roads that crisscross the sod areas; if you are interested, stop and inquire. You may also see Great Blue Herons from the large rookery (225+ nests) a few miles across the valley, American Kestrel, and a smattering of songbirds.

Shades Rd. soon enters a beautiful deciduous woods, with stands of mature Sugar Maple, Black Walnut, ashes, oaks, Slippery Elm, and many other species. You can park at either of two pullouts, one at 2.4 miles north of Rt. 611 and the second at 2.7 miles, and walk along the lightly traveled road. In May the woods are alive with many migrant passerines, while in June and July you will find a diverse selection of breeding birds. Many of the species noted for Jenny

Jump State Forest also nest along Shades Rd.; in addition there have been Northern Parula (two pairs in 1984) and Yellow-throated Vireo.

About 3.8 miles north of Rt. 611 an overgrown field on the right has several pairs of nesting Golden-winged Warblers, plus White-eyed Vireo and Swamp Sparrow. Beyond the I-80 overpass are more fields, where American Goldfinch is abundant and Grasshopper Sparrow has been found on occasion, along with Willow Flycatcher.

Worthington State Forest

This 5,830-acre state forest in Warren County, which includes the New Jersey side of the famous Delaware Water Gap, contains some of the most scenic and rugged terrain in the state. Elevations range from about 300 feet along the Delaware River to 1,549 feet, and include the 1,527-foot Mt. Tammany, which overlooks the gap. Worthington State Forest takes in a variety of habitats, from the bottomlands along the river, through steep hillsides with climax deciduous forest and hemlock-shrouded ravines, to the dry ridgetops of the Kittatinny Mountains. Nestled in the forest is beautiful Sunfish Pond, a glacial lake lying at 1,382 feet in a broad valley between two ridges. Most of the land adjoining Worthington State Forest is in the Delaware Water Gap National Recreation Area, which may eventually comprise as much as 70,000 acres of land along the Delaware in Pennsylvania and in Sussex and Warren counties in New Jersey.

Birdlife in Worthington State Forest is as diverse as the terrain. Old Mine Rd. along the Delaware River is excellent for migrants in spring and fall; it supports an interesting variety of breeding birds and is a good area for winter finches during invasion years. Bald Eagles from the population that winters in Sullivan County, New York, are regularly seen this far downriver. Most of the state forest, including all the higher elevations, is accessible only on foot; reaching it usually involves a strenuous hike of several miles. Consequently the area receives insufficient attention from birders. Those who spend the time and effort to explore Worthington State Forest, however, will find many birds of interest.

Directions

Take Interstate 80 west toward Pennsylvania and the Delaware Water Gap. Just after you pass through the gap, watch for a rest area

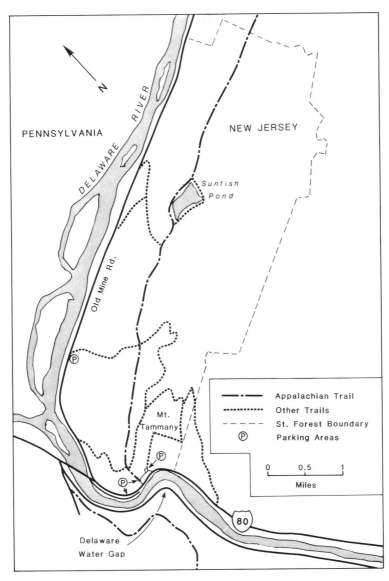

MAP 12. Worthington State Forest

sign on the right, and pull in. If you miss the rest area, take the next exit (the last one in New Jersey) and turn left from the exit ramp, following the signs for the National Recreation Area Information Center. Drive past the Information Center (or stop and get a map) to the next intersection. Turn left, follow the road under the highway to a stop sign, turn right, and drive a short distance to the rest area.

Birding

If you are prepared for a strenuous hike, this is a good place to start. There are two parking lots, with a trail leaving from each. Tammany Trail (marked by red blazes) starts at the first parking area and climbs almost 1,200 feet to the summit of Mt. Tammany in just one mile. It is a steep, rocky, moderately difficult trail and is not particularly birdy. You might find nesting Wild Turkey, Winter Wren, Hermit Thrush, or Dark-eyed Junco, however.

The trail that leaves from the second parking area (0.2 miles further along) is Dunnfield Hollow Trail, which follows the Appalachian Trail for about three-quarters of a mile. Dunnfield Creek is a clear, rock-strewn stream that still supports native Brook Trout. The creek begins high on the Kittatinny Ridge near Sunfish Pond, and falls more than 1,000 feet to the Delaware River in less than 4 miles. Dunnfield Hollow Trail branches from the Appalachian Trail on the right as an abandoned road (marked by blue blazes), that follows Dunnfield Creek for another 1.5 miles to an old sawmill. It then climbs a steep ravine and rejoins the Appalachian Trail after about three-quarters of a mile. Turn left (southwest) on the Appalachian Trail (marked by white blazes) to return to your car. If you are adventuresome, a right turn at the junction with the Appalachian Trail will take you on a 1.8-mile hike to Sunfish Pond.

Another 0.4 miles up the Dunnfield Hollow Trail there is a fork, where the blue-blazed trail goes right and Dunnfield Hollow Trail bears left. The blue-blazed trail leads to the summit of Mt. Tammany, where it connects with Tammany Trail (which leads to the first parking area). You can thus hike a 3.5-mile loop via Tammany Trail and the blue-blazed trail, or a 5-mile loop via Dunnfield Hollow Trail to the sawmill and back on the Appalachian Trail.

The blue-blazed trail, Dunnfield Hollow Trail, and Appalachian

Trail have many more birds than Tammany Trail, as they pass through a variety of habitats, including the dry ridgetop oak woods; dark hemlock glens; and mature deciduous woods of oak, maple, beech, Yellow Birch, and others. The understory consists of rhododendron or Mountain Laurel in some areas, and deciduous trees and shrubs such as Flowering Dogwood and Witch Hazel in others.

Typical breeding birds of Worthington State Forest include Wood Duck; Broad-winged Hawk; Ruffed Grouse; Wild Turkey; American Woodcock; Black-billed and Yellow-billed Cuckoos; Eastern Screech, Great Horned, and Barred Owls; Chimney Swift; Ruby-throated Hummingbird; Pileated Woodpecker; Acadian and Least Flycatchers; Brown Creeper; Cedar Waxwing; Solitary (hemlocks) and Yellow-throated Vireos; Chestnut-sided, Black-throated Green, Blackburnian, Cerulean, Black-and-white, Worm-eating, Hooded, and Canada Warblers; American Redstart; Northern Waterthrush; Rose-breasted Grosbeak; and many other, more common, species. Some of the less common nesting species which should be searched are Cooper's Hawk, Northern Goshawk, Red-shouldered Hawk, Whip-poor-will, Winter Wren, Eastern Bluebird, Hermit Thrush, Nashville Warbler, Northern Parula (along the Delaware River), White-throated Sparrow, and Purple Finch.

To explore more of the state forest, continue on I-80 for 0.7 miles from the Dunnfield Natural Area parking lot to Exit 1, the last exit in New Jersey; turn right from the exit ramp onto Old Mine Rd. Go north for about one mile to the Far View parking lot, on the right. A half-mile stretch of Old Mine Rd. just north of I-80 is open only to one-way traffic, which is controlled by a traffic light.

Any of the stops along Old Mine Rd. may have migrants in spring and fall, especially where the road passes close to the Delaware River. In fall, winter, or spring, walk down to the river to look for Common Goldeneye or Common Merganser and maybe even a Bald Eagle. Osprey is a regular migrant along the river in April and September–October. The hemlock groves and spruce plantings along Old Mine Rd. are worth checking for northern finches in winter; Pine Grosbeak, Red Crossbill, and White-winged Crossbill have been found, and Pine Siskin and Evening Grosbeak are annual visitors.

Golden-crowned Kinglet nested in the spruce grove about 1.2 miles north of the Far View parking lot in 1984. Hooded Warbler is a common breeding bird along this stretch of Old Mine Rd., and

Northern Parula has recently begun nesting after an absence of many years. Yellow-breasted Chat can be found in some of the brushy fields along Old Mine Rd., and Prairie Warbler is regular in the fields near Van Campens Glen. Kentucky Warbler is usually present every year, but is rare and hard to find. Common Mergansers can sometimes be seen courting in the Delaware River from about Pokono Island north, and broods have been seen early in the summer.

About 100 yards north of the Far View parking lot, an abandoned road (with an iron gate) on the right starts up the side of the hill, where Brown Creeper nests. After about a mile (and 1,000 feet of elevation), the road intersects the Appalachian Trail at the same point as the trail from Dunnfield Hollow. An interesting hike can be made by turning left on the Appalachian Trail and continuing about 1.8 miles to Sunfish Pond, a delightful spot to enjoy your lunch. This beautiful glacial lake was nearly turned into a pumped storage reservoir during the 1960s, but the resulting uproar caused the plans to be changed and the pond is now a protected natural area within the state forest.

The 1.5-mile hike around Sunfish Pond is interesting, but not very birdy. To complete your hike, return south along the Appalachian Trail for about one-half mile to Campsite No. 2, which you passed on your way north. Here a trail marked by blue blazes leads to the right. This trail, an abandoned road, leads downhill to Old Mine Rd. in about 1.4 miles (stay left when the road forks after about a mile). Turn left and walk the 1.9 miles back to your car along Old Mine Rd., which has little traffic and good birding.

If you have time, you may wish to continue north along Old Mine Rd. and explore other areas within the Delaware Water Gap National Recreation Area. A particularly attractive spot is Van Campens Glen, which is on the right about 8.6 miles north of the Far View parking lot. Two miles past Van Campens Glen is the restored village of Millbrook, where in summer National Park Service personnel re-enact the daily chores common a hundred years ago. At Millbrook, the Blairstown-Millbrook Rd. (Rt. 602) turns south and crosses the Kittatinny Mountains at Millbrook Gap before descending into Blairstown. From Blairstown, you can follow Rt. 521 back to I-80.

Black River Wildlife Management Area

Black River Wildlife Management Area (WMA) in western Morris County near Chester, covers 3,000 acres of river bottom, freshwater marsh, swampy woodland, upland deciduous woods, and fields. Nearly 200 species of birds have been found here during the past few years, and an amazing variety (about 100 species) nest. Spring and summer are the best seasons at Black River, but it is worth visiting at any time of the year.

Although birders have long visited the Black River area occasionally, not until 1979 did David Harrison begin the thorough field studies that have revealed the full potential of this attractive spot. Among the more interesting breeding species are Least Bittern; Virginia Rail; Sora; Eastern Screech, Great Horned, and Barred Owls; Alder Flycatcher; Marsh Wren; Chestnut-sided (common), Cerulean, Worm-eating, Kentucky, Hooded, and Canada (abundant) Warblers; Northern and Louisiana Waterthrushes; Yellow-breasted Chat; Bobolink; and Grasshopper Sparrow.

Note: Black River is a very popular WMA, and is heavily used by hunters from October through December—except on Sundays, when no hunting is allowed. On other days during this season, confine your visits to the paved roads. There are portable toilets near the Firearms Training Area at the Headquarters, except in winter.

Directions

There are several points of access to Black River WMA and it boasts many good birding spots. The area most frequently visited by birders includes the bridge over the Black River at Pleasant Hill Road and the abandoned railroad bed that parallels the river, starting a short distance south of the bridge. To reach this point:

MAP 13. Black River WMA

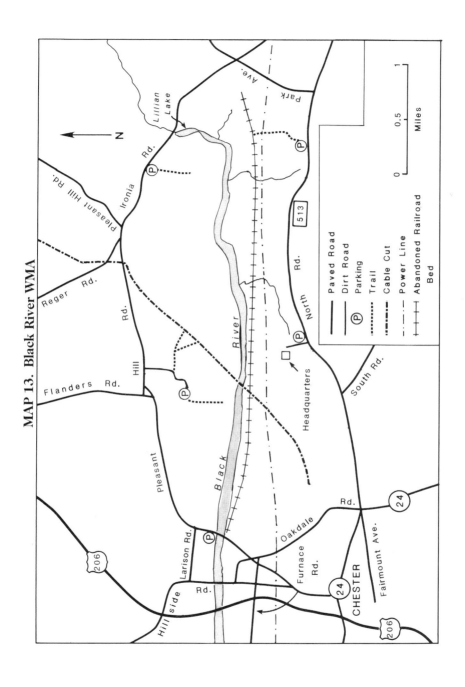

From southern New Jersey or the Philadelphia area, take the New Jersey Turnpike or the Garden State Parkway north to Interstate 287. Follow I-287 north to Exit 18B (US 206 North, Bedminster, and Netcong), about one mile north of Interstate 78. Go 10 miles north on US 206 to the intersection with Rt. 24 in Chester, then continue straight ahead on Rt. 206 for 0.8 miles to the intersection with Furnace Rd. Turn right, go about 0.2 miles to the second stop sign, and turn left onto Pleasant Hill Rd. Follow this for one-half mile; just after crossing the bridge over the Black River, turn left into an unpaved parking area.

From central New Jersey, take US 206 and I-287, or I-78 and I-287 north to I-287 Exit 18B (US 206 North, Bedminster, and Netcong). Continue as described in the preceding paragraph.

From northeastern or northwestern New Jersey, take Interstate 80 to Exit 27 (US 206 South). Go south on Rt. 206 for about 7 miles to Furnace Rd., the first intersection after crossing the bridge over the inconspicuous Black River (0.3 miles). Turn left and proceed as described above.

Birding

From the Pleasant Hill Road parking area, where Least Flycatcher and Warbling Vireo usually nest, walk back to the bridge across the Black River. This is a good spot for waterfowl (especially Ring-necked Duck and Hooded Merganser) and Spotted and Solitary Sandpipers in migration, and in the breeding season for Least Bittern; rails; Willow Flycatcher; Tree and Rough-winged Swallows, Barn Swallow (under the bridge), Marsh Wren, Yellow Warbler, Common Yellowthroat, Red-winged Blackbird, Swamp Sparrow (abundant), and Song Sparrow. Continue across the bridge to a gate on the left. Go around the gate, and walk east along the trail provided by an abandoned railroad bed.

You can walk this trail for several miles, following the Black River on the left, to Ironia Road. It is excellent during spring migration, when about 30 species of warblers and many other songbirds can be found, and is one of the best areas for breeding birds in the WMA. During June, more than 70 nesting species can be found along the first 2 miles of the trail.

Other nesting birds along this stretch of the river are Green-backed Heron; Canada Goose; Wood Duck; Common Moorhen (scarce); both cuckoos (most years); Eastern Kingbird; Cedar Waxwing; Yellow-throated Vireo; Blue-winged, Chestnut-sided, Black-and-white, and Canada (abundant) Warblers; Ovenbird (abundant); Rose-breasted Grosbeak; and Field Sparrow; Eastern Screech, Great Horned, and Barred Owls all can be heard in this area at night, but seeing one or finding a nest is difficult. Less than one-half mile along the railroad bed, Ruby-throated Hummingbird has nested regularly in a swampy area on the right (south) side of the trail. Louisiana Waterthrush is usually here also. At least one pair of Alder Flycatchers nests each year in the swampy woods between one-half and three-quarters of a mile in from Pleasant Hill Road, making this one of the most reliable spots for that species in New Jersey. Acadian Flycatcher is another occasional breeder here; the only other place in the state where breeding Acadian, Alder, Willow, and Least Flycatchers are known to occur together is the Great Swamp (see that chapter). The railroad bed trail is also noteworthy for having one of the highest densities of nesting Canada Warblers in the state.

Worm-eating, Kentucky, and Hooded Warblers nest on a hillside above the railroad bed. To reach this point, go about one and a quarter miles in from Pleasant Hill Road to an underground cable right-of-way, marked by yellow or orange numbered markers on top of poles. Follow the right-of-way uphill for about 400 yards to a knoll on the left, where the warblers nest. (This spot can also be reached from the parking area at the headquarters, as discussed later.)

You can easily retrace your steps to your car and explore some other birding spots in Black River WMA, including sites along Pleasant Hill Rd., Ironia Rd., Dover-Chester Rd. (3 areas), and a small section west of US 206 which is accessible from Furnace Rd. Descriptions of these sites follow.

Pleasant Hill

To reach this area from the parking lot by the bridge, continue north on Pleasant Hill Rd. for about 1.7 miles, to a dirt road on the right marked by a Black River WMA sign. Follow this road for 0.3 miles to a large parking lot, where you should park near the entrance.

The grove of pines at the parking lot has had Long-eared Owls in winter. Walk back up the entrance road for about 200 yards to an orange gate on the right that marks the beginning of one of the many mowed trails that crisscross this portion of the WMA. Using a compass, follow the trails in a generally eastward direction for a little less than one-half mile until you come to an underground cable right-of-way. Along the way, in the fields and hedgerows, you may encounter Red-tailed Hawk, Tree Swallow, Purple Martin, Eastern Bluebird, Brown Thrasher, White-eyed Vireo, Grasshopper and Field Sparrows, Indigo Bunting, Bobolink, and Eastern Meadowlark.

Turn right at the cable right-of-way, which cuts a 30-foot-wide swath through some mature deciduous woodland, and head south toward the river. There is no path along the cable cut, so by late summer the Bracken Fern and Hay-scented Fern may be waist high. After about one-half mile, a steep hill leads down to the river. Species to be expected here include Willow Flycatcher, Brown Creeper, House Wren, Yellow-throated Vireo, Cerulean, Worm-eating, and Canada Warblers, and many others already mentioned.

Another interesting area can be reached by turning left (northeast) instead of right at the cable cut. Follow the cut northeast for about a quarter-mile, until you come to a stream. Turn right and follow the stream for a half-mile down to the river. The going is not easy, but along the way you may find Alder Flycatcher, Brown Creeper, White-eyed Vireo, Cerulean Warbler, Yellow-breasted Chat, and other species.

Ironia Road

Return to Pleasant Hill Rd. and go right. Drive about 1.8 miles, bearing right after 1.3 miles onto Ironia Rd. (Pleasant Hill Rd. forks left), to a WMA parking lot on the right. Explore the woods, fields, and hedgerows, starting at the orange gate at the east end of the lot. In the fall, this area is good for migrants, including Philadelphia Vireo. Nesting species include Belted Kingfisher, Purple Martin, Brown Creeper, Brown Thrasher, White-eyed Vireo, Canada Warbler, Indigo Bunting, and Bobolink.

Continue on Ironia Rd. for 0.5 miles to a bridge across the Black River. On the right is Lillian Lake, which is really just a wide section of the river; it is good for migrant waterfowl in spring. Northern Waterthrush is usually found near the bridge. Beware the No Parking signs here, and do not leave your car, or you may get a parking ticket.

Ironia

The next birding stop in our tour of Black River WMA is reached by continuing east from the bridge on Ironia Rd. for about 0.9 miles to the stop sign at Park Ave. Turn right and go 0.8 miles to the junction with Rt. 513, the Dover-Chester Rd. Turn right and drive about 0.4 miles to a WMA parking lot on the right. Park near the far (east) end of the lot.

Go through the gate at the northeast corner of the lot and follow the mowed path. Bear left at the first two trail junctions until you start down a long, tree-lined path that is obviously an old road. The road eventually narrows to a trail, and emerges, after about 0.4 miles, onto the cleared right-of-way for the power line previously mentioned. Continue on the trail as it descends toward the river and enters a superb stand of bottomland deciduous woods. Another 300 yards will bring you to trail along the abandoned railroad bed. By turning left and walking for about 1.5 miles, you will come to a stream at a rise in the path. Along the way you may encounter Ruffed Grouse, Northern Waterthrush, Canada Warbler, and many of the species previously noted. In winter, Eastern Screech, Great Horned, Barred, and Northern Saw-whet Owls have been found in this area; the first three species presumably nest here as well.

At the stream, the power line is very close to the railroad bed; about 50 yards before you reach the stream, you will pass a trail on the left. You can walk up the trail to the right-of-way, and return along the power line clearing. Some of the species that nest along the power line are Red-tailed Hawk; Black-billed Cuckoo; Chestnut-sided, Prairie, Cerulean, and Hooded Warblers; Yellow-breasted Chat; Scarlet Tanager; Indigo Bunting; Rufous-sided Towhee; and Field Sparrow.

Headquarters

The headquarters of Black River WMA is reached by continuing west along Rt. 513 for about 1.9 miles to a parking lot on the right. From the west end of the lot, take the trail to the dirt road that leads toward the headquarters. This area is excellent for sparrows in winter, and for Winter Wren in migration. It also has nesting Broad-winged Hawk, Ring-necked Pheasant, Eastern Phoebe, and Yellow-breasted Chat. Walk along the dirt road for about 300 yards until you come to a three-way fork. Continue straight ahead on the middle fork toward a Firearms Training Area sign, and follow the trail for about 200 yards downhill to the power line cut. Turn left and follow the power line for about one-third of a mile to the underground cable cut. The hillside on your left—the same spot described in the initial section— has nesting Worm-eating, Kentucky, and Hooded Warblers. By turning right at the cable cut and heading north down the hill, you will reach the abandoned railroad bed along the Black River.

To return to Rt. 206, continue west on Rt. 513 for about 1.7 miles to a 5-way intersection at Rt. 24. Go straight ahead on Rt. 24 for about one mile to the intersection with Rt. 206.

Jockey Hollow
(Morristown National Historical Park)

The Jockey Hollow section of Morristown National Historical Park preserves more than 1,000 acres of land rich in history. It was here that General George Washington set up quarters for his Continental Army during the winters of 1777–78 and 1779–80. The Morristown area provided a source of food, water, and fuel wood, while the nearby Watchung Ridges enabled the lookouts to observe the activities of the British, 30 miles to the east in New York City. In addition to its historical attributes, the park is also an excellent place to observe spring migration and has an interesting variety of breeding birds.

Jockey Hollow today probably looks much the way it did 200 years ago when Washington's troops camped here, except that the forest is a gradually maturing second-growth woodland of maples, oak, hickories, and towering Tuliptrees rather than the mature forest that existed then. The American Chestnut that dominated the forest in Colonial times is gone, a victim of the chestnut blight; only short-lived sprouts remain as reminders of this magnificent tree.

A few fields around the old Wick farm and several parade grounds are the only open areas in the park. The rest is upland deciduous forest that harbors a good variety of migrant and breeding birds in spring and summer. Among the more noteworthy species are Winter Wren (March–April and October), Pileated Woodpecker (all year), Brown Creeper (all year), Louisiana Waterthrush (April–July), Northern Waterthrush (May–September), Hooded Warbler (May–August), and Kentucky Warbler (May–July). Fall migration is more easily observed elsewhere; in winter, Jockey Hollow is as barren of birds as it is of leaves.

MAP 14. Jockey Hollow

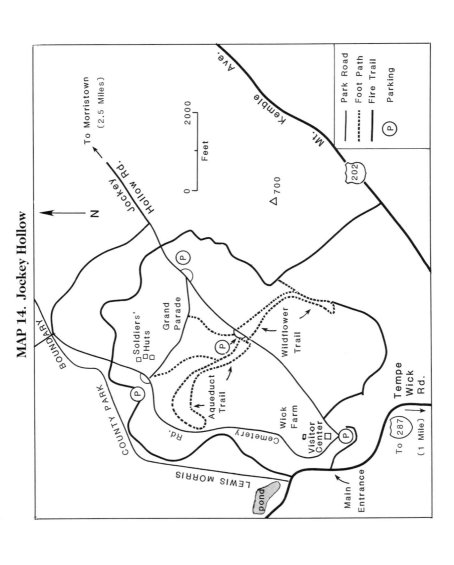

Directions

From the north, take Interstate 287 south to Exit 29 (Harter Rd.). From the exit ramp go left onto Harter Rd. and follow it for about 0.9 miles to Mount Kemble Ave. (Rt. 202). Go left (south) for about 2.2 miles to the traffic light at Tempe Wick Rd. Turn right and go 1.4 miles to the sign at the park entrance road, on the right. Follow the entrance road for 0.3 miles to the Visitor Center parking area. The Visitor Center is open from 9 A.M. to 5 P.M. daily, except Thanksgiving, Christmas, and New Year's Day. Park roads are open every day of the year; the official opening time is 9 A.M., but in practice the gates are open by 7:30 A.M. or earlier, and close at sunset.

From the south, take I-287 north to Exit 26B (Rt. 202, N. Maple Ave.). Watch for the brown signs with white lettering that direct you to the exit for Jockey Hollow—do *not* take Exit 26A (N. Maple Ave., Basking Ridge), which comes just before the Rt. 202 exit. Follow N. Maple for 0.2 miles to the traffic light at Rt. 202. Turn right and go about 1.8 miles to the traffic light at Tempe Wick Rd. Turn left and proceed as described in the preceding paragraph.

Birding

An extensive network of trails and fire roads covers the park (see Map 14). The most productive for birding are generally the Aqueduct Trail and the Wildflower Trail, both of which parallel a stream that has some swampy areas and that passes between wooded hillsides with a variety of birds. To reach the parking lot where these trails start, take Cemetery Rd. from the Visitor Center for 1.2 miles to the junction of Grand Parade Rd. Go right on Grand Parade for about 0.6 miles to Jockey Hollow Rd. Turn right and go about 0.4 miles to the parking lot, on the right.

The starting point for the Aqueduct Trail is at the far end of the parking lot. The trail gradually works its way uphill along the stream to a point just below Cemetery Road, then turns back to finish near its starting point. Round trip is about 1.3 miles; the walking is easy, but the trail can be very muddy in spring.

The Wildflower Trail is located on the opposite (south) side of Jockey Hollow Road. One end of it is near the entrance to the parking lot; the other is a couple of hundred feet beyond the parking lot, just past the bridge over the stream. I usually start at the bridge and check for Eastern Phoebes. The Wildflower Trail is somewhat more strenuous than the Aqueduct Trail, but is by no means difficult. There is a short loop (about one-half mile) and a long loop (about one mile). This trail, too, can be very muddy in spring. You must cross the stream on rocks in several places, which can be tricky if the water is high.

The two trails have similar birds. Late winter and early spring is a good time to look for woodpeckers, as they tend to be active and noisy. Red-bellied, Downy, Hairy, and Pileated Woodpeckers and Northern Flicker are all fairly common; Yellow-bellied Sapsucker is an uncommon migrant. The park is especially known for its resident Pileated Woodpeckers. Listen for their loud, bugle-like call (slower than the similar call of the Flicker) or slow, resonant drumming. They often forage near the ground on trees killed by Gypsy Moths. Ruffed Grouse is another fairly common permanent resident that is frequently heard drumming in spring, but is seldom seen.

By early April, the first Eastern Phoebes and Louisiana Waterthrushes will have arrived and your chances of finding a migrant Winter Wren are good. Broad-winged Hawk, a common breeder, usually turns up by the middle of the month. Most migrant and breeding songbirds do not begin to appear until the end of April, and the middle two weeks of May is the time of greatest activity.

The list of migrants includes many flycatchers (Yellow-bellied mainly in fall), all the thrushes (Gray-cheeked rare), both kinglets, five vireos (Philadelphia in fall only), most of the warblers, and a variety of sparrows, blackbirds, and finches. Solitary and Spotted Sandpipers and Common Snipe have been found along the streams in spring, and a variety of hawks can be expected overhead during fall migration.

Many of the spring migrants remain to nest. The breeding birds, some of which are permanent residents, include: Black-billed and Yellow-billed Cuckoos; Least and Acadian Flycatchers; Eastern Kingbird; Tree and Barn Swallows; Brown Creeper; Carolina and House Wrens; Eastern Bluebird; White-eyed, Yellow-throated, Warbling, and Red-eyed Vireos; Blue-winged, Yellow, Chestnut-sided, Black-and-white, Worm-eating, Kentucky, Hooded (rare), and Canada Warblers; American Redstart; Northern and Louisiana Waterthrushes;

Rose-breasted Grosbeak; Indigo Bunting; Chipping, Field, and Song Sparrows. Most of the other familiar species of deciduous woodlands are here as well.

Two of the more sought-after breeding species, Hooded and Kentucky Warblers, are among the rarest. Hooded is the rarer of the two; it has occasionally nested along the trail that runs from the Aqueduct Trail to the Hospital (see map). Kentucky Warbler has been found there as well, and also near the north end of the Wildflower Trail and along the fire trail between the parking lot on Jockey Hollow Rd. and the Grand Parade.

Winter is the bleakest season at Jockey Hollow, as in all New Jersey deciduous forests. A few wintering hawks may be present, including any of the accipters. Saw-whet Owls have been found roosting in the Eastern Red Cedars near the Wildflower Trail. Field, Fox (rare), Song, White-throated, and American Tree Sparrows and Dark-eyed Juncos inhabit the woods and field edges at this season, and are occasionally joined by winter finches, such as Purple Finch, Common Redpoll, Pine Siskin, and Evening Grosbeak.

To return to the Visitor Center from the parking lot for the Aqueduct and Wildflower Trails, continue on Jockey Hollow Rd. for about 0.7 miles. There are two other entrances to the park (see Map 14); one of these is through Lewis Morris County Park, a 750-acre unit of the Morris County Park System. The habitat here is similar to that in Jockey Hollow, but the park also has numerous picnic areas and playing fields. The other entrance is from Western Ave., which runs south from Morristown to the northeastern boundary of the park, where it becomes Jockey Hollow Rd.

Scherman-Hoffman
Sanctuaries

These twin sanctuaries of the New Jersey Audubon Society include more than 250 acres of upland deciduous forest, fields, and flood-plain in the northeastern corner of Somerset County. The diversity of habitat provided by these nature preserves attracts a wide variety of both migrant and nesting birds; more than 175 species have been recorded, of which about 60 nest in a typical year. Among the more interesting breeding species are Great Horned Owl; Pileated Wood-pecker; Acadian Flycatcher; Brown Creeper; Eastern Bluebird; Ce-rulean, Worm-eating, and Kentucky Warblers; and Louisiana Water-thrush.

Spring migration at Scherman-Hoffman can be outstanding, with at least 25 species of warblers occurring in May, including the elu-sive Mourning Warbler. Other noteworthy spring migrants include Olive-sided Flycatcher (regular in late May–early June), Winter Wren (April–May and October–November), and Yellow-bellied Fly-catcher (May).

Fall migration is also excellent at the sanctuaries, but the dense vegetation makes the birds harder to see than in spring. The first waves of warblers appear in mid-August, while September and Oc-tober can produce spectacular flights of kinglets, thrushes, vireos, Yellow-rumped Warblers, and blackbirds of several species. Among the more sought-after migrants are Olive-sided Flycatcher (August), Yellow-bellied Flycatcher (mainly September), and Connecticut Warbler (rare, in September).

Other interesting species that have occurred in recent years in-clude winter finches, such as Common Redpoll, Pine Siskin, Red Crossbill, White-winged Crossbill and Pine Grosbeak (the latter two rare). A few Black Vultures, which were formerly rare anywhere in the state, have joined a winter Turkey Vulture roost in nearby Ber-nardsville for the past few years and are occasionally seen from the sanctuaries.

MAP 15. Scherman-Hoffman Sanctuaries

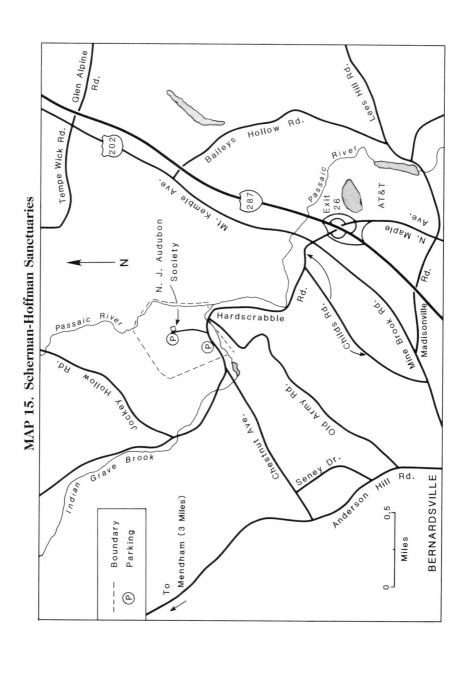

Directions

From the north, take Interstate 287 south to Exit 26B (Bernards-ville). From the exit ramp go a short distance to a traffic light at Rt. 202, then proceed straight ahead through the light onto Childs Rd. Go 0.2 miles, and bear right onto Hardscrabble Rd. After about 0.8 miles you will cross a bridge; the second driveway (uphill) on the right after the bridge is the entrance to the Hoffman Sanctuary.

From the south, take I-287 north to Exit 26B (Rt. 202, N. Maple Ave.)—do *not* take Exit 26A (N. Maple Ave., Basking Ridge), which comes just before the Rt. 202 exit. Follow N. Maple Ave. for 0.2 miles to the traffic light at Rt. 202 and continue straight ahead as just described.

The Hoffman Sanctuary houses the office, bookstore, educational facilities, and rest rooms. The offices are open from 9:00 A.M. to 5:00 P.M., Tuesday through Saturday, and from noon to 5:00 P.M. on Sunday; trail maps are available here. To reach the parking lot for the trails, continue on Hardscrabble Rd. about 100 yards past the Hoffman driveway to the parking lot on the right. If you arrive before 9:00 A.M., you may remove the chain across the entrance to the parking lot—it is not locked. The trails are open every day until 5:00 P.M.

Birding

There are several marked trails, each of which offers some different habitat.

The Nature Trail is a good place to start, especially early in the morning before traffic develops on Hardscrabble Road. The entrance to the trail is directly across the road from the main parking area. This short loop trail along Indian Grave Brook has an abundance of thick undergrowth that provides cover for migrants and becomes a center of activity in spring. Louisiana Waterthrush is usually on territory along the brook after the first week in April, and Winter Wren is possible from late March to mid-April, but the main waves of migrants do not start before the beginning of May. The list is too long to enumerate, but among the more sought-after species are Kentucky and Mourning Warblers, both of which are found here annually during the last 10 days of May.

You can return to the parking lot by way of the Museum Trail, where you are likely to hear a Worm-eating Warbler deliver his dry, rattling song from the hillside above the parking lot. This species, an annual breeder at the sanctuaries, usually arrives in late April and departs by mid-August.

From the parking lot, take the trail toward the Hoffman Fields. In spring, the woods along the way ring with the marvelous songs of Wood Thrushes and Veeries; other woodland species are here as well: Eastern Wood Pewee, Great Crested Flycatcher, Red-eyed Vireo, Scarlet Tanager, Northern Oriole and many others. Just after crossing the driveway to the Hoffman Nature Center, the trail branches; the right path goes through the fields and the left path is part of the Dogwood Trail.

This area is good for Orchard Oriole in May, nesting Eastern Bluebird from March through June (present most of the year), Yellow-throated Vireo, Cerulean Warbler (in recent years), Blue-winged Warbler, and a variety of other migrant and breeding species. Some of the common nesting birds around the borders of the fields are House Wren; Gray Catbird; Northern Mockingbird; Brown Thrasher; Yellow Warbler; Common Yellowthroat; Northern Cardinal; Indigo Bunting; Rufous-sided Towhee; Chipping, Field, and Song Sparrows; Red-winged Blackbird; House Finch; and American Goldfinch.

At the junction of the Field Loop and the Dogwood Trail, continue along the Dogwood Trail, which gradually climbs the ridge above the sanctuary buildings. The top of the ridge is at an elevation of 600 feet, almost 300 feet above the Passaic River, which borders the Hoffman Fields. Along the way you will pass through deciduous woodland dominated by White and Red Oaks, Red Maple, American Beech, and Tuliptrees, the latter occurring as tall, straight giants that tower over the forest.

There are many other varieties of trees and shrubs along the Dogwood Trail, some of which provide food and shelter to Pileated, Downy, Hairy, and Red-bellied Woodpeckers. The Pileated Woodpeckers are most easily seen in March and April, when the pairs are busy courting and building their nests. Other birds to be found along the Dogwood Trail are Ruffed Grouse, Great Horned Owl (mainly in winter), Worm-eating Warbler, Kentucky Warbler (may nest), and Hooded Warbler (occasionally nests).

Most of the familiar species of the upland deciduous forest can be found along the Dogwood Trail, including Broad-winged Hawk,

Yellow-billed Cuckoo (numbers fluctuate), Black-and-white Warbler, American Redstart, and Rose-breasted Grosbeak. The trail eventually returns to the parking lot by way of the Museum Trail, or you can take a detour on the Old Field Loop Trail that has many of the species already mentioned.

Another trail that can be interesting in spring is the River Trail, that runs from Hardscrabble Road along the Passaic River, then upslope to a junction with the Dogwood Trail. This trail should not be attempted without wading boots. It has Wood Duck and Louisiana Waterthrush in spring, plus a good variety of nesting and migrant thrushes, vireos, and warblers. Recently, Acadian Flycatcher has begun nesting along the river.

In fall, any of the trails can be good for migrant passerines. The areas along the streams are prime spots for some of the less common transients such as Yellow-bellied and Olive-sided Flycatchers, Winter Wren (October–November), Philadelphia Vireo, and Connecticut Warbler (rare, in September). Winter brings a variety of sparrows to the feeders at the Hoffman Sanctuary and, in flight years, flocks of Pine Siskins, Purple Finches, and Common Redpolls. Evening Grosbeaks visit the feeders in most years, usually during late fall and early spring; Red Crossbill, White-winged Crossbill and Pine Grosbeak all have occurred (the latter two only once).

To look for Black Vultures in the nearby Turkey Vulture roost, turn right onto Hardscrabble Road from the parking lot and go about 0.1 miles to the first left turn, Chestnut Ave. Follow Chestnut uphill for about one mile to the junction with Seney Dr. on the left. The vulture roost is usually in the backyards of the houses on the north side of Chestnut Ave., opposite Seney. If the vultures are not there, they are often somewhere in or around a square, about 400 yards on a side, bounded by Chestnut, Seney, Rolling Hill Rd., and Anderson Hill Rd. The birds are present from about late November to late March; they stay in the roost until about 9 A.M. on winter mornings, but don't return until late afternoon.

Round Valley Recreation Area

Round Valley Reservoir is the largest body of fresh water in the state. It is located within the Round Valley Recreation Area, which covers more than 3,600 acres in northeastern Hunterdon County and offers a variety of outdoor activities such as swimming, boating, hiking, and camping. There is an entry fee for the Recreation Area in summer. For birders, however, it is the other three seasons that are of interest.

The reservoir attracts diving birds, mainly loons, in spring and fall. Flocks of gulls begin to gather in late fall and remain through the winter. Rarities that have appeared here in the past 10 years are Pacific Loon, Red-necked Grebe, Red-necked Phalarope, and Lesser Black-backed Gull.

Directions

Take Interstate 78 west to Exit 20A (Lebanon), 10 miles west of Interstate 287. Go about 0.3 miles to the traffic light at Rt. 22 and turn right. Follow Rt. 22 west for about 0.8 miles to the jughandle turn for Round Valley Recreation Area. Take this access road for about 0.8 miles to the junction with Rt. 629 (no street sign). Turn left onto this road, then immediately right into the parking area.

Birding

Scan the cove at the boat launch area, where there is an unobstructed view of the reservoir. Round Valley is the prime inland location for Common Loon in New Jersey. Counts of 100 or more are not exceptional in October–November; smaller numbers are present in

MAP 16. Round Valley Recreation Area

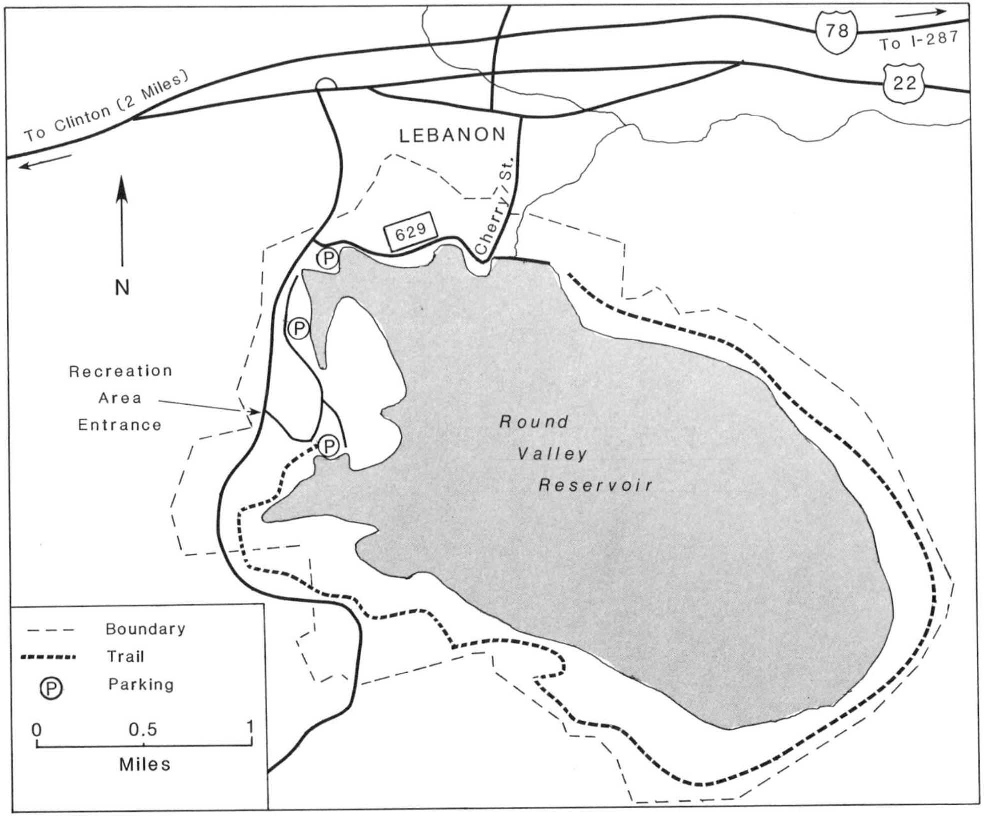

Round Valley Reservoir

LEBANON

Cherry St.

629

To Clinton (2 Miles)

78

22

To I-287

Recreation
Area
Entrance

N

Boundary
Trail
P Parking

0   0.5   1
Miles

spring. Some Red-throated Loons are usually mixed in with the Commons (as many as 40 have been seen), and a Pacific Loon was present for two weeks in November 1978. A few Horned Grebes stop off at the reservoir in spring and fall, and Red-necked Grebe, a rare annual visitor, has been recorded from October to March.

The number of gulls at Round Valley begins to build in late fall and may surpass 1,000. Herring Gull is the most common species, followed closely by Ring-billed. Great Black-backed Gull is found in lesser numbers and Bonaparte's Gull (high count of 50), Iceland Gull, and Lesser Black-backed Gull have also been seen. Double-crested Cormorants drop into the reservoir occasionally, as do Tundra Swans and a variety of diving ducks, but overall, nearby Spruce Run Reservoir is much more attractive to most kinds of waterfowl.

Before leaving the boat launch cove, scan the shoreline of the reservoir for Snow Buntings, which often appear in winter. Turn right onto Rt. 629 and follow the road along the edge of the water, stopping at intervals to scan for birds. You will be looking through a chain-link fence from now on, however, so the viewing is not great.

When you reach the dam (1.1 miles), turn around and go back to the Round Valley access road. Turn left and go about 0.8 miles to the Recreation Area entrance. Go in, take the first right turn (0.5 miles), and proceed for 0.3 miles to a parking lot overlooking a narrow section of the reservoir. The extensive pine groves to your left may have northern finches or owls in winter. A hiking and riding trail begins here that follows the south and east sides of the reservoir for about nine miles.

Rest rooms at the Recreation Area are open year-round. A trip to Round Valley is easily combined with one to nearby Spruce Run Recreation Area.

Spruce Run
Recreation Area

Spruce Run Recreation Area encompasses almost 2,000 acres of reservoir and shoreline near Clinton in northern Hunterdon County. It is probably the best inland location in the state for observing migratory waterbirds, rivaled only by Assunpink Wildlife Management Area. Together with adjacent Clinton WMA, which contains 1,115 acres, Spruce Run offers a diversity of habitat with a wide variety of birdlife.

Migratory waterfowl occur at Spruce Run from September to April, many species staying until frozen out in winter. The variety includes most of the species of ducks and geese that regularly occur in New Jersey, except for a few sea ducks. Loons and grebes are also present at these times. Late summer usually brings an influx of herons and egrets, as well as an excellent collection of migratory shorebirds if the water levels in the reservoir are low (as they often are).

Some of the species that have occurred here in recent years, including a few not often seen at inland sites in New Jersey, are Red-necked Grebe (almost annual), Tricolored Heron, Eurasian Wigeon (now annual), Oldsquaw, Black Scoter, Lesser Golden-Plover, Piping Plover, Whimbrel, Buff-breasted Sandpiper (annual), Red Phalarope, Pomarine Jaeger, Lesser Black-backed Gull, Forster's Tern, Least Tern, Black Skimmer, and Northern Shrike.

Note: The Recreation Area is crowded with bathers and boaters in summer. The WMA is heavily used by hunters, especially from October through December (except on Sundays). Be sure to wear bright clothing, preferably blaze orange, if you enter the area on a hunting day.

Directions

Take Interstate 78 west from its interchange with Interstate 287 for 13 miles, to Exit 17 (Rt. 31 North, Clinton, and Washington). Go

MAP 17. Spruce Run Recreation Area

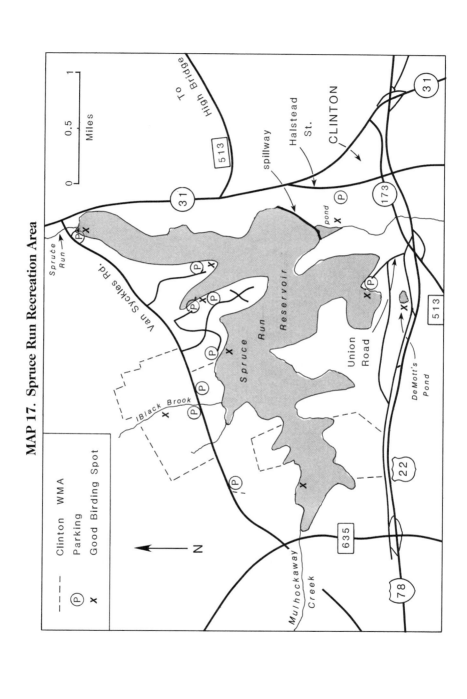

Clinton WMA
Parking
Good Birding Spot

north on Rt. 31 toward Washington for about 3.5 miles to the traffic light at Van Syckles Rd., a well-marked left turn with signs for Spruce Run Recreation Area. Turn left and go about 200 yards to a parking area on the left.

From the Trenton area, it is quicker to take Rt. 31 north all the way to Van Syckles Rd., a distance of about 37 miles from downtown Trenton.

From northwestern New Jersey, take US 206 to Netcong, Rt. 46 to Hackettstown (8 miles), Rt. 57 to Washington (10 miles), and Rt. 31 south to Van Syckles Rd. (about 7 miles).

Birding

The most productive areas for shorebirds, herons, and egrets are the places where Spruce Run and Mulhockaway Creek flow into the reservoir. The stream that you cross just after turning onto Van Syckles Rd. is Spruce Run; Mulhockaway Creek is discussed shortly. In late summer and fall (roughly mid-July through September), when the water level in the reservoir is below capacity, a large expanse of grassy mudflats is exposed along the shore; these are extensive where Spruce Run flows into the reservoir.

From the first parking area on Van Syckles Rd., walk out onto the mudflats (knee boots are advisable). Here you may find an interesting variety of shorebirds—at least 27 species have been recorded at the reservoir in the past 10 years, many of them at this spot. Black-bellied and Semipalmated Plovers; Killdeer; Greater and Lesser Yellowlegs; Spotted, Semipalmated, Western, Least, and Pectoral Sandpipers; Dunlin; Short-billed Dowitcher; and Common Snipe are some of the more common, regularly occurring species. The "goodies" that bring birders to this spot are Lesser Golden-Plover and Baird's and Buff-breasted Sandpipers, which occur annually. Other shorebirds that are found here with some frequency include Ruddy Turnstone (rare); Sanderling; Solitary, White-rumped, and Stilt Sandpipers; and Long-billed Dowitcher. This northeastern corner of the reservoir usually attracts herons and egrets as well in late summer, although Mulhockaway Creek is better.

Continue west along Van Syckles Rd., watching for waterfowl offshore along the way. After about one mile you will come to a road for the boat launch area on the left. Follow this road for about one-half mile to the launch site, at the end of a peninsula. This peninsula is an excellent place to observe waterfowl offshore and is a gathering place for gulls and terns. Caspian, Common, Forster's, Least (once), and Black Terns all have appeared here, usually in late summer—early fall; Caspian Tern occurs annually, in spring and fall; and Pomarine Jaeger was found once. The launch area is excellent for Horned Lark and Snow Bunting in winter. The cove to the west, known as Boat Launch Cove, has been a favorite area for Eurasian Wigeon in recent years.

Return to Van Syckles Rd. and go another 0.4 miles to the entrance to the Recreation Area, on the left. A fee is charged here in summer for this popular swimming area, and the gate does not usually open until 8 A.M. Just past the tollbooth, turn right and follow the road to a parking area that overlooks the western end of the reservoir. This is a good spot for finding migratory waterfowl, especially diving birds such as Common and Red-throated Loons; Common, Hooded, and Red-breasted Mergansers; and even the occasional Oldsquaw, White-winged Scoter, or Black Scoter.

When you return to the main entrance road, continue straight across it, following the sign for family picnicking. Picnic area 3 provides a good view of the birds in Boat Launch Cove, including the Eurasian Wigeons. In addition to the overlook and several picnic areas, the Recreation Area includes a large bathing beach, a boat rental area, and a campground (all except the campground are open to the public). Although most of the natural vegetation has been destroyed and replaced with grass, there are a few fields and patches of woodland left; these can be good for songbirds, especially sparrows, in migration. A Northern Shrike wintered here one year.

Go back to Van Syckles Rd. and continue west for about one-half mile to where Black Brook flows into the reservoir. There is a parking area on the left before you reach the brook and a smaller one on the right after you cross the brook; you are now in the Clinton WMA. Park in the smaller area on the right, and walk up the dirt road that runs north along Black Brook. Yellow-breasted Chat is a common breeder in the Multiflora Rose tangles along this road, and the many other species here include Willow Flycatcher, Acadian Flycatcher (up the brook), White-eyed Vireo, and Chestnut-sided Warbler.

To find shorebirds and herons in the fall, continue on Van Syckles

Rd. for 0.9 miles to an unmarked parking area on the left, just before the administration building for the WMA. If you come to the sign for the Clinton WMA, you have gone too far. From the parking area, walk west along the road for about 200 yards, 50 feet past the WMA sign. Turn left just before a line of trees and walk southeast toward the reservoir.

Follow the tire tracks and trails for about one-half mile. This will bring you to the reservoir near the north bank of Mulhockaway Creek, where a large expanse of mudflat is usually exposed in late summer. This is frequently the best spot for shorebirds, but the walking can be difficult—knee boots are definitely advisable. It is also the best area for wandering herons and egrets. All of New Jersey's herons and egrets, except Yellow-crowned Night-Heron, have occurred here; Tricolored Heron is rare, however. Do not attempt this walk on a Saturday or weekday during hunting season, as it is unsafe.

Take Van Syckles Rd. back to Rt. 31 and turn right. After about 1.8 miles bear right onto Halstead St. Go another 0.4 miles to the Clinton Community Center on the right, and park in the lot. Walk across the ballfield to a chain-link fence overlooking the outlet pond of Spruce Run Reservoir. This is often the best spot for waterfowl; a noteworthy attraction is the flock of Redheads that often gathers in the spring and that has numbered more than 100. Other diving ducks are fond of this spot as well, perhaps because it is not as deep as most of the reservoir. Puddle ducks come to roost but not to feed, and the Eurasian Wigeon is a regular visitor.

Continue down Halstead, which soon becomes Lehigh St., for about 0.4 miles to the intersection with Old Rt. 22, also called Rt. 173. Turn right and go 0.7 miles to the intersection with Rt. 513. Go right again for 0.1 miles; just past the Town and Country Bank, turn right onto Union Rd. Follow this for 0.4 miles to a gate, from which a dirt road leads 0.3 miles to a parking lot along the reservoir. This is another good waterfowl observation spot and may have shorebirds when the water is low. Both Baird's and Buff-breasted Sandpipers have been seen here.

Go back to Rt. 173 and turn right. After 0.3 miles, you will come to a small pond on the right, DeMott's Pond. Despite its modest size, this Clinton city park is a good spot for Snow Goose, Wood Duck,

Eurasian Wigeon, other ducks, and a small variety of gulls, mainly Ring-bills.

To rejoin I-78 westbound, take the entrance ramp just west of De-Mott's Pond. For I-78 eastbound, turn around and go back to the intersection of Rt. 173 and Rt. 513. Turn right and go under the highway, then take the left turn onto the entrance ramp.

A trip to Spruce Run is easily combined with one to nearby Round Valley Recreation Area.

NOTE: The gate at the end of Union Rd. (p. 98) is no longer open. Park on Union Rd. and walk to the reservoir.

Alpha

(Oberly Rd.)

Oberly Rd. is a short farm road in extreme southwestern Warren County. Although it is only 1.5 miles long, in winter it is one of the best inland locations in the state for Snow Bunting and Lapland Longspur. During the summer, an interesting variety of grassland nesting species can be found here, including Eastern Meadowlark; Vesper, Savannah, and Grasshopper Sparrows; and Bobolink. In migration a variety of ground-feeding birds pass through.

Directions

Take Interstate 78 west toward Phillipsburg. One-half mile after the (temporary) end of the highway, which becomes Rt. 22, you will come to a traffic circle. Go two-thirds of the way around the circle, and turn right on Alt. Rt. 22 toward Alpha. After 0.8 miles turn left at a traffic light onto Rt. 519; follow this for 1.5 miles through Alpha. Continue past the Alpha Lumber Co., under Interstate 78, then take the first right onto Rt. 635. Go about 1.3 miles and turn onto unmarked Oberly Rd., on the right.

Birding

The entire 1.5-mile length of Oberly Rd. traverses private land, so do not stray from the road. The birds you will find here depend as much on the condition of the fields as on the season. For the first mile the road passes through cultivated fields, but one or more of these may lie fallow. In winter, the acres of corn stubble are attractive to Horned Lark and occasionally Eastern Meadowlark. Snow Bunting and Lapland Longspur (uncommon but regular) prefer the barest of fields. In winter, when the farmers spread manure the birds tend to gather around the freshest deposits. After a fresh snow, the plow-scraped road shoulders also may be productive. The best way to find the birds is to drive slowly along Oberly Rd. (and also along Rt. 635), stopping to scan the fields at intervals. Snow Buntings never stay in one place for more than a few minutes, so you will see them fly up and land repeatedly.

Along this stretch of road, Water Pipit is occasional in early winter, Northern Harrier is common, and Rough-legged Hawk is present in most years. Short-eared Owl is often seen in winter; to look for owls, park in a spot with a wide view of the area about one-half hour before dark. The owls course over the fields as they hunt, pausing occasionally to perch on a post or on the ground.

After about a mile, the road passes between farm buildings. The last half-mile has sparrows at all seasons. The small fields here are bordered with shrubs and trees and provide better cover than the open fields on the south end of the road. In winter look for American Tree, Field, Savannah, Song, White-throated, and White-crowned (uncommon) Sparrows and Dark-eyed Junco. Vesper Sparrow is rare in winter and Dickcissel has been found once.

During migration, all the species mentioned above (except Dickcissel) are regular. In addition, look for Chipping, Grasshopper, Fox, Lincoln's (mainly fall), and Swamp Sparrows, and Bobolink. In fall there may be migrating raptors overhead; they tend to follow the nearby ridges and the Delaware River, only one mile to the west.

In summer several of the grassland species remain to nest, depending on the condition of the fields. Fallow fields are likely to have Grasshopper Sparrow, Bobolink, and Eastern Meadowlark. Horned Lark and Vesper Sparrow like cornfields, while Savannah Sparrow seems to prefer large alfalfa fields. The latter two species are now very uncommon nesting birds in New Jersey.

At its north end, Oberly Rd. ends at Carpentersville Rd. Turn right, go 0.4 miles to a fork, then bear right onto Rt. 642. Follow this for about 0.9 miles into Alpha to the intersection with Rt. 519. To rejoin Interstate 78 (Rt. 22), go left for 0.4 miles, then right onto Alt. Rt. 22, which merges with I-78 in about a mile.

For an alternate route through additional birding territory, turn left on Carpentersville Rd. and follow it through more fields and then along the Delaware River for about 2.5 miles. At the village of Carpentersville, turn left onto Rt. 635 and follow it back to Rt. 519 near the Alpha Lumber Co.

Additional Birding Spots in Northwestern New Jersey

Allamuchy Mountain State Park

This large, undeveloped state park covers more than 7,000 acres in Morris, Sussex and Warren counties. It consists mainly of mature deciduous woodlands, with some fields, conifer plantings, and a few native Eastern Hemlock groves. The park has a healthy population of Wild Turkeys, and supports an interesting diversity of breeding birds, including Winter Wren. Because much of the land is difficult to reach and because the park is so little known, its full birding potential has not been explored.

Directions

There are two main points of access. Take Interstate 80 west to Exit 19 (Rt. 517). From the exit ramp, turn left toward Hackettstown. Go about 1.4 miles and turn onto an unmarked dirt road on the left, which is the entrance road to the state park. Follow it for about one-half mile to a display board showing some of the roads that you can drive or walk. The other point of access can be reached by turning right onto Rt. 517 from the I-80 exit ramp. Drive north on Rt. 517 for about 1.3 miles, turn onto a dirt road on the right, and go 0.2 miles, watching the fields on either side for Wild Turkey. At the end of the road, turn left onto another dirt road and park. Just ahead is a dirt road on the right. Hike this road uphill, then bear right onto a trail that leads up toward the top of Allamuchy Mountain. Be sure to take a compass so you don't get lost.

Hacklebarney State Park

More scenic than birdy, Hacklebarney covers 569 acres in southwestern Morris County. The main feature of the park is a beautiful hemlock gorge along the Black River—the type of place that might attract winter finches during an invasion year.

Directions

From the intersection of US 206 and Rt. 24 in Chester, take Rt. 24 west for about 0.7 miles to Hacklebarney State Park Rd. Turn left onto this road, and drive about 1.2 miles to the park entrance, on the left.

Abraham Hewitt State Forest

Although this scenic, undeveloped forest contains almost 2,000 acres of land on Bearfort Mountain in northwestern Passaic County, it is seldom visited by birders. Its birdlife is similar to that in adjacent Pequannock Watershed areas, with such common breeding species as Ruffed Grouse, Pileated Woodpecker, Ovenbird, Hooded Warbler, and many others. An interesting 4-mile hike starts at the State Line Trail on Rt. 511, circles Surprise Lake and West Pond, and then returns to the State Line Trail. A trail map is available at either Wawayanda State Park or Ringwood State Park.

Directions

Take Rt. 23 west to Union Valley Rd. (Rt. 513). Follow Union Valley for 9 miles, through West Milford, to the junction with Rt. 511 at Greenwood Lake. Turn left onto Rt. 511 (Lakeside Rd.) and go about 2.5 miles to just over the New York State line, where there is a place to park on the right. Walk back into New Jersey to a marina on the left, then cross the road. At the far side of the marina parking lot is a stream; walk along it until blue-on-white markers on the trees indicate the beginning of the State Line Trail.

Silas Condict Park

A 7-acre lake, a few fields, and mature upland deciduous woods make up the small (265 acres) but attractive Silas Condict Park in the Highlands of northern Morris County. There are numerous hiking and cross-country skiing trails. Birdlife is similar to that of Mahlon Dickerson Reservation, but less diverse because of the park's much smaller size.

Directions

From the junction of Rts. 23 and 511 in Butler, go west on Rt. 23 for about one mile to Kinnelon Rd. Turn left and drive about one mile to the park entrance, on the right—the first right turn after Ricker Rd.

The Tourne Park

The Tourne is a 463-acre unit of the Morris County Park System that contains a variety of habitats, including upland deciduous forest and a fine stand of hemlocks. The park extends into Boonton, Denville, and Mountain Lakes, and has many hiking and nature trails, as well as family picnic sites. A map of the area can be obtained from the Morris County Park System (see chapter on Mahlon Dickerson Reservation for information).

Directions

Take Interstate 287 to the Intervale Rd. exit in Parsippany, about 2 miles north of I-80. From the exit ramp turn left onto Intervale Rd., cross over the highway, and take the first right turn, Fanny Rd. Follow Fanny Rd., which soon merges with Powerville Rd., for about 1.2 miles to the park entrance, on the left.

Merrill Creek Reservoir

This new reservoir on Scotts Mountain, Warren County, is a promising area for waterfowl and, possibly, migrant passerines. See the directions on p. 440, and continue up the hill to the reservoir.

Barred Owl

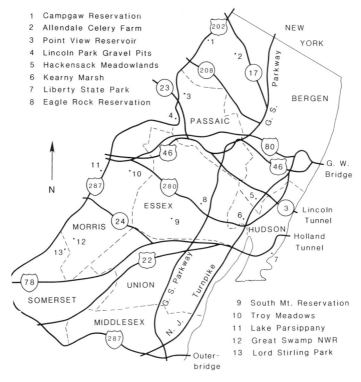

1 Campgaw Reservation
2 Allendale Celery Farm
3 Point View Reservoir
4 Lincoln Park Gravel Pits
5 Hackensack Meadowlands
6 Kearny Marsh
7 Liberty State Park
8 Eagle Rock Reservation

9 South Mt. Reservation
10 Troy Meadows
11 Lake Parsippany
12 Great Swamp NWR
13 Lord Stirling Park

MAP 18. Northeast Region

Northeast

Campgaw Reservation

The 1,351 acres of this Bergen County park contain most of Campgaw Mountain, a two-mile-long ridge in the northwestern part of the county. Ramapo Valley Rd. forms part of the northwestern boundary of the reservation. The Ramapo River runs along this road, separating Campgaw Mountain from the Ramapo Mountains. Elevations in the park range from about 300 feet along Ramapo Valley Rd. to 751 feet atop Campgaw Mountain. Most of the habitat consists of deciduous forest in various stages of succession, but there are a few patches of hemlocks. The borders of the ski area and the power line right-of-way provide some shrubby fields and edge habitat.

Like Eagle Rock Reservation, nearby Ramapo Reservation, and other similar places in northeastern New Jersey, Campgaw Reservation is best during spring and fall migration. Among its breeding birds are Ruffed Grouse, Pileated Woodpecker, and Golden-winged Warbler.

Directions

Take the Garden State Parkway to Exit 160 (Fair Lawn). From the exit ramp turn left onto Paramus Rd., then go about one-half mile to the exit for Rts. 4 and 208 (Fair Lawn and Hawthorne); this will put you on Rt. 4. After about 0.3 miles, bear right onto Rt. 208 toward Oakland. Follow Rt. 208 for about 8 miles to the Ewing Ave. exit. Turn right onto Ewing Ave., go about 0.3 miles, and turn left onto Franklin Ave. Proceed for about 0.8 miles and turn right onto Pulis Rd. Continue for 1.5 miles, turn left onto Campgaw Rd., and drive 1.7 miles to the Campgaw Reservation entrance road, on your left. Proceed for about one-half mile, staying left at the junction with the road to the ski area, until you come to a parking lot on the left for the Deer Picnic Area. There are some restrooms about 200 yards farther along the entrance road.

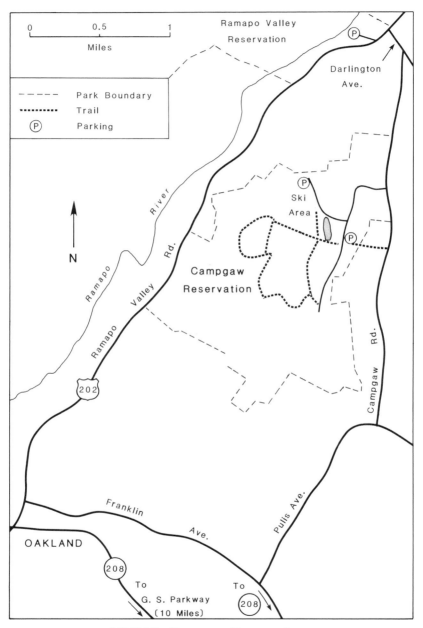

MAP 19. Campgaw Reservation

Birding

The trees and shrubs around the parking lot are good for migrant songbirds. Take the marked Hemlock Trail for several hundred yards; soon you will come to a small pond on the right and then to the marked junction with Indian Trail on the left. The area around this junction is one of the best birding spots in the park.

Walk up Indian Trail (yellow blazes), which climbs the ridge, roughly paralleling the ski slopes, in about one-half mile. At the top, you can turn left on Rocky Ridge Trail (blue blazes), or continue straight ahead a short distance to Old Cedar Trail (red blazes). Old Cedar Trail is the longer of the two, as it descends the ridge on the western slope, heads south for a while, then climbs the ridge to join Rocky Ridge Trail. From this junction, Rocky Ridge Trail continues south, then heads back down the eastern slope to rejoin the main park road just west of the campground. The total distance from Indian Trail to the main road is about 2.3 miles; it is another 0.4 miles back to the parking lot.

During May and August–September, you may expect to find here most of the common migrant songbirds that pass through New Jersey. Connecticut Warbler has been recorded, and sought-after species such as Olive-sided and Yellow-bellied Flycatchers, Gray-cheeked Thrush, and Philadelphia Vireo probably occur in fall. Additional breeding birds to look for are Broad-winged Hawk; Belted Kingfisher; Brown Creeper; Veery; Wood Thrush; Yellow-throated Vireo; Blue-winged, Yellow, Chestnut-sided, and Black-and-white Warblers; American Redstart; Ovenbird; Northern Waterthrush; Common Yellowthroat; Scarlet Tanager; Rose-breasted Grosbeak; Indigo Bunting; Northern Oriole; and American Goldfinch.

Nearby Ramapo Reservation (also a Bergen County park) and Ramapo Mountain State Forest (see Additional Birding Spots in Northeastern New Jersey) offer further birding opportunities in this area.

Allendale Celery Farm

The Allendale Celery Farm is a haven for wildlife amidst the residential and industrial developments of northwestern Bergen County. Although it was once actually a celery farm, the site has lain fallow since 1951, and is now a 78-acre wildlife preserve owned by the Borough of Allendale. The centerpiece of this little park is a 48-acre marsh of Cattails and *Phragmites* that attracts a variety of migrant and nesting birds.

Almost 200 species of birds have been observed at the Celery Farm since 1953, mainly by Stiles Thomas and members of the Fyke Nature Association. Among the interesting nesting species are Wood Duck, King Rail (rare), Virginia Rail, Sora, Willow Flycatcher, Marsh Wren, and Northern Waterthrush. Although it is not known as a hotspot for rarities, the Celery Farm has attracted some noteworthy species over the years, including Glossy Ibis, Black Rail, Northern Goshawk, Upland Sandpiper, Wilson's Phalarope, Common Barn Owl, Common Raven, Sedge Wren, Northern Shrike, and Connecticut Warbler.

Directions

Take the Garden State Parkway to Exit 163 (Rt. 17). Follow Rt. 17 north for about 7.2 miles to the Allendale exit. Go west on E. Allendale Ave. for exactly one mile to Franklin Turnpike, turn right, and go about 0.2 miles to the small parking lot, on the right.

Birding

Cross a small wooden bridge to reach the main trail, a two-mile loop installed by the Fyke Nature Association. It follows the perimeter of the marsh that forms the southern two-thirds of the preserve. Two

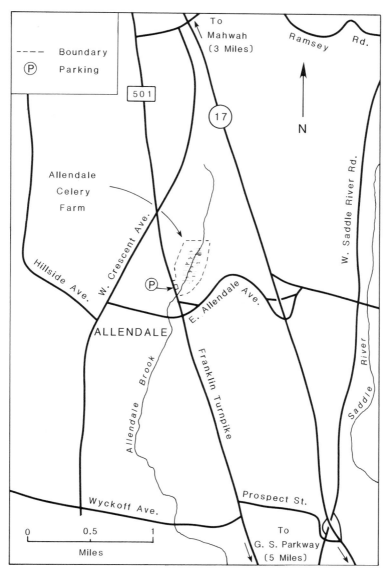

MAP 20. Allendale Celery Farm

unmarked trails branch off on the north side of the marsh into a wet deciduous woodland. A leisurely walk around the loop trail takes about two hours; the path may be muddy in places, so waterproof footwear is helpful.

In April, look for migrant American Bittern (uncommon) and Common Snipe (common); this is also when the nesting Wood Ducks are setting up housekeeping. A variety of sparrows are present, mainly on the edges of the fields around the northern and western parts of the tract. These include Field, American Tree, Savannah, Song, Swamp, and White-throated Sparrows and Dark-eyed Junco. Song and Swamp Sparrow remain to nest in good numbers.

Other common nesting birds are Canada Goose, Mallard, Yellow Warbler, Common Yellowthroat, and Red-winged Blackbird. Many of the common birds of lowland deciduous forest can be found in the wooded northern section.

Fall migration brings large flocks of ducks and Canada Geese into the marsh at dusk; this is the time for the greatest variety of waterfowl. It is also the best time to look for some of the less common migrants that show up regularly, including Olive-sided Flycatcher (September), Lincoln's Sparrow, and White-crowned Sparrow. Bobolinks are common in September and early October. Spectacular blackbird roosts have occurred here at times, as in the fall of 1981 when up to a million European Starlings, Common Grackles, and other blackbirds gathered in the evenings.

Winter is unexciting at the Celery Farm, especially after the water freezes. There are always sparrows and some of the common permanent residents, but you won't run up a long list of species. Still, a rarity might show up at this welcome oasis on a cold winter day.

Point View Reservoir

This 400-acre reservoir is located in Wayne, Passaic County. Point View is an excellent spot for migrating ducks, especially Common Merganser and Ring-necked Duck, and for gulls in winter and early spring. At least 19 species of shorebirds have been seen here, mainly in fall. Like most of New Jersey's reservoirs, Point View is very difficult and frustrating to bird. A high chain-link fence and lack of vantage points combine to give the birder a hard time. Those who make the effort may be rewarded with some impressive sights, however, such as the flock of 1,200 Common Mergansers present on March 20, 1981.

Directions

Take Interstate 80 west to Rt. 23 in Wayne. Go north on Rt. 23 for about 3.8 miles to a traffic circle, then take the first right turn out of the circle onto Ratzer Rd. Follow Ratzer for about 1.5 miles to Alps Rd., turn left, and proceed for 0.9 miles to the traffic light at the Paterson-Hamburg Turnpike. Continue straight through this light onto a road that circles behind the Preakness Shopping Center. When you come to the stop sign at Berdan Rd. (about 0.4 miles), turn left. After about 0.2 miles, just before the Wayne Hills High School on the right, a gate on the left leads into the reservoir property. The gate will be closed and locked, but there is room to park.

Birding

The gate is one of the better spots for viewing the reservoir, and there is usually some shorebird habitat along the edge to the right. A spotting scope is helpful for studying the ducks, which may be far out on the water; after awhile, you'll get used to looking through the fence with your scope.

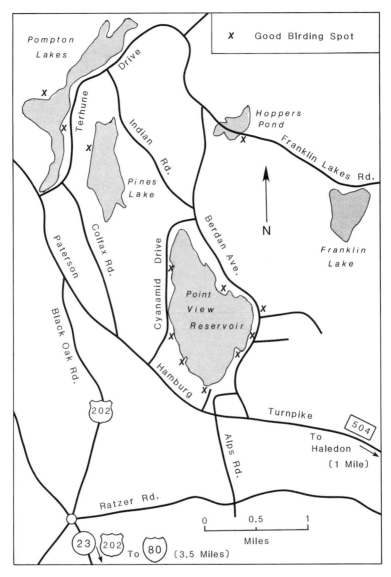

MAP 21. Point View Reservoir

March–April and October–November are the best times for waterfowl. Although most ducks occur regularly in migration, the most abundant species are Common Merganser, Ring-necked Duck, Mallard, and American Wigeon. Hooded Merganser is a regular visitor in spring and fall, and such unusual species as Eurasian Wigeon, Oldsquaw, and White-winged Scoter also have occurred. Point View is probably the best inland spot in the Bergen–Passaic County area for Common Loon, and Horned Grebe stops by in both migrations.

August and September are the months for shorebirds, especially if the water level is low enough to expose some fresh shoreline. Semipalmated, Least, and Pectoral Sandpipers, Dunlin, and both yellowlegs are regular visitors, and such rarities as Lesser Golden-Plover, Hudsonian Godwit, Baird's Sandpiper, Ruff, and Red-necked Phalarope have occurred. Large flocks of gulls gather to roost on the reservoir in winter and early spring. Look for Iceland and Glaucous Gulls, especially in March, when the ice is breaking up; you might find a Lesser Black-backed Gull among them. Black Tern has occurred once in spring, but late summer and fall is when other terns are sometimes observed. Forster's, Common, and Caspian Terns have occurred rarely.

To reach some of the other vantage points for viewing the reservoir, continue north along Berdan Ave. (Rt. 502) for about 0.4 miles to a vegetable stand on the right at the junction of Valley Rd., where you can park. The hill on the north side of Valley Rd. provides an unimpeded, but distant, view of the water. In another 0.5 miles, on the left, is the Van Riper–Hopper House, owned by the Wayne Historical Society. The parking lot has room for about 10 cars, and the area along the fence in back of the house provides a fair view of the reservoir when the vegetation is not too dense.

Continue along the reservoir from the Van Riper–Hopper House for about 0.7 miles to the entrance to the American Cyanamid Corporation Headquarters on the left. Cyanamid Dr., as the road is called, is private, but you may drive through the property on weekdays. The road passes by a couple of vantage points for scanning the reservoir. If a guard should question your presence, explain politely what you are doing. On weekends the gate on the south side of the drive is closed, so you will have to return to Berdan Rd.

Take Berdan Rd. back to the Paterson-Hamburg Turnpike, then turn right and go about 0.4 miles to Manor Dr., the first right turn after the traffic light at Alps Rd. Follow this short road to its dead end, where you can get another view of the reservoir. Return to the Turnpike and turn right. Go about 0.4 miles to the Schuyler-Colfax Junior High School on the right; the grounds in back of the school provide another vantage point. Another 0.2 miles along the Turnpike, you will come to the south end of Cyanamid Dr. on the right. Turn right and drive a 0.3 miles to the edge of the reservoir, just before a pumping station. This spot provides one of the better views, although you will still be looking through the chain-link fence. Continue along Cyanamid Dr. for another 0.2 miles to the last gate before some woods at the entrance to the American Cyanamid property. Here, too, you can obtain a reasonably unobstructed view of the water. On weekdays, you can continue through on Cyanamid Dr. to Berdan Rd.

A visit to Point View Reservoir during the spring or fall migration can be combined with stops at several other local spots to make a good day's birding. Lincoln Park Gravel Pits, which is only 2 miles southwest off the Newark-Pompton Turnpike, is covered in a separate chapter. Pines Lake is about a mile north of Point View off Indian Rd., the first left turn after Cyanamid Dr. Pompton Lake can also be reached from Indian Rd., about one-half mile beyond Pines Lake. Hopper Pond is in Franklin Lakes; continue on Berdan Rd. for about 0.9 miles past Indian Rd. to Franklin Lakes Rd. and turn right. The road crosses Hooper Pond in about 200 yards. All these lakes attract migrating waterfowl.

Lincoln Park
Gravel Pits

The Lincoln Park Gravel Pits or "the pits," as the area is affection-ately known to North Jersey birders, is an abandoned sand and gravel quarry along the Pompton River in northeastern Morris County. It consists of several large and small pools separated by a steep, narrow dike known as the knife edge, and interspersed with numerous islands. The edges of the ponds support sedges, rushes, and thickets of willow. There are open grassy areas, weedy fields, and some deciduous woodland along the river and the northern boundary. This varied habitat in an area covering only about 200 acres attracts an amazing array of herons, waterfowl, raptors, shore-birds, sparrows, warblers, and many other passerines.

More than 225 species have been recorded at the pits in the past 15 years. The spring migration can be very good from March to May, especially for waterfowl; huge concentrations of Common Mergan-ser appear in March. However, the July—November fall migration boasts the greatest variety of species. The first southbond shore-birds and herons begin to appear during July, followed by waves of migrant passerines in August and September. Waterfowl are abun-dant in September and October; many linger until frozen out in winter. October is probably the most interesting month, as this is when most of the eastern sparrows occur, along with a few other noteworthy species.

The list of rare or unusual species that have occurred at Lincoln Park in recent years is impressive: Golden Eagle; Yellow Rail; Ruff, Sedge Wren; Black-headed Grosbeak; Dickcissel; and Clay-colored, Lark, and Henslow's Sparrows. Other noteworthy species are Red-necked Grebe; White-rumped and Baird's Sandpipers; Wilson's and Red-necked Phalaropes; Yellow-bellied Flycatcher (annual); Phila-delphia Vireo (annual); Orange-crowned (annual) and Connecticut (several every fall) Warblers, Vesper (regular in fall); Grasshopper,

MAP 22. Lincoln Park Gravel Pits

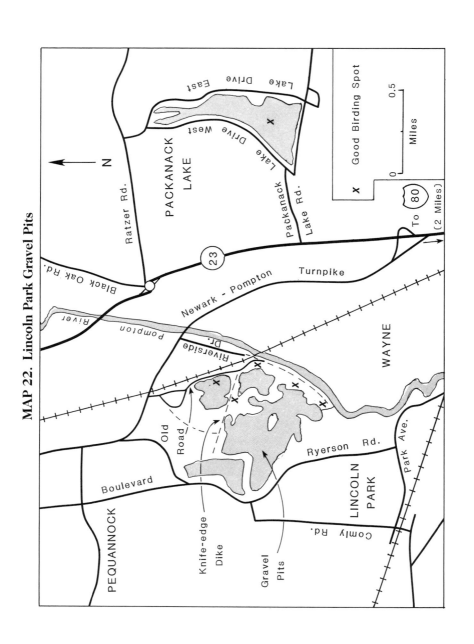

N

Ratzer Rd.

PACKANACK LAKE

Lake Drive East

Lake Drive West

Black Oak Rd.

23

Packanack Lake Rd.

Newark – Pompton Turnpike

Pompton River

Riverside Dr.

WAYNE

Old Road

Knife-edge Dike

Boulevard

PEQUANNOCK

Gravel Pits

Ryerson Rd.

LINCOLN PARK

Comly Rd.

Park Ave.

X Good Birding Spot

0   0.5
Miles

80

To
(2 Miles)

Sharp-tailed (rare inland in New Jersey), Lincoln's (common in fall), and White-crowned (common in fall) Sparrows; Snow Bunting (winter); Lapland Longspur (fall); and Common Redpoll (rare in winter).

Directions

A large portion of the pits is actually in the town of Pequannock, and that is where the birding access is. From the east or south, take Interstate 80 or the Garden State Parkway and I-80 west to Rt. 23 north (4.4 miles west of the Parkway on I-80). Go north on Rt. 23 for about 2.0 miles to the Newark-Pompton Pike. Follow this north for about 2 miles until you cross the stone bridge over the Pompton River. Turn left onto Riverside Dr. and go 0.2 miles. Park on either side of the road, just before the pavement ends.

From the west, take I-80 east to Exit 47 (Rt. 46, Montclair, and the Caldwells). Travel east on Rt. 46 for about 7.1 miles to the exit for Rt. 23 north. Follow the signs for Rt. 23 north (this can be very tricky), and go about 2 miles to the exit for the Newark-Pompton Pike. *Note that there is no exit from I-80 to Rt. 23 north.*

Birding

From the end of the pavement, walk straight ahead along the dirt road for a hundred yards or so. Cross over the railroad tracks and through some trees onto the old road that forms the boundary of the gravel pits on the north and east sides. From here you can see most of the area; to your right at the bend in the road is the knife-edge dike, to your left the road parallels the Pompton River for about one-half mile to the outflow.

There are several different hiking options, and if you have time you can cover the whole area. The road down to the outflow is probably the most productive. Between the road and the river as you walk south is a stand of large deciduous trees with a shrubby understory. The trees and bushes are excellent for migrant fly-catchers, vireos, warblers, tanagers, orioles, and grosbeaks. A Black-headed Grosbeak was seen here for a week in August–September, 1981.

On your right as you walk toward the outflow you will pass by brushy overgrown pits, then a grassy field, and then more brushy overgrown areas good for sparrows and other ground-feeding birds, and for skulkers such as wrens, thrushes, and Orange-crowned, Connecticut, and Wilson's Warblers.

Numerous trails lead down to the edges of some of the small pools and to the big pool that occupies much of the southern portion of the tract. Here you may find a variety of shorebirds in season. At least 19 species of shorebirds have been found at the pits, including several that are unusual inland. In addition to those already noted, Semipalmated Plover, Upland Sandpiper, Willet, Dunlin, Short-billed and Long-billed Dowitchers, Stilt Sandpiper, Western Sandpiper, and Sanderling have occurred. Regular species include Black-bellied Plover; Killdeer; Greater and Lesser Yellowlegs; Solitary, Spotted, Semipalmated, Least, and Pectoral Sandpipers; Common Snipe; and American Woodcock.

The large pond attracts migrant waterfowl, including a good selection of diving ducks. Up to 1,500 Common Mergansers have occurred in spring. Such inland rarities as Oldsquaw, White-winged Scoter, and Black Scoter have been recorded, in addition to all the usual divers. The pond is also a favored fishing spot for Ospreys in fall.

Once you reach the outflow, you will probably have to turn back, unless the water is low enough for you to cross the stream. This outflow area is where Yellow Rail (one record) and Sedge Wren have occurred. If you cross the stream, you can walk around the large pond; however, it is a better use of your time to return to the starting point and continue along the road toward the knife edge.

Beyond the knife edge is another large pool with an overgrown brushy shore. An abandoned dredge sits near the road, rusting away. The brushy area between the knife edge and the dredge is excellent for sparrows in fall: Seventeen of the eighteen species that regularly occur in New Jersey have been found at the pits; only Seaside Sparrow is missing. Lincoln's and White-crowned Sparrows are sometimes common in October.

Walk out on the knife edge, which is good for passerine migrants (including Connecticut Warbler in September) and which provides a vantage point for scoping most of the pits. If the water level is not too high, you can walk all the way to the west end of this dike, then bear right across an area of dirt fill that has occasionally had Water Pipit in late fall. You will soon reach the old road that will lead you along the perimeter of the pond, past the old dredge, and back to your starting point. After about mid-morning the dirt bikes racing up and down the road can be a real nuisance; do your birding early.

The future of the Lincoln Park Gravel Pits is uncertain. Most of the land is in private hands, although a portion in Lincoln Park is municipally owned. The northern part, in the town of Pequannock, would provide some good industrial sites and such use can be anticipated. There is also the possibility that part of the site may be purchased under the state Green Acres program.

WARNING: The Lincoln Park Gravel Pits was closed to the public in 1987 and remains closed as of December 1988.

Hackensack Meadowlands
(De Korte State Park)

When birders talk about the Hackensack Meadowlands, they are usually referring to parts of the extensive Hackensack River marshes that are included in the new De Korte State Park. This area is known as much for its foul odors as for its interesting fowl. The garbage dumps and tidal flats here attract myriad gulls and shorebirds. Among the unusual species that have appeared here during the past 15 years are White Ibis; Fulvous Whistling-Duck; Lesser Golden-Plover (annual); Hudsonian (annual) and Marbled Godwits; Baird's (annual), Curlew, and Buff-breasted Sandpipers; Ruff; Wilson's and Red-necked Phalaropes; Franklin's, Common Black-headed (regular in winter), Thayer's, Iceland (regular), Lesser Black-backed (regular), and Glaucous (regular) Gulls; Blue Grosbeak (an annual nester); Dickcissel (nested in 1974); and Yellow-headed Blackbird.

Directions

To reach De Korte State Park from everywhere but northwestern New Jersey, take the New Jersey Turnpike to Exit 16W (Secaucus and Rutherford). Take Rt. 3 west for about 1.5 miles, then take the exit for Rt. 17 South. Follow the ramp back over Rt. 3 to a traffic light at Polito Ave., where there is a sign for De Korte State Park. Turn left, and go about 0.6 miles to the end of Polito at Valley Brook Rd., turn left, and continue about 1.7 miles to the end at the parking lot for De Korte State Park and the Hackensack Meadowlands Development Commission (HMDC); drive past the building and park near the southeast corner of the lot.

Alternatively, you can take the Garden State Parkway to Exit 153 (Rt. 3), then go east on Rt. 3 for about 5 miles to the second exit for Rt. 17 South (Lyndhurst); there is a sign for De Korte State Park and

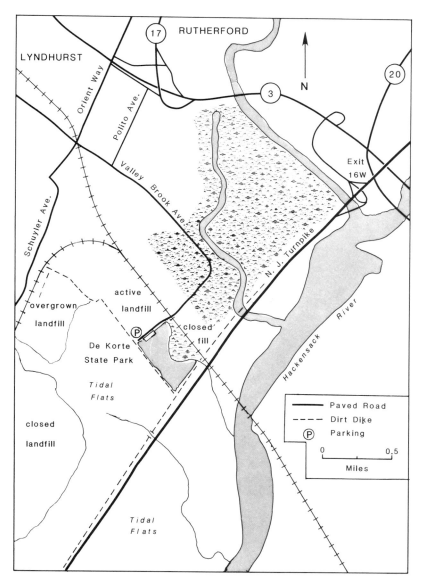

MAP 23. Hackensack Meadowlands

the Hackensack Meadowlands Commission. Proceed straight ahead at the traffic light onto Polito Ave. Go about 0.6 miles to the end of Polito at Valley Brook Rd., turn left, and continue about 1.7 miles to the end.

From northwestern New Jersey, take Interstate 80 east to US 46 in Wayne, then exit onto Rt. 3 in Clifton. Follow Rt. 3 for about 6.5 miles to the Rt. 17 South exit in Lyndhurst and proceed as above.

Birding

The best birding areas in the 2,000-acre De Korte State Park are now an impounded pool known as the shorebird pool (99 acres), a large tidal flat (581 acres), an active garbage dump (90 acres), and an overgrown landfill with marshy pools (66 acres). Some of these land uses will change substantially in the next few years; however, the impoundment and tidal flat are in a marshland preservation zone and will continue to attract shorebirds and gulls.

Late summer and fall is the shorebird season at the meadowlands. The modern new headquarters of the HMDC and its adjacent Environmental Center are on the shore of the large, shallow impoundment known to birders as the shorebird pool. It is a good spot for migrant waterfowl in spring, shorebirds in the fall (July through October), and gulls in winter. To bird it thoroughly, you must walk around the perimeter, a little more than one and a half miles.

The water level in the shorebird pool is regulated by floodgates. If a low level is maintained in August and September, the pool provides good feeding and resting areas for migrant shorebirds. At high tide, the nearby tidal flats along the Hackensack River are submerged, and many birds seek refuge in the impoundment. Some species use the impoundment at all tides. In recent years, the water level has been kept high to reduce the threat of botulism, and the shorebirding has been much less productive. However, you can still find most of the common species and, occasionally, phalaropes. Breeding birds include Pied-billed Grebe, Common Moorhen, Gadwall, Ruddy Duck, and Blue-winged Teal. Snowy and Common Egrets, Black-crowned Night-Heron, and Glossy Ibis are regular visitors in late summer and early fall.

To bird the shorebird pool, walk south from the parking lot a short distance to a dike that runs east-west, then turn left. As you walk east toward the New Jersey Turnpike, which you can see about one-half mile ahead, the pool will be on your left and the large tidal flat on your right. Large numbers of shorebirds, mainly Lesser Yellowlegs, Least and Semipalmated Sandpipers, and Short-billed Dowitchers, gather on the flats to feed when the tide is out. Just before you reach the Turnpike, the dike ends at a junction with a dike running north-south. Here you can turn left to continue the walk around the shorebird pool or turn right and walk along the edge of the tidal flat for about 0.3 miles. The viewing conditions in the morning are usually better on this side of the flat, especially later in the season. The tidal flats to the south on both sides of the Turnpike are part of the Sawmill Creek WMA; they can be reached on foot from the Belleville Pike (see Kearny Marsh chapter).

The overgrown landfill is about one-half mile west of the parking lot, and is reached by walking west along the dike on the south side of the parking lot. Access to the landfill is via a dirt road at the west end, just before you come to some railroad tracks. Blue Grosbeaks have nested for about 15 years at the edge of a bluff about a mile south along these tracks or, more recently, on the landfill itself. The dense growth of *Phragmites* on the landfill makes it excellent during fall migration for sparrows, including White-crowned and Lincoln's. Short-eared Owls roost in the reeds in winter and sometimes can be flushed out by walking the muddy paths through the fill.

Winter is the season for gulls at the meadowlands, when tens of thousands of the scavengers come to feed at the garbage dump or roost on the pools and mudflats. The shorebird pool is especially good for viewing the gulls when it is partly or completely frozen. Even larger numbers roost on the frozen tidal flats, but the light is not as good, because you are usually looking into the sun. Days when the dump is working (Monday through Friday, Saturday until 1 P.M.) are best for seeing the greatest numbers and variety of gulls, although it is sometimes frustrating to search for rare gulls among the thousands of birds hustling for the best pickings or swarming overhead like a cloud of giant white insects. The vast majority are Herring Gulls, with lesser numbers of Great Black-backed and Ring-billed Gulls. Mixed in among them in winter are always a few Iceland and Glaucous Gulls and up to three or four Lesser Black-backed

Gulls. For the past few winters, several observers have reported Thayer's Gull, a bird that undoubtedly occurs regularly, but which is difficult to identify. New Jersey's first Franklin's Gull was found in the shorebird pool in February 1975.

Other winter visitors to the Hackensack Meadowlands are Red-tailed Hawk, Rough-legged Hawk, which can be quite common in flight years, and American Kestrel. A few ducks and shorebirds linger around the pools if the water isn't frozen, and numerous sparrows feed on the landfill on cold winter days.

Kearny Marsh

Kearny Marsh, the finest freshwater marsh in New Jersey, is located near the southern end of the Hackensack Meadowlands, in heavily urban Hudson County. It was created accidentally in the early 1970s, when the pumps draining an area surrounded by railroad and road-bed embankments failed to keep pace with greatly increased drainage into the site. Today, the marsh covers 342 acres, has an average water depth of about 30 inches, and is bordered on one edge by a 63-acre abandoned landfill overgrown with weeds, shrubs, and small trees.

Since its creation, Kearny Marsh has become an outstanding breeding ground for a number of different waterbirds, some of which, such as Pied-billed Grebe and Ruddy Duck, rarely nest elsewhere in the state. It also provides a roost for large numbers of herons and egrets in late summer, has a good-to-excellent shorebird migration in May and July—August, and harbors a variety of unusual species in winter. If your esthetic and olfactory senses are not easily offended by the litter, rubble, and nearby active garbage dump, the marsh is an interesting place to visit at any season, but especially in summer.

Among the birds that have nested at Kearny Marsh during the past 10 years, the following are especially noteworthy: Pied-billed Grebe (common), Least Bittern (common), Black-crowned Night-Heron, Gadwall, Green-winged Teal, Ruddy Duck, Common Moorhen (abundant), American Coot (formerly abundant, now rare), and Blue Grosbeak. Some of the rare or unusual species that have been found here during that time are White Ibis; Black-necked Stilt; Ruff; Wilson's, Red-necked, and Red Phalaropes; Iceland, Lesser Black-backed, and Glaucous Gulls; Gull-billed Tern; and Yellow-headed Blackbird.

Directions

From the north and south, take the New Jersey Turnpike to Exit 15W (Interstate 280, Newark, the Oranges). Coming north, be sure

MAP 24. Kearny Marsh

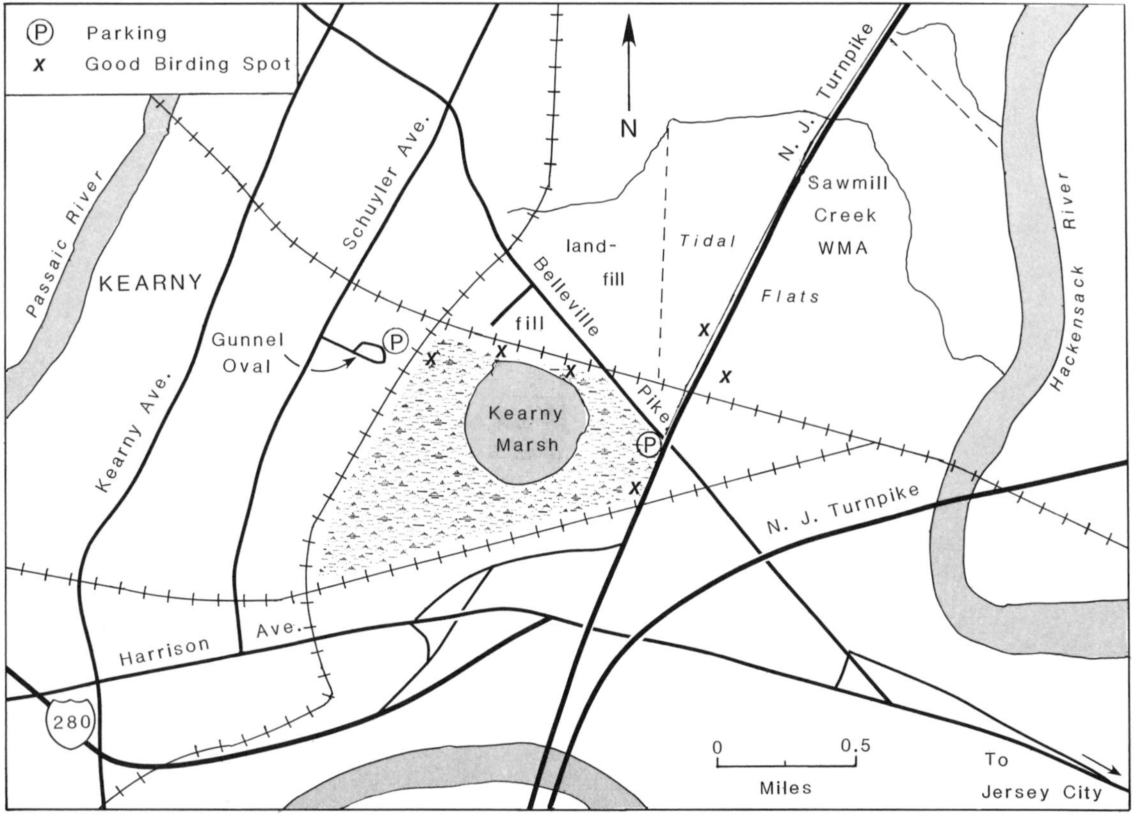

Parking — Ⓟ
Good Birding Spot — X

KEARNY

Passaic River

Schuyler Ave.

Gunnel Oval

Kearny Ave.

Harrison Ave.

280

Kearny Marsh

Belleville Pike

land-fill

fill

Tidal Flats

Sawmill Creek WMA

N. J. Turnpike

Hackensack River

N. J. Turnpike

To Jersey City

N

0   0.5
Miles

to stay left when the Turnpike forks just north of Exit 14. After the tollbooth, stay to the right, following the signs for Harrison Ave. Go west on Harrison Ave. for about 0.7 miles to the first traffic light, at Schuyler Ave. Turn right onto Schuyler and drive north for about 1.2 miles to a traffic light and a sign on the right at the entrance to Gunnel Oval, a Kearny city park. Turn right into Gunnel Oval, drive around to the northeast corner of the park near the tennis courts, and park.

From the west, take Interstate 280 east to the Harrison Ave. exit in Harrison. Go left on Harrison Ave. for about 0.8 miles to the traffic light at Schuyler Ave. Turn left onto Schuyler and proceed as described above.

Birding

Birding at Kearny Marsh is done mainly from the railroad embankment that forms the north boundary. From the tennis courts walk east for a short distance to an abandoned railroad bed near the western edge of the marsh. If a low water level coincides with shorebird migration, this can be an outstanding spot. Turn left (north), and go about 200 yards to a concrete railroad bridge. Climb the steep embankment on the right, up to the railroad tracks. Unlike the tracks below, these are active, so watch out for trains. Walk east, toward New York City. North of this embankment is the landfill.

The entire shorebird area can be scoped from the top of the embankment. This northwest corner is where the rare shorebirds noted above have been seen. Other species that appear here regularly are Black-bellied and Semipalmated Plovers; Killdeer; Greater and Lesser Yellowlegs; Solitary, Spotted, Semipalmated, Least, White-rumped (rare), and Pectoral Sandpipers; Short-billed Dowitcher; and Common Snipe.

Continue walking east along the railroad tracks. From here you can see the entire expanse of the marsh, which is largely overgrown with *Phragmites*, except for one large pond, a network of canals, and a few smaller areas of open water. In and around the large pond, you can see the nesting species in summer. In addition to the species noted above, other nesting waterbirds are Green-backed Heron, Canada Goose, Mallard, American Black Duck and Blue-winged

Teal. Other species that have occurred during the breeding season and may have nested are Snowy Egret, Little Blue Heron, Wood Duck (in muskrat houses), Northern Shoveler, and Sora.

Kearny Marsh is especially valuable because of its large numbers of several unusual breeding birds. The 25 or so pairs of Pied-billed Grebes is now the only significant breeding population in New Jersey (single pairs nest at a half-dozen other places). Similarly, the 10–15 pairs of Ruddy Ducks represent virtually the entire nesting population for the state. The number of Least Bitterns is difficult to estimate because of the species' secretive nature; however, there probably are one or two dozen pairs—certainly the healthiest population in New Jersey. Common Moorhen is abundant and the numbers of American Coot (formerly 400+ pairs) far exceed those anywhere else in the state. Late afternoon and evening in spring and summer is a good time to visit the marsh, since many of the birds are active and conspicuous at that time.

Several dikes cross the marsh and support a few Common Elderberry bushes. On one of these dikes is the only mixed heronry in northern New Jersey. Black-crowned Night-Heron (up to 40 pairs) and Glossy Ibis (5+ pairs) are long-term residents, but the other species noted above have probably nested. In late summer, the heronry becomes a roost for large numbers of herons and egrets from elsewhere, including Great Blue Heron, Great Egret, Tricolored Heron, and as many as 500 Snowy Egrets. On the evening of September 19, 1977, three immature White Ibis came in to roost.

The marsh itself is host to Marsh Wren, Yellow Warbler, Common Yellowthroat, Swamp Sparrow, and Red-winged Blackbird, while the landfill accommodates Indigo Bunting, American Goldfinch and Northern Mockingbird. Also present in most years are one or two pairs of Blue Grosbeaks, here approaching the northern limit of their breeding range in the East. During the 1970s, American Woodcock nested on the fill and Barn Owls were in the adjacent warehouse. Common Nighthawks nest on the tops of buildings in the surrounding cities and can be seen hawking insects over the marsh every evening in summer. Migrant birds regularly found on the landfill are Bobolink (May and July to October), a variety of warblers in the tree copses (May and September), and a good mix of sparrows including White-crowned and Fox Sparrows, in fall and winter.

Numerous species of gulls and terns appear at Kearny Marsh during migration and in winter. In May or late summer, Caspian, Common, Forster's, and Black Terns appear; Gull-billed Tern has been seen once. In winter, a few Iceland, Lesser Black-backed, and Glaucous Gulls are found amidst the large flocks of gulls on the pond.

When it is not completely frozen, the marsh usually contributes some unusual species to the Lower Hudson Christmas Count total. Among these are some of the breeding birds that try to overwinter, such as Pied-billed Grebe, Black-crowned Night-Heron, Blue-winged Teal, and Common Moorhen. Yellow-headed Blackbird has been found a few times in winter as well as in spring and summer. Northern Harrier and Rough-legged Hawk are frequently seen here in winter.

Another good point of access to the east side of Kearny Marsh is along the Transco right-of-way, which parallels the New Jersey Turnpike. To reach it, drive north on Schuyler Ave. for one mile to the traffic light at the Belleville Pike and turn right. Go about 1.4 miles, then park at the power substation on the right, just before you reach the New Jersey Turnpike. Walk south along the right-of-way. This is a good spot for Least Bittern and other marsh birds.

The Sawmill Creek WMA, which lies along both sides of the New Jersey Turnpike north of the Belleville Pike, is excellent for shorebirds and waterfowl in migration, especially May and July– October. To reach it, walk north along the Transco right-of-way for about 0.2 miles to some railroad tracks. The shorebird areas are north of the tracks, which provide access to the east side of the Turnpike. Low tide is best (tides here are about three hours later than at Sandy Hook).

A visit to Kearny Marsh can be combined with a trip to the marshes and ponds at De Korte State Park, in Lyndhurst, which is covered in the Hackensack Meadowlands chapter. To reach De Korte from Kearny, go north for about 2.6 miles on Schuyler Ave. to its end at the Schuyler Diner. Turn left onto Page Ave., go one block and turn right onto Orient Way. Go about 0.3 miles to the traffic light at Valley Brook Ave. and turn right. Follow Valley Brook for about two miles to its end at De Korte State Park.

Liberty State Park

This 736-acre state park, one of New Jersey's newest, lies, almost literally, in the shadow of the Statue of Liberty, along the banks of the Hudson River in Jersey City. In addition to offering an impressive view of Miss Liberty and the Manhattan skyline, it is a good birding spot from late fall through spring. Red-necked Grebe; Great Cormorant; Eurasian Wigeon; Lesser Golden-Plover; Little, Common Black-headed, Iceland, and Glaucous Gulls; Snowy Owl; and Boreal Chickadee are some of the more interesting birds that have been found here and at adjacent Caven Cove and Caven Pier. Caven Cove is currently the best place in the state to find both Little and Common Black-headed Gulls, and Caven Pier has Snow Buntings, Purple Sandpiper and, occasionally, Lapland Longspur in winter.

Most of Liberty State Park, which extends over abandoned railroad yards, is still undeveloped. Current proposals for the area include a golf course and other forms of recreational development; however, a small portion of the land has been set aside as a natural area, which, along with the waterfront, should continue to provide good birding in the future.

Directions

Take the New Jersey Turnpike Extension east from Exit 14 of the Turnpike for about 5 miles to Exit 14B (Jersey City). Stay left at the tollbooth, and turn left onto Bayview Ave., following the signs for Liberty State Park. After about 300 yards, keep to the right at a small traffic circle, where the road becomes Morris Pesin Dr. Continue about 0.3 miles farther, then turn into the first parking lot on the right.

MAP 25. Liberty State Park

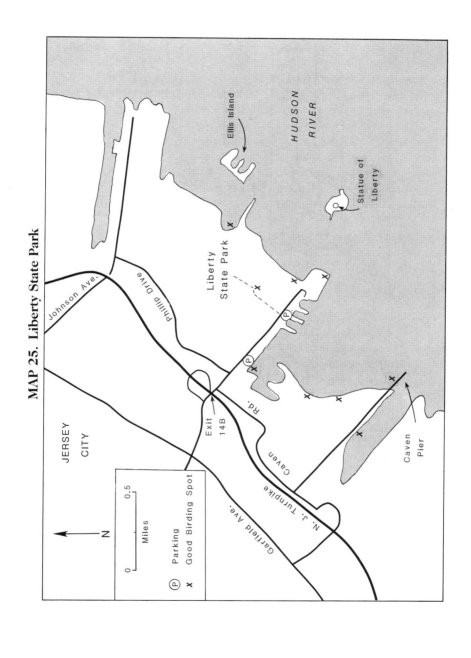

Birding

Scan the cove between the parking area and the jetty to the south for grebes, ducks, and gulls. A Red-necked Grebe spent the entire winter of 1981–82 here, and others are occasionally seen. Scope the jetty, which is several hundred yards distant, for white-winged gulls. Also, look for Snowy Owl, which occurs fairly regularly (one Snowy made the jetty his favorite perch for over a month in January–February 1981). Double-crested Cormorants (year-round) and Great Cormorants (October–May) also use the jetty as a resting place. Dunlin, Black-bellied Plover, and occasionally Purple Sandpiper frequent the jetty at high tide in the winter.

The cove between the jetty and Caven Pier (visible about one mile south) is known as Caven Cove. It is accessible from Caven Pier, but the Little and Common Black-headed Gulls that frequent the cove sometimes fly closer to Liberty State Park, so keep an eye out for them.

Continue east along the entrance drive for about 0.4 miles to the parking lot at the park office. Ring-billed Gulls gather to roost on the parking lot in winter, and should be checked for something rare. Walk south to the edge of the water, and scan for waterbirds—many species of grebes, loons, and waterfowl show up in the waters off the state park during migration, and some of them stay for the winter. Among the more common ones are Brant, Canada Goose, Green-winged Teal, American Black Duck, Mallard, Gadwall, American Wigeon (plus the occasional Eurasian Wigeon), Canvasback, Greater and Lesser Scaup, Common Goldeneye, Bufflehead, Red-breasted Merganser, and Ruddy Duck. Even Redhead, Oldsquaw, and all three scoters are found here regularly.

Follow the edge of the water east to the overlook along the river, and scan for ducks and gulls; this is a good place to see Little Gull, especially in late spring. Continue around the edge until you reach a marsh along the north side of the entrance road. This area is good for many of the puddle ducks and for Clapper Rail, and is also the best place to see Northern Harrier and Short-eared Owl in winter.

Walk west along the road overlooking the marsh for about 200 yards beyond the headquarters, to the beginning of the interpretive trail, which leads to the new Interpretive Center. The many pine and shrub plantings along the trail, the marsh along the eastern edge, and the small freshwater pond at the north end of the trail promise to make this area a haven for migrant birds—a small oasis of food and shelter along the heavily urbanized waterfront of the Hudson River. Many sparrows and other songbirds can be found here from September through November, with lesser numbers during the winter. Lincoln's and White-crowned Sparrows have proven to be regular migrants here, and a Boreal Chickadee discovered in late November 1983 stayed through the following March.

The area to the north and west of the Interpretive Center, the largest part of the park, is still undeveloped. Gulls roost in winter on some of the abandoned railway yards, and a boat line runs tours of upper New York Bay from the old ferry terminal at the north end of the park. To reach this area, drive back to the small traffic circle mentioned in the directions. Turn right at the circle onto Burma Rd., which soon becomes Phillip Dr.; this ends at Audrey Zapp Dr. where a right turn leads to the ferry terminal, about 2 miles from the traffic circle.

To bird Caven Pier and Caven Cove, go back to the traffic circle and turn right toward Jersey City. After about 100 yards, turn left onto Caven Point Rd., just before the Turnpike. Follow this road south for about 0.8 miles to the first left turn, where there is a sign and a guardhouse for the U.S. Army Reserve. If a soldier is on duty, stop at the guardhouse and show him your binoculars; he will wave you on. The road you are on runs for about three-quarters of a mile to its end at Caven Pier. Along the way, you will pass a small estuary on the right that is a favorite spot of Common Black-headed Gulls, although they are difficult to spot through the fence. Stop at a small brick building on the right and look for the pipe outlet where the Black-headeds appear at low tide.

Park at the end of the road, and walk out the pier to check for waterbirds offshore. In winter, Snow Bunting and Lapland Longspur roost on the pier, and Purple Sandpiper can usually be found near its end or roosting on the floating wreckage on the north side. Walk north from the pier along the shore of Caven Cove to search for Little and Black-headed Gulls, which are usually among the flocks of migrant or wintering Bonaparte's Gulls. Late spring and early summer (especially about May 10 to June 5) is the best time for Little Gull. A variety of shorebirds, including Lesser Golden-Plover, pause in migration to feed on the tidal mudflats of Caven Cove.

The Caven Pier area is bleak and unsightly, and not a place you should bird alone. With the development that is slated for the future, it will likely become more attractive to people, but less attractive to birds.

NOTE: Caven Pier was severely damaged by storms during the winter of 1992–93 and is now closed off by a fence and no trespassing signs. It is unlikely that it will ever reopen, but the pier can be scoped from the end of the road.

A paved road now connects the main parking area with the ferry terminal, but the pines and shrubs along the road can still attract migrants and wintering sparrows.

Jamaica Bay
Wildlife Refuge
(Long Island, N.Y.)

Although Jamaica Bay is not located in New Jersey, no regional book that includes the New York City area would be complete without a section on this famous birding spot. The 12,000-acre refuge, a unit of Gateway National Recreation Area, is unquestionably the best shorebirding area readily accessible to most residents of New Jersey, and one of the best anywhere on the East Coast. A permit (free) is required and can be obtained at the headquarters. A spotting scope is indispensable.

A good variety of species occurs here in spring, but it is the fall migration that attracts birders from hundreds of miles around. From July through October, a steady procession of southbound plovers, sandpipers, godwits, and phalaropes stop at Jamaica Bay to feed and rest for up to two weeks before continuing their journey to the southern United States, the Caribbean, or South America. More than 40 species have been recorded at the refuge, of which about three dozen occur in a typical season.

Jamaica Bay is also an outstanding spot for many other kinds of birds, including migrant passerines that are attracted to the abundant plantings that provide food and cover in the midst of a heavily urbanized area. Approximately 320 species have been recorded at the refuge in the past 30 years. Among the regularly occurring birds are such sought-after species as Lesser Golden-Plover; American Avocet; Hudsonian and Marbled Godwits; Baird's, Curlew, and Buff-breasted Sandpipers; Ruff; Wilson's and Red-necked Phalaropes; and Saw-whet Owl. The long list of rarities includes American White Pelican; Wood Stork; White and White-faced Ibis; Fulvous Whistling-Duck; Cinnamon Teal; Common and King Eiders; American Swallow-

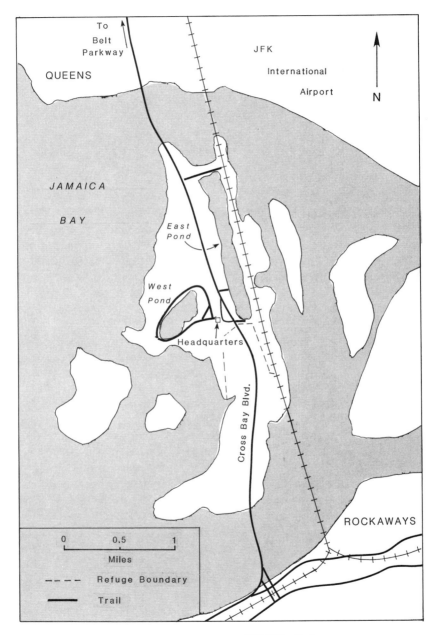

MAP 26. Jamaica Bay Wildlife Refuge

tailed Kite; Black-necked Stilt; Little and Rufous-necked Stints; Sharp-tailed Sandpiper; Sage Thrasher; Townsend's Warbler; Western Tanager; and Lark Bunting.

Directions

From northern New Jersey, take the Goethals Bridge (Interstate 278) from Elizabeth to Staten Island. Continue east on I-278 across Staten Island and over the Verrazano Narrows Bridge. Stay to the left when crossing the bridge and exit onto the Belt Parkway. Follow the Belt Parkway east for 14 miles to Cross Bay Blvd. (exit for the Rockaways). Take Cross Bay Blvd. south for about 3.5 miles to the entrance (on the right) to the parking lot for Jamaica Bay Wildlife Refuge. The entrance is not well marked, so after you have gone a little more than three miles on the Boulevard, watch carefully for the large wooden sign on your right. Park in the lot (open from about 8 A.M. to 6 P.M.) and obtain a permit at the headquarters. Rest rooms are provided here.

From central and southern New Jersey, take the Outerbridge Crossing (Rt. 440) from Perth Amboy to Staten Island, then follow Rt. 440 north for about 8 miles to I-278. Take I-278 east across Staten Island and continue as described above.

Birding

Jamaica Bay has two principal birding areas, the West Pond and the East Pond. The West Pond is good for herons, egrets, shorebirds, and waterfowl. Extensive plantings of pine and shrubs around the eastern side of the pond provide food and shelter for a variety of migrant and wintering songbirds. The East Pond is also good for waterfowl, and is the best spot for shorebirds during the fall migration.

To bird the West Pond, walk out the back door of the headquarters building, check the book of bird sightings on the post to your right, then continue along the trail toward the pond. After passing pine and shrub plantings for a couple of hundred yards, you will see the open water of the West Pond on your right. Scan the shoreline for herons, egrets, and shorebirds, and check the water for grebes, cormorants, geese, and ducks. Gull-billed Tern breeds here irregularly, but is seen frequently.

The beach to your left is good for shorebirds in migration and for Least and Common Terns during the breeding season. The waters of surrounding Jamaica Bay have good numbers of Brant and diving ducks during the colder months. Keep your eye out for Boat-tailed Grackles, which have recently started nesting on nearby Ruffle Bar and probably in the trees around the West Pond itself. The grackles are at the northeastern limit of their range in this area.

Completing your circuit of the West Pond, you will pass through a half-mile-long area of pine and shrub plantings known as the North and South Gardens. This area is excellent from fall through spring for migrant and wintering songbirds, and one or two Saw-whet Owls are usually found roosting in the pines from November through March. The complete round-trip back to the headquarters is about 1.5 miles.

The East Pond is about 1.5 miles long and varies in width from about 100 to 200 yards. During most of the year the water level is kept high to accommodate the waterfowl. Starting in late June, however, the level is gradually lowered to expose more shoreline and mudflats. This attracts thousands of shorebirds from July through October, and has made the East Pond the best shorebirding spot in the region. The alternating freshwater flooding (winter–spring) and drawdown and drying out (summer–fall) has successfully controlled botulism, a deadly bacterial disease of birds that thrives in shallow ponds.

The best time to visit the East Pond is from two or three hours before high tide to one or two hours after high tide. A rising tide forces shorebirds off the tidal mudflats of Jamaica Bay and into the East Pond, where they feed and rest, until the falling tide again exposes the mudflats of the bay. There are always shorebirds present on the pond, even at low tide, but the greatest concentrations and variety occur at high tide. High tide at Jamaica Bay occurs about 45 minutes later than that at Sandy Hook, which you can find listed in most metropolitan area newspapers; tides at Sandy Hook occur at about the same time as at Cape May Point and 20 minutes later than at Barnegat Light.

To reach the East Pond from the parking lot, walk east to Cross Bay Blvd. and cautiously cross this busy road. Turn right and walk south to the southwest corner of the pond, where there is a trail through the reeds to the shoreline. You should be prepared to get your feet wet and muddy while walking around the East Pond. Some birders prefer to wear old sneakers and slog through it all, while others prefer gum shoes or knee boots.

Walk across the south end of the pond and continue up the east shore, pausing to look at shorebirds wherever you encounter them. The area of old pilings about one-quarter of the way up the east side of the pond is excellent. One of the marvelous features of Jamaica Bay is that you can get close to many of the shorebirds because they have become habituated to people's presence. By careful observation here, you can learn to identify the shorebirds not only by species, but also by age groups. Adult shorebirds of most species migrate a month or more earlier than the young of the year, and it is interesting to follow the changing composition of the flocks as the season progresses.

Among the more common species found on the East Pond in fall are Black-bellied and Semipalmated Plovers; Greater and Lesser Yellowlegs; Ruddy Turnstone; Red Knot; Sanderling; Semipalmated, Least, Pectoral, and Stilt Sandpipers; Dunlin; and Short-billed Dowitcher. Species found regularly, but in smaller numbers, include American Oystercatcher; Whimbrel; Willet; Hudsonian Godwit; Spotted, Western, and White-rumped Sandpipers; Long-billed Dowitcher; and Common Snipe. Rarities found annually, usually from one to a few, are Lesser Golden-Plover; American Avocet; Marbled Godwit; Baird's, Curlew, and Buff-breasted Sandpipers; Ruff; and Wilson's and Red-necked Phalaropes.

Jamaica Bay is widely known as *the* place to see Curlew Sandpiper. Every year one or more of these colorful Eurasian shorebirds shows up at the East Pond, often in full breeding plumage. Mid-July through August is the best time. When a Curlew is discovered, its presence is quickly announced on the New York Rare Bird Alert—(212) 832-6523; the birds normally stay about a week. Extreme rarities that have been found at Jamaica Bay in recent years include a Sharp-tailed Sandpiper in July of 1981 and 1983, a Little Stint in July 1983 and in June 1985, and a Rufous-necked Stint in July 1985.

When you reach the northeast corner of the East Pond at the outflow valve, you must leave the shoreline as the mud is impassable. Walk out to the road on the north dike, turn left, and go about 100 yards to a trail through the *Phragmites* on the left, which leads to the northwest corner of the pond. Continue birding south along the west shore of the pond, paying closest attention to the peninsula that almost reaches across the entire pond about one-quarter of the way south. You can walk about three-quarters of the way south along the pond, although the reeds and mud make the going tough for the last quarter-mile. If you decide to slog your way through, you will eventually come to an open grassy area with a park bench, from which you can scan the pilings on the east side of the pond. The Little Stint favored this spot. A wide trail leads out to Cross Bay Blvd., a short distance north of the entrance to the parking lot. If you prefer a shorter walk, a quick trip from the parking lot directly to this spot can provide you with most of the shorebird species, especially at high tide.

If you decide not to fight the reeds and mud along the west shore, turn around when you have run out of shoreline and return to the trail at the northwest corner of the East Pond. Walk out to the north dike, turn left, and proceed out to Cross Bay Blvd. The entrance to the parking lot is a little over one mile south (to your left).

Nearby Jacob Riis Park and Breezy Point Park are also worth visiting if you have time, especially in fall. Inquire at the Jamaica Bay headquarters for directions to these other units of Gateway National Recreation Area.

Eagle Rock Reservation

This 408-acre preserve of the Essex County Park Commission sits atop the First Watchung Mountain in West Orange (with small sections extending into Verona and Montclair) at an average elevation of about 600 feet. Because of its position along this basalt ridge, Eagle Rock Reservation is an excellent place to find migrant passerines in spring and, especially, in fall. Although the lack of habitat variety limits the diversity of nesters, the list of breeding birds includes some interesting species such as Acadian Flycatcher (occasional); Northern Waterthrush; Worm-eating, Hooded, and Kentucky Warblers (all three irregular); and Canada Warblers.

Directions

From Interstate 280 Exit 8B (Prospect Avenue, Route 577), in West Orange, drive north on Prospect Ave. for 0.4 miles to the second traffic light (Eagle Rock Ave.), and turn right. Go 0.3 miles, and turn left into the entrance to Eagle Rock Reservation.

Birding

Follow the entrance road for about 0.4 miles, part of the way around a large oval drive, and park on the left opposite a small brick building, where another road (Crest Drive) turns off to the right. Along the way you will pass a stone wall where you can look out to the east for a spectacular view of the New York skyline. Just past the stone wall is a two-story stone building, known as the "Casino."

Eagle Rock Reservation has about 7 miles of bridle trails and another 3.5 miles of foot trails, which together cover every part of the park. The bridle trails are wider, better maintained, and easier to

MAP 27. Eagle Rock Reservation

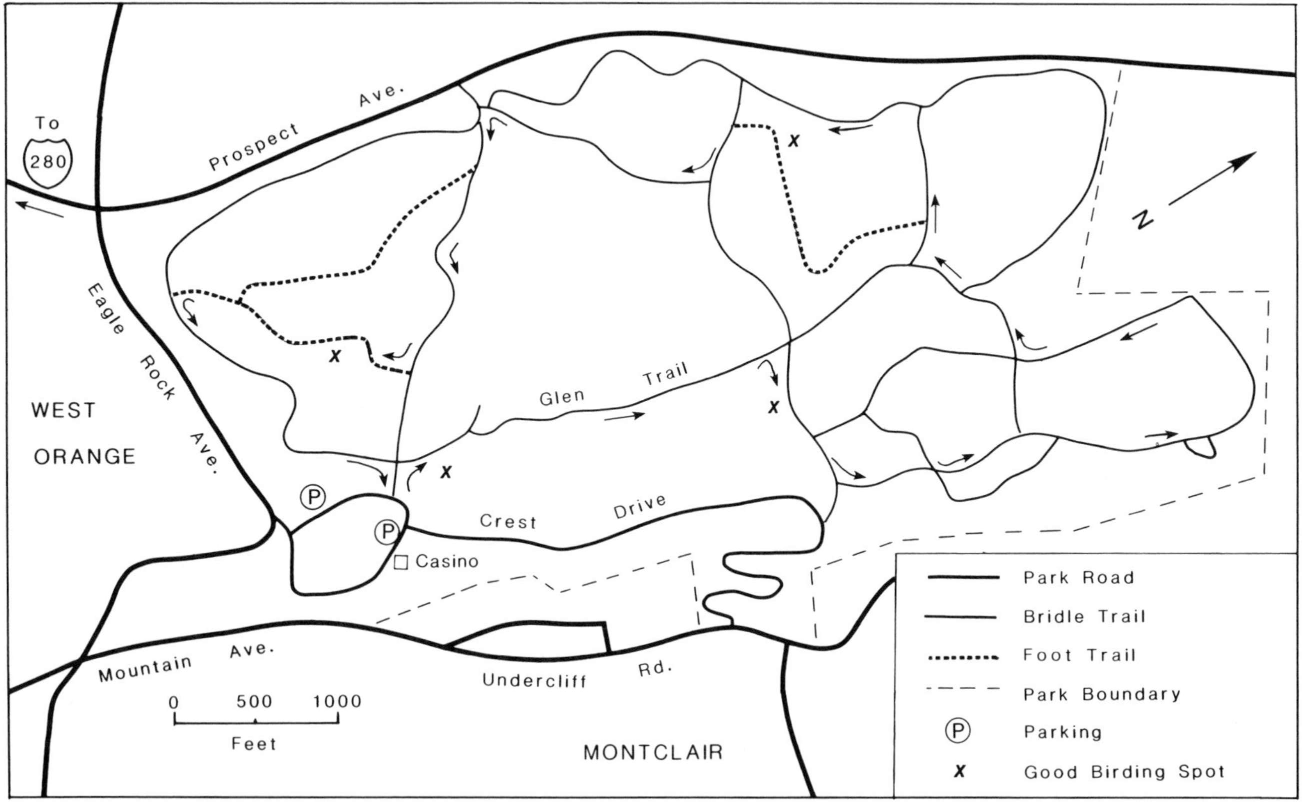

follow than the foot trails, and since they cover most of the same ground, I suggest using the bridle trails. There is very little equestrian traffic, especially early in the morning. The trails are easy to follow with the help of a compass and the fairly good trail map available from the Essex County Parks Department. Avoid trails near noisy Prospect Ave.

The vegetation of the park is a mixture of woods and thickets typical of the Piedmont hills of northeastern New Jersey. It reflects second-growth woodland in every stage of development, with mixed oaks, Black Birch, aspen, and various shrubs along the dry ridgetops, and a richer forest of oaks, maples, birches, beech, Tuliptree, Sweet Gum, ash, Flowering Dogwood, Sassafras, sycamore, and many other trees and shrubs in the cooler and wetter basins and ravines. Many of the migrant and breeding birds at Eagle Rock are found in the thickets along the streams and ravines. The route suggested on the map for this chapter covers all these habitats.

Walk along the oval entrance road to a gravel path on the right, which leads past an old stone privy. Stay right on the gravel trail at the next intersection; this is marked as the Glen Trail on the map, but there are no posted signs. Glen Trail is one of the best birding areas in the park. Follow this trail along a stream for about 200 yards, then bear right where the gravel trail leads left to a park maintenance building.

The suggested route, which follows bridle paths, can be covered in a couple of hours. Some of the likely breeding birds are Broad-winged Hawk; Black-billed and Yellow-billed Cuckoos; Eastern Screech and Great Horned Owls; Pileated Woodpecker; Blue-winged (rare), Black-and-white (rare), Worm-eating, Kentucky, Hooded, and Canada Warblers; American Redstart (rare); Northern Waterthrush; Rose-breasted Grosbeak; Indigo Bunting; and many other, more common, species.

In migration, look for Turkey Vulture; Osprey; Sharp-shinned, Red-shouldered, and Red-tailed Hawks; American Kestrel; Whippoor-will; Ruby-throated Hummingbird; Yellow-bellied Sapsucker; Olive-sided, Yellow-bellied, and Least Flycatchers; Eastern Phoebe; various swallows; Red-breasted Nuthatch; Winter Wren (April and October best); kinglets; all the thrushes; Cedar Waxwing; vireos (including Philadelphia in September); warblers (all the northern breeders, including Mourning in spring); Fox, Lincoln's (rare), and

Swamp Sparrows; Purple Finch; and Evening Grosbeak. Winter visitors include Golden-crowned Kinglet, American Tree and White-throated Sparrows, Dark-eyed Junco, and occasional winter finches such as Pine Siskin and Common Redpoll.

Eagle Rock Reservation is open from 6 A.M. to 10 P.M. To obtain a copy of the trail map, write or phone the Essex County Dept. of Parks, Recreation, and Cultural Affairs, 115 Clifton Ave., Newark, NJ 07104, (201) 482-6400.

South Mountain Reservation

South Mountain Reservation encompasses 2,047 acres in the southwestern part of Essex County. A little over three miles long from north to south, it extends from the crest of the First Watchung Mountain on the east to that of the Second Watchung on the west. The west branch of the Rahway River runs the entire length of the preserve. Most of the reservation is covered with mature deciduous woods, and small areas of thickets, fields, and conifer plantings. Because of its location along the mountain ridges, South Mountain is a good spot for migrant songbirds in spring and fall. The reservation supports most of the breeding birds expected for this primarily deciduous woodland habitat; in winter, the park is quiet and birds are scarce.

Dick Ryan, Director of the Turtle Back Zoo, which is adjacent to the park on the north, has birded South Mountain for many years and has compiled a list of more than 230 species that have been recorded in the park. The list includes many rare or uncommon species, some of which have occurred only once. Many of the records of waterfowl, shorebirds, gulls, and terns are from the Orange Reservoir, located next to the zoo. The reservoir is very difficult to bird, since most of it is surrounded by a high fence that restricts the view; there are a few good vantage points for scanning the water, however. The remainder of the reservation has many places to park, picnic areas, and 20 miles each of bridle and hiking trails.

Directions

A good place to park and explore some of the trails and streams in South Mountain is the Tulip Springs picnic area.

From the south or east, take the New Jersey Turnpike or the Gar-

149

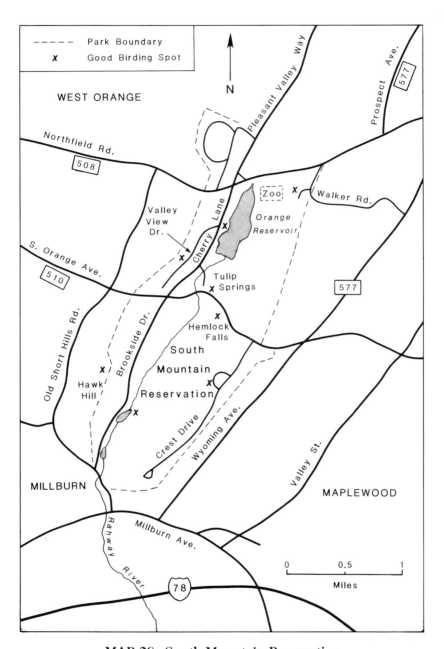

---- Park Boundary
X   Good Birding Spot

WEST ORANGE

N

Pleasant Valley Way

Prospect Ave.

577

Northfield Rd.

508

Cherry Lane

Zoo

X Walker Rd.

Valley View Dr.

X

Orange Reservoir

S. Orange Ave.

510

X

Tulip Springs
X

577

Old Short Hills Rd.

Brookside Dr.

Hemlock Falls
X

South

Mountain

X

Hawk Hill
X

Reservation

X

Crest Drive

Wyoming Ave.

Valley St.

MILLBURN

MAPLEWOOD

Rahway River

Millburn Ave.

0   0.5   1

Miles

78

MAP 28. South Mountain Reservation

den State Parkway to Interstate 280. Go west on I-280 to Exit 10 (Northfield Avenue, Orange, S. Orange, and Montclair). At the exit ramp traffic light, turn left onto Northfield Ave. and go about 2.4 miles until you pass the South Mountain Skating Arena and Turtle Back Zoo on the left. Exit right just after you pass the left turn for the zoo entrance, turn left onto Pleasant Valley Way, and proceed to the traffic light. Continue straight through the light, where the road name changes to Cherry Lane. Drive about 0.9 miles, then turn left onto a park road that leads about 100 yards to the parking lot and picnic area at Tulip Springs (bear right when the road forks just after you turn off Cherry Lane).

From the west, take I-280 east to Exit 8A (Prospect Ave.). Go south on Prospect Ave. for about 1.5 miles to Northfield Rd. and turn right. The Cherry Lane intersection is about 1.4 miles ahead; proceed as described above.

Birding

The Tulip Springs and Hemlock Falls areas are excellent for migrant warblers and other songbirds in the spring. From Tulip Springs there are two ways to reach the Hemlock Falls area. You can walk along the river from the picnic area, which will lead you under South Orange Ave., and turn left onto a bridle trail about 200 yards past the underpass. Or, you can bird your way from the picnic area through the pine woods uphill along a trail marked by a yellow dot and cross South Orange Ave. on the equestrian bridge. The yellow-dot trail begins just south of the parking area at Tulip Springs, on the opposite side of the road. All these areas are best explored with the help of a trail map, which is available from the Essex County Department of Parks, Recreation and Cultural Affairs, 115 Clifton Avenue, Newark, NJ 07104.

One of the best areas in the reservation during the breeding season is the slope to the west of Crest Dr., south of South Orange Ave. There are several points of access to the numerous trails that traverse the hillside and lead down to the ponds along the Rahway River. To get to Crest Dr. from the Tulip Springs picnic area, return to Cherry Lane and turn left. Go about one-third mile to South Orange Ave. and turn left. Drive up the hill for about one mile, then turn right onto Crest Dr. In one-quarter mile you will come to a loop road that circles Summit Field; there are several parking areas along this loop. Alternatively, you can continue on Crest Dr. for 1.5 miles to the circle at the end of the road, where there is parking.

Other good birding spots in the reservation include the rhododendron thickets along Valley View Dr. (turn off Cherry Lane at the Oakdale sign, about 0.5 miles north of Tulip Springs) and the Hawk Hill area in the southwestern part of the park. The migrant and breeding birds at South Mountain are much the same as those at nearby Eagle Rock Reservation; refer to that chapter for a list of some of the species you should expect to find.

Troy Meadows

Troy Meadows, near Parsippany in eastern Morris County, has long been famous as the premier freshwater marsh in the state. Like the Great Swamp, it is a remnant of Glacial Lake Passaic that once covered more than 200 square miles of north-central New Jersey. The marsh is an excellent place in spring and early summer to see and hear many of the freshwater marsh birds that are otherwise difficult to find. Also, the swampy woods and overgrown fields around the edges of Troy Meadows are good for migrants in spring and fall. In winter, a variety of sparrows and wintering raptors augment the limited number of permanent residents and lingering summer visitors.

Some of the nesting marsh birds that draw birders to Troy Meadows are American Bittern (now very rare), Least Bittern (now rare), Wood Duck, King Rail (formerly nested), Virginia Rail, Sora, Alder Flycatcher, Willow Flycatcher, and Marsh Wren. Among the migrants are Loggerhead Shrike (rare), Philadelphia Vireo, Orange-crowned Warbler (rare), Lincoln's and White-crowned Sparrows, and Rusty Blackbird. Northern Harrier, Rough-legged Hawk, and (occasionally) Short-eared Owl are prime attractions in winter. Rarities that have occurred at Troy Meadows include Bald Eagle, Golden Eagle, Sandhill Crane (two records), Sedge Wren (formerly nested), Northern Shrike, and Yellow-headed Blackbird.

Unfortunately, the construction of Interstates 80 and 280 has significantly reduced the size of Troy Meadows, and has had substantial negative effects both environmentally and esthetically. It is now difficult to hear the early-morning calls of distant marsh birds because of the traffic from the highways. Nearby development and consequent siltation have also reduced the value of the area to wildlife; it remains, however, an interesting and worthwhile area to bird, and can still produce most of the expected marsh birds.

MAP 29. Troy Meadows

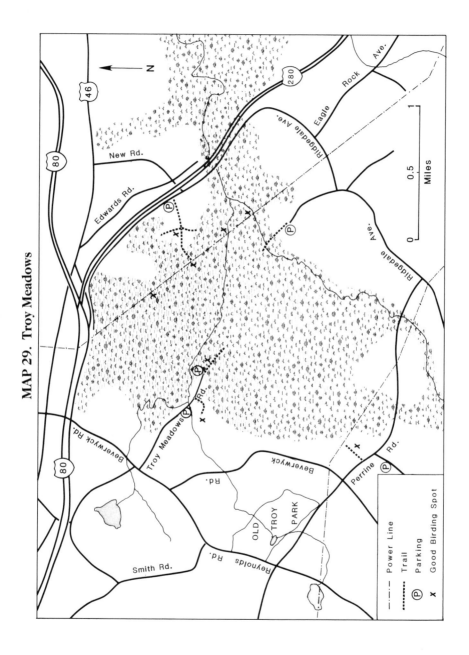

Directions

There are several points of access to Troy Meadows; to reach the best area:

From Bergen or Passaic Counties, take I-80 west to Exit 47 (US 46 West). Make a U-turn at the first opportunity, and head east on US 46. About 0.3 miles after you go under I-80, bear right onto Edwards Rd. (sign to East Hanover and Florham Park). Go 0.8 miles to the stop sign at New Rd., and turn right. Cross over I-280, and turn right onto a service road. Do *not* turn right onto the entrance ramp to I-280, but carefully continue just beyond it to a parking area on the left, *after* you turn right to parallel I-280. Here an old dirt road leads south into the woods. When parking and walking, watch out for broken glass and other litter.

From the rest of northeastern or southern New Jersey or the Philadelphia area, take either the Garden State Parkway or the New Jersey Turnpike north to I-280. Go west on I-280 to Exit 1 (Edwards Rd.); turn left, cross over I-280, and proceed as described above.

From central New Jersey, take I-287 north to Exit 37A (I-80), then go east on I-80 for about 2 miles to Exit 47B (US 46 East, The Caldwells, Montclair). Go east on US 46 for about 0.8 miles to the first traffic light, at New Rd. Turn right and go 0.7 miles to Edwards Rd. Continue straight ahead across I-280 as described above.

From northwestern New Jersey, take I-80 east to Exit 47B (US 46 East) and proceed as just described.

Birding

The best area for marsh birds is the boardwalk that runs for more than 2 miles along a power line that crosses the meadows from I-280 on the northwest to Willow Pl., off Ridgedale Ave. in East Hanover, on the southeast. Although the narrow boardwalk is usually in good repair, there are no side railings and you will occasionally find a plank missing; be alert to this possibility or you may suddenly find yourself up to your waist in the muck.

Early morning is the best time to visit Troy Meadows, as this is when the marsh birds are most vocal. The hour before dawn is a good time to listen for the *coo-coo-coo* of Least Bittern and the "pumping" call of American Bittern. Late April and May are best for these species, and for Virginia Rail and Sora. After dawn, patience is usually rewarded with a glimpse of some of these species; a tape recording of the calls is also helpful in luring them into view, but use tapes sparingly so as not to disturb the birds unduly.

To reach the boardwalk, follow the dirt road from the parking area into the woods for a couple of hundred yards. Along the way, you will pass through wet deciduous woodland that is excellent for migrant songbirds, including a wide variety of warblers. When you come to a field, take the middle path across it toward some more woods, continuing a short distance through these to the edge of a large marsh. Here you will find some planks that lead about 25 yards out to the boardwalk. If the water is high, as it often is in early spring, the planks may be submerged, and you may need to wear rubber boots.

You can walk the boardwalk for about a mile in either direction. Turning right (northwest) toward I-80 will take you through some of the better areas for bitterns and rails, which prefer the cattail areas to those overgrown with *Phragmites*. In addition to the species already noted, birds resident in the marsh during the nesting season are Great Blue Heron (not yet known to nest), Green-backed Heron (common), Mallard, Blue-winged Teal, Belted Kingfisher (nests nearby), Eastern Kingbird, Tree Swallow, Yellow Warbler, Common Yellowthroat, Swamp Sparrow, and Red-winged Blackbird (the last four abundant). Willow Flycatcher and Marsh Wren are very common in this section of the meadows; Alder Flycatcher is rare. One especially impressive feature of the marsh in spring is the number of muskrat houses; hundreds of them occupy every available patch of water as far as the eye can see.

Walking southeast on the boardwalk will eventually lead you to Troy Brook and then the Whippany River, lined with Silver Maples and willows. Here you can usually find Solitary and Spotted Sandpipers in May, Warbling Vireo, and possibly Rough-winged Swallow.

Retracing your steps to your car, you can take sidetrails to the left or right to explore more of the wooded areas at this site. To your right at the open field is an old homestead with some large evergreens that occasionally harbor Long-eared Owls or a Great Horned Owl in winter. Broad-winged and Red-tailed Hawks nest in the woods nearby. You may be fortunate enough to encounter a Red Fox; this attractive resident is common at Troy Meadows.

Troy Meadows Road

To reach the next stop at Troy Meadows, return to your car, drive back over I-280 on New Rd. for about 0.6 miles to the traffic light at US 46, and turn left. Go west on US 46 for about 2 miles to the traffic light at Beverwyck Rd. and turn left. Go about 0.8 miles and turn left onto Troy Meadows Rd. After about one-half mile you will cross a pipeline right-of-way; beyond this the pavement ends and the road enters a swampy woodland. You can park at the pipeline or continue another 0.3 miles to the end of the road, which is near a gun club, and park on the right.

Bird along the road between the pipeline and the gun club, then walk along the line of trees that heads southeast from the end of the road out into Troy Meadows. This tree line follows what was once a road that crossed the meadows. Here you will find many of the species that occur in the northern part of the marsh, but not as much variety.

Perrine Road

This spot on the southern edge of Troy Meadows can be reached by returning to Beverwyck Rd. and turning left. Drive south on Beverwyck for about 0.8 miles (Beverwyck makes a sharp left after about 250 yards), then turn left onto Perrine Rd. (shown on some maps as Troy Rd.). After about 0.2 miles you will pass an old driveway on the left; do not park here but continue a short distance to Algonquin Pkwy. on the right and park.

Return on foot to the old driveway and walk along it toward the shrubby overgrown fields on the left. Yellow-breasted Chat usually nests among the thickets of rose bushes, and Indigo Bunting sings from the treetops. Walk east (parallel to Perrine Road) down a hill toward a swampy area. Least and Willow Flycatchers nest here, and sparrows are abundant in the fall. Lincoln's Sparrow is a regular at this spot in October, along with Chipping, Field, Savannah, Fox, Song, Swamp, White-throated, and White-crowned (uncommon) Sparrows and Dark-eyed Junco. Orange-crowned Warbler has been found in the weedy fields in fall.

All the areas described in this chapter are owned by a private conservation organization but are open to the public, except during the deer-hunting season in early December. The topographic maps (Caldwell and Morristown quadrangles) and some scouting will turn up several other points of access. There are no rest rooms. To return to I-80, go back to Beverwyck Rd. and drive north for about 1.6 miles to the entrance for I-80 West. To reach I-80 East, continue another 0.2 miles to US 46 and go right (east) for a mile to the entrance ramp. If you are heading south, turn left off Perrine Rd. onto Beverwyck and go one mile to Rt. 10. Turn right and go about 1.5 miles to I-287, where you can take the southbound entrance toward Morristown.

Lake Parsippany

This small, artificial lake in eastern Morris County attracts a surprising diversity of waterfowl, primarily in late fall/early winter before the lake freezes, and in early spring after the ice has thawed. Averaging less than one-half mile across and nowhere very deep, Lake Parsippany is especially popular with diving ducks. When the water is frozen, gulls use the ice as a roosting area, and large numbers of them gather on the thawing ice in late February or March.

Directions

From the south take Interstate 287 through Morristown. Take Exit 36 (Lake Parsippany) to the traffic light at Parsippany Rd. Turn left, cross over I-287, then take the first left turn onto Freneau Rd. (0.3 miles). Go immediately left onto Califon Rd. for 0.3 miles, then bear right at the T-intersection onto Georgene Ct., which ends at Lake Shore Dr. after one short block. Continue straight ahead on Lake Shore Dr. This is the starting point for the loop drive. Lake Shore Dr. runs all the way around the lake; the complete loop is 2.3 miles.

From the north or east, take Interstate 80 to I-287 in Parsippany, then take I-287 south for one mile to Exit 36B (Lake Shore Dr., Lake Parsippany). The exit puts you on Georgene Ct. at Califon Rd. Georgene Ct. ends at Lake Shore Dr. in one short block. Continue as described above.

Birding

There are several good vantage points for scanning the lake; a spotting scope is helpful. The best place is just past the spillway, 0.2 miles from the starting point at Lake Shore Dr. There is a strip of grass and trees along the right and space to park between the

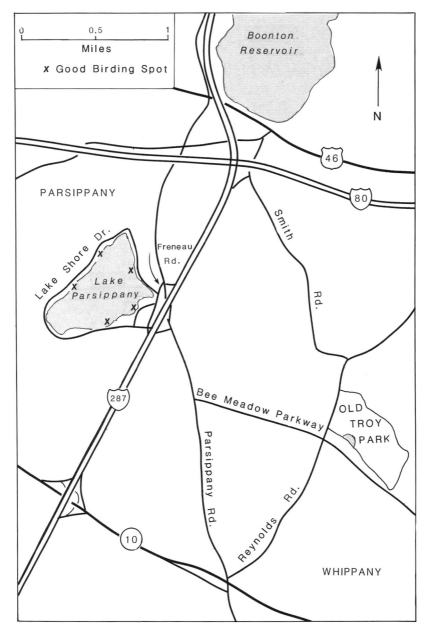

MAP 30. Lake Parsippany

Johnson Beach baththouse and a boathouse belonging the Lake Parsippany Property Owners Association. "No Trespassing" signs are posted, but at the seasons you will be there no one shows any concern for birders. From here continue around to the opposite shore, where the road is close to the lake from mile 1.0 to mile 1.6. Another good viewing spot is at Drewes Beach, 2.0 miles from the start.

During October the first migrant diving ducks appear. Ruddy Duck is common, with flocks of up to 500, and is joined in November by good numbers of Common Mergansers. Bufflehead, Lesser Scaup, Canvasback, and Ring-necked Duck are present in small numbers, while Redhead, Common Goldeneye, and Hooded and Red-breasted Mergansers drop in occasionally. Other diving birds also appear: American Coot can be abundant, Common Loon and Horned and Pied-billed Grebes are regular, and Red-necked Grebe has been found a few times. A variety of dabbling ducks stop in for brief visits, but only the resident Mallards remain.

After the lake freezes over in December, gulls gather to roost on the ice. In some years there are hundreds, in other years only a few dozen; this variation may be related to activity at garbage dumps within commuting distance. The greatest number and variety of gulls are present from the beginning of the thaw until the ice is completely gone—anytime from mid-February to late March.

Ring-billed and Herring Gulls are by far the most common, with smaller numbers of Great Black-backed Gulls. The rare gulls are what keep you going back to check the lake again and again, however. Glaucous, Iceland, and Lesser Black-backed have all occurred; on the day the last ice melted in March 1978, 3 Glaucous, 1 Iceland, and 2 Lesser Black-backs were present at the same time. Lesser Black-backed was a regular winter visitor during the late 1970s, but although this species has increased elsewhere, none has appeared at Lake Parsippany in recent years.

In spring, as soon as there is open water, the diving birds start to reappear. Most of the same birds present in fall also occur in spring. Common Mergansers are especially plentiful, and March–April is the best time to look for Red-necked Grebe (very rare).

After completing the loop, you will be back at the intersection of Georgene Ct. and Lake Shore Dr. To return to I-287 southbound, turn left and follow Georgene Ct. two short blocks to the entrance ramp. To reach I-287 northbound, turn left onto Califon Rd., follow it back to Freneau Rd., then turn right onto Parsippany Rd. Cross over the interstate and take the entrance ramp on the right marked I-287 North.

Great Swamp National Wildlife Refuge

Great Swamp National Wildlife Refuge is a 7,000-acre refuge consisting primarily of hardwood swamp, marsh, and some open water; in addition it has areas of upland deciduous woods, overgrown fields, and pastures maintained by periodic mowing. The swamp escaped becoming the metropolitan area's fourth major airport only through the efforts of concerned citizens; today it is a haven for wildlife in the midst of southern Morris County's ever-expanding suburbia.

The refuge is divided into a wilderness area and a management area. The wilderness area was established by an Act of Congress in 1968, and comprises the eastern two-thirds of the swamp. It has a number of maintained trails, but is otherwise left untouched. The management area, the western one-third of the swamp, has several large ponds, where water levels are controlled to provide optimal habitat for the resident and migrant waterfowl, and numerous fields that are mowed periodically to provide feeding and nesting habitat for a wide variety of wildlife. At present, access to the management area is limited. You can drive along Pleasant Plains Rd., which bisects the area, and you can walk the trails and visit the observation blinds at the Wildlife Observation Center off Long Hill–New Vernon Rd.

More than 200 species of birds occur on the refuge, plus a wide variety of mammals, reptiles, amphibians, and fish. About 90 species of birds nest here. The mammals most likely to be encountered are the abundant White-tailed Deer and Muskrat, plus Gray Squirrel, Eastern Chipmunk, Raccoon, and Eastern Cottontail. Opossum, Long-tailed Weasel, Striped Skunk, and Red Fox are all common, but highly nocturnal. River Otters are seen on occasion. Among the more interesting reptiles and amphibians are the state-endangered Bog Turtle and Blue-spotted Salamander.

MAP 31. Great Swamp NWR

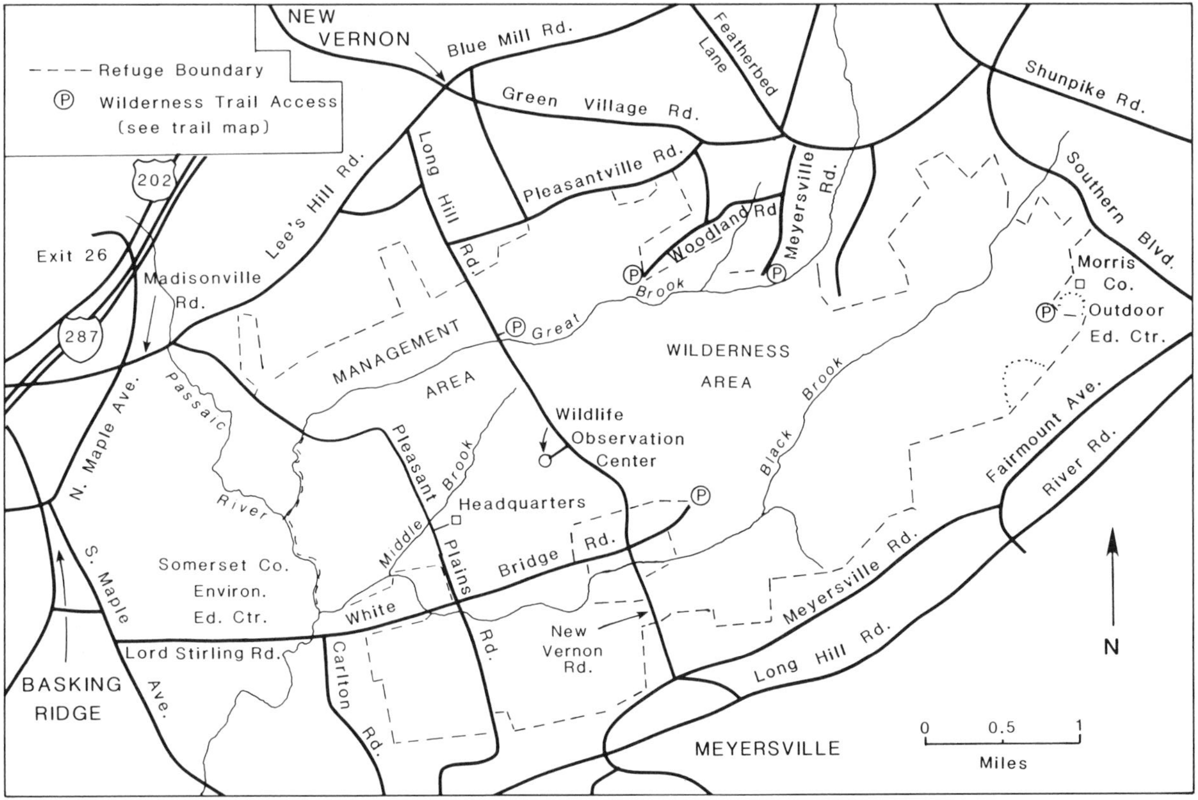

NEW VERNON

Shunpike Rd.

Southern Blvd.

Morris Co. Outdoor Ed. Ctr.

Fairmount Ave.

River Rd.

Featherbed Lane

Meyersville Rd.

Blue Mill Rd.

Green Village Rd.

Woodland Rd.

Pleasantville Rd.

WILDERNESS AREA

Black Brook

Meyersville Rd.

Long Hill Rd.

MEYERSVILLE

Great Brook

Long Hill Rd.

Wildlife Observation Center

MANAGEMENT AREA

Headquarters

Plains

Bridge Rd.

New Vernon Rd.

Middle Brook

Pleasant

White

Carlton

Rd.

Lee's Hill Rd.

Madisonville Rd.

Passaic River

Somerset Co. Environ. Ed. Ctr.

Lord Stirling Rd.

S. Maple Ave.

N. Maple Ave.

Exit 26

202

287

BASKING RIDGE

--- Refuge Boundary

(P) Wilderness Trail Access
    (see trail map)

N

0   0.5   1
Miles

Directions

All directions for locations within Great Swamp NWR start at the Wildlife Observation Center (WOC) on Long Hill–New Vernon Rd. in Harding Township, Morris County. The WOC can be reached as follows.

From the east, take Rt. 24 west to the Morris Ave. exit in Summit; this puts you on River Rd. Follow River Rd. south for 1.1 miles, cross the bridge over the Passaic River into Chatham, and take the first left, also called River Rd. After a stop sign at 1.3 miles, continue straight ahead on River Rd. for 0.5 miles and bear right at the fork when the road curves to the left; you are still on River Rd. Continue for 1.4 miles and turn right onto Fairmount Ave. Take the second left turn (0.2 miles) and follow Meyersville Rd. 2.5 miles to the circle in Meyersville. Turn right onto New Vernon Rd. and go 1.9 miles to the WOC entrance, on the left, marked by a small stone gate. On the way, you will cross White Bridge Rd. and the name of the road you are on will change (there are no markers, however) from New Vernon Road to Long Hill Rd. when you cross from Passaic Township into Harding Township by the refuge sign.

From the north, take Interstate 287 south to Exit 29 (Harter Rd.), and stay to the right as you come around the cloverleaf onto Harter Rd. Go 0.3 miles and turn right onto James St. Proceed 1.1 miles and turn right on Blue Mill Rd. Follow Blue Mill Rd. for 0.8 miles, staying left at the fork and proceeding through the blinking yellow light, where the road name changes to Lee's Hill Rd. Go 0.4 miles and turn left onto Long Hill Rd. opposite the Harding Township School. The WOC entrance is 2.2 miles ahead, on the right.

From the south, take Interstate 287 north to Exit 26A (N. Maple Ave., Basking Ridge). Follow N. Maple for 0.5 miles to the first traffic light. Turn left onto Madisonville Rd. and go 2.7 miles (the name changes to Lee's Hill Rd. when you cross a small dam). Turn right onto Long Hill Rd. (opposite the Harding Township School) and proceed 2.2 miles to the WOC entrance, on the right.

Birding

The Great Swamp can be interesting at any season, but the most productive times to visit are during spring migration in April and

May and during the nesting season, primarily May through July. The nesting season is a time of great activity in the swamp—about 100 species are known or suspected to have nested here within the past 10 years. In fall there are many migrant passerines and waterfowl, but the dense vegetation makes them hard to see. In winter, raptors and sparrows abound. The area is called a swamp for good reason, and many of the trails will be wet or muddy.

Wildlife Observation Center

The WOC has a large parking lot, an information kiosk, rest rooms, and trails to two observation blinds. The blinds are helpful for viewing some of the birdlife, especially in the spring and also in the winter if the bird feeders are filled. Take the right trail, past the rest rooms, to the boardwalk that leads to one blind. In spring and summer, watch for Virginia Rail and Common Yellowthroat around the boardwalk; Swamp Sparrow is here at any season. The blind may permit close looks at Great Blue Heron, Green-backed Heron, Wood Duck, Green-winged and Blue-winged Teal, Mallard, or perhaps something unusual—Ring-necked Duck and Horned Grebe have both appeared here in migration.

Returning to the parking lot area, take the left trail leading to the other blind. This is a longer trail (about 0.3 miles), and leads through a wet woodland that has many of the common birds of the swamp. The blind looks out over some small ponds and fields. Wood Ducks can be closely observed here, especially in the spring, and Great Blue Herons from the nearby heronries are frequently seen feeding. The Great Swamp is the best place in the state and one of the best in the country for observing Wood Duck. More than 500 pairs usually nest on the refuge and can be easily found in the spring on the many ponds or sitting on top of the nest boxes provided for them. During their midsummer molt they become hard to see, but by August the adults and young are everywhere. Many remain well into the fall, and a few into the winter. Great Blue Herons have been nonbreeding year-round residents for many years, but in 1982 they established a nesting colony in the management area. This heronry had 55 nests in 1985, and another colony has started in the wilderness area.

Rarities show up here on occasion—Bald Eagle, Northern and

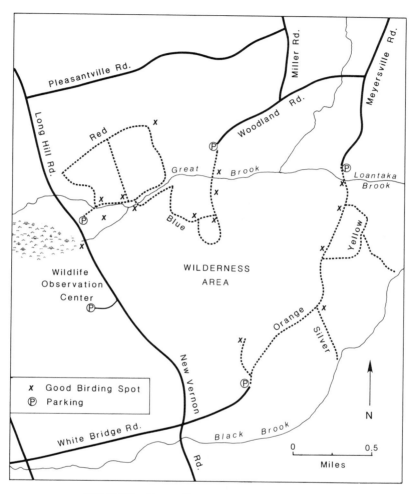

MAP 32. Great Swamp NWR Trail Map

Loggerhead Shrikes, and Yellow-headed Blackbird have all been seen from the blind. If the bird feeder near the blind is kept filled in winter, it offers the chance to see some of the local birds at close range. Red-bellied Woodpecker, Blue Jay, Black-capped Chickadee, Tufted Titmouse, White-breasted Nuthatch, Red-winged Blackbird, and Northern Cardinal are all regular visitors to the feeder, as are Tree, White-throated, Swamp, and Song Sparrows.

Primitive Access (no longer open, see page 173)

The Primitive Access area is a good place to find many of the characteristic birds of the Great Swamp. From the WOC, go left on Long Hill Rd. for 0.6 miles to the parking area on the right, which has room for 10 cars. Walk back along Long Hill Rd. to the bridge, and scan the large impoundment (known to refuge personnel as Pool 1) on the west (management) side of the road. In spring, before the vegetation grows too tall, a variety of waterfowl can be seen here, including Wood Duck and Green-winged and Blue-winged Teal. Common Moorhen and Green-backed and Great Blue Herons are usually visible, and with luck you might see or hear an American or a Least Bittern. Osprey fish over the pond in the spring, and Bald Eagle is seen here once or twice a year. Great Egrets appear here in the late summer, as do occasional Black-crowned Night-Herons and Glossy Ibis. Hundreds of ducks gather here in the fall, although the dense vegetation makes it difficult to see them.

Return to the parking area, where Yellow-throated Vireo is often found, and take the trail which leads to the left. You will soon come to a trail marker with a map showing the alternative routes. You can make two loops following the red blazes on the trees; the longer loop is about two miles, the shorter, about half that. As you continue along the trail, listen for woodpeckers. Five species may be nesting in the woods to your left: Red-bellied, Downy, Hairy, and Pileated Woodpeckers, plus Northern Flicker. This is an especially good place to see and hear the Pileated; no matter how many times you encounter this magnificent crow-sized woodpecker, watching one drumming on an old dead tree or flying through the forest is a thrilling experience.

The trail soon comes to an open area on the right, an old landfill now overgrown with willows, grasses, and *Phragmites*. This area has nesting Willow Flycatcher, Yellow Warbler, and Swamp Sparrow, Common Snipe and Solitary Sandpiper feed around the edges of the landfill in spring, and a variety of sparrows can be found here in fall, including Lincoln's and White-crowned Sparrows in October and Tree Sparrow from November through March. Flocks of Common Nighthawks occur here in mid-May and again in late August–early September.

Shortly after the marked trail crosses Great Brook, you will come to the first junction. Stay right as the trail continues through some mature woods, then follows the brook for a while. In spring migration this area has flycatchers (including Olive-sided), thrushes, vireos, and warblers. In August and September watch for Yellow-bellied Flycatcher and Philadelphia Vireo.

You will soon come to a brushy field, where the trail forks: for the short loop take the left fork, for the long loop, the right fork. If you have time, take the long loop, which runs through a greater variety of habitats. If you do, you will soon come to the junction of a trail marked with blue blazes, which goes to Woodland Rd. (see next section). The red-blazed trail takes you through wet woodlands with fairly mature stands of oak and maple, and through some scrubby areas dominated by Gray Birch, before eventually returning to the beginning of the loop near Great Brook.

Some of the nesting birds along the red trail are Wood Duck; American Woodcock; Yellow-billed Cuckoo; Eastern Screech and Barred Owls; Least Flycatcher; Eastern Kingbird; Tree Swallow; Brown Creeper; Carolina Wren; Eastern Bluebird; Northern Mockingbird; Brown Thrasher; White-eyed Vireo; Blue-winged, Chestnut-sided, and Black-and-white Warblers; American Redstart; Rose-breasted Grosbeak; Chipping, Field and Song Sparrows; plus all the common species of deciduous woods and shrubby fields listed on p. 12.

The many migrant passerines include 10 species of flycatcher (8 nest on the refuge), all 6 eastern swallows (Purple Martin, Tree Swallow, and Barn Swallow nest), all the thrushes (Gray-cheeked rare), both kinglets, 6 vireos (4 nest), more than 30 species of warblers (about 10 nest), 12 sparrows (4 nest), and 8 icterids (blackbirds), of which all but Rusty Blackbird remain to nest. About 25 warbler species are noted in any given year; Golden-winged, Mourning, and Kentucky are rare spring migrants, and Connecticut Warbler is rare in the fall.

Woodland Road

From the WOC, go left on Long Hill Rd. for 1.4 miles to Pleasantville Rd., the first intersection. Turn right, go 1.7 miles, and make the first right turn, Miller Rd. Proceed on Miller for 1.0 miles, then go right on Woodland Rd. for one-half mile to the end. The trail is marked by blue blazes; there is a one-mile loop, or you can continue all the way to the bridge across the Great Brook, where the blue-blazed trail intersects the red-blazed trail described above.

A short distance down the path from the parking lot, a side path to the right leads to an overgrown field and (if you have wading boots) to a wooded island in the marsh. At the far side of the island is a marsh along Great Brook where Wood Duck, Virginia Rail, Sora and Eastern Bluebird nest, and where two White Ibis were found in July 1977. About 100 down the main trail a fallen tree serves as a foot-bridge across Great Brook. To your left is a large expanse of marsh. If the water is low, this may hold a small variety of shorebirds in the spring, including Greater and Lesser Yellowlegs; Solitary, Spotted, and Least Sandpiper; and occasionally a Semipalmated or Pectoral Sandpiper, Dunlin, or Short-billed Dowitcher.

The blue-blazed trail loop passes through a grove of large old American Beech trees where Scarlet Tanagers and Veeries abound; otherwise, the birds are mainly the same as those noted for the red-blazed trail.

Meyersville Road

The old Meyersville Rd., marked by orange blazes, can be reached from either end. To reach the north end, follow the directions for Woodland Rd., but turn left at the intersection of Miller Rd. and Woodland Rd. and go 0.5 miles to Meyersville Rd. Turn right and continue 0.7 miles to the parking area. To reach the south end from the WOC, go right on Long Hill Rd. for 0.8 miles to White Bridge Rd. Turn left and proceed 0.6 miles to the parking area.

Meyersville Rd. passes through a variety of habitats, including Red Maple swamp, drier deciduous woods, overgrown fields, marsh, and even an old orchard and some Norway Spruce plantings. The road itself is only about a mile and a half long, but two side trail loops (shown on trail map) and a couple of dead-end spurs increase the total trail length to about 5 miles. Because of the diversity of habitats, most of the breeding birds of the Great Swamp can be found here.

Starting from the southern end, you will be near the newest Great Blue Heron rookery and may see the birds flying to and from feeding areas. Near the beginning of the trail, there is usually a Least Flycatcher in the wet woods on the right. Eight species of flycatcher were found nesting along this road in 1983, including all four of the state's breeding *Empidonax* flycatchers. A short distance ahead a loop trail branches off to the left through a field and near some ponds surrounded by willows. Alder and Willow Flycatchers have been found nesting here, although Alder is not present every year. Willow Flycatcher is common and widespread throughout the swamp, but the only other spot for Alder Flycatcher at the present time is in the management area. Acadian Flycatcher was found nesting in 1983 for the first time in many years, in a wooded area containing some large maples near the north end of Meyersville Road. The other flycatchers nesting here are Eastern Wood-Pewee, Eastern Phoebe, Great Crested Flycatcher and Eastern Kingbird.

Meyersville Rd. is a good place for hawks (Red-tailed, Red-shouldered and American Kestrel) and owls (Eastern Screech, Great Horned, and Barred), and provides your best chance in the refuge for finding Ruffed Grouse. The marsh on the east side of the road opposite the orchard, about one half mile from the northern end, has Least Bittern and Virginia Rail. King Rail occurs in migration and may occasionally nest. Near the northern end of the road, a footbridge crosses Loantaka Brook; the marsh here sometimes has bitterns and Marsh Wrens.

Pleasant Plains Road

A drive along Pleasant Plains Rd. through the management area can be very productive for hawks in winter and for Eastern Bluebird at any other season. Red-tailed Hawk and American Kestrel are common along the road from November to March (both species also nest here); other species to be looked for are Red-shouldered Hawk, Rough-legged Hawk (rare), and Northern Harrier. Turkey Vultures from the nearby Bernardsville roost are conspicuous during most winters, and have been joined in recent years by up to six Black Vultures. During the fall of 1983, about 50 Red-headed Woodpeckers appeared in the refuge, mainly in the management area. They remained throughout the winter and could often be seen along Pleasant Plains Rd. Whether this formerly uncommon bird will maintain its sudden abundance remains to be seen.

To reach Pleasant Plains Rd. from the WOC, turn right onto Long Hill Rd. and go 0.8 miles to White Bridge Rd. Turn right and go 1.1 miles to the next intersection, which is Pleasant Plains Rd. Go right again, and in 0.3 miles you will come to a gate at the refuge boundary. This gate and the one at the other side of the refuge are open only from 8:00 A.M. to dusk. The distance between the gates is 1.5 miles, and the road is dirt. A short distance past the south gate a long driveway on the right leads to the refuge headquarters. The office is open from 8:00 A.M. to 4:30 P.M. weekdays, and has bird checklists, trail maps, and other information.

As you drive along Pleasant Plains Rd., watch the wires and trees for Eastern Bluebird. The refuge maintains a very successful nest-box program and now has several dozen pairs of bluebirds nesting in both boxes and natural cavities. The birds are conspicuous most of the year, especially in the late summer after the young have fledged, though the numbers in winter are somewhat reduced. Other species in the fields, woods, and artificial ponds along the road are Canada Goose, Wood Duck, American Woodcock, Great Horned Owl (in old Red-tailed Hawk nests), Tree Swallow (in boxes), Eastern Meadowlark, and Bobolink, plus many of the more common species. In early May, swallows of all six species swarm over the fields in search of insects. All but Cliff Swallow are seen throughout the summer, although Bank and Northern Rough-winged Swallows do not nest within the refuge boundaries.

Watch the fields for Red Fox early in the morning, especially in spring when the kits are about and have yet to learn to fear humans. Just before the north gate, there is a pond on the left that is favored by Ring-necked Duck and occasionally other divers such as Ruddy

Duck and Hooded Merganser, during migration. The north gate is at the bridge over Great Brook, where Warbling Vireo and Orchard Oriole may be present. The gate is closed to public travel, so you must retrace your route to the south gate.

Two of the more sought-after birds of the Great Swamp, American Woodcock and Barred Owl, are quite common, but most easily found at dusk or after dark, respectively. The male woodcock can be seen performing his courtship flight over virtually any field adjacent to wet woodlands starting in early March and continuing into May. The flights usually begin about 30 minutes after sunset and continue well after dark. The owls are common throughout the refuge, and can usually be found near the WOC or the Primitive Access parking area. If you plan to be in the refuge after dark, however, you will need a permit, which can usually be obtained by stopping at the headquarters on Pleasant Plains Rd. and explaining your interests to the officer in charge.

If you have toured the refuge and still want to visit other birding spots in the area, there are three good ones nearby: Jockey Hollow (Morristown National Historical Park), Scherman-Hoffman Sanctuaries, and Lord Stirling Park, each of which is described in its own chapter. The Morris County Outdoor Education Center is on the eastern border of the swamp and provides access to the Laurel Trail, which is in the refuge. To reach the center from the WOC, go right for 1.9 miles to Meyersville, and left on Meyersville Rd. for 2.5 miles to Fairmount Ave. Go left on Fairmount for 1.7 miles to the traffic light at Southern Blvd., then left for 0.9 miles to the OEC entrance, on the left.

Information about Great Swamp National Wildlife Refuge can be obtained by writing to the Refuge Manager, Great Swamp NWR, Pleasant Plains Rd., RD 1, Box 148, Basking Ridge, N.J. 07920.

NOTE: The Primitive Access parking area has been closed; however, a new parking area was opened in 1990 at the pipeline cut above 1.2 miles north of the WOC on Long Hill Rd. on the west side, just outside the wilderness area. A trail begins here and connects with the trail shown on the map as the red trail, which is now marked with blue blazes and connects with the trail from Woodland Road. Except for the landfill area, the remaining trails are still open.

Lord Stirling Park

This 900-acre park, which adjoins the Great Swamp National Wildlife Refuge, has nearly 9 miles of hiking trails, including more than one and one-half miles of boardwalk. Bordering the Passaic River, the park contains a variety of both marshy and woodland habitats that support a birdlife similar to that of the NWR. Approximately half the park is reserved for equestrian trails, where no pedestrians are allowed, and the remaining half is devoted to the conservation and nature programs of the Somerset County Environmental Education Center.

Nearly 200 species of birds have occurred at the park, of which about 75 nest. The breeding species include Wood Duck; Great Horned and Barred Owls; Red-bellied Woodpecker; Willow and Least Flycatchers; Brown Creeper; Eastern Bluebird; White-eyed, Yellow-throated, Red-eyed, and Warbling Vireos; and Prothonotary Warbler. Spring and fall migrations bring a variety of waterfowl, hawks, a few shorebirds, and many passerines. Winter is a quiet time, with only a few raptors and sparrows to augment the population of permanent residents. Rarities seen here in recent years include Bald Eagle, Golden Eagle, and Peregrine Falcon.

Directions

Take Interstate 287 to Exit 26A (N. Maple Ave., Basking Ridge). Follow N. Maple Ave. for about 1.7 miles to a fork, where you bear left onto S. Maple Ave. Continue another 1.0 miles to Lord Stirling Rd. and turn left. The Center is one mile ahead on the left.

Birding

The Environmental Education Center building and trails are open 9 A.M.–5 P.M. weekdays, 10 A.M.–4 P.M. on Saturday, and 1–5 P.M. on

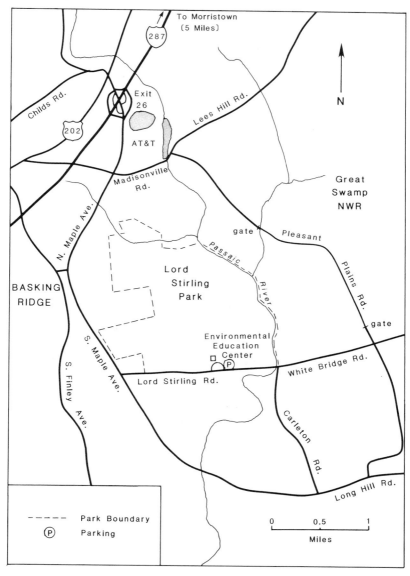

MAP 33. Lord Stirling Park

Sunday; they are closed on most holidays. The trails are open to permit holders, however, from sunrise to sunset, every day of the year. An annual permit, which also provides access to the two observation blinds, costs $5 per person or family in 1985.

If you do not have a permit, register at the Center and obtain permission to use the trails. A small fee is charged. In spite of the boardwalks and numerous bridges, you may encounter muddy conditions along some of the trails; rubber boots are recommended. The route suggested below is just one of many that you can take using the trail map, which is available at the Center, as are rest rooms.

From the Environmental Education Center, which has Barn Swallow nesting under the eaves, walk out the red and yellow trail along Branta Pond on the left, where Canada Goose and Tree Swallow nest. Turn right where the red and the yellow trail diverge, following the yellow. Stay right at the next two junctions, as you cross a field where Eastern Kingbird, Northern Mockingbird, Brown Thrasher, Eastern Bluebird, Blue-winged Warbler, Common Yellowthroat, Eastern Meadowlark, American Goldfinch, Field Sparrow, and Song Sparrow nest.

When you pass Lily Pad Pond, you may flush Green-backed Heron or Wood Duck. Continue past the observation blind, and leave the yellow trail at the next junction on the right. This trail follows along the edge of a woods near the Passaic River, and is an excellent spot for migrant songbirds in spring. The breeding birds here include Red-bellied Woodpecker, Eastern Phoebe, Tree Swallow, Barn Swallow, Yellow-throated and Warbling Vireos, Prothonotary and Yellow Warblers, and Rose-breasted Grosbeak. Three or four pairs of Prothonotary Warblers nest along the stretch of the Passaic River between Lord Stirling Road and the East Observation Tower.

Turn right at the next trail junction, then right again on a trail that leads you 200 yards further to the East Observation Tower. Here you may see Mallard, Wood Duck, Eastern Kingbird, Prothonotary and Yellow Warblers, and Song and Swamp Sparrows. Continue along the trail from the observation tower, taking a right turn at each new trail junction.

This route will take you along the edge of a field, where Ruby-throated Hummingbird, House Wren, White-eyed Vireo, Common Yellowthroat, Northern Cardinal, Rufous-sided Towhee and Field Sparrow are breeders. Then you will enter a swampy Red Maple woodland; Barred Owl is a common resident in such habitat in the Great Swamp basin; it will probably take you many visits to see one, but you have a fair chance of hearing one giving its *who cooks for you, who cooks for you-allll* call, especially in April–May. Barred Owls have a wide repertoire of other hoots and screams, which they often give even in the middle of the day, so be alert to the noises of the swamp.

You will soon come to a boardwalk across a marshy area; stay right at the next fork and follow the boardwalk down to the river. In June, you might find a female Wood Duck with her brood; in August, the banks are aflame with the scarlet of Cardinal Flower. Continue along the boardwalk for another 250 yards, then turn right at the next junction. After a couple of hundred yards you will emerge into a large, open area where cattails are interspersed with Swamp Rose, Buttonbush, and willows. Great Blue and Green-backed Herons come to feed here, and nesting species include Virginia Rail, Sora, Willow Flycatcher, Eastern Kingbird, Marsh Wren, Gray Catbird, Cedar Waxwing, Yellow Warbler, Common Yellowthroat, Red-winged Blackbird, and Swamp and Song Sparrows.

The trail soon enters a forest of Pin Oak and Red Maple. Here and in the slightly drier stands of oaks, hickories, and birches farther along the red trail, you will encounter many of the common woodland species of the Great Swamp. Among the breeding birds are Yellow-billed and Black-billed Cuckoos, Brown Creeper, Yellow-throated Vireo, Black-and-white Warbler, American Redstart, Rose-breasted Grosbeak, and many other, more common, species.

The trail completes a long loop, then comes to another boardwalk junction; turn right, then right again at the next junction. From this point it is about 300 yards to the red trail. Follow the red trail through a variety of woods and fields for about one mile back to the Environmental Center. The entire tour covers a little over three miles; it can be birded in 2–3 hours, depending on your pace.

In May, you will encounter many migrants in the woods, especially thrushes, vireos, and warblers. The park bird list includes 28 species of warblers, most of which occur as common spring migrants. Many of these same species return as fall migrants in August and September. They are followed in October by a variety of sparrows that includes Savannah, Vesper, Tree, White-crowned, White-throated, Fox, and Lincoln's, plus Dark-eyed Junco.

A small number of waterfowl and raptors pass through during the fall migration, as do a smattering of shorebirds. October and November bring Rusty Blackbird, Purple Finch, and Evening Grosbeak. Winter birds usually include only the permanent residents, plus a few hawks and sparrows.

This well-maintained park has a varied and interesting birdlife, but it is not adequately covered by birders. Wandering immature Bald Eagles have shown up here increasingly during spring and summer in recent years, and diligent searching might turn up other rarities.

Additional Birding Spots in Northeastern New Jersey

Green Brook Sanctuary

A private, densely wooded preserve atop the New Jersey Palisades in Alpine and Tenafly, Bergen County, this 165-acre sanctuary provides excellent birding and spectacular views of the Hudson River and nearby Manhattan. Owned by the Palisades Nature Association, Green Brook is open only to members, who pay tax-deductible annual dues. More than 230 species of birds have been recorded here, including most of the common species that regularly migrate through New Jersey and all the winter finches. Rarities have included Swallow-tailed Kite, Golden Eagle, Boreal Chickadee, Orange-crowned Warbler, Henslow's Sparrow, and Yellow-headed Blackbird. Write the Palisades Nature Association at P.O. Box 155, Alpine, NJ 07620 for information about membership.

Mills Reservation

Mills Reservation, a 157-acre unit of the Essex County Parks system, is similar to Eagle Rock Reservation, which is about 3 miles to the south. Both preserves sit atop the First Watchung Mountain, but Mills is almost entirely within the township of Cedar Grove. It is best during the songbird migrations in May and in August–September. The birds at Mills are much the same as those at the larger Eagle Rock Reservation, but because Mills has less habitat and less varied terrain, the diversity of birdlife is somewhat smaller. Nearby Cedar Grove Reservoir is a good spot for gulls in winter, and the road that runs along the east side of the reservoir is good for songbirds in migration.

Directions

Take the Garden State Parkway north to Exit 151 (Watchung Ave., Montclair). From the exit ramp, turn left onto Watchung Ave., and drive about 2.2 miles until the road ends at Upper Mountain Ave. Turn right and go about 1.7 miles to the traffic light at Normal Ave. Turn left and drive 0.3 miles to the poorly marked entrance to the parking lot for Mills Reservation on the left. If you are coming from farther north, you can take the Parkway to Exit 154 (US 46 West). Go west on Rt. 46 for 1.3 miles, and take the exit for Valley Rd. Turn left onto Valley Rd. and go about 1.1 miles to Normal Ave. Turn right onto Normal and drive 0.6 miles to the entrance to Mills, on the left. Reservoir Dr., which runs along the east side of Cedar Grove Reservoir, is 0.2 miles farther west on Normal Ave.

Old Troy Park

This 100-acre county park in eastern Morris County is known for its excellent passerine migration, especially in fall. It gained fame during the 1970s as the home of a male Lawrence's Warbler; this bird (or its progeny) returned to the park in spring for a dozen years, last appearing in 1981. Thirty or more species of warbler are found here during August and September, along with most *Empidonax* flycatchers and many thrushes, vireos, and sparrows.

Among the sought-after species seen here in recent years are Yellow-bellied (regular in fall) and Acadian (summer) Flycatchers; Gray-cheeked Thrush (mainly fall); Philadelphia Vireo (regular in fall); Kentucky, Connecticut (fall), and Mourning Warblers; Summer Tanager (spring); and Lincoln's Sparrow.

Directions

Old Troy Park is shown on Maps 29 and 30. Take Interstate 80 west to Exit 47 (Parsippany). Go about one mile to the traffic light at Beverwyck Rd. and turn left (from the west, take I-80 to Exit 45, Beverwyck Rd., and turn right). Take Beverwyck road for one mile to a fork, and bear right onto Reynolds Rd. Follow this for 0.6 miles to the park entrance on the left. A display board at the parking lot shows a map of the park; there are many trails, but they are not marked. If the gate is closed, continue another one-tenth of a mile to another gate on the left, where there is room to park.

From the south, take I-287 to Exit 35 (Rt. 10 East, Whippany). Take Rt. 10 for about 0.7 miles to the Parsippany exit, then turn left onto Parsippany Road (Rt. 511). Just after crossing over Rt. 10 (200 yards), take the right turn onto Reynolds Rd. The park entrance is about 1.4 miles ahead, on the right.

Oradell Reservoir

Noted for waterfowl in migration and for gulls in winter, this reservoir is very difficult to bird because of limited access and a surrounding chain-link fence. The conifer plantings around the reservoir have had Boreal Chickadee and Black-backed Woodpecker and are good for winter finches during invasion years. Your best bet is probably to park at the Haworth Golf Club, then walk back to Lake Shore Dr. and bird the reservoir on foot. With a little exploring, you may be able to find some other points of access.

Directions

Take the Garden State Parkway to Exit 165 (Oradell Ave.). Go east on Oradell for 2.5 miles to Grant Ave. and turn left. After 0.2 miles, bear left onto Lake Shore Dr. Go about 0.8 miles to the parking lot at the golf club and park. Walk back to Lake Shore Dr., which can be walked in either direction. Use a good Bergen County map to explore the rest of the reservoir.

Overpeck County Park

This 811-acre unit of the Bergen County Park Commission contains several remnant marsh areas along Overpeck Creek, historically an outstanding area for ducks, rails, and other waterbirds. The areas along the east bank are accessible from parking lots at several sections of the park; exploring the west bank is best done with a good street map and care in observing No Parking signs.

Directions

Take Interstate 80 or the New Jersey Turnpike to I-95 and the exit for Fort Lee Rd. eastbound in Teaneck. Drive about one-quarter mile across the creek into Leonia and turn right into the park entrance.

Palisades Park Overlooks

Two overlooks along the Palisades Interstate Parkway are good spots during migration for loons, waterfowl, hawks, and songbirds. State Line Overlook is best in fall, the Alpine Overlook best in spring. The bigger birds tend to be high and difficult to spot, while the passerines move through the trees along the top of the Palisades or fly along the cliff top.

Directions

Take Interstate 95 to the exit for Palisades Interstate Parkway at the west end of the George Washington Bridge. Drive north on the Parkway for about 5.5 miles to the Alpine Overlook, a well-marked exit on the right. State Line Overlook, another 3.5 miles north on the Parkway, is also well marked.

Ramapo Mountain State Forest

This long, narrow state forest stretches more than 5.5 miles along the ridgetops of the Ramapo Mountains. Although it covers 2,336 acres, the forest averages only about one-half mile in width. It has many marked trails and includes the Ramapo Lake Natural Area. A trail map is available at Ringwood State Park. The birdlife here is similar to that in nearby Ringwood State Park, Campgaw Reservation, and Ramapo Valley Reservation.

Directions

Follow the directions for the Skyline Drive Hawk Lookout in the Hawk-Watching section. There are two parking areas; the main one (well marked by signs) is on the left, 0.3 miles after you turn off West Oakland Ave. onto Skyline Dr. A second, unmarked, place to park is on the left, 1.1 miles past the first parking area. Connecting trails at both spots lead to Ramapo Lake.

Ramapo Valley Reservation

Located in the northwestern corner of Bergen County, this park contains more than 2,000 acres of bottomland and hillside along the Ramapo River and the slopes of the Ramapo Mountains. Many trails traverse the varied terrain, where the birdlife is similar to that in Ringwood State Park and in nearby Campgaw Reservation. A trail map is available at the headquarters or at the Bergen County Wildlife Center on Crescent Avenue in Wyckoff. The gate opens at 8:00 A.M.

Directions

Follow the directions for Campgaw Reservation, but instead of leaving Rt. 208 at Ewing Ave., continue another 2 miles to US 202 in Oakland. Turn right onto US 202 and drive about 5.0 miles to the park entrance, on the left.

Rifle Camp Park

This Passaic County park sits atop the First Watchung Mountain just south of Paterson. Its habitat and birds are similar to those of Eagle Rock Reservation. The songbird migration is excellent in spring and fall, and in fall, hawks are visible from the Nature Center. Nearby Garret Mountain Reservation is much like Rifle Camp, but also has a pond that occasionally attracts waterfowl and an overlook that provides a spectacular view of northeastern New Jersey.

Directions

Take Interstate 80 to Exit 56A (Squirrelwood Rd., West Paterson). Drive south on Squirrelwood Rd. for 0.4 miles to its end at Rifle Camp Rd. Turn left and go about 0.9 miles to the park entrance on the left, just past a fire station. The Nature Center is located at the last parking lot, about one mile from the entrance.

Watchung Reservation

Largest of Union County's parks, Watchung Reservation encompasses almost 2,000 acres between the ridges of the First and Second Watchung Mountains. The reservation is an excellent spot to observe the songbird migration in spring and fall, and supports an interesting diversity of breeding birds. Nesting species include Ruffed Grouse, American Woodcock, Red-bellied and Pileated Woodpeckers, Chestnut-sided Warbler, Louisiana Waterthrush, and many other common species of fields and deciduous woodlands. Prothonotary Warbler, Worm-eating Warbler (slopes along Glenside Ave.), and Kentucky Warbler (near the Deserted Village) have all been found nesting, but may not occur every year. All the winter finches have occurred here, usually in the spruces at the Deserted Village or in the pines and birches at the nursery near the Trailside Nature and Science Center. Unfortunately, much of the reservation, including some of the better birding areas, is being severely disrupted by the construction of Interstate 78.

Directions

To reach the Trailside Nature and Science Center, where trail maps of the reservation are available, take US 22 to New Providence Rd. in Mountainside. Turn north onto New Providence Rd. and go about one mile (the name of the road changes to Ackerman Ave. after about 0.7 miles) to the end at Coles Ave. Turn right and drive about 0.2 miles to the parking lot for the Nature Center, on the left. To reach the Deserted Village, take W. R. Tracy Dr. through the reservation to Glenside Ave. Turn left and go about 0.9 miles to unmarked Cataract Hollow Rd. on the left, directly opposite Glenside Rd. on the right. Follow Cataract Hollow Rd. for a couple of hundred yards to a parking area on the right where the road bends right; proceed on foot.

West Essex County Park

This 1,300-acre park comprises several unconnected units along the Passaic River in northwestern Essex County. The park has a number of good birding areas, including the Essex County part of Hatfield Swamp and the 150-acre Becker Tract, an abandoned farm with woods and overgrown fields. The Becker Tract is excellent for both field and woodland migrants, while the birdlife of Hatfield Swamp is similar to that of nearby Troy Meadows. To bird these areas, stop at the Essex County Center for Environmental Studies, which is in the park, to obtain a map and directions.

Directions

Take Interstate 280 to Exit 3 (Eisenhower Parkway). Go south on Eisenhower for one-half mile to the traffic light at Eagle Rock Ave. and turn right. Drive about one-half mile to the Center for Environmental Studies on the left, just before the bridge over the Passaic River.

Bobolink

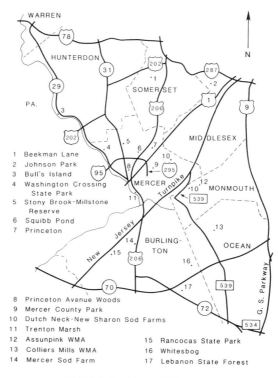

1   Beekman Lane
2   Johnson Park
3   Bull's Island
4   Washington Crossing
     State Park
5   Stony Brook-Millstone
     Reserve
6   Squibb Pond
7   Princeton

8   Princeton Avenue Woods
9   Mercer County Park
10   Dutch Neck-New Sharon Sod Farms
11   Trenton Marsh
12   Assunpink WMA
13   Colliers Mills WMA
14   Mercer Sod Farm

15   Rancocas State Park
16   Whitesbog
17   Lebanon State Forest

MAP 34. Central Region

Central

Beekman Lane

This small, but beautiful tract of farmland in Somerset County is one of the best places in the state for breeding grassland species. The Beekman Lane area, near the town of South Branch in Hillsborough Township, was "discovered" in 1981 by Wade Wander. Since then the farms north of New Centre Rd., along Beekman Lane on the east and Orchard Rd. on the west, have held nesting Upland Sandpiper; Vesper, Savannah, and Grasshopper Sparrows; Bobolink; and Eastern Meadowlark in most years. These farmlands, especially those along Beekman Lane, are being rapidly turned into housing developments, so enjoy them while you can.

Directions

From northeastern or southern New Jersey, take the Garden State Parkway or the New Jersey Turnpike to Interstate 287. Follow I-287 west past Bound Brook to Exit 10 (US 22 West), then go west on US 22 for 3 miles to US 202/206 South. Drive south for 0.7 miles to the Somerville traffic circle, and take the third exit (US 206) out of the circle. Go 0.4 miles to the next traffic light at Somerset St., and turn right toward the borough of Raritan. Follow Somerset St. into Raritan for 0.6 miles (Chimney Swift is a common borough resident in summer), and turn left at Nevius St. (Rt. 625). In about 0.1 miles, you will cross the bridge over the Raritan River, where you should look for Rough-winged Swallow from May through August, and where the road name changes to River Rd. (what else?). From the bridge, drive 2.5 miles along River Rd. to the junction with Beekman Lane, on the left.

From northwestern New Jersey, take I-287 south to Exit 13 (US 202/206), then follow US 202/206 south for 1.9 miles to the Somerville traffic circle and proceed as described above.

From the Trenton area, take US 206 north to Amwell Rd. in Hillsborough (the Hillsborough School is on the far right corner). Turn

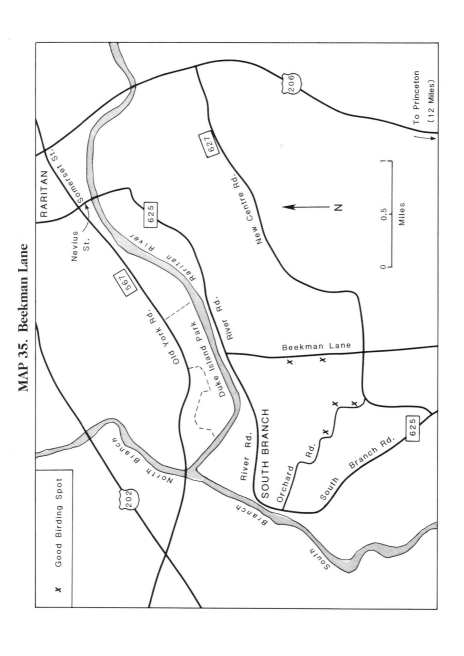

MAP 35. Beekman Lane

left and go about 1.8 miles to Beekman Lane, on the right. Turn onto Beekman and continue about 1.6 miles to the intersection with New Centre Rd. At this point you can continue north on Beekman Lane or turn left to reach Orchard Rd. (see below).

Birding

Going south on Beekman Lane you will emerge into farmland on both sides of the road. House Sparrow and European Starling are the two most common birds, but keep alert for other species. Song Sparrow is plentiful and there is often an American Kestrel. About 0.4 miles along is a field on the left where Grasshopper Sparrow has nested, and Vesper Sparrow sometimes sings from the tree line on the right. Further along, you should encounter both Bobolink and Eastern Meadowlark.

When you reach New Centre Rd. (1.3 miles from River Rd.), turn right and go 0.5 miles to where the paved road curves left and a dirt road (Orchard Rd.) continues straight ahead. Take Orchard, which soon makes a right-angle turn. The next 0.3 miles, from the house on the left to a left turn in the road, is where Upland Sandpiper, Savannah and Grasshopper Sparrows, Bobolink, and Eastern Meadowlark have been found for the past few years, mainly from May to July. After the left turn, the road continues through farmland for another 0.4 miles until it turns right and enters a residential area. Vesper Sparrow has been found along this latter section of fields and hedgerows.

In another mile, you will come to River Rd. Here, a right turn will take you back to Raritan, while a left turn will head you south toward Sourland Mountain Preserve, a 1,500-acre undeveloped property of the Somerset County Park Commission. To reach the preserve, go south on River Rd. for about 0.4 miles, then bear left onto South Branch Rd. (still Rt. 625). After about 2.4 miles, turn right onto Amwell Rd. (Rt. 514) at the sign for the municipal building. Go 0.7 miles, and turn left onto East Mountain Rd. After about 0.7 miles the park property begins on the right and continues for the next 1.5 miles, with numerous inholdings, along the west side of the road. Park where you can, and explore the property lying west of East Mountain Rd. wherever you see county park signs; avoid trespassing on private property.

Johnson Park

Lesser Black-backed Gull is the star attraction at Johnson Park, which is in the floodplain of the Raritan River in Highland Park and Piscataway. However, there are many other birds in this 600-acre Middlesex County park. In winter, Iceland Gull is regular, Glaucous Gull is rare but regular, and there are several unconfirmed reports of Thayer's Gull. During migration, a variety of shorebirds and songbirds stop here. More than 150 species, including about 55 that nest, have been recorded in the park during the past 50 years, principally by Carl Woodward, Jr., and also, more recently, by Charles Leck.

Directions

From northeastern New Jersey, southwestern New Jersey, or the Philadelphia area, take the New Jersey Turnpike to Exit 9 (New Brunswick). Stay right at the tollbooth, and turn onto Rt. 18 west. Go about 2.9 miles to the exit for Rt. 27 north to Highland Park, then stay in the left lane as you cross the bridge over the Raritan River. Turn left at the end of the bridge onto River Rd., proceed 0.6 miles (passing under a railroad trestle) to the first traffic light, and turn left into Johnson Park.

From coastal New Jersey, take the Garden State Parkway north to Exit 127 (Interstate 287). Go west on I-287 for about 2.6 miles to the New Jersey Turnpike, then south on the Turnpike for 4.8 miles to Exit 9. Proceed as above.

From northwestern New Jersey, take I-287 south to the exit for Rt. 18 to Highland Park. Go about 3.5 miles on Rt. 18, then continue straight ahead on River Rd. when Rt. 18 turns right to cross the Raritan at the traffic light and new bridge. The next right turn is an entrance into the park, but to reach the same entrance given above, continue another mile to the next traffic light and turn right.

MAP 36. Johnson Park

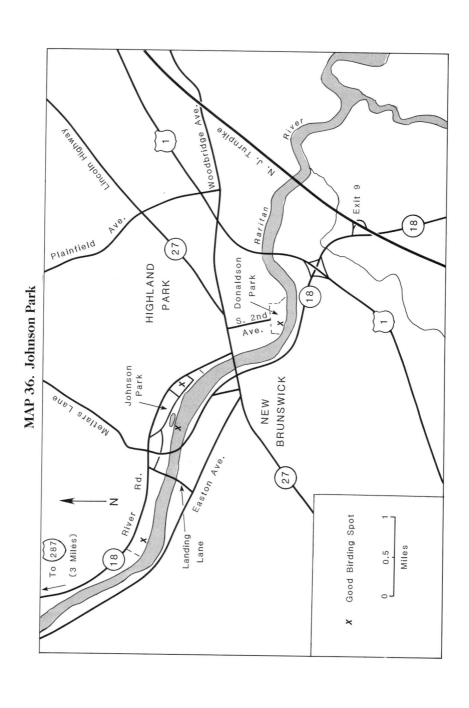

Birding

From October through March, hundreds of gulls gather to roost at Johnson Park, particularly when the garbage dumps a few miles downstream are not operating. The gulls are especially fond of an island in the river, opposite the zoo, which provides a good resting spot at low tide. During high tide the gulls either float on the water or join the flocks in the nearby parking lots or playing fields. High tide occurs here about two or three hours later than at Sandy Hook.

As you drive into the park from the traffic light at River Rd., check the field on the right for gulls, especially in rainy weather. A little further on you can see the river on the left; watch for concentrations of birds on the water. Sometimes in spring, when the outgoing current is strong, the birds play a game reminiscent of leapfrog on a moving sidewalk, in which they fly up the river, float downstream to the railroad bridge, then fly back upstream again to the front of the line.

About one-half mile from the entrance, you will see the zoo on the right and a pond on the left. The pond usually has many Canada Geese and Ring-billed Gulls; maybe a California Gull will show up here someday. Park on the right at the far (west) end of the pond, and walk to the river, where you will see the island if the tide is low. This island and the ballfields that you passed earlier are the best places in New Jersey to see Lesser Black-backed Gull. The ballfields are especially good during, or just after, heavy rains.

Since the first Lesser Black-backed Gull appeared here in December 1978, there have been numerous sightings of up to three birds; I have seen birds of every age group from first winter to full adult (fourth winter or older). Although most birds are seen from late October to mid-March, there are even midsummer and early September records. The gulls are unpredictable, however, and it may take several trips to find one.

Most of the gulls at Johnson Park are Herring, Ring-billed, and Great Black-backed, but in fall and spring you may find up to several hundred Laughing Gulls. In winter Iceland Gull is a regular visitor, with up to three birds at a time (usually in first-winter dress), and Glaucous Gull has occurred several times.

Johnson Park has a moderately good fall shorebird migration for an inland location. Of regular occurrence are Killdeer; Greater and

Lesser Yellowlegs; Semipalmated Sandpiper (the most common species here); and Spotted, Western, Least, and Pectoral Sandpipers. There are many records for Lesser Golden-Plover and a single record of Red-necked Phalarope. Common and Forster's Terns are also occasional late-summer visitors to the river.

The main area for songbirds lies to the west of Landing Lane, the first street west of the Rt. 18 bridge. To reach the birding spots, continue west along the park road from the zoo, and stay left at the next intersection. You will pass under the Rt. 18 bridge, then come to a stop sign at Landing Lane. Continue straight ahead across Landing Lane, and park in one of the lots for the picnic groves. The best birding is between here and the west end of the park near the administration building.

Another nearby winter spot for gulls, including Lesser Black-backed, is Donaldson Park in the town of Highland Park. It is neither as large nor as productive as Johnson Park, but is nearer to the garbage dumps. At high tide or in rainy weather, gulls gather to roost on the park's many playing fields.

To reach Donaldson Park, return east along River Rd. to the traffic light at Rt. 27 (Raritan Ave.) in Highland Park, and turn left. Go four blocks to S. 2nd Ave. and turn right. Take S. 2nd Ave. about 0.6 miles to its end, and continue straight ahead into the park. Search the river and the playing fields for gulls.

Bull's Island

(Delaware and Raritan Canal State Park)

Bull's Island is an 80-acre section of the Delaware and Raritan Canal State Park about 20 miles up the Delaware River from Trenton. The "island" was created by the digging of the canal during the nineteenth century. It is one of the most accessible examples of the riparian habitat along the Delaware and is best known among birders for the variety of interesting species that nest here, especially Acadian Flycatcher, Cliff Swallow, and several species of warbler: Yellow-throated, Parula, Cerulean, and Prothonotary. It is also an excellent place to observe the spring migration.

Directions

From the north, take Interstate 287 or Rt. 22 to their intersections with US 202 in Somerville, then follow Rt. 202 south for 26 miles to the exit for NJ Rt. 29 north. Go north for about 6 miles to the entrance to Bull's Island, on the left. Cross the bridge over the canal and continue straight ahead to the parking area.

From the northern part of the New Jersey shore, take I-195 west to Trenton, then follow the signs to I-295. Go west on I-295 (becomes I-95) for 9 miles to the exit for Rt. 29 north. Stockton is 10 miles north on Rt. 29, and Bull's Island another 3 miles. From southern New Jersey or the Philadelphia area, go north on I-95 from Philadelphia, then take the Rt. 29 North exit just after crossing the Delaware. Proceed as described above.

MAP 37. Bull's Island

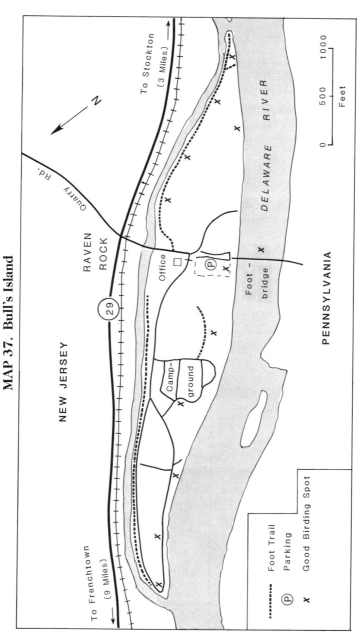

Birding

The best time to visit Bull's Island is from late April through June. Mid-May is best for the spring migration, while the many nesting songbirds are especially conspicuous and easy to find in late May and early June. The park receives little attention during the fall migration, when the dense foliage make birding difficult. Winter is the dullest season, with only a few resident songbirds and occasionally a roosting owl. The river may harbor some waterfowl, especially Canada Goose, Common Goldeneye, and Common Merganser, and there are usually good numbers of wintering raptors along Rt. 29 (mainly vultures and Red-tailed Hawks, but sometimes Bald Eagles).

The most interesting feature of Bull's Island is its small population of nesting Yellow-throated Warblers. The first males arrive during the last week of April and begin singing from the tops of the tall American Sycamores which dominate the island. These birds are of the race *albilora* (formerly called "Sycamore Warbler"). This race is the typical breeding subspecies of the Mississippi Valley and is here near the extreme northeastern limit of its range. The nearest significant population of *albilora* is in West Virginia, so the Delaware Valley birds represent a disjunct colony. "Sycamore" Warblers are distinguished from the race *dominica*, which breeds in southern New Jersey, by having white instead of yellow lores (that part of the face between the eye and the bill), and by their slightly different song.

The northern two-thirds of Bull's Island is now largely developed for picnicking and camping. A pleasant picnic area is located just beyond and to the right (north) of the parking area as you enter; Chipping Sparrow is a common nester in the evergreen plantings scattered around the nearby field. The paved road on the right just past the headquarters leads to the campground; to enter it, you must stop for a permit. This campground is usually full from late spring through the summer, so reservations are advised if you plan to stay. For birders, though, the campground is mainly a place to walk through to observe some of the migrant and nesting species (please be courteous to the campers, who have paid for the privilege of staying there, and do not enter occupied campsites). Yellow-throated and Cerulean Warblers, although found everywhere on the island in recent years, are more common on the northern part with its many huge sycamores. Northern Rough-winged Swallow also can usually be found at the north end.

Between the campground and the picnic area is a low area which is under water when the Delaware River floods. Thickly wooded, this spot is a favorite of migrant waterthrushes. In 1983, a pair of Northern Parulas was observed building a nest using some of the flood debris left hanging from the trees—the first confirmed nesting attempt for New Jersey in many years. The species was once a common breeder throughout the state, but disappeared with the decline of the *Usnea* lichen (Old Man's Beard) that they prefer for building their nests. Northern Parulas have also been found in summer along the Delaware Bayshore in Cumberland County, in Worthington State Forest, and in the Delaware Water Gap National Recreation Area in Warren and Sussex counties. One hopes this attractive species is adapting to new construction materials in the absence of its old favorite and may again become a common summer resident.

The large oak and maple trees bordering the parking area usually have nesting Cerulean Warbler and Northern Oriole, and sometimes Orchard Oriole. At the far end of the parking lot, the footbridge leading across the Delaware River to Pennsylvania is a good place to look for waterfowl in winter, soaring raptors at any season, and swallows in spring. Barn and Cliff Swallows nest under the bridge, while both Rough-winged and Tree Swallows nest nearby and can be seen hawking insects over the river. Bank Swallow is usually present as well, but is not as common as the other swallows. Over the past 10 years, this has been the most reliable spot in the state for Cliff Swallow, now listed as an endangered breeding species in New Jersey. Fortunately, just a few miles downstream, this trend shows signs of reversing: Large new colonies of Cliff Swallow are nesting under the bridges at Lambertville and Stockton. The Lambertville colony has grown to almost 200 nests, thanks in part to assistance from the New Jersey Division of Fish, Game and Wildlife. Cliff Swallows frequently attach their nests to the weathered surfaces underneath steel bridges; when these surfaces are repainted, the nests will not adhere to the paint and the birds abandon the site. To deal with this problem, the state has installed numerous artificial nests made of concrete, which the swallows glady accept.

The most interesting birding area on Bull's Island is the southern one-third, most of which has been designated a Natural Area. To bird this area, walk back toward the entrance from the parking lot. Just opposite the headquarters some dirt fill has been dumped by the edge of the road. At the end of this fill a trail leads down the bank to the canal, which it follows to the southern end of the island, passing among mature sycamores, Silver Maples, River Birches, and Box Elders. The path is lined with Jewelweed, Poison Ivy and Stinging Nettle, so be careful what you touch. Jewelweed is supposed to soothe the stings of the nettle; if you should contact some nettle (you'll feel the burning right away), crush some Jewelweed leaves and rub them on the spot—maybe it will help. Another interesting feature of this walk along the canal is the large Ostrich Ferns, which are at their best along this stretch of the Delaware and which unfurl their fiddleheads in late spring.

Yellow-throated Warbler may be anywhere along this stretch of the island, but they are hard to spot as the males sing from the tops of the sycamores; a little squeaking or pishing may bring one down for a closer look. In most years one or two pairs of Prothonotary Warbler nest in holes in the trees along the canal. This is our only hole-nesting warbler and, like the Yellow-throated, arrives in late April; listen for its monotonous, but distinctive, song. You will have to wait until at least the second week in May to find Acadian Flycatcher, another Bull's Island regular. Although this species is fairly common in southern New Jersey, Bull's Island was formerly the only reliable spot for it in the northern part of the state. It has been expanding its range, however, and is now found along many of the streams in the Kittatinnies and in the Highlands, especially in hemlock glens.

Warbling Vireo and Cerulean Warbler nest on the southern part of the island, and Northern Parula may be here as well. Other species common in these woods are Wood Duck and Spotted Sandpiper (along the canal), Red-bellied Woodpecker, Fish Crow, Carolina Wren, Veery, Blue-gray Gnatcatcher, Yellow-throated Vireo, and Louisiana Waterthrush.

After reaching the end of the trail, you will have to turn back, either retracing your steps along the towpath or following one of the makeshift trails closer to the river; any of these routes will lead you back to the parking lot. There are modern rest rooms in the campground and two primitive outhouses at the northern end of the picnic area.

Upon leaving the park, you may want to turn north and follow Rt. 29 for about 10 miles to Frenchtown, watching for roosting and soaring raptors, including Black Vulture. This is where Black Vultures were first seen regularly in New Jersey (in July, 1978) and—although they have increased tremendously and are now found over much of the state—it is still one of the best spots for them. As many as 25 have been seen in a Turkey Vulture roost on an island in the Delaware about 0.2 miles north of the Mile 28 marker, 3 miles south of Frenchtown.

If you are heading south you may want to visit the Cliff Swallow colony in Lambertville. Take Rt. 29 south into Lambertville and turn right on Bridge St., which leads to the bridge over to New Hope, Pennsylvania. Just before the bridge, turn left into the municipal parking lot and drive down to the lower level. From the riverbank here you can see many of the nests and the hordes of swallows streaming in and out of them.

Washington Crossing State Park

Situated on the east bank of the Delaware River, eight miles north of Trenton, this 807-acre park preserves the site of a famous event in American history. On Christmas night, 1776, George Washington and his Continental Army crossed the river from Pennsylvania and marched toward Trenton, where they defeated the Hessians in a daring surprise attack—an event considered by many historians as the turning point of the Revolutionary War. Continental Lane, which runs the entire length of the park (about one mile), is the road over which Washington's soldiers marched. In addition to being an important historical site, Washington Crossing State Park is also a good birding area.

The park includes manicured lawns and gardens, fields, evergreen groves, and upland deciduous woods that attract a diversity of birds. Although it is not known as a place to see rare or unusual birds, except for occasional winter finches, it provides a good selection of the species that occur in the central Delaware Valley.

Directions

From northern New Jersey, take US 1 or US 206 south to Interstate 295, north of Trenton. Turn right onto I-295 and proceed to Exit 3 (Scotch Rd.). From the exit ramp turn right onto Scotch Rd. Drive 1.3 miles to Rt. 546 (Washington Crossing–Pennington Rd.), and turn left. Go 1.9 miles to the intersection with Rt. 579, and continue straight ahead on Rt. 546 for one-half mile to the park entrance, on the right.

From the northern part of the New Jersey shore, take I-195 west to Trenton, then follow the signs for I-295 around Trenton and proceed as described above.

MAP 38. Washington Crossing State Park

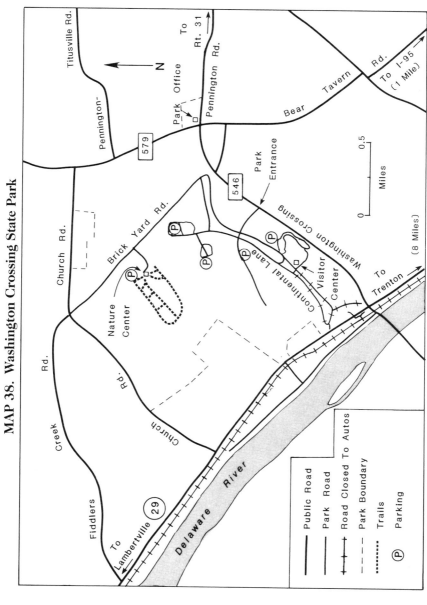

From southern New Jersey or the Philadelphia area, take Interstate 95 north to the first exit in New Jersey, Exit 1 (Rt. 29). Take Rt. 29 north for about 2.5 miles to traffic light at to 546, turn right, and go 0.8 miles to the park entrance, on the left. Alternatively, from southern New Jersey, you can take the New Jersey Turnpike or I-295 north to US 206. Follow US 206 into Trenton, then, about 1.8 miles past the White Horse Circle, bear left on Lalor St. In about 1.2 miles, turn right onto Rt. 29, then drive about 10 miles to the intersection with Rt. 546 noted above. This route is recommended only during the early morning on a Saturday or Sunday, because it becomes congested at other times.

Birding

Drive down the park entrance road for about 0.2 miles to Continental Lane and turn left. Go about 0.3 miles to the parking area on the left for the Visitor Center. After stopping in the Center, walk along Continental Lane for 0.3 miles to an overlook; continue across a pedestrian bridge that takes you over Rt. 29 to Washington's landing site on the banks of the Delaware. The numerous conifer plantings along Continental Lane have had Red and White-winged Crossbills in winter; Common Redpoll has also been found in this area. Red-breasted Nuthatch, Brown Creeper, and Golden-crowned Kinglet can almost always be found here during the colder months. The Red Pine and spruce groves (some of which have been recently cut) have been one of the most reliable places in New Jersey for Long-eared Owl in winter.

Some of the best birding in Washington Crossing State Park is in the Natural Area, which encompasses about one-quarter of the park. To reach the Nature Center, where the trails through the Natural Area begin, drive north on Continental Lane from the Visitor Center parking lot for about 0.6 miles, to where the road loops around to return to the entrance. Turn right onto Brick Yard Rd. at the Nature Center sign, drive one-half mile, and turn left into the Nature Center driveway; the parking lot is about 300 yards ahead. Although the official opening time is 10:00 A.M., the road into the Nature Center is open by 8:00 A.M., and you are welcome to use the trails. If you arrive after the Center opens, you can stop in and get a trail map.

A network of trail loops traverses the Natural Area. If you don't have the trail map, you can make a general circuit of the trails by following the yellow trail (stay right at the first junction) to the white trail, the green trail, the blue trail, and then the red trail, which leads back to the Nature Center. These trails pass through a variety of mature and scrubby second-growth deciduous woodland.

The Natural Area may be an excellent spot for migrant songbirds in spring, but most birders choose to go to Princeton for spring migration, so relatively little is known about Washington Crossing. In summer, the breeding birds include most of the expected species for this habitat, including Ruffed Grouse; American Woodcock; Yellow-billed Cuckoo; Eastern Screech and Great Horned Owls; Red-bellied Woodpecker; Fish Crow (along the river); Black-capped and Carolina Chickadees; Carolina Wren; Brown Thrasher; Yellow-throated Vireo; Warbling Vireo (along the river); Blue-winged, Yellow, Black-and-white and Prairie Warblers (the last in cedars near the open-air theater) American Redstart; and Rose-breasted Grosbeak.

The fall migration of songbirds also is inadequately covered at Washington Crossing. In late fall, ducks, geese, and gulls can be found along the Delaware River. To reach the parking lot that overlooks the river, return to the park entrance and go right onto Rt. 546. Drive 0.8 miles to the traffic light at Rt. 29, then continue straight ahead for a short distance to a parking lot, on the right. From the banks of the river you can scan the water in both directions. Canada Goose, Mallard, Common Goldeneye, and Common Merganser are the most common waterfowl.

Along Rt. 29 between the park and Lambertville, a distance of about 7 miles, you can frequently find Black Vultures roosting or soaring with the abundant Turkey Vultures.

Stony Brook—
Millstone Watersheds
Reserve

This 480-acre reserve near Pennington, Mercer County (owned by the Stony Brook—Millstone Watersheds Association), is one of the few places in New Jersey where Henslow's Sparrow has nested or attempted to nest in the last 20 years. Several other interesting species breed here, including Eastern Bluebird, Yellow-breasted Chat, Vesper Sparrow (rarely), Savannah Sparrow, Grasshopper Sparrow, Bobolink, and Eastern Meadowlark, plus a good variety of the common field and woodland species typical of the central part of the state. Saw-whet Owl is a regular winter visitor to the cedar woods, and Long-eared Owls are present some years.

Directions

There are two entrances to the reserve, one on Wargo Rd. and the other on Titus Mill Rd.

From northeastern New Jersey, take US 1 south to Interstate 295 north of Trenton. Follow I-295 (becomes I-95) west for 5 miles to Rt. 31. Go north on Rt. 31 for about 4.2 miles and turn right onto Titus Mill Rd.; continue about 1.4 miles to the driveway on the left that leads to the headquarters and parking lot. For the Wargo Rd. entrance, continue past the headquarters driveway for 0.3 miles to Wargo Rd. and turn left. Go about one-half mile to a gate on the left, just where the road takes a sharp right turn. There is limited parking on either side of the road before the turn. Walk through the gate to enter the reserve.

From the Philadelphia area, take I-95 north across the Delaware River, exit at Route 31 North, and proceed as described above.

MAP 39. Stony Brook–Millstone Watersheds Reserve

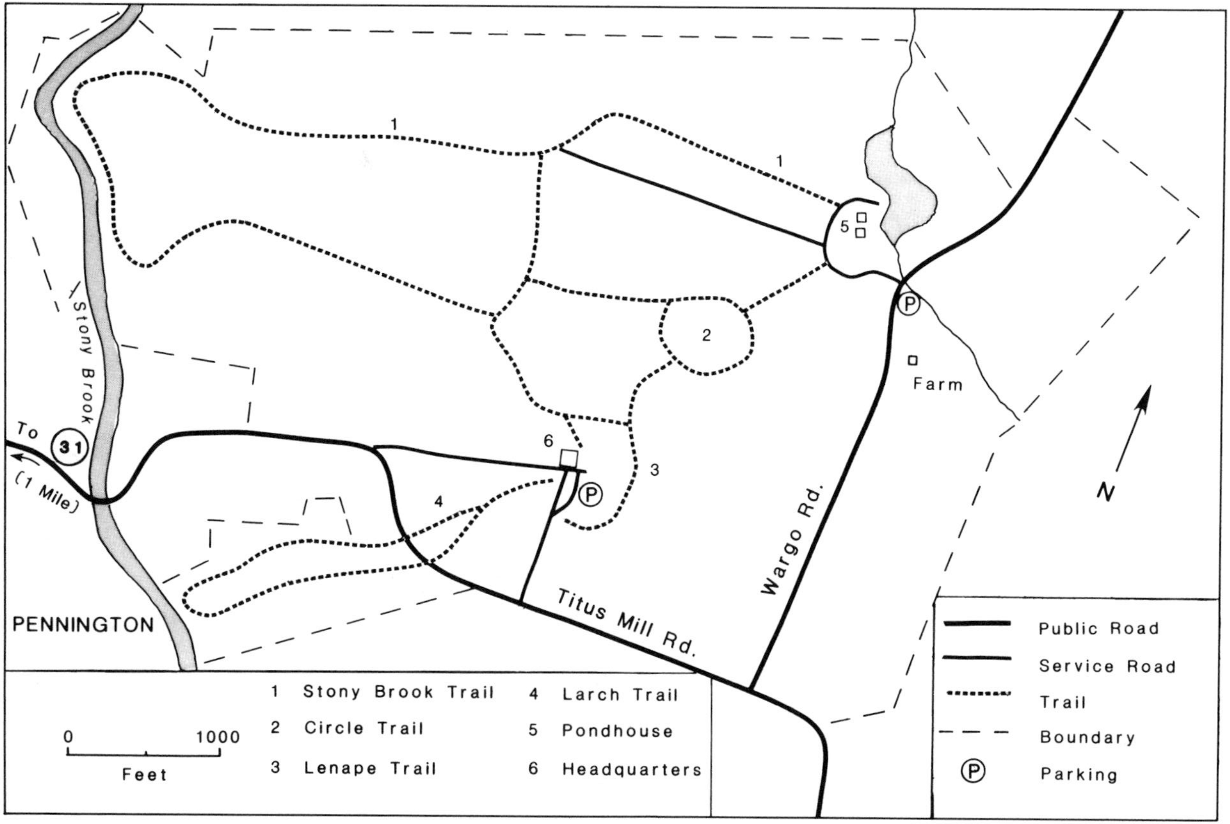

Legend:
- Public Road
- Service Road
- Trail
- Boundary
- (P) Parking

N

Farm

Wargo Rd.

Titus Mill Rd.

1 Stony Brook Trail   4 Larch Trail
2 Circle Trail   5 Pondhouse
3 Lenape Trail   6 Headquarters

Stony Brook

PENNINGTON

To (31)
(1 Mile)

1000

0

Feet

From the north coast, take I-195 west to its terminus in Trenton, then follow the signs for I-295 north around Trenton to Rt. 31.

From southern New Jersey, take the Atlantic City Expressway or I-295 north to Interstate 676, then cross the Ben Franklin Bridge to Philadelphia. Exit onto I-95 northbound and proceed as described above. Alternatively, you can take I-295 north to its present terminus at US 130 in Bordentown, then follow the signs for I-295. After you come to the continuation of the interstate (about 6 miles), go north for 10 miles to the Rt. 31 exit.

Birding

The reserve offers a mixture of weedy fields, cultivated fields (leased to nearby farmers), second-growth deciduous woods along the Stony Brook, scrubby Red Cedar woods, pine plantings, and a small pond with adjacent marshy area. Several marked trails pass through these diverse habitats. Here you will find most of the usual field and woodland birds of central New Jersey.

To bird the reserve in spring or summer, enter via the service road at the Wargo Rd. gate. This road curves around to the left, passing through vestiges of an old orchard and past the beginning of the Circle Trail on the left. Both Black-billed and Yellow-billed Cuckoos are likely to be here, and sometimes an Orchard Oriole. Vesper Sparrow used to nest in the field bordering the Circle Trail and may still occur on occasion.

Continue on the service road, past another service road on the left (called Red Rd. after the red shale that colors the soil here), then past two old silos on the right (about 300 yards from the entrance). Next, you'll go by the starting point of the Stony Brook Trail on the left, some buildings on the right, and come to the pond. Canada Goose, Mallard, Tree Swallow (in boxes), and Swamp Sparrow nest around the edges of the pond and King Rail has occurred in the marshy areas.

Return to the starting point of the Stony Brook Trail. This trail runs west across some fields for almost a mile, then enters the woods and leads to Stony Brook; it turns south for one-quarter mile, then returns toward Wargo Road through the cedar woods and edges of the fields. The fields have nesting Eastern Bluebird; Field, Savannah, Grasshopper, and Song Sparrow; Bobolink; and Eastern

Meadowlark. Henslow's Sparrow nested here in the early 1970s and has made several other attempts during the past decade. Yellow-breasted Chat nests in the Multiflora Rose at the edge of the field about two-thirds of the way to the woods.

Many other species of birds nest in the woods surrounding the fields, including Wood Duck, Red-tailed Hawk, American Kestrel, American Woodcock, four species of woodpeckers, and a long list of songbirds. Turkey Vulture, Belted Kingfisher, Northern Rough-winged Swallow, and Bank Swallow, which are not known to nest on the reserve, are frequent visitors.

The fall migration brings a modest hawk flight, various warblers, an array of sparrows (including Vesper), and an occasional rarity such as Northern Phalarope and Western Kingbird.

In winter, the reserve is quiet. A few bluebirds usually remain, and in the fields a variety of sparrows can be found, especially American Tree, Field, Song, Swamp, and White-throated, and Dark-eyed Junco. White-crowned Sparrow is an occasional visitor.

Every winter one or two Saw-whet Owls seek shelter in the cedars at the southwestern end of the fields. They are usually not very far in, but there are so many cedars and the foliage is so dense that you can look for hours without finding an owl. Since this area is closer to the headquarters parking lot than to the gate at Wargo Rd., walk behind the headquarters to the trail and go left (see map). Along the trail you'll encounter a grove of planted pines that often harbors a Great Horned Owl in winter. Wintering Long-eared Owls are sometimes found along the Larch Trail, on the opposite side of Titus Mill Rd. from the headquarters.

Yellow-breasted Chat and Willow Flycatcher nest in scrubby overgrown fields nearby. Take Wargo Rd. north from the gate to its end at Moore's Mill–Mount Rose Rd. and turn left. Go about one-half mile to an area of dense shrubby growth with young trees on both sides of the road. Park carefully alongside the road, as the shoulders are narrow and traffic is moderately heavy. Look and listen for the chat and the flycatcher; don't try leaving the road because the wild rose bushes and briars are almost impenetrable and full of ticks as well.

A short distance farther on the left are some fields and a place to pull off the road before you come to a farmhouse. Bobolinks usually nest on the far side of the fields, and can be seen flying about or perched on the fences.

Squibb Pond

A 12-acre pond at the E. R. Squibb & Sons World Headquarters in Lawrenceville is a favorite stop for birders visiting Princeton's Institute Woods in fall, winter, or spring. For its size, Lake Lawrence (or Squibb Pond, as it is known to birders) attracts a surprising variety of waterfowl, including a good selection of diving ducks (especially Ring-necked Duck and Ruddy Duck). Huge flocks of Canada Geese roost on the pond in winter. In early May, all the eastern swallows can be seen hawking insects over the water.

Directions

From the junction of US 206 and Rt. 27 (Nassau St.) in Princeton, go south on Rt. 206 toward Trenton for about 2.6 miles to the traffic light at Province Line Rd. Continue straight ahead for a couple of hundred yards to the entrance to Squibb on the right. Drive in the entrance road toward the pond until the road forks, then bear left. Stop where you can get a clear view of the pond and park on the pavement. **Do not park on the grass.**

Birding

The list of regular visitors to the pond includes Pied-billed Grebe, Horned Grebe (uncommon), Double-crested Cormorant, Snow Goose (uncommon), Canada Goose (abundant), Wood Duck (occasional), Green-winged Teal, Mallard (nests), all the other puddle ducks (occasional), Canvasback, Redhead (uncommon), Ring-necked Duck (especially March and November), Lesser Scaup (rare), Oldsquaw (rare), Common Goldeneye (uncommon), Bufflehead, Hooded Merganser (rare), Common Merganser, Red-breasted Merganser (uncommon), and Ruddy Duck (a few present from fall through spring if the water is not frozen).

Squibb Pond is also a reliable place in spring for Spotted Sandpiper, and for Water Pipit along the edges in fall. Although the pond occasionally attracts a few other shorebirds, it lacks the habitat that would entice them to remain. The pond is not noted for rarities, but Greater White-fronted Goose, Red-necked Phalarope, and Iceland Gull have occurred. Note that all the swans on the pond (5 species in 1985) are introduced.

Princeton

(Institute Woods and Rogers Refuge)

When birders talk about "Princeton," they are usually referring to the Charles H. Rogers Wildlife Refuge, which is owned by Princeton Township, and the adjacent Institute Woods, which belong to the Institute for Advanced Studies. Covering almost 550 acres, these areas constitute the best spot in New Jersey for observing the spring migration of warblers and other songbirds. On a good day in May, you can see as many as 25 species of warblers here—a few people have even had 30. The Rogers Refuge includes a freshwater marsh that attracts many waterbirds. The two areas support an interesting diversity of breeding birds and are also excellent for fall migrants. In winter the woods are quiet; however, you can count on the common resident and wintering species, a few owls, and, occasionally, winter finches.

Almost 200 species have been recorded in these combined areas in the past 30 years, mainly through the efforts of Ed Bloor, Ray Blicharz, and their associates. Among the regular breeding birds are Wood Duck; Broad-winged Hawk; Virginia Rail; Sora; Eastern Screech, Great Horned, and Barred Owls; Least Flycatcher; Warbling Vireo; Prothonotary and Kentucky Warblers, and Orchard Oriole. Mourning Warbler is an annual visitor in late May and early June, as are Yellow-bellied Flycatcher, Philadelphia Vireo, and Connecticut Warbler in fall. Rarities have included Boreal Chickadee, Yellow-throated Warbler, Summer Tanager, Pine Grosbeak, Red Crossbill, White-winged Crossbill, and Common Redpoll.

Directions

The most popular of several parking places at Princeton is along West Dr. near the entrance to the Rogers Refuge. To reach this spot:

MAP 40. Princeton (Institute Woods and Rogers Refuge)

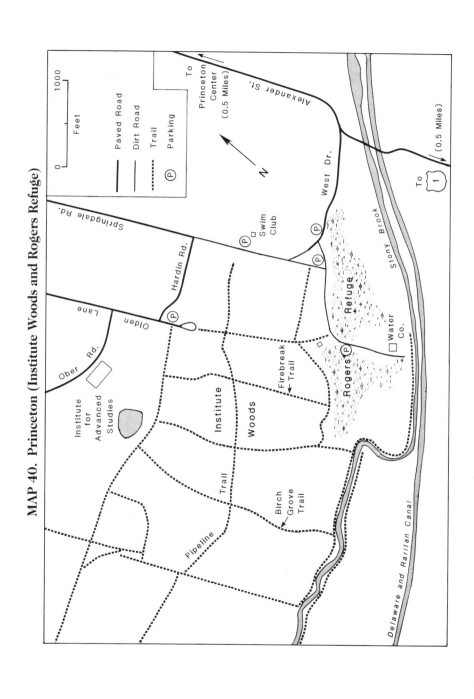

From northeastern New Jersey, take US 1 south toward Princeton to the traffic light at Alexander St. Turn right onto Alexander St. (shown as Alexander Rd. on some maps), and go about 0.7 miles to West Dr., the first left turn after you cross two bridges, one over the Delaware and Raritan Canal and the other over Stony Brook. Drive about 0.3 miles to where the road forks and becomes dirt. Park along the side of the road here; the left fork leads to the Rogers Refuge.

From northwestern New Jersey, take US 206 south to the intersection with Rt. 27 (Nassau St.) in Princeton. Turn left onto Nassau St., then almost immediately right onto Mercer St. Drive about 0.2 miles to Alexander St. and turn left. Go about one mile to West Dr. and turn right. Proceed as described above.

From the New Jersey shore, take Interstate 195 west to Trenton, then follow the signs for Interstate 295. Take I-295 to the exit for US 1 North. Go north for 4 miles to the jughandle exit for Alexander St. westbound, and continue as described above.

From southern New Jersey or the Philadelphia area, take I-95 or I-295 north around Trenton to the exit for US 1 North. Go north for 4 miles to the jughandle exit for Alexander St. westbound, and continue as described above.

Birding

Everybody has a preferred way of birding Princeton, so the best thing to do is to familiarize yourself with some of the main roads and paths, then develop your own plan for covering Rogers Refuge and the Institute Woods. The network of paths can be bewildering to the newcomer and there are no good maps available. The map that I have drawn is accurate as far as the major features are concerned; the positions of some trails may be a little off, but you should be able to find your way around. In the following paragraphs, I suggest a way of covering most of the paths; it will take you about two hours to complete the walk—longer if the birding is good.

If you arrive here at dawn on a Saturday or Sunday morning in early to mid-May, you will probably find dozens of birders already present; later in the morning the numbers will reach into the hundreds. *This is because there is simply no other place in New Jersey where you can expect to find the numbers and variety of migrant songbirds that visit Princeton in May.* Birding these woods on a good day can be truly exciting, as the trees and shrubs seem to be bursting with thrushes, vireos, warblers, tanagers, grosbeaks, and orioles. It is best to arrive early, however, because the birds' songs and calls, which are used to identify and locate most species, often decline after about nine o'clock. Being able to identify species by their songs is a valuable skill here.

From West Dr., walk along the road that leads to the Charles H. Rogers Wildlife Refuge and the Elizabethtown Water Company. The section of road from West Dr. to the marsh, about one-quarter mile, is often the best spot at Princeton for migrant songbirds in spring. The first three weeks in May are best, but there are early birds in late April and latecomers such as Olive-sided Flycatcher and Mourning Warbler later in May.

At the bend in the road where the marsh begins, a trail on the right leads to a brick pump house. Kentucky Warbler nests in this spot in some years, and Yellow-throated Vireo sings from the tall trees overhead. Just ahead you will come to the marsh, which is where the rails nest. Tree Swallow and Purple Martin are abundant after early April, nesting in the many boxes and martin houses provided for them. Other common breeding birds around the marsh are Eastern Kingbird, House Wren, Blue-gray Gnatcatcher, Yellow Warbler, Common Yellowthroat, Song and Swamp Sparrows, Red-winged Blackbird, Northern Oriole, and American Goldfinch. Least Flycatcher was formerly a reliable breeding bird at the north end of the marsh, but has become much less so in recent years. Willow Flycatcher, on the other hand, has become more common and Ruby-throated Hummingbird nests annually.

Continue along the dirt road toward the water company; the large willow trees along the road usually have nesting Warbling Vireo and Orchard Oriole. When you come to Stony Brook, stop and listen for Prothonotary Warbler, which often nests in this area. Turn right and follow Stony Brook Trail along the stream; this is an excellent area in migration for thrushes, vireos, and warblers. After several hundred yards you will intersect a trail that crosses Stony Brook on a suspension bridge to your left, where Prothonotary Warbler sometimes nests. Make a brief detour on this trail by turning right and walking a short distance to a stream and marshy area on the right—an excellent area for migrant Solitary Sandpipers in the spring.

Return to the trail along Stony Brook, turn right, and bird along the brook. After another hundred yards or so, you will come to the junction of the birch grove trail on the right. In spring, the catkins on the Gray Birches and Big-toothed Aspens harbor many insects that in turn attract many feeding birds.The birch grove trail intersects the pipeline trail, the major trail running northeast-southwest through Institute Woods. Turn left onto the pipeline trail, and you will soon come to a spot where a stream passes under the trail and the path bends right. In addition to being an outstanding area for migrant songbirds, this is also a regular nesting spot for Kentucky Warbler. As you continue along this trail, you will come to a magnificent stand of American Beech on the right. The trees are very old, and this area may have never been logged. Turn right at the next trail junction, go about 50 yards, and cross through some woods to another trail on the right. Here you will be in an area that has nesting Blue-winged Warbler and often Kentucky Warbler.

The next trail junction will be at the edge of the Princeton Battlefield State Park. Turn right and follow the trail that leads along the edge of some fields and shrubby woods to the next trail junction, on the right; this is again the birch grove trail. Follow this trail for a few hundred yards to some pine plantings on the left. This grove is probably the most reliable spot in New Jersey for Saw-whet Owl in the winter. Although these tiny owls are difficult to locate as they sit quietly in dense pines or cedars, at least one bird has been found every winter for the past 20 years.

Just past the pine grove, the birch grove trail intersects the pipeline trail. Turn left and bird your way through the mixed deciduous woods for several hundred yards. After passing a couple of junctions with smaller trails, you will come to a wide, clear trail known as the firebreak trail. Turn right onto this trail, which passes between a mature deciduous stand on the right and some old pine plantings on the left.

The firebreak trail is one of the best birding trails at Princeton. As you walk along it, you will soon come to the edge of the marsh at Rogers Refuge, where the firebreak turns left and parallels the edge of the marsh. You will eventually cross a small stream and intersect with another path. A left turn here will lead to some dense conifer plantings where Great Horned Owl and occasionally Long-eared Owl (winter) can sometimes be found. A right turn will lead to a gate that may be locked. (It was formerly kept locked for much of the year, but opened in the spring. For the past few years, it has been unlocked all year.) Continuing through the gate, the trail leads out to the dirt road in Rogers Refuge.

If instead of turning onto the side path you continue straight ahead on the firebreak, you will pass some dense tangles on the right that are a favorite spot for Mourning Warbler in late May and early June. After crossing a small stream, you will come to another gate that has been left unlocked in recent years. Through the gate, you will emerge onto a dirt road and parking area which joins the entrance road to Rogers Refuge almost immediately to your right. If you parked along West Dr., your car is a few hundred feet up the entrance road, to your left. Alternatively, you can turn left after passing through the gate and bird along the dirt road (which soon intersects West Dr.) as far as the swim club.

If the gates are locked, take the path through the conifers mentioned two paragraphs ago, and follow it as it emerges from the woods and crosses a field to a paved road. This is Olden Lane, an alternate entrance to Institute Woods. After passing by two houses, you will see a parking area on the right and a trail on the left that leads along the edge of the woods. Continue along Olden Lane past the brick building to the first road on the right (Hardin Rd.), then turn right. Hardin Rd. ends in about one-quarter mile at Springdale Rd., which is the dirt road mentioned in the preceding paragraph. Turn right onto Springdale, continue past the swim club, then stay left at the fork. You will soon emerge onto pavement; this is West Dr., and the entrance road to Rogers Refuge is just ahead on the right.

Among the species that breed on Rogers Refuge or in the Institute Woods (in addition to those already mentioned) are Green-backed Heron, Canada Goose, Mallard, Black Duck, Blue-winged Teal, American Kestrel, Ring-necked Pheasant, American Woodcock, Black-billed and Yellow-billed Cuckoos, Chimney Swift, Belted Kingfisher, Red-bellied and Pileated (rare) Woodpeckers, Eastern Phoebe, Northern Rough-winged Swallow, Fish Crow, Carolina Chickadee, Brown Creeper (rare), Carolina Wren, Brown Thrasher, Cedar Waxwing, White-eyed Vireo, Black-and-white Warbler, American Redstart, Rose-breasted Grosbeak, and Indigo Bunting.

Some other interesting birding spots in the Princeton area are Squibb Pond, Stony Brook–Millstone Watersheds Reserve, Herrontown Woods, and Rosedale Park. The first two areas are covered in their own chapters, the second two in the chapter Additional Birding Spots in Central New Jersey.

Princeton Avenue Woods
(Lawrence Township)

Princeton Avenue Woods is the name given to a small patch of woodland on the northern edge of Trenton by Ray Blicharz, who has birded the area for many years. Covering several dozen acres, the area is actually in Lawrence Township. As the last piece of greenery a southbound bird encounters before reaching Trenton, however, these woods are an oasis in a desert of urban development. For this reason, they have become one of New Jersey's best inland places for fall migrant songbirds, especially some of the more sought-after species.

Some of the many species that may be encountered here from mid-August to the end of October are Red-headed Woodpecker, Olive-sided and Yellow-bellied Flycatchers, Winter Wren, Gray-cheeked Thrush, Philadelphia Vireo, Orange-crowned and Connecticut Warblers, and Lincoln's Sparrow.

Directions

From northern New Jersey, take US 1 south toward Trenton. Just north of Trenton, when US 1 and Alt. US 1 divide, stay right on Alt. US 1. Go about 2.2 miles to the traffic-circle intersection with US 206, turn north onto US 206, and go 0.3 miles to Princeton Ave. (Rt. 583). Turn left and drive about 0.2 miles to the third right turn, Betts Ave., which has a sign for the Trenton Police Athletic League Field. Take Betts Ave. 0.3 miles to its end at the PAL Field, and park.

From southern New Jersey, take the Garden State Parkway and Interstate 195, the New Jersey Turnpike, or Interstate 295, to US 206 on the south side of Trenton. Follow US 206 through Trenton to the junction with Princeton Ave. (Rt. 583). Turn left and continue as described above. Alternatively, you may want to follow the signs for

MAP 41. Princeton Avenue Woods

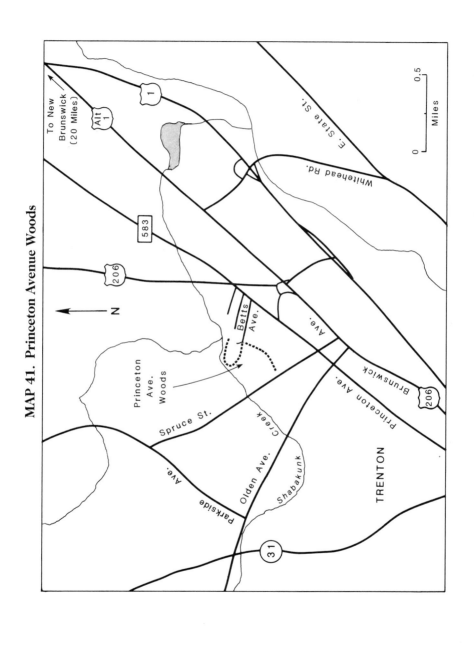

I-295 and take I-295 to the north side of Trenton, where you can go south on US 1 and proceed as described above.

From the Philadelphia area, take US 1 north through Trenton to the exit for US 206 North, and proceed as described above.

Birding

A couple of trails wander through the Princeton Avenue Woods, which are bounded on the north and west by Shabakunk Creek, but some of the best birding is along the edges of the open area that includes the ballfield. Here you may find more birds than in the woods by quietly walking along the edge of the woods and patiently waiting for the birds to appear or perhaps squeaking to coax them into the open. One good birding trail is essentially the continuation of Betts Ave. It passes through some open scrubby woods, then loops around through denser woods and comes out near the ballfield. An even better path is a partially obscured one that leads off to the left from the end of Betts Ave. It passes through second-growth deciduous woods, then some scrubby and weedy fields, before emerging at the back of the Farmers' Market on Spruce St. This path is excellent for all the flycatchers, vireos, warblers, and sparrows mentioned below.

The flycatcher and warbler migration begins in mid-August. Olive-sided Flycatchers are regular—sometimes there are several competing for a single perch—and *Empidonax* flycatchers can be abundant; telling them apart becomes a chore. Among the "empis" are plenty of Yellow-bellied Flycatchers, usually in late August and early September.

From the end of August through September, vireos and warblers appear in numbers, and a good day should produce five species of vireos and 20 or more species of warblers. There are always Philadelphia Vireos (as many as 5 in a single day) and a few Solitary Vireos, the latter mainly in October. The fall warbler list at Princeton Avenue Woods includes virtually all the species that regularly occur in New Jersey. Connecticut Warbler is an annual visitor in September, and Orange-crowned Warbler is regular (but rare) in October. Also passing through the woods in September are many Scarlet Tanagers, Rose-breasted Grosbeaks, and Northern Orioles.

Late September and early October bring the thrushes, mainly

Veery and Swainson's Thrush, but always a few Gray-cheeked Thrushes, too. By mid-October, Hermit Thrush is a regular. This is also the season for sparrows, with the first big waves in early October. Most of them will be the common ones—Chipping, Field, Song, Swamp, White-throat, and Dark-eyed Junco—but keep your eye out for Lincoln's and White-crowned, both of which occur annually in small numbers. By November there will be Tree and Fox Sparrows. Late in the fall you may find Purple Finch, Pine Siskin, or Evening Grosbeak.

Bakers Basin

Another local birding spot that is good in the fall, and better than Princeton Avenue Woods in the spring, is the towpath of the Delaware and Raritan Canal at nearby Bakers Basin. Go back to the traffic-circle intersection of US 206 and Alt. US 1, then go north on Alt. US 1 for about 3.0 miles to the traffic light at Bakers Basin Rd. (Rt. 546). Turn right and go 0.2 miles, crossing the bridge over the canal; park on the left, just past the canal. You can walk the towpath in either direction, but south (right, as you crossed the bridge) is usually the best.

The towpath, which is part of the 60-mile-long Delaware and Raritan Canal State Park, is an excellent spot for migrant songbirds, especially in early May. In addition to all the usual migrants, it has nesting Warbling Vireo and Orchard Oriole.

NOTE: Since this chapter was written, much of Princeton Avenue Woods to the south of Betts Ave. has been destroyed by a housing development. The woods around the ballfield remain, and still attract the species noted above, but the value of the area has been diminished.

Mercer County Park

This large park in central Mercer County has attracted increasing attention in recent years because of its interesting variety of breeding birds and the occasional appearance of rare or unusual species. Mercer County Park includes more than 2,500 acres of fields, deciduous woodlands, and streams in West Windsor Township, about 7 miles northeast of Trenton. The centerpiece of the park is 300-acre Lake Mercer, a prime birding spot. Although a portion of the park is devoted to recreational facilities, a large part will not be developed and will continue to be good for birding.

The many fields and woodland edges are excellent in migration for sparrows. These areas also have nesting Yellow-breasted Chat, Blue Grosbeak, and Vesper Sparrow. Rarities found here in the past few years include Franklin's Gull, Scissor-tailed Flycatcher, and Henslow's Sparrow. The low water level in Lake Mercer in the fall of 1984 attracted many shorebirds, including dozens of Lesser Golden-Plovers. The water level in the lake was raised over the winter of 1984–85, and development of the recreational areas will further alter the conditions here, but Mercer County Park will still be one of the best birding spots in central New Jersey.

Directions

From northern New Jersey, take the New Jersey Turnpike south to Exit 8 (Hightstown, Rt. 33). Follow Rt. 33 west into Hightstown. From the junction with Rt. 571 in Hightstown, continue on Rt. 33 for 1.8 miles until the road merges with US 130. Go 0.9 miles farther and exit right at the sign for Windsor. Drive another 0.9 miles to the center of Windsor, and turn right onto Church St. (Rt. 641). Church St. soon becomes Windsor Rd., and after 2.2 miles it intersects Rts. 535 (Old Trenton Rd.) and 526 in Edinburg. Turn left onto Rt. 535 and go one-half mile to the park entrance, on the right.

MAP 42. Mercer County Park

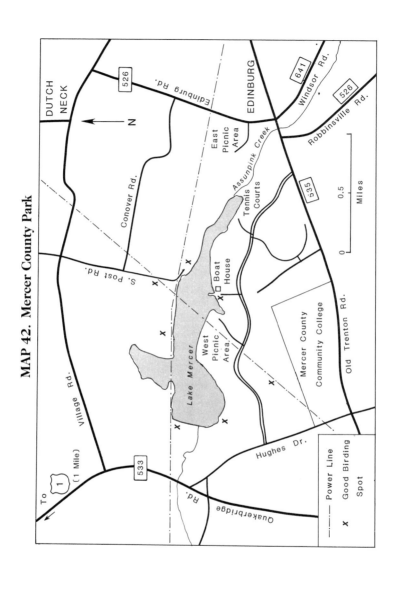

DUTCH NECK

526

Edinburg Rd.

N

EDINBURG

641

Windsor Rd.

526

Robbinsville Rd.

Conover Rd.

East Picnic Area

Assunpink Creek

Tennis Courts

535

0.5   0   Miles

S. Post Rd.

x
x

x

Boat House
x

Lake Mercer

West Picnic Area

x

Mercer County Community College

Old Trenton Rd.

x

Village Rd.

To 1 (1 Mile)

533

x   x

Hughes Dr.

Quakerbridge Rd.

——— Power Line

x   Good Birding Spot

From coastal New Jersey, take the Garden State Parkway to Interstate 195, then go west on I-195 for about 25 miles to Exit 5 (US 130 North)—the first exit after the New Jersey Turnpike. Drive north on Rt. 130 for 0.9 miles, then turn left onto Rt. 526. In about 0.3 miles, where Rt. 526 joins Rt. 33 at an angle, immediately turn right, staying on Rt. 526. Go 3 miles to the intersection with Rt. 535, Old Trenton Rd. Turn left and continue one-quarter mile to the park entrance, on the right.

From southwestern New Jersey or the Philadelphia area, take the New Jersey Turnpike north to Exit 7A (I-195). Go west on I-195 for 2 miles to Exit 5 (US 130), and proceed north on US 130 as described in the preceding paragraph.

Mercer County Park can also be approached from the west via US 1. Exit onto Quakerbridge Rd. (Rt. 533), and go southeast for about 2.2 miles to Hughes Dr. Turn left and drive about 0.7 miles to the park's west entrance, on the left.

Birding

The main road across the park is a wide boulevard about 2 miles long. Drive in about a mile from either Rt. 535 on the east or Hughes Dr. on the west, to the road that leads to the parking lot for the boathouse on the north side of the road. Park in the lot, which is where a Scissor-tailed Flycatcher spent two weeks in the fall of 1984, and walk down to Lake Mercer. The paved walkway that extends into the lake provides an excellent vantage point for scanning the water and shore in all directions.

In late summer and early fall, small numbers of herons and egrets appear at the lake to feed, some of them lingering for months. Great Egret and Great Blue Heron are the two most common species, but Little Blue Heron and Snowy Egret are also regular visitors. A variety of shorebirds can be found at Lake Mercer from July through October. During the summer and fall of 1984, the exposed mudflats and grassy areas attracted more than a dozen species of shorebirds, including up to 90 Lesser Golden-Plover. Some of the common visitors are Black-bellied and Semipalmated Plovers; Killdeer; Greater and Lesser Yellowlegs; and Semipalmated, Least, and Pectoral Sandpipers. Although the water level is now higher than in 1984, the habitat along the edges of the lake will continue to attract migrant shorebirds.

In addition to the shorebirds, gulls and (occasionally) terns roost on Lake Mercer, Ring-billed Gull is the common species, but other regulars are Herring Gull in the colder months and Laughing Gull in the warmer months. Bonaparte's Gull has occurred, and 3 Franklin's Gulls were present briefly in October, 1984. Least and Forster's Terns have been found on the lake in late summer and fall, and Caspian Tern is to be expected. Lake Mercer also attracts migrant waterfowl in March–April and October–November, and it may become a more important stopover after the water level is stabilized. During the hunting season, many ducks from nearby Lake Assunpink may flee to Mercer County Park. Some of the regular visitors are Tundra Swan, Canada Goose, Wood Duck, Green-winged Teal, Mallard, Northern Pintail, Blue-winged Teal, Ring-necked Duck, Hooded Merganser, and Ruddy Duck. Pied-billed Grebe and Double-crested Cormorant are also regular migrants in spring and fall.

Between the boathouse and Hughes Dr. there are fields on both sides of the road, and woods along the south shore of Lake Mercer. Grasshopper and Vesper Sparrows nest in the fields along the north side of the road, and a few White-crowned Sparrows are usually found here from late fall into spring. A walk along the power line right-of-way on the south side of the road can be especially productive for Blue Grosbeak and other nesting species, and for an excellent variety of migrant sparrows in October. Eastern Bluebird is occasionally seen near the dam at the west end of Lake Mercer and may soon nest in the boxes that have been provided.

To visit another part of the park, drive out the west entrance to Hughes Dr. and turn right. Go about 0.7 miles to Quakerbridge Rd., turn right, and continue about three-quarters of a mile farther to Village Rd., then turn right. Go about 1.7 miles on Village Rd. to the intersection with Post Rd., and turn right onto S. Post Rd. Follow S. Post Rd. for about one mile to its end at a dirt parking area on the north shore of Lake Mercer.

The woods and fields here are good for nesting and migrant birds; the power line rights-of-way also provide good paths for exploring this part of the park. Walking west under the power lines you will soon come to a depression that can be a bit wet and very weedy. This is an excellent spot for migrant sparrows, including White-crowned and Lindoln's; a Henslow's Sparrow was found here in Otober 1983. Blue Grosbeaks nest along the right-of-way. In addition to those species already mentioned, Northern Bobwhite, Brown Thrasher, Yellow-breasted Chat, and Eastern Meadowlark are among the approximately 60 species that nest in the park.

The final point of access to the park is the east picnic area. To reach it from the parking lot on the north shore, go north on S. Post Rd. for about one-half mile to Conover Rd. on the right. Turn right and proceed to Edinburg Rd., Rt. 526. Turn right and drive about 0.6 miles to the entrance to the picnic area, on the right. The birding potential of this area has not been explored. If you continue past the entrance to the picnic area for another 0.2 miles, you will come to the junction of Rts. 526, 535, and 641 in Edinburg.

Dutch Neck—
New Sharon Sod Farms

Certain species of shorebirds frequently forage on sod farms, and those around the towns of Dutch Neck in Mercer County and New Sharon on the Mercer-Monmouth County line are worth birding in late summer and early fall. Regular visitors include Lesser Golden-Plover (mainly September–October), Upland Sandpiper (mainly August), Baird's Sandpiper (September), and Buff-breasted Sandpiper (mainly September). Unfortunately, these grass-covered acres are dwindling rapidly, replaced by housing developments or fields of soybeans. The few remaining spots have declined in their attractiveness to birds, partly because of the use of pesticides, which reduce the insect populations. The Mercer Sod Farm near Columbus in Burlington County is a much better birding spot; however, the proximity of the New Sharon sod farms to Assunpink and of the Dutch Neck sod farms to Princeton makes it easy to stop there when visiting these areas.

Directions

To reach the New Sharon sod farms, follow the directions for Assunpink WMA to the junction of Herbert Rd. and Rt. 539. Turn east onto Herbert Rd.

Birding

The first half-mile of Herbert Rd. runs through extensive fields of cultivated sod. Although these sod farms do not attract many birds, possible visitors, especially if there are any rain pools, include Black-bellied Plover; Killdeer; Greater and Lesser Yellowlegs; and Semipalmated, Least, White-rumped, and Pectoral Sandpipers; plus any of the species mentioned above. Lesser Golden-Plover is the most regular of the sought-after species. To explore more of the sod farm on the south side of Herbert Rd., turn right onto Sharon Station Rd., about 0.6 miles from Rt. 539. In spring, large flocks of Ring-billed Gulls and a few Laughing Gulls gather to feed in the cultivated fields a little farther east on Herbert Rd. Upland Sandpiper has been seen here in May.

Return to Rt. 539 and turn right. After about 1.2 miles are some cultivated fields on the left that extend for almost a mile along Rt. 539. This used to be the Princeton Sod Farm, which covered large areas on both sides of the highway; during the 1970s this was the best spot for grassland shorebirds, including all the rarities.

To visit the remaining New Sharon area sod farms, turn around and go south on Rt. 539 from Herbert Rd. for about 0.6 miles, through the village of New Sharon, to Walters Rd. on the right; usually the fields on either side of Walters Rd. are planted in sod for the first quarter-mile. Continue south on Rt. 539 for another one-half mile to Gordon Rd.; there is often sod on the right, just beyond Gordon Rd. and along Gordon Rd. Interstate 195 is about one mile farther south on Rt. 539.

The main Dutch Neck sod farm can be reached by going north on Rt. 539, 0.2 miles past Herbert Rd., to Sharon Rd. on the left. Follow Sharon Rd. for 0.8 miles to the first right turn, Windsor Rd. Follow this for about 5 miles, across US 130, to the traffic light in Edinburg. Continue diagonally right through the light onto Rt. 526, Edinburg Rd. Go about 1.5 miles to the junction with Village Rd. and turn left. Continue 0.4 miles to the next intersection and bear right, as does Rt. 526, onto S. Mill Rd. The sod farm is 0.3 miles ahead on the right.

This sod farm has been the most productive in the Dutch Neck area in the past few years. Recent high counts have been 30 Lesser Golden-Plovers, 1 Baird's Sandpiper, and 7 Buff-breasted Sandpipers, all in 1982. Pectoral Sandpiper is also seen here occasionally, but Upland Sandpiper is no longer regular. If there are rain pools, an even wider variety of shorebirds can be expected, including Semipalmated, Least, and White-rumped Sandpipers and both yellowlegs. An August hurricane in the early 1970s produced a spectacular fallout at this sod farm of more than 100 Black Terns, Wilson's and

Red-necked Phalaropes, dowitchers, plovers, and many other shorebirds, including Western, Baird's, and White-rumped Sandpipers. As is usual in such situations, the birds lingered for only two days before departing.

Other sod farms, along Village Rd., can be reached by turning around, driving 0.3 miles back to Village Rd., and turning right. The sod farms extend along both sides of the road for the next mile, but these have not been nearly as productive as the S. Mill Rd. farm.

In general, the New Sharon sod farms have not been especially productive since the late 1970s and their acreage is dwindling. Although the Dutch Neck sod farms may be slightly better, fewer sod fields remain each year. In fact, by the time you read this, the Dutch Neck sod farms may have been consumed by the housing developments which are rapidly encroaching from all sides.

As the area becomes more suburbanized, Mercer County Park is becoming an increasingly important local birding spot. It is good for a variety of migrant and breeding birds, and may attract some of the grassland shorebirds to its acres of grass, provided the fields are not too heavily treated with pesticides. The main entrance to the park, on Old Trenton Rd. can be reached by returning to Edinburg on Rt. 526, turning right at the traffic light on Rt. 535 (Old Trenton Rd.), and going about 0.5 miles to the entrance, on the right.

As of the end of 1988, the Dutch Neck sod farms have been destroyed by housing developments. Many of the New Sharon sod farms still exist, but they have not been productive in recent years. The most productive sod farm in the area is Reed's Sod Farm in Allentown, just south of I-95 and 3 miles south of New Sharon on Rt. 539. The farm lies to the east of Rt. 539 and the north of Rt. 526 on the northeast side of town and can be scoped from several vantage points along both roads. Be aware that Allentown is one of the worst speed traps in central New Jersey.

Trenton Marsh
(John A. Roebling Memorial Park)

John A. Roebling Memorial Park (or Trenton Marsh, as it is known to birders) is an excellent place to observe spring migration in late April and early May and is well known for its variety of nesting marsh birds. This unit of the Mercer County Park System is located in Hamilton Township on the southeast side of Trenton. It is the most accessible part of a large system of wetlands that extends for about three miles along the Delaware River between Trenton and Bordentown and up to one mile inland. Some of the local specialties are Pied-billed Grebe, Least Bittern, American Bittern (now very rare), King Rail (rare), Virginia Rail, Sora, Common Moorhen, and Marsh Wren.

The park comprises about 300 acres of marshes, ponds, streams, second-growth bottomland deciduous woods, and thickets of viburnum and other shrubs. More than 210 species of birds have been recorded here, mainly by Ray Blicharz and members of the Trenton Naturalists Club. Many birders come here in late April, because the birds arrive here about one week earlier than in the northern part of the state.

Directions

From the north, take the New Jersey Turnpike south to Exit 7A (Interstate 195) and follow I-195 west for 5 miles to Exit 2 (US 206, S. Broad St.), which is where the highway now ends. Turn left at the exit, then go 0.1 mile to the traffic light and turn right onto S. Broad St. Follow this west (through the White Horse Circle, where it becomes US 206) for 2.3 miles to Sewell Ave. on the left. (Sewell Ave. is in the 1800 block, one block east of the conspicuous green steeple of Holy Angels Church.) Turn left onto Sewell and follow it through

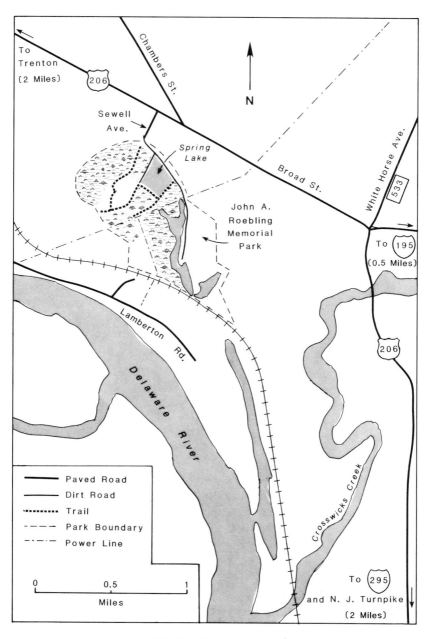

MAP 43. Trenton Marsh

three stop signs to its end (0.2 miles), where a dirt road bears off to the left and down a hill. Follow the dirt road and park at the beginning of the causeway that separates Spring Lake on the left from a marshy pond on the right.

Alternatively, you can take either Rt. 31 or Rt. 206 south into Trenton, where these routes intersect; then follow Rt. 206 south. From the point where Rt. 206 crosses over US 1, Sewell Ave. is about 2.0 miles, on the right.

From the Philadelphia area, take US 1 north across the tollbridge into Trenton, then take the first exit; bear right, following the signs for Rt. 29. After about 0.2 miles, turn left onto the John Fitch Parkway (Rt. 29), which soon becomes Lamberton St. Turn left onto Lalor St. (about one mile total from exit ramp), following the signs for Rt. 206 South. Go 1.1 miles to S. Broad St. and turn right. Sewell Ave. is 0.2 miles ahead on the right.

From southern New Jersey take the New Jersey Turnpike north to Exit 7 (Bordentown). Turn right onto Rt. 206 and go about 5 miles to the White Horse Circle. Sewell Ave. is another 1.6 miles ahead on the left.

From the north shore, take Interstate 195 west to the end and proceed as above.

Birding

Spring Lake is known for migrant waterfowl (especially Ring-necked Duck in March–April and October–November) and for nesting Pied-billed Grebe. The marshy area to the right has nesting Blue-winged Teal and Common Moorhen. Willow Flycatcher, Yellow Warbler, and Carolina Wren are common around the borders of the marsh. As you walk along the edge, watch for Least Bittern, Green-backed Heron, and Spotted Sandpiper (all nesters), Black-crowned Night-Heron, and Common Snipe, all of which are common migrants in late April–early May.

At the far end of the causeway (about 400 yards) a path leads off to the left along the lake and a footbridge leads straight ahead across a creek, Cross the footbridge and follow the path into the woods—it is excellent for migrant songbirds in spring and fall, but the first stretch is very muddy.

Rusty Blackbirds are abundant in the wet woodland in late April, and with luck you might flush an American Woodcock. Early migrants such as Sharp-shinned and Broad-winged Hawks; Yellow-bellied Sapsucker; Eastern Kingbird; Golden-crowned and Ruby-crowned Kinglets; Blue-gray Gnatcatcher; Hermit Thrush; White-eyed and Solitary Vireos; Yellow, Palm, Yellow-rumped, and Black-and-white Warblers; Louisiana and Northern Waterthrushes; and Purple Finch are regular here and easy to see before the leaves come out. In May, you can expect cuckoos, Ruby-throated Hummingbird, flycatchers, and a long list of migrant thrushes, vireos, warblers, and other songbirds.

The path through the woods is unmarked, but the area is not extensive and you're not likely to get lost. Eventually, you will have to return to the footbridge. When you do, turn right and take the path along the lake. All the eastern swallows are usually present by the end of April, and can be seen hawking insects over the ponds. Migrant Ospreys find the fishing good, and sit in one of the tall dead trees to enjoy their catch.

After about a hundred yards, the trail forks. Bear right toward the power lines. This trail follows the border of an extensive marsh where many species nest, including Least Bittern, Wood Duck, Blue-winged Teal, King Rail (rare), Virginia Rail, Sora, American Coot, Eastern Kingbird, Tree Swallow, Marsh Wren, Yellow Warbler, Common Yellowthroat, and Swamp Sparrow.

Return to your car and drive along the dirt road. Just past Spring Lake is a storm-sewer outlet where the marshes begin; this is an excellent spot in winter for Common Snipe, Rusty Blackbird, and even an occasional yellowlegs. About 0.7 miles from the causeway, you will come to a picnic area. In addition to being a pleasant spot to enjoy your lunch, the woods around the picnic grounds are excellent for migrant warblers in spring and fall and for Yellow-bellied Flycatcher and Philadelphia Vireo in fall.

There are no rest rooms at Trenton Marsh, but the woods in back of the picnic area are pretty dense. To leave the park, go back 0.2 miles from the picnic area and take the gravel road to the right. This will lead you to Wescott Ave. (0.2 miles), where you should go left for one short block to Park Ave. A right turn on Park will take you back to S. Broad St. in 0.3 miles.

Assunpink Wildlife Management Area

The Assunpink WMA comprises more than 5,400 acres of lakes, fields, hedgerows, and deciduous woodlands situated near the geographic center of New Jersey. Most of the tract is located in extreme western Monmouth County, but part is in Mercer County. Assunpink is an excellent inland place to observe migrant waterfowl, and is also fairly good for shorebirds. Its diversity of habitats attracts an interesting selection of breeding birds.

Some of the species that occur regularly at Assunpink are Ring-necked Duck (up to 450), Common Merganser (up to 1,300), Kentucky and Hooded Warblers, Yellow-breasted Chat, Blue Grosbeak, Vesper and Grasshopper Sparrows, and Orchard Oriole. The latter seven species all nest locally, although Vesper Sparrow is hard to find in the breeding season. Rarities that have occurred here include Mississippi Kite, Western Kingbird, Ash-throated Flycatcher, and Henslow's Sparrow.

Assunpink is a relatively new WMA. Much of the land was acquired during the 1960s, and the lakes were impounded during the early 1970s. A diligent survey of the area from 1974 to 1978 by Wade Wander revealed its many birding possibilities, and Assunpink is now a regular birding stop.

NOTE: As a Wildlife Management Area, Assunpink is heavily used by hunters from October through December (except on Sundays, when no hunting is allowed). On other days at this season confine your visit to the parking lot at Lake Assunpink or to the roads through the tract, and always wear some bright clothing.

Directions

To reach the parking lot at Lake Assunpink:

From the north, take the New Jersey Turnpike south to Exit 8 (Hightstown), and follow Rt. 33 into town. Go left at the junction

MAP 44. Assunpink WMA

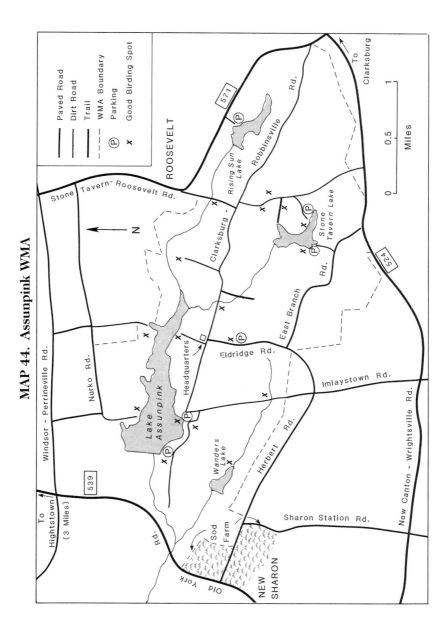

Paved Road

Dirt Road

Trail

WMA Boundary

ⓟ Parking

x Good Birding Spot

ROOSEVELT

Stone Tavern - Roosevelt Rd.

571

ⓟ

Rising Sun Lake

Robbinsville Rd.

Clarksburg - Robbinsville Rd.

To Clarksburg

1

0.5

0

Miles

N

Stone Tavern Lake

ⓟ

ⓟ

East Branch Rd.

524

Imlaystown Rd.

Windsor - Perrineville Rd.

Nurko Rd.

Lake Assunpink

Headquarters

Eldridge Rd.

ⓟ

ⓟ

Herbert Rd.

Wanders Lake

New Canton - Wrightsville Rd.

Sharon Station Rd.

Old York Rd.

Sod Farm

NEW SHARON

539

To Hightstown

(3 Miles)

with Rt. 539, proceed one short block through the traffic light at Stockton St., then continue about 0.2 miles and turn left on Rt. 539. Follow Rt. 539 south for about 4.8 miles to Herbert Rd. Turn left onto Herbert Rd., go about 2.0 miles to Imlaystown Rd., turn left, and proceed 1.2 miles to the parking lot at Lake Assunpink. Imlaystown Rd. is sometimes flooded about one-half mile north of Herbert Rd. If so, drive back to Herbert Rd. and turn left (the name changes to East Branch Rd.). After about one-half mile, continue straight ahead on Eldridge Rd. when East Branch Rd. turns right. In about 0.8 miles, you will come to Clarksburg-Robbinsville Rd., directly opposite the WMA headquarters. Turn left, and go 0.7 miles to the parking lot at Lake Assunpink.

From the southwest, take the New Jersey Turnpike north to Exit 7A (Interstate 195). Go east on I-195 for 2 miles to Exit 8 (Rt. 539). Take Rt. 539 north for about 2.1 miles to the junction with Herbert Rd. Turn right and proceed as described above. From the Trenton area, take I-195 east to Rt. 539.

From the southeast, take the Garden State Parkway to Exit 58 (Route 539). Follow Rt. 539 north for about 45 miles to the junction with Herbert Rd., 2.1 miles north of I-195.

From the east, take I-195 west from Garden State Parkway Exit 98 for about 22 miles to Exit 11 (Imlaystown Rd., Monmouth Co. Rt. 43). Take Imlaystown Rd. north for about 2.6 miles to the parking lot at Lake Assunpink.

Birding

Lake Assunpink is the main attraction for birders. A wide variety of migrating ducks, geese, and other waterbirds stop here, especially in spring. The peak waterfowl seasons are February through April and October through December. A few species breed around the periphery of the lake.

Red-throated Loon is a rare visitor, mainly November to March, but Common Loon is regular in small numbers both in fall and in spring; a few are usually seen in May, and occasionally one lingers into mid-summer. Pied-billed Grebe is present year-round, though it is most common in November and March–April; Lake Assunpink is one of the few places in New Jersey where this species has nested in recent years. Horned Grebe is a common migrant in spring and fall, while Red-necked Grebe is rare, but regular, usually appearing in March or April. Nonbreeding Double-crested Cormorants show up in the spring and can be found throughout the summer. Even Great Cormorant has occurred once.

Great Blue Heron is a year-round resident at Assunpink (most common in late summer), and Green-backed Heron is a common summer resident. Many of the other herons and egrets can also be found here, especially in late summer when these species are prone to wander. American Bittern, Great and Snowy Egrets, Little Blue Heron, Black-crowned and Yellow-crowned (rare) Night-Heron, and Glossy Ibis are all regular visitors to the shore of Lake Assunpink. The best place for most of these birds is the marshy east end of the lake, which is difficult to reach (see map).

The waterfowl migration starts as soon as the lakes are open, usually by mid-February. It peaks in March and continues strong through April; by mid-May, mainly the local breeders remain. In September, the first migrant teal and wigeon appear, but the biggest numbers and variety of species occur in October and November. In recent years, however, hunting pressure has chased most of the birds off Lake Assunpink in the fall. Some remain until the lake freezes over, and a few stay for the winter in ice-free years. Species that occur regularly are Tundra Swan (uncommon), Snow Goose (rare), Canada Goose (abundant), Wood Duck (nests), Green-winged Teal, American Black Duck (nests), Mallard (nests), Northern Pintail, Blue-winged Teal (nests), Northern Shoveler (rare), Gadwall (uncommon), American Wigeon, Canvasback, Redhead, Ring-necked Duck, Greater Scaup, Lesser Scaup, Oldsquaw (rare), Black Scoter (rare), Common Goldeneye (uncommon), Bufflehead, Hooded Merganser (uncommon), Common Merganser (common), Red-breasted Merganser (uncommon), and Ruddy Duck. The other lakes on the tract, especially Stone Tavern Lake and Wander's Lake, may also harbor waterfowl in season, but they are neither as large nor as productive as Lake Assunpink.

A smattering of migrant shorebirds stop off along the lakeshore; any area that has some mud may attract a few. The species seen here include Black-bellied and Semipalmated Plovers; Killdeer (nests); Greater and Lesser Yellowlegs; Solitary, Spotted (nests), and Upland Sandpipers (the last more common on nearby sod farms);

Sanderling (rare); Semipalmated, Western, Least, White-rumped (rare), and Pectoral (common in spring) Sandpipers; Dunlin; Stilt Sandpiper (rare); Long-billed Dowitcher (rare); Common Snipe; American Woodcock (nests); and Wilson's and Red-necked Phalaropes (both rare). Several other species are occasionally seen on the nearby farm fields and sod farms. Unfortunately, the sod farms (see Dutch Neck–New Sharon Sod Farms) are rapidly dwindling in both acreage and birding productivity. Species that were formerly regular there in fall are Lesser Golden-Plover and Upland, Baird's and Buff-breasted Sandpipers.

Small numbers of gulls and terns show up at Lake Assunpink in spring and again in late summer and fall. Ring-billed and Herring Gulls are the regulars, but Laughing Gull occurs in small numbers and Bonaparte's Gull is occasional; Common Black-headed Gull has occurred twice and Iceland Gull once. Common, Forster's, Caspian, and Black Terns appear annually in late summer and fall, but they are generally scarce; there are also records for Least and Gull-billed Terns.

In May, June and July, it is the breeding landbirds that bring birders to Assunpink. The nesting species include American Kestrel (the commonest raptor); Northern Bobwhite (common); Whip-poor-will; Belted Kingfisher; Willow Flycatcher; Purple Martin; Carolina Chickadee; White-eyed, Yellow-throated, and Warbling Vireos; Prairie, Worm-eating, Kentucky, and Hooded Warblers; Yellow-breasted Chat; Blue Grosbeak; Vesper (rare) and Grasshopper Sparrows; Eastern Meadowlark; and Orchard Oriole.

Blue Grosbeak frequently inhabits the hedgerow on the east border of the Lake Assunpink parking lot. To see some of the other breeding species, leave the parking lot and proceed back down Imlaystown Rd. Go about 200 yards, then turn right onto another dirt road. Just after the road bends right are some large trees where Orchard Oriole and Warbling Vireo usually nest. After about 0.5 miles, the road climbs a little rise to a parking area shaded by two large old Sugar Maples and a Red Mulberry. Orchard Oriole is here, too, and there is always Grasshopper Sparrow in the fields between the parking area and the Lake Assunpink dam.

If you haven't yet found an Orchard Oriole or Warbling Vireo, walk north toward the south end of the dam, then out along the dam, listening for their songs; most of the orioles encountered will be yearling males in green plumage, but a few older males in their chestnut dress can be expected. Take advantage of your hike along the dam to scan for waterbirds. From the parking area, you can drive a short distance further to some fields on the left, where sparrows can be found, or you can walk south towards Wanders Lake, which is hidden from view by the vegetation.

Return to Imlaystown Rd., turn left toward Lake Assunpink, then right at the intersection onto Clarksburg-Robbinsville Rd. (no sign). The WMA headquarters is about 0.7 miles on the left; stop in for a map of the area if your visit is on a weekday. Along the way, listen for Willow and Least Flycatchers, Yellow-breasted Chat, Grasshopper Sparrow, and Blue Grosbeak. Just before the headquarters a dirt road on the left leads 0.3 miles to the shore of Lake Assunpink; this is a good vantage point to scan for ducks, herons, and hawks.

Go back to the main road; directly opposite the headquarters turn right onto Eldridge Rd. (no sign) and go about one-quarter mile to a parking area on the left. Listen here for Blue Grosbeak in the hedgerow and Grasshopper Sparrow in the grassy fields. Henslow's Sparrow has been seen in the wet fields on the right, just before the parking lot.

Drive back toward the headquarters, turn right, and go about 0.2 miles to a bridge across a marshy stream. Willow Flycatcher, Virginia Rail, and several other species breed here. About 200 yards farther on is a trail on the right, where you might find Blue Grosbeak, Indigo Bunting, Orchard Oriole, and plenty of Poison Sumac. As you drive east, the fields along the road just before the next intersection may have Grasshopper Sparrow. About 1.5 miles past the headquarters, turn left on Stone Tavern–Roosevelt Rd., and drive about 0.3 miles to where Assunpink Creek crosses the road. Acadian Flycatcher and Prothonotary Warbler have been seen here in summer.

Drive back to Clarksburg-Robbinsville Rd. and turn left. Go about 100 yards and turn right onto the continuation of Stone Tavern–Roosevelt Rd. The road soon enters a deciduous woods that has nesting Yellow-throated Vireo, Kentucky Warbler, and Hooded Warbler. After about 0.4 miles, you will emerge from the woods at the top of a hill overlooking Stone Tavern Lake, which is largely hidden from view by trees and bushes. The entire perimeter of the lake is good for birds, and usually has Orchard Oriole and Blue Grosbeak in a few places; Western Kingbird has been seen here in winter. There are two spots where you can drive down to the lake, which is an excellent spot for Ring-necked Duck (see map). The first is 0.3 miles ahead on the right, at the bottom of the hill.

There are numerous other places in Assunpink WMA that can be explored. The eastern third of the tract receives inadequate attention from birders, as does the area north and east of Lake Assunpink. The disjunct western section in Mercer County gets no attention at all. In fall and winter Nurko Rd. on the north side of Lake Assunpink (see map) is excellent for sparrows, including Lincoln's (October) and White-crowned. The tree rows along the north side are also good for fall migrants; such sought-after species as Yellow-bellied Flycatcher, Mourning Warbler, and Connecticut Warbler occur regularly.

Assunpink is an excellent place to observe raptors during the fall migration and in winter. Turkey Vulture, Northern Harrier, Red-tailed Hawk, and American Kestrel are the commonest species, but Osprey and Sharp-shinned Hawk are common in migration, Cooper's Hawk and Merlin uncommon, but regular. Broad-winged and Red-shouldered Hawks nest on the area, and there are usually several reports of Bald Eagle every year. A few Rough-legged Hawks are seen every winter, while early spring brings a few Short-eared Owls. Barn, Great Horned, and Eastern Screech-Owls are common, but elusive, permanent residents; Long-eared and Saw-whet Owls are regular winter visitors, most often found roosting in conifers.

Other than raptors and sparrows, Assunpink has little to offer in winter if the water is frozen. It's not long, however, before the late winter thaws bring the first of the migrant waterfowl.

Colliers Mills Wildlife Management Area

Colliers Mills WMA covers more than 12,000 acres of northwestern Ocean County, near the northern edge of the New Jersey Pine Barrens. Most of the upland areas are covered with the typical Pitch Pine and Scrub Oak vegetation of the Barrens, while the wetter areas support Atlantic White Cedar. There are also a few areas with deciduous woods, and some hardwood swamps. Several impoundments provide habitat for migrant waterfowl.

The birds of Colliers Mills are basically those of the Pine Barrens, and are described in detail in the chapters on Lebanon State Forest and Whitesbog. Noteworthy breeding birds include Red-headed Woodpecker (occasional), Eastern Bluebird, Northern Waterthrush, Blue Grosbeak, and Orchard Oriole. The area is not heavily birded during the breeding season, which is when you might find something really unusual. If you live nearby, this would be a good place to do some exploring during June and July, instead of visiting the more well-known spots.

Note: As a WMA, Colliers Mills is heavily used by hunters, mainly from October through December. If you visit during the hunting season, stay on the roads and wear bright clothing, or confine your trips to Sundays.

Directions

From northern New Jersey, take the New Jersey Turnpike south to Exit 7 (Interstate 195). Go east on I-195 for about 2 miles to Exit 8 (Rt. 539). Follow Rt. 539 south through Allentown (watch for a sharp left turn) for about 10 miles to Colliers Mills Rd., which is about 1.4 miles south of the intersection of Rt. 539 and New Egypt–Lakewood Rd. (Rt. 528). Turn left onto Colliers Mills Rd. (there is

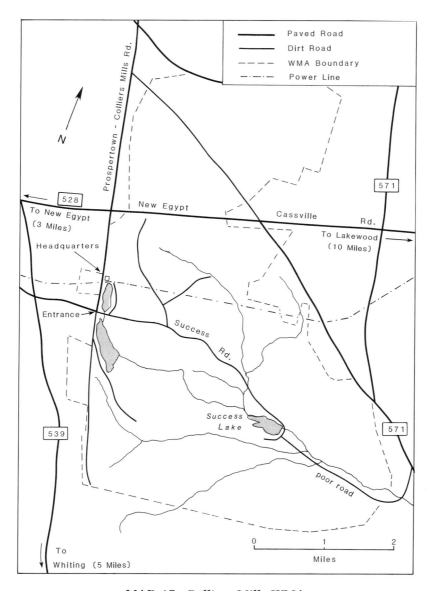

MAP 45. Colliers Mills WMA

a WMA sign) and go about 0.9 miles to the entrance to the WMA, which is straight ahead on the dirt road.

From southwestern New Jersey or the Philadelphia area, take Rt. 70 east to the intersection with Rt. 539 near Whiting. Turn left (north) on Rt. 539 and go about 8.5 miles to Colliers Mills Rd.

From southern New Jersey, take Rt. 539 north from the Garden State Parkway for about 32 miles to Colliers Mills Rd.

Birding

Orchard Oriole usually nests in the trees around the bridge at the south end of Colliers Mills Lake, which is where you enter the WMA. Take the first left turn, just past the bridge, and drive along the lakeshore about 0.3 miles to a small parking area, on the left. Walk to the north side of the parking area, to where a dirt road has been blocked by a pile of sand. Walk along the blocked road to search for birds of the Pine Barrens. Along your drive in, and along this walk, you will notice fields off to the right. A very active and productive bluebird trail is maintained by Tom Mulvey of the staff at Colliers Mills, and some of the boxes are located in these fields.

You will soon come to a power line cut, where you can turn right and explore more of the area. When you come to a dirt road after about a half-mile, you can either retrace your steps, or turn right and walk through more of this pine-oak habitat. In about 0.7 miles, you will come to a junction with another dirt road, where you should turn right. Called Success Road on some maps, this is the same entrance road that led you into the WMA. From here it is about a mile to the spot where you turned left after crossing the bridge. The road passes through a large cut-over area, where you might find Red-headed Woodpecker.

Return to your car and drive back 0.3 miles to the dirt entrance road (Success Rd.). A left turn leads you across the WMA from west to east to Rt. 571, a distance of about 5.3 miles. There are many interesting stops along the way. Most of the birds you will encounter on Success Rd. are the common species of the Pine Barrens, especially Brown Thrasher, Gray Catbird, Prairie Warbler, Pine Warbler, and Rufous-sided Towhee. After about 2.5 miles, you will reach Success Lake on the right, where you might find Green-backed Heron,

Wood Duck and other waterfowl, Osprey, Belted Kingfisher, and various swallows in migration.

About 2.8 miles from the entrance, you will come to a small dam at the outlet stream of Success Lake. A dirt road continues for another few hundred yards around the edge of the lake. A second dirt road turns left just past the dam, and east for about 2.6 miles to Rt. 571; after about one-half mile, however, the road becomes very soft sand and is difficult to manage without a four-wheel-drive vehicle. A short distance beyond Success Lake, this road crosses through a Red Maple swamp where Northern Waterthrush has been found nesting, one of its southernmost breeding sites in New Jersey. If you are able to continue as far as Rt. 571, a right turn (east) will take you to the town of Lakehurst, a few miles farther.

There are several other roads and trails throughout Colliers Mills WMA that you can explore with the help of a USGS topographic map (Cassville quadrangle) or the *Guide to Wildlife Management Areas* (see Bibliography). Visit this area in the spring or summer and you might find something interesting. Both Red Crossbill and White-winged Crossbill were found nesting a few miles to the southeast of Colliers Mills during the 1930s and 1940s, and these and other northern finches have been found in winter.

Mercer (Columbus) Sod Farm

The Mercer Sod Farm (better known to birders as the Columbus Sod Farm because of its proximity to that Burlington County community) has been the best place in New Jersey to see migrating grassland species of shorebirds. These birds, which nest in fields or on grassy tundra, stop here on their southbound migration in late summer and early fall to search for insects on the green fields of cultivated grass or on the bare fields recently stripped of grass. Among the regular visitors are such sought-after species as Lesser Golden-Plover (late August–October), Upland Sandpiper (mainly August), and Buff-breasted Sandpiper (mainly September). How much longer these precious fields will remain grass-covered in the face of the inexorable onslaught of creeping suburbia remains to be seen.

Directions

To reach the Mercer Sod Farm (see Map 46): From northern New Jersey, take the New Jersey Turnpike south to Exit 7 (Bordentown). Stay left through the tollbooth and merge onto US 206 South. Go south, past the town of Columbus, for about 5.7 miles to Rt. 670, the Jacksonville-Jobstown Rd. Continue through the intersection, where there is a stop light, for about 100 yards and park on the right shoulder of US 206, just beyond an old building.

From the Philadelphia area, take either the Tacony-Palmyra Bridge to Rt. 38 or the Ben Franklin Bridge and US 30 to Rt. 38. Follow Rt. 38 past Mount Holly to Rt. 530, and continue another 3 miles to US 206. Turn left onto US 206 and go north about 3 miles to the intersection with Rt. 537. Continue straight ahead; the sod farm begins after about one-half mile, and continues as far as Rt. 670, a distance of about 1.5 miles from Rt. 537. It is easiest to bird from the south-

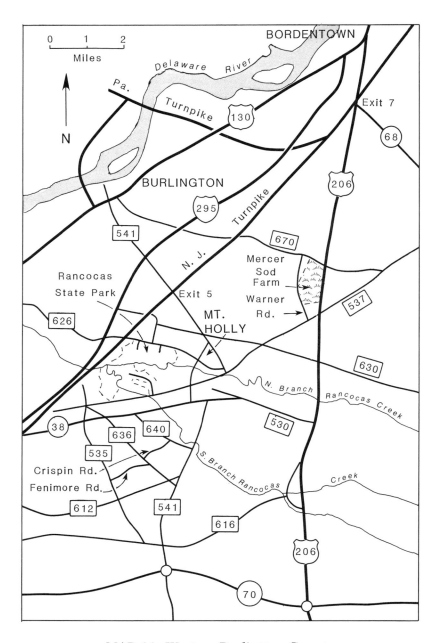

MAP 46. Western Burlington County

bound lane, so turn left onto Rt. 670, make a U-turn and then turn right onto Rt. 206.

From south coastal New Jersey, take the Atlantic City Expressway northwest to Exit 28 (Hammonton), then follow Rt. 54 and US 206 north for about 30 miles to Rt. 537. Continue as described in the preceding paragraph.

From north coastal New Jersey, take Interstate 195 west to the New Jersey Turnpike, then the Turnpike south to Exit 7 and proceed as described in the directions for northern New Jersey.

Birding (see note, page 249)

The sod farm stretches for about a mile along the west side of US 206. Stay on the shoulder of the highway (do not leave the road to bird the fields), and watch out for the traffic along this heavily traveled road. Because the birds are frequently at some distance, a spotting scope is essential. Upland Sandpipers are usually on the fields of grass, whereas the other species are frequently found on the bare fields as well as on the grass.

The best time to visit the sod farm is from mid-August to mid-September, but anytime from late July to late September can be productive, because arrivals and departures of the various species are unpredictable. For example, in 1982, Lesser Golden-Plover was seen only from August 31 to September 5, with a maximum count of 15. In most years, however, the arrival date is about August 20 and the final departure date about September 20. In 1983 and 1984, the peak counts were in late October! The highest count of this species in recent years was 150 on October 25, 1984; counts of 10 to 20 are more usual.

Killdeer nest around the Mercer Sod Farm and a few birds are always present; from August to October, however, migrants increase their numbers to as many as 250. The first of the migrant shorebirds to arrive at Mercer Sod Farm is Upland Sandpiper. A few are usually found in early July, but the main influx occurs in early to mid-August. Numbers dwindle toward the end of August, and the last ones are gone by mid-September. The record count is 100 on September 1, 1974.

Buff-breasted Sandpiper has been found as early as August 1, but a more normal arrival time is in late August. Numbers fluctuate from year to year, from one in 1982 to as many as fifteen on September 7, 1980. This is the rarest, and consequently the most sought-after, of the grassland shorebirds that frequent the sod farm. Other shorebirds that occur regularly in August and September are Black-bellied Plover and Pectoral Sandpiper. Of irregular or infrequent occurrence are Semipalmated Plover; Greater and Lesser Yellowlegs; Solitary, Spotted, Least, and White-rumped Sandpipers; Short-billed Dowitcher; and Common Snipe. Horned Lark, Vesper Sparrow, and Eastern Meadowlark are among the few passerines you might see on the fields at this season. In winter, Horned Lark, Water Pipit, and Snow Bunting are possibilities.

Another accessible part of the Mercer Sod Farm lies along Warner Rd., which roughly parallels US 206 to the west. Continue south on 206 to Rt. 537 and turn right. Go 0.3 miles to Warner Rd. and turn right again. After a few hundred yards, you will come to the west side of the sod farm, part of which is visible from the road. In about 0.4 miles, there is a bridge over a stream, and another small section of the sod farm is on the right. In the past, this area has attracted most of the birds mentioned above. To return to Rt. 206, continue north on Warner Rd. to the next intersection at Rt. 670 (Jacksonville Rd.), and turn right. The intersection with Rt. 206 is 0.9 miles ahead. If you should try to reach Warner Rd. from the north by driving west on Rt. 670 from US 206, be aware that there may not be a street sign; Warner Rd. is the first left turn.

Another area that occasionally has some of the same species as the Mercer Sod Farm is in Lumbertown Township, about a 15-minute drive from the Mercer Sod Farm. To reach this area (where Lesser Golden-Plover, Killdeer, and Upland Sandpiper have been seen), go south on US 206 for 3 miles from Rt. 537 to Rt. 530, then turn right. After about 2 miles, Rt. 530 becomes Rt. 38; continue on Route 38 for another 3.8 miles then turn left onto Fostertown Rd. (Rt. 636).

The best spots, shown on the map of Western Burlington County, are Crispin Rd., which is on the left about 1.5 miles on Fostertown Rd. from Route 38; Fenimore Rd., which is on the right about 0.2 miles beyond Crispin Rd.; Fostertown Rd. (Rt. 636) from Fenimore Rd. to Route 541; and Mt. Laurel–Eayrestown Road (Rt. 612), which crosses Fostertown Rd. about 0.7 miles beyond Fenimore Rd. (turn right at the intersection).

Red-tailed Hawk, Northern Harrier, and American Kestrel are regular on the sod farms in winter. Horned Lark, Water Pipit, Snow Bunting, and Lapland Longspur are rare, but occur annually. Look for them on freshly manured fields, especially when there is some snow cover.

NOTE: As of late 1990, little of the Mercer Sod Farm remains in cultivation, as development is impending. Some of the other areas mentioned above still have shorebirds occasionally.

Rancocas State Park

Rancocas State Park in western Burlington County encompasses almost 1,100 acres of oak and Virginia Pine woods, overgrown fields, lowland deciduous forest, and freshwater streams and marshes along the two branches of Rancocas Creek—the only Pine Barrens stream that drains westward. Since 1977, the New Jersey Audubon Society has operated the Rancocas Nature Center at an old farmhouse in the northeast corner of the tract. Because the park is not well known, and had little public access in the past, the birding possibilities at Rancocas are not fully appreciated. The full-time staff of naturalists at the Nature Center has gradually increased awareness of Rancocas among birders but the park could still benefit from more thorough coverage.

Because of its location near the Delaware River, Rancocas harbors many migrant songbirds in spring. The breeding species are diverse, but not unusual. The fall migration is not as good as the spring, but the colder months can be very productive, with northern finches and other wintering species.

Directions

Take the New Jersey Turnpike to Exit 5 (Mt. Holly and Burlington). From the exit ramp, go right (east) on Rt. 541 (Mt. Holly–Burlington Rd.). Go about 1.5 miles to the second traffic light, and turn right onto the Mt. Holly Bypass, marked "To Rt. 38" (still Rt. 541). Drive 0.7 miles to the next traffic light, and turn right onto Rancocas Rd. The entrance to the Rancocas Nature Center is one mile ahead on the left. Alternatively, you can take Interstate 295 to Exit 45A (Rancocas Rd.). Go east for 1.7 miles to the entrance to the Nature Center, on the right.

MAP 47. Rancocas State Park

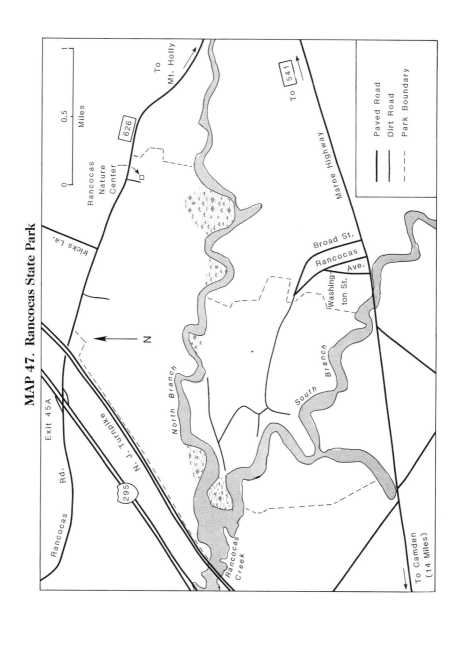

Birding

The nature trail and other trails in the northern part of the park cover a good selection of the habitats available at Rancocas. The nature trail begins at the southeast corner of the parking lot and forms a loop of about 0.6 miles; a side trail about one-third of the way along (going clockwise) adds another 0.4 miles to the walk. The side trail leads to the marshes along the North Branch of Rancocas Creek, where you will find abundant Wild Rice, Arrow Arum, and other marsh plants.

In spring, Wood Duck, Green-winged Teal, Gadwall, Blue-winged Teal, Northern Pintail, Ring-necked Duck, and other species of waterfowl visit Rancocas Creek. Other migrants along the streams include Great Blue Heron, Osprey, Greater and Lesser Yellowlegs, and Common Snipe. Although Rancocas is a little east of the main Delaware Valley flyway, it gets a good spillover of spring migrant songbirds, with as many as 24 species of warblers from late April through May, including Yellow-throated and Prothonotary Warblers, Louisiana Waterthrush, and Yellow-breasted Chat.

Breeding birds at Rancocas include Green-backed Heron, Wood Duck, Red-tailed Hawk, Northern Bobwhite, American Woodcock, Yellow-billed Cuckoo, Eastern Screech and Great Horned Owls, Chimney Swift, Belted Kingfisher, Red-bellied Woodpecker, Wood Thrush, Brown Thrasher, Yellow and Black-and-white Warblers, Blue Grosbeak (since about 1980), Indigo Bunting, and Swamp Sparrow.

Fall migration is unspectacular, but it does bring many Bobolinks to the Wild Rice marshes along the creek, a good selection of warblers (especially Cape May and Yellow-rumped) from mid-September to mid-October, and a variety of sparrows to the fields and feeders later in the season. From November to March, you may find Northern Harrier and Sharp-shinned, Cooper's, and Red-tailed Hawks hunting in the woods and marshes. Other species to look for at that season are Red-breasted Nuthatch, Eastern Bluebird, Hermit Thrush and (in flight years) Red and White-winged Crossbills, Common Redpoll, and Pine Siskin.

To reach some of the other spots in Rancocas State Park, return to Rancocas Rd. and turn left (west). Drive 0.8 miles to the entrance to another Rancocas State Park parking area on the left (the sign now reads "Powhatan-Renape Rankokus Reservation"). Continue down the entrance road, park at the end, then explore the numerous unmarked trails that traverse the fields and woodlands.

The southern portion of the park can be reached from the Nature Center by turning right (east) onto Rancocas Rd. and going 1.1 miles to Rt. 541 (the Mt. Holly Bypass). Turn right, and go 0.8 miles to Rt. 537 (Marne Highway). Drive about 1.1 miles, then turn right on Rancocas Ave., the first right turn after Broad St. After about 0.6 miles, Rancocas Ave. becomes dirt and enters the state park. Passable dirt roads continue almost to the confluence of the North and South branches of Rancocas Creek (about 1.2 miles), but use caution when the roads are wet and muddy. Park along the roads and explore the woods and the marshes along the creek.

Whitesbog

Whitesbog is a unique birding area in the New Jersey Pine Barrens that offers a variety of habitats. It is better known historically as the place where the first successful blueberry crops were cultivated. Now it comprises more than 3,000 acres of both abandoned and cultivated cranberry bogs, blueberry fields, reservoirs, swamps, ponds, streams, cedar bogs, fields in many stages of succession, and oak and Pitch Pine forest. The area, in northeastern Burlington County, is a part of Lebanon State Forest and is operated as the Conservation and Environmental Studies Center.

More than 200 species of birds have been observed around Whitesbog, but it is mainly the waterfowl that attract birders to the site. Nowhere else in New Jersey can you observe Tundra Swan at such close range. The most remarkable feature of the area is the flocks of Gull-billed Terns that have appeared here during August in recent years; although this tern is considered to be an exclusively coastal species, Whitesbog is more than 20 miles from the nearest salt water.

Most of the records of birds that have occurred at Whitesbog have been compiled by Len Little, who has lived here for many years.

Directions

From the north, take the New Jersey Turnpike south to Exit 7A (Interstate 195). Go east on I-195 for about 2 miles to the second exit (Rt. 539). Take Rt. 539 south for about 20 miles to Rt. 70. Go right (west) on Rt. 70 for 5 miles to Rt. 530, on the right. Take Rt. 530 west for about 1.2 miles, then turn right at the sign for the Conservation and Environmental Studies Center. Follow this road for about 0.4 miles to the town of Whitesbog.

From the Philadelphia area or southwestern New Jersey, take Rt. 70 east toward Lakehurst. Go 16 miles beyond the intersection of US 206 and Rt. 70 to Rt. 530, on the left. Turn onto Rt. 530 and go 1.2 miles to the entrance to Whitesbog, as above.

MAP 48. Whitesbog

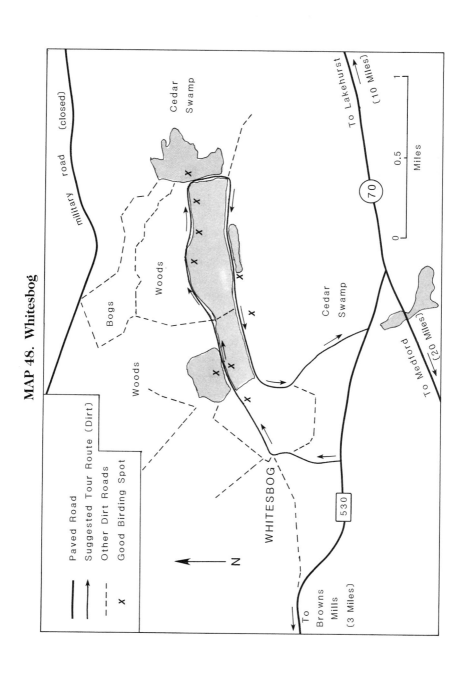

From the north shore, take the Garden State Parkway to Exit 88 (Rt. 70), then follow Rt. 70 west for 19 miles to Rt. 530. From southeastern New Jersey, take the Garden State Parkway to Exit 58 (Rt. 539), then follow Rt. 539 north for 23 miles to Rt. 70 and proceed as above.

Birding

The map shows a three-mile tour, suggested by Len Little, that covers most of the interesting birding areas. By parking in appropriate places and hiking into the surrounding woods and fields, you can thoroughly investigate Whitesbog. Use caution in driving the narrow sandy roads through the bogs, especially during wet weather, because you can easily become mired.

Upon reaching the buildings at Whitesbog, turn right and follow the dirt road for about 0.5 miles until you come to a reservoir on the left. The bogs and reservoirs are the best places for birding, and harbor the many species of waterfowl and shorebirds that occur here. Tundra Swans can be found in late winter or early spring, as soon as the water is open. Their numbers may approach 400 in March and they can be studied at incredibly close range, especially if you stay in your car. The swans prefer the flooded cranberry bogs in the center of the suggested tour route. Among the other waterfowl that occur in large numbers on these ponds are Canada Goose, Wood Duck (nests), Green-winged Teal, American Black Duck (nests), Mallard (nests), Northern Pintail, Blue-winged Teal, and Ring-necked Duck (up to 50). Hooded Merganser is regular in spring, and a variety of other ducks occur in limited numbers.

The spring migration of landbirds is not particularly noteworthy at Whitesbog, but the diversity of nesting species is greater than at most other places in the Pine Barrens. Nesters include Pied-billed Grebe (rare as a breeder anywhere in the state), Green-backed Heron, Virginia Rail, Killdeer, Spotted Sandpiper, and American Woodcock. Ring-necked Pheasant, Ruffed Grouse, Northern Bobwhite, Eastern Screech-Owl, and Great Horned Owl are year-round residents.

Yellow-billed Cuckoo, Whip-poor-will, Common Nighthawk, and Chimney Swift are summer visitors in and around Whitesbog. The common woodpeckers are Red-bellied, Downy, and Hairy, but Red-headed is an occasional visitor and is increasing in neighboring parts of Lebanon State Forest. The list of nesting songbirds includes all the characteristic species of the Pine Barrens.

In late summer when the reservoirs are partly drained, small numbers of shorebirds stop in on their way to the coast. At least 16 species have been observed, the most common being Greater and Lesser Yellowlegs, and Semipalmated, Least, and Pectoral Sandpipers.

Since 1980, flocks of Gull-billed Terns have been appearing at Whitesbog in late summer. The first birds arrive in July, and peak numbers occur in mid-August; most depart by the beginning of September. In New Jersey, this species is normally confined to the salt marshes in the southern part of the state, where it nests in small numbers. The birds that come to Whitesbog take advantage of the shallow water in the bogs and reservoirs to feed on the abundant frogs, tadpoles and insects. The flock of 70 Gull-billed Terns counted here on August 10, 1981, was the largest ever recorded in the state.

Fall brings a few migrating raptors and many of the same species of waterfowl that occur in spring, although in smaller numbers. Golden Eagle and Bald Eagle have occurred during the winter, but otherwise only a few of the common resident species are present.

After completing the loop around the cranberry bogs, return to Rt. 530. There are no public rest rooms at Whitesbog, but there are some at the Lebanon State Forest Headquarters off Rt. 72, just east of Rt. 70. Shinn's Rd. (covered in the chapter on Lebanon State Forest) is just west of the headquarters and has nesting Red-headed Woodpecker, Eastern Bluebird, and Summer Tanager.

Lebanon State Forest

Lebanon State Forest covers almost 30,000 acres in the heart of the New Jersey Pine Barrens in Burlington and Ocean counties. Like most of the pinelands, Lebanon receives relatively little attention from birders because of the uniformity of habitat and lack of diversity of birdlife. However, a number of unusual species have been found nesting in the state forest in recent years, mainly through the fieldwork of Wade and Sharon Wander and Ted Proctor. Their findings suggest that other surprises might await the inquisitive birder who is willing to explore some out-of-the-way places.

Unusual species that nest in Lebanon State Forest are Common Nighthawk, Red-headed Woodpecker, Brown Creeper, Eastern Bluebird, Black-throated Green Warbler, and Summer Tanager. Other birds that have been found nearby and should be sought here in summer are Hermit Thrush, Northern Waterthrush, and Canada Warbler.

Directions

Our tour of Lebanon State Forest begins at the traffic circle where Rts. 70 and 72 intersect, known as the Four Mile Circle. To reach this point:

From northern New Jersey, take the New Jersey Turnpike south to Exit 7 (Bordentown). Stay left through the tollbooth and merge onto US 206 South. Go 10 miles to the intersection with Rt. 530, and turn left toward Pemberton. At the traffic light in Pemberton (3 miles) continue straight ahead on Rt. 644 toward Magnolia and Ongs Hat. After 7 miles you will come to the Four Mile Circle.

From the Philadelphia area, take Rt. 70 east from Camden for about 30 miles to the 70–72 circle.

From the New Jersey shore, take either Rt. 70 southwest from Exit 88 of the Garden State Parkway for 27 miles, or take Rt. 72 northwest from Exit 63 of the Parkway for 22 miles.

MAP 49. Lebanon State Forest

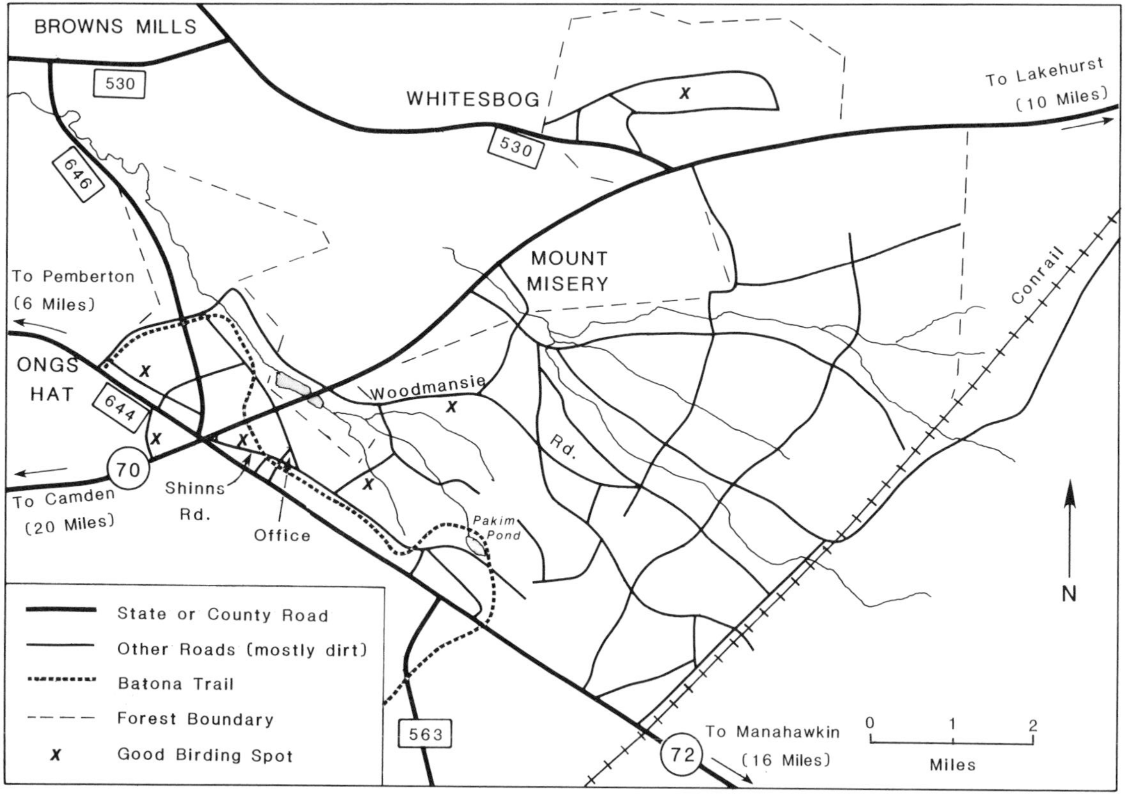

Birding

Most of the roads in Lebanon State Forest are unpaved and un-marked. At the headquarters (see below) you can get a map that shows the main roads, but it is better to use USGS topographic maps of the area (Lebanon State Forest is covered on the Browns Mills, Whiting, Chatsworth, and Woodmansie quadrangles). These are usually on sale at the forest headquarters.

From the Four Mile Circle, go east on Rt. 70 for about 100 yards to a dirt road (Shinns Rd.) on the right. Turn onto it and almost imme-diately you will come to a junction where another dirt road goes left (paralleling Rt. 70), a second dirt road goes right toward Rt. 72, and Shinns Rd. continues straight ahead (paralleling Rt. 72); follow Shinns Rd.

Parts of the oak-pine woods along the road have been selectively cut. This has provided habitat that is attractive to Red-headed Wood-pecker and Summer Tanager; several pairs of both these species are usually here in spring and summer. The first 0.8 miles are espe-cially good; stop periodically and listen for the raucous call of the woodpecker and the Robin-like song or *tick-tucky-tuck* call of the tanager. Eastern Bluebirds also find the open woodlands desirable, and can often be found along Shinns Rd.

Other birds to be found along Shinns Rd. include Broad-winged Hawk; Yellow-billed Cuckoo; Blue-winged, Pine, Prairie, and Black-and-white Warblers; Indigo Bunting; Chipping Sparrow; and other typical Pine Barrens species.

About one mile in from Rt. 70, Shinns Rd. intersects a paved road and continues as a paved road. The new headquarters building, which has rest rooms, maps, and information, is just beyond the in-tersection, on the left. A hundred yards beyond the headquarters is an intersection with another dirt road, and a partially cleared area on the right that attracts Red-headed Woodpecker and Summer Tanager. Continue about 0.6 miles to yet another intersection with a dirt road and turn left. In about 0.6 miles you will cross the bridge over Shinns Branch, a typical Pine Barrens stream bordered by a dense cedar swamp.

About 200 yards beyond the bridge a sand road on the right paral-lels the edge of the swamp for almost a mile. Park along the dirt road and explore the sand road. You will have to wander off the road into the woods on the right to get close to the swamp. If you do, you may encounter Brown Creeper, Black-throated Green Warbler, and possibly Northern Waterthrush or Canada Warbler, in addition to many of the species mentioned above. Brown Creeper has also been found along Shinns Rd. during the breeding season, but this species is more closely associated with cedar swamps in the Pine Barrens. The creeper was formerly a rare nesting bird even in the highlands of northwestern New Jersey, but has extended its range during the past 30 years to cover most of the state (although it is still very uncommon on the coastal plain).

Lebanon State Forest has many more cedar swamps that you can explore with the help of topographic maps. These include McDonald's Branch, about 1.5 miles east of Shinn's Branch; the North, Middle, and South Branches of Mount Misery Brook, which converge at Mount Misery, about 3.5 miles northeast of the forest headquarters; and Goose Pond, about one mile north of Pasadena, which lies along the abandoned Central Railroad of New Jersey. Long-eared Owl and Acadian Flycatcher have been found at Goose Pond in summer, and Sharp-shinned Hawk and Saw-whet Owl are possibilities. Hooded Warbler and Prothonotary Warbler should also be looked for, although neither has been found nesting in this part of the Pine Barrens.

Several places in Lebanon State Forest have cranberry bogs and associated reservoirs that provide habitat similar to Whitesbog, which is covered in a separate chapter. The most accessible of these is Reeves Bogs (at the X-symbol on the map below Woodmansie Rd.); to reach this area, go north from the bridge across Shinns Branch for 0.3 miles and turn left on another dirt road. Go 0.6 miles to a T-intersection and turn right onto Woodmansie Rd. The bogs begin on the right in about 200 yards.

Another good spot for some of the interesting breeding birds can be reached by returning to the Four Mile Circle and heading northwest on Magnolia Rd. (Rt. 644). Turn left on the first dirt road (about three-quarters of a mile), then go another quarter-mile to a clear-cut area and park. This spot has nesting Red-headed Woodpecker, Eastern Bluebird, Summer and Scarlet Tanagers, Northern Oriole, and many other species.

In addition to those species already noted, some of the other regular breeding birds of the Pine Barrens are Green-backed Heron; Red-tailed Hawk (uncommon); Ruffed Grouse; Wild Turkey (now being widely reintroduced); Northern Bobwhite; American Woodcock; Black-billed Cuckoo; Ruby-throated Hummingbird; Willow Flycatcher; Eastern Phoebe; Purple Martin; Tree, Northern Rough-winged, and Barn Swallows; Fish Crow; Carolina Wren; Northern Mockingbird; White-eyed Vireo; Yellow Warbler; American Redstart; and Swamp Sparrow. Most of these species are less widely distributed in the Barrens than those cited above as being typical of the area. Two other species that should be searched for in areas with dense pines are Red Crossbill and White-winged Crossbill, especially during the spring and summer after a flight year. Both species were found nesting a few miles northeast of Lebanon State Forest in the late 1930s and early 1940s (White-winged only once). It seems likely that both have nested in the Pine Barrens in the intervening years, but the territory is vast and summer birders few.

The Batona Trail, a well-marked foot trail, traverses 41 miles of varied habitats and landforms of the Pine Barrens. It begins at Ongs Hat on the western edge of Lebanon State Forest and covers 9.4 miles within the forest, passing near the headquarters building. The trail then turns south toward Wharton State Forest, reaching almost to Batsto before it heads east to its end at Evans Bridge on Rt. 563. Camping is permitted at several spots along with way; a trail map and camping permit can be obtained at the Lebanon State Forest headquarters.

If you camp in the state forest or stay in the area until dark, you may hear some of the nocturnal birds of the Pine Barrens. The most conspicuous voices of the night are those of Eastern Screech-Owl, Barred Owl, Common Nighthawk, and Whip-poor-will, which nest in the forest. The nighthawk is a rare breeder elsewhere in the state, but is locally common in the Barrens. Saw-whet Owl has also been found in the Pine Barrens during the nesting season, and is probably more common than birders realize. Do a little exploring and see if you can find one.

Additional Birding Spots in Central New Jersey

Helmetta

A large (3,000+ acres) outlier of Pine Barrens habitat in southern Middlesex County, Helmetta contains many of the typical species of the Barrens. This is probably the northernmost spot in the state where Whip-poor-will is a common breeding bird; other nesting species include Ruffed Grouse, Common Nighthawk (probable), Purple Martin, Pine Warbler, and Summer Tanager (in 1983). Common Loon, Great Blue Heron, and Osprey occur regularly in migration. The woods are accessible from Helmetta Blvd., Port St., and Washington Ave. Many sand roads lead off these paved roads into the woods. The sand roads can be walked, but not driven (access is blocked). Part of the land is owned by the Middlesex County Dept. of Parks and Recreation.

Directions

From Exit 8A of the New Jersey Turnpike, go east on Rt. 32 (Forsgate Dr.) for about 1.6 miles to the intersection with Half Acre Rd. Turn left and drive about 0.7 miles to Gatzmer Ave. Turn left, go one block, then turn right onto Lincoln Ave. Follow Lincoln, which soon becomes Helmetta Rd. and then Spotswood-Cranbury Rd., for about 2 miles to Maple St. in Helmetta. Turn left and drive about 0.1 miles to Helmetta Pond, on the left. To explore the pine woods, continue another 0.3 miles to Helmetta Blvd. and turn left. Drive 0.3 miles to a dirt road, on the left, that leads into the woods. Port St. is another 0.4 miles ahead. To reach Washington Ave., turn left on Port and drive about one-half mile to the left turn onto Washington. Port and Washington have little traffic, so you can park and bird along the road.

Herrontown Woods

This Princeton Township park contains 142 acres of upland deciduous forest, pine plantings, and overgrown fields. Specialties include Ruffed Grouse and Pileated Woodpecker, but otherwise the birdlife is similar to that of Institute Woods in Princeton (covered in a separate chapter). There are 3 miles of marked trails.

Directions

Take US 1 to the intersection with Rt. 522 (Ridge Rd.) near Kingston, Middlesex County. Go west on Ridge Rd. for about one mile to Rt. 27 in Kingston. Turn left, drive about one-half mile on Rt. 27, crossing the bridges over the Delaware and Raritan Canal and the Millstone River, then take the first right turn, River Rd. Go about 0.2 miles then turn left onto Herrontown Rd. The entrance to the park is about 1.2 miles ahead on the left.

Orchard Road

This spot, which should not be confused with Orchard Rd. in Hillsborough, Somerset County, is located near the town of Linvale, Hunterdon County. It is one of the best spots in the state to find nesting grassland species such as Upland Sandpiper, Savannah and Grasshopper Sparrows, Bobolink, and Eastern Meadowlark; look for them from May through July.

Directions

At the town of Linvale, which is on Rt. 31, 14 miles north of Trenton and 9 miles south of Flemington, go north on Linvale Rd., the main street. After about 2 miles you will come to Orchard Rd.—the third right turn after you leave Linvale. Turn right onto Orchard Rd., which is only about a mile long, and drive a short distance until you see fields on both sides of the road. Search for the grassland birds for the next half mile.

Rosedale Park

The Mercer County Park Commission maintains this 475-acre park, which has been the most reliable place in New Jersey to see Loggerhead Shrike. An individual of this species has wintered in the park at least three out of every four years for the past twenty years, including every winter from 1981 through 1985. Eastern Bluebird is another specialty of the park, along with a variety of raptors in winter, including an occasional Northern Goshawk.

Directions

Follow the directions for Squibb Pond in Lawrenceville (page 210), but instead of turning into Squibb, continue south on US 206 to the next right turn, Carter Rd. Go north on Carter Rd. for about 1.7 miles and turn left onto Cold Soil Rd. (sign for Rosedale Park). Drive about 1.4 miles to Blackwell Mills Rd., turn right, and go about 0.4 miles to a spot on the right where there is room to park several cars and there is a chain across a gate, just before you come to a house. Park here and walk north along the edges of the overgrown fields, searching for the shrike in winter. A sunny, warm, still day is ideal, and the far edge of the fields near the cedars is usually the best place to look.

Thompson Grove Park

This small municipal park near Freehold, Monmouth County, has nesting Grasshopper Sparrow, plus many other species of songbirds in migration.

Directions

From the intersection of Rt. 33 and US 9 in Freehold, go west on Rt. 33 for about 4 miles to the exit for Rt. 527, Millhurst Rd. and Sweetmans Lane. Take the jughandle turn through the traffic light and go south on Millhurst for about 0.3 miles to Kinney Rd., on the left. Turn onto Kinney, then take the next right turn, Thompson Grove Rd., to the park entrance, on the right.

Turkey Swamp Park

A Monmouth County Park containing several hundred acres, Turkey Swamp adjoins the state-owned Turkey Swamp Wildlife Management Area. Together these areas encompass more than 2,000 acres of pine-oak woodland, swamps, and overgrown fields. Birdlife is similar to that of nearby Allaire State Park.

Directions

From the intersection of US 9 and Rt. 33 in Freehold, go south on US 9 for about 0.8 miles to Rt. 524 (Elton-Adelphia Rd.). Turn right and go 0.6 miles to Georgia Rd., on the left. Turn onto Georgia Rd. and drive about one mile to the park entrance, on the right.

Woodfield Reservation

The mature upland deciduous forest in this Princeton Township park attracts many of the same migrant songbirds as the more famous Institute Woods. Nesting species have included Pileated Woodpecker, Worm-eating Warbler, Louisiana Waterthrush and Kentucky Warbler.

Directions

From the junction of US 206 and Rt. 27 in Princeton, go south on US 206 for about one-half mile to the traffic light at Elm St. Turn right on Elm. After about 0.6 miles, the road name changes to Great Rd.;

in another mile, the road bears slightly right and Old Great Rd. joins on the left. Turn onto Old Great Rd. and drive about one-half mile to Woodfields Reservation entrance, on the left. In winter, watch for vultures along Great Rd.; many Black Vultures have been seen with the Turkey Vultures.

Black Skimmers

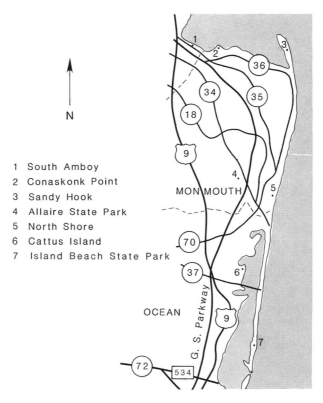

1 South Amboy
2 Conaskonk Point
3 Sandy Hook
4 Allaire State Park
5 North Shore
6 Cattus Island
7 Island Beach State Park

MAP 50. North Coast Region

North Coast

South Amboy

In the late 1960s and 1970s Little Gull and Common Black-headed Gull drew birders to the tidal mudflats at the southeast end of South Amboy on Raritan Bay. Shorebirding also proved to be good here, and there are numerous records for Curlew Sandpiper in addition to a long list of other shorebirds. Gulls and terns, including Black Tern, roost on the flats at low tide. The overgrown fill that borders the shoreline counts Horned Lark as a year-round resident, with Snow Bunting a regular winter visitor. Lapland Longspur is occasional among the mixed flocks of larks and buntings in winter. This area has received much less attention from birders in recent years, in part because of the litter, debris, and uncontrolled shooting of guns, but mainly because the rare gulls are seen less frequently. In general, it is one of the more unsavory birding spots and not a place to go alone.

Directions

From the north, take the Garden State Parkway south to Exit 123 (US 9), then take the first exit off Rt. 9 toward South Amboy, the Bordentown-Amboy Turnpike. Follow this road, which becomes Bordentown Ave., for about 1.4 miles to Broadway in South Amboy. Turn left, go two short blocks to John St., turn right, and go two blocks to the end. Turn right onto Rosewell St., then left at the next street, George St. Bear right at the boat club, follow the bumpy, glass-littered road across the landfill as far as you dare, then park.

From the south, take the Parkway north to the service area at Mile 123. Enter the service area and drive to the commuter parking area at the north end. Follow the commuter access road out the north end of the parking area to the Bordentown-Amboy Turnpike, and proceed as above.

From the Philadelphia area, take the New Jersey Turnpike north to Exit 10 (Edison), then follow Rt. 440 east for about 2 miles to the

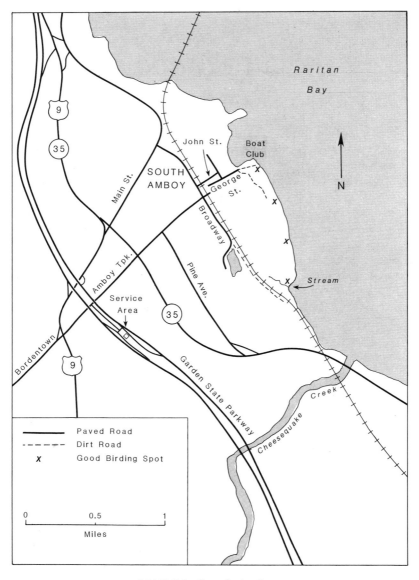

MAP 51. South Amboy

Garden State Parkway South. Go 4 miles south on the Parkway to Exit 123.

Birding

The best birding spot is the mudflat around the mouth of a small stream almost a mile southeast of the end of George St. You can drive part of the way on the dirt road, but eventually you will have to park and walk. Watch out for broken glass and do not leave anything of value exposed in your car while you are gone. You may encounter people target shooting or aimlessly firing guns; proceed at your own risk.

Walk down to the shore, then head southeast along the water's edge, scanning ahead for shorebirds. Although gulls and terns tend to concentrate around the stream, shorebirds may be found anywhere along the way, provided some stones or mudflats are exposed. The best times for the shorebirds, gulls, and terns are the three hours before (better) and after low tide. (Low tide at South Amboy occurs approximately one-half hour later than the published tides for Sandy Hook.) The shorebirds to be expected here are generally the same as those mentioned for Conaskonk Point; Curlew Sandpiper is found here in May every two or three years.

When you reach a point where the shoreline bends sharply to the right, you are approaching the stream where the gulls and terns gather. If there are any around, you should spot them sitting on the mudflats offshore. Little Gull and Common Black-headed Gull have been found here at all seasons, but the best time for them is May, when they mingle with migrant flocks of Bonaparte's Gulls which feed in Raritan Bay and pause to rest on the South Amboy mudflats when the tide is out. Numbers of Little Gull have declined steadily since the early 1970s, and they are no longer found here every year. One Little and one Black-headed Gull were present in May 1984, however; they were at the boat club, which now seems to be the best place here to see them.

May is also a good time to find Black Tern at South Amboy, although the species is an uncommon spring migrant anywhere in New Jersey. Late July and August are better for Black Tern and for any other wandering terns. Shorebirding is also good in late summer, but birders find other places more attractive and productive.

In winter, rafts of scaup and other diving ducks float offshore, and gulls are abundant. Flocks of Horned Larks and Snow Buntings feed in the weedy areas near the foot of George St. or on the playing fields south of the end of Rosewell St.; occasionally there is a Lapland Longspur or two in with them.

The stream mouth where the gulls gather also can be reached by turning right instead of left on Broadway. Follow Braodway for four blocks to Locust Street, where it jogs left around a building and runs along the railroad tracks. In about 300 yards, the road bends to the right and continues around a pond; before you reach the pond, turn left onto a dirt road that parallels the tracks. This road is reasonably rough and littered with junk. After about one-half mile you will see the cove at the stream off to your left; park on the side of the road, cross the tracks carefully, and make your way down to the shore.

Conaskonk Point

This area of salt marsh and beach at Union Beach on Raritan Bay, between Sandy Hook and South Amboy, is good for migrant terns and shorebirds from late spring through early fall. It provides a good vantage point for watching southbound loons and waterfowl in fall. Winter finds rafts of scaup and other diving ducks offshore, a few raptors over the salt marsh, and Horned Lark and Snow Bunting on the beach. Gulls, including an occasional rarity, are present at all seasons. Conaskonk makes a good spot to spend an hour or two as part of a trip to Sandy Hook or South Amboy.

Some of the noteworthy species recorded at Conaskonk in recent years are American Oystercatcher, Hudsonian and Marbled Godwits, Baird's and Curlew Sandpipers, and Little and Common Black-headed Gulls. Caspian, Royal, and Black Terns occur in later summer. Among the few species of breeding birds is the sometimes elusive Sharp-tailed Sparrow, which is abundant here.

Directions

Take the Garden State Parkway to Exit 117 (Keyport and Hazlet), and take Rt. 36 east (follow signs for Sandy Hook, Gateway National Recreation Area). Go about 2.7 miles from the tollbooth to the jughandle turn for Union Ave. north toward Union Beach. After about 0.8 miles, Union Ave. bears slightly left and becomes Front St.; continue another one-half mile to the intersection with Florence Ave. and park on the right overlooking the water.

Birding

The parking areas along the waterfront in Union Beach provide a good view of the waters of Raritan Bay and the fishing weirs offshore. From spring through fall, but especially in late summer, terns can be

275

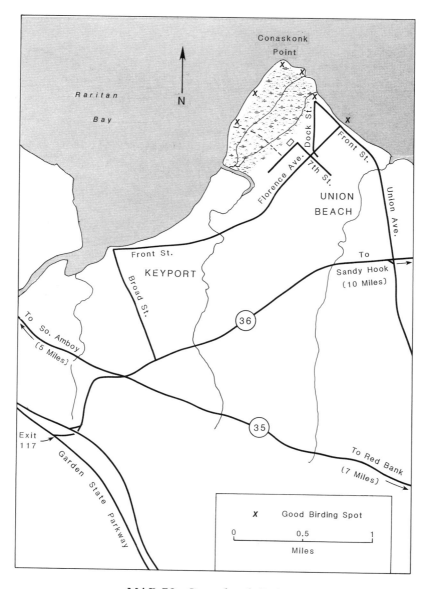

MAP 52. Conaskonk Point

seen sitting on the beach or fishing in the surf. Common and Least Terns are the dominant species, since both breed nearby, but Caspian, Royal, and Black Terns are annual visitors.

Gulls are most common in winter, when Iceland, Glaucous, and Lesser Black-backed should be looked for, but Little Gull and Common Black-headed Gull occur among migrant flocks of Bonaparte's Gulls in spring or late fall. Nearby South Amboy (covered in a separate chapter) has long been known as a place to see Little and Black-headed Gulls, but is no longer reliable. Double-crested Cormorants can be seen sitting on the fishing weirs at all seasons, and are joined by a few Great Cormorants in winter. Ospreys, both migrants and nesting birds from nearby Sandy Hook, also perch on the weirs.

After scanning the bay, continue on Front Street another one-half mile to its end and park in the dirt parking area. Walk north along the beach, scanning the sod banks and mudflats for shorebirds, mainly Black-bellied and Semipalmated Plovers, Semipalmated and Least Sandpiper, and Short-billed Dowitcher. In about a hundred yards, you will come to a creek; at low tide you can cross the creek with knee boots, but be sure you return before the tide comes in. (The tides here are about one-half hour later than at Sandy Hook.) After a short walk along the beach, you will come to Conaskonk Point.

The sandbar at the point is a favorite resting place for gulls, terns, Black Skimmers, and shorebirds. Here you may find Greater and Lesser Yellowlegs, Willet (nests in the saltmarsh), Ruddy Turnstone, Red Knot, Sanderling, White-rumped and Stilt Sandpiper and Dunlin, in addition to the species noted above. This is the spot where most of the rarities have been found. From the point you can continue along the beach toward Keyport, where you will encouter more good shorebird habitat.

If the tide is high, the point and the shore of Keyport Harbor can be reached from the west. Return to your car and take the first right turn (Dock St.) off Front St. Follow Dock St. back to Florence Ave., and take the first right off Florence onto 7th St. At the end of 7th St. you will see a sewage treatment plant; just to the west, a dirt road leads out to the beach. Park near the beginning of the dirt road, walk a couple of hundred yards to the shore, and turn right toward the point.

The salt marsh in back of the beach has a few breeding birds.

Clapper Rail, Willet, Marsh Wren, Sharp-tailed Sparrow, and Seaside Sparrow nest in the wetter areas; Fish Crow and Song Sparrow inhabit the edges. Northern Harriers hunt over the marsh in fall and winter, Rough-legged Hawk is sometimes present in winter, and Merlin and Peregrine Falcon have been seen in migration. A variety of sparrows can be found in the weedy areas in winter, and Horned Lark and Snow Bunting frequently feed on the beach.

Sandy Hook
(Gateway National Recreation Area)

Sandy Hook is not only an exciting place to discover birds, it is also unique from a geographical and historical perspective. The five-mile long peninsula of Sandy Hook juts northward toward the center of Lower New York Bay, occupying a commanding position at the gateway to New York harbor that has determined its history for three hundred years. Since the late 1600s, Sandy Hook has been the site of forts, lighthouses, and later a Coast Guard station. Today, as a 1,600-acre unit of Gateway National Recreation Area, it is an interesting historical spot and an extremely popular summer bathing beach. One benefit of the many years of military occupation is that, unlike most of the barrier beaches in New Jersey, much of Sandy Hook has escaped development and retains an impressive array of habitats including holly forest, deciduous woods, beach, mudflats, and dunes.

As a coastal peninsula along a principal flyway, "The Hook" is an outstanding place to find migrant birds in spring and fall. There is an excellent hawk migration in March and April, followed by waves of songbirds in May. In fall, the songbird migration holds strong from early August to the end of October, with an ever-changing kaleidoscope of species. Sandy Hook supports an interesting diversity of breeding birds during summer, although it is not regularly birded at that season because of the beach crowds. In winter, it is a good place to look for seabirds and waterfowl, the rarer gulls, winter finches, Snow Bunting and longspurs.

The more sought-after species that occur regularly at Sandy Hook include Red-necked Grebe; Great Cormorant; Little, Iceland, Glaucous, and Lesser Black-backed Gulls; Yellow-bellied Flycatcher; Gray-cheeked Thrush; Philadelphia Vireo; Orange-crowned, Connecticut, and Mourning Warblers; Lincoln's Sparrow; and Lapland

279

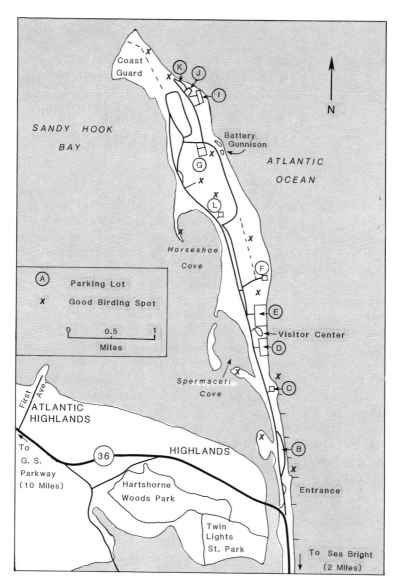

MAP 53. Sandy Hook

Longspur. Rarities found here in recent years are Eared Grebe; American Swallow-tailed Kite; Western Kingbird; Scissor-tailed Fly-catcher; Townsend's Warbler; LeConte's, Clay-colored, and Lark Sparrows, and Chestnut-collared Longspur. The variety of both expected and unexpected species makes Sandy Hook an exciting place to bird at any season.

Directions

Take the Garden State Parkway to Exit 117 (Keyport, Rt. 36). Go east on Rt. 36 for 13 miles, then follow the signs for the exit on the right just after you cross the bridge over the Navesink River. The exit road leads under the bridge and then to the entrance to Gateway National Recreation Area, Sandy Hook Unit, in about 0.3 miles. An entrance fee is charged in summer.

Birding

The first parking lot on the right, Lot B, is 0.2 miles past the entrance. From late fall to early spring search here for loons, grebes, scoters and other sea ducks, and gulls; this is one of the best spots on the coast for Red-necked Grebe. Lot C, one-half mile north of the Lot B exit, is another good place to check the ocean off the break-water; I have seen Little Gull here in winter. Great Cormorants often roost on the mudflats around Spermaceti Cove in winter, and Brant and Greater Scaup are usually abundant.

From Lot C, continue north for about 1.7 miles, past the Visitor Center on the right, to the right turn for Lot F (South Beach); after about 0.4 miles, you will reach the parking lot. After parking, walk back along the road for about 200 yards, and turn right on a path that leads north into the woods. This area is excellent for spring and fall migrant songbirds, including some of the less common species such as Yellow-bellied Flycatcher, Gray-cheeked Thrush, Philadelphia Vireo, Connecticut Warbler (mainly September), and Mourning Warbler (late May–early June). Look and listen for chickadees; the resident species at Sandy Hook is the Black-capped Chickadee, while the resident species on the nearby mainland at Highlands is the Carolina Chickadee. The trail continues for a little over one-half mile, and eventually meets the paved road to North Beach. Near its northern end are some groves of planted pines that attract migrants, and crossbills in winter during invasion years.

Return to parking Lot F and walk south along the beach for a short distance to a trail that leads inland toward a large area surrounded by a chain-link fence. This is the maintenance area (**X** on the map between lots E and F), which is also accessible from parking Lot E near the Visitor Center. The fence along the maintenance area, especially on the eastern side, is excellent for migrant sparrows in October; in addition to all the common species, White-crowned and Lincoln's Sparrows are regular, and Lark and Clay-colored Sparrows usually appear each year.

Drive back to the main road from Lot F and turn right. In about 0.7 miles you will come to a right turn for North Beach. Continue straight ahead just past this junction, turn right into Lot L, and park. The complex of buildings inside the chain-link fence was formerly a radar site for Fort Hancock. Follow the marked Camper's Trail north from the east end of the parking area along the fence; this can sometimes be good for migrant warblers and sparrows. In September and October, American Kestrels and Sharp-shinned Hawks are usually much in evidence, chasing prey around the radar site. When the trail forks after a hundred yards or so, stay right.

In another hundred yards, across a paved path, you will see a large, rusty metal building ahead to the left; head toward this building, and follow the path leading around its left side. The holly woods here, with its dense tangle of catbriar and other undergrowth, harbors many songbirds in migration, including skulkers such as Gray-cheeked Thrush, Connecticut Warbler, and Mourning Warbler.

You will soon emerge into a clearing with a yellow brick building on the left. Just ahead on the right, another trail goes about 50 yards into the dense woods; this is another place to check for migrants. At this point, you can either retrace your steps back to Lot L or detour at the yellow brick building onto a driveway which leads out to the main road. At the road, turn left and walk about 0.4 miles to Lot L. Horseshoe Cove, on the bay side of the road opposite Lot L, is a good place in winter for loons, grebes, geese, ducks, cormorants, and gulls. An Eared Grebe spent a month here during the winter of 1984–85.

Drive out of Lot L and turn left, then immediately turn left again onto the road to North Beach. After about 1.2 miles, you will pass a sewage treatment plant and then Battery Gunnison, a former gun emplacement. In another tenth of a mile, at the intersection with a sign for a right turn to North Beach, continue straight ahead for a short distance and turn into Lot G. Park near the southeast corner of the lot (the entrance is on the northwest corner) and check the fence around the peculiar concrete structure at the south end of the lot. These rectangular concrete boxes were holding tanks for fish or other marine life, but they are now overgrown with weeds and are excellent for migrant sparrows; I have seen Clay-colored Sparrow here. The paths that lead through the woods to Battery Gunnison and to the sewage treatment area have many songbirds in migration, and in October the fences around the sewage treatment plant are good for sparrows.

Drive out the exit of Lot G and continue straight ahead toward North Beach. After 0.4 miles, bear right onto the dirt road to Lot I, the North Beach parking lot. Park here and walk north along the edges of the dunes. You can walk the beach for almost a mile to the fence at the Coast Guard station. There are two ponds hidden in the dunes about halfway up the beach, and the hollows in the dunes around some of the former gun emplacements are outstanding for migrants in spring and fall. The dunes are an excellent spot for viewing the hawk migration, especially in April (the biggest flight month) and in September–October. American Kestrel is by far the most common species, but all the regular coastal migrants are well represented, including Cooper's Hawk, Merlin, and Peregrine Falcon. American Swallow-tailed Kite has been seen almost annually in April in recent years from the hawk watch site on a knoll near the lighthouse, about 0.3 miles southwest of Lot I.

Along the dunes in October you will also find many migrant songbirds, including Orange-crowned Warbler, sparrows, such as White-crowned, Lincoln's and even Lark. In winter, there are always Snow Buntings and Horned Larks here, and Lapland Longspurs are often among them. In January 1984, a Chestnut-collared Longspur was found in a flock of Snow Buntings about one-half mile north of Lot I and stayed for almost a month. The following year a Le Conte's Sparrow wintered a little father up the dunes.

As you drive out of Lot I, Lots J and K are on the right. The large parade ground to the north of Lot K attracts fall migrant sparrows, including Vesper Sparrow. Many migrants can also be found along the fence blocking the road at the north end of the parade ground.

Some of the common breeding birds at Sandy Hook are Green-backed Heron, Northern Bobwhite, Clapper Rail, Killdeer, American Woodcock, Herring Gull, Common and Least Terns, Whip-poor-will, Eastern Kingbird, Black-capped Chickadee, Brown Thrasher, White-eyed Vireo and American Redstart. Other interesting breeding species include Piping Plover, Yellow-breasted Chat and Boat-tailed Grackle.

One of the best birding places at Sandy Hook, especially in fall migration, is the spot known as the garden, which was discovered by birders after this chapter was written. To reach it, take the road (not shown on the map) that leads west for about 200 yards from the north-south road at Lot J past an abandoned tennis court (also a good spot for sparrows) to the northeast corner of the loop shown on the map. On the southwest corner of this intersection is a parking area and the garden. Do not enter the garden, which is farmed by nearby residents, but bird around the perimeter.

Allaire State Park

This 3,035-acre park in southern Monmouth County contains an interesting mixture of oak-pine woodland, upland deciduous forest, and bottomland deciduous woodland along the Manasquan River. It is the site of a restored village that preserves a glimpse into the life of a mid-nineteenth-century iron mining and smelting village. It is an excellent spot in spring for migrant warblers and other songbirds, and supports a diverse population of breeding birds. Fall migration is also good, but the area attracts fewer birders at that season, when the nearby coastal locations are more productive. Noteworthy breeding birds at Allaire are Acadian Flycatcher; Prothonotary, Kentucky, and Hooded Warblers; and Northern Waterthrush. Yellow-throated Warbler has nested at least once.

Directions

From northern or southern New Jersey, take the Garden State Parkway to Exit 98 (Interstate 195). Follow the sign for I-195, then go west on I-195 for almost 3 miles to Exit 31B (Rt. 547). Turn right onto Rt. 547 and go a couple of hundred yards to Allaire Rd. (Rt. 524). Turn right and go about 1.2 miles to the main park entrance, on the right. Follow the entrance road for several hundred yards to the large parking area at Allaire Village. The gate is open from 8:00 A.M. to sunset.

From west-central New Jersey, take I-195 east to Exit 31B (Rt. 547) and proceed as just described.

Birding

From the parking area at Allaire Village, walk west (to your right as you drive into the parking lot) along the path. This trail is the former

MAP 54. Allaire State Park

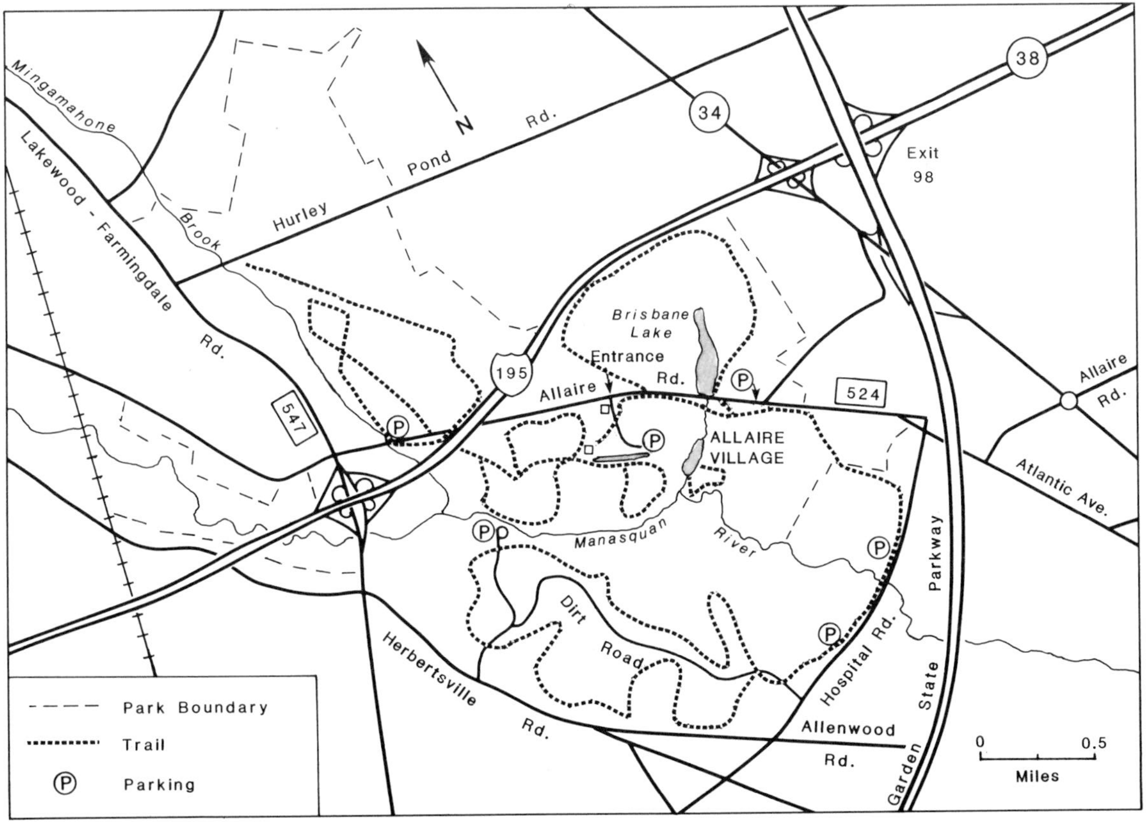

Allaire Rd.

Atlantic Ave.

38

Exit 98

Garden State Parkway

524

Hospital Rd.

Allenwood Rd.

P

P

34

Brisbane Lake

ALLAIRE VILLAGE

Manasquan River

P

Entrance Rd.

P

P

Allaire Rd.

Dirt Road

195

P

Herbertsville Rd.

Pond Rd.

N

Hurley Brook

547

Mingamahone Brook

Lakewood - Farmingdale Rd.

0   0.5
Miles

- - - Park Boundary

······· Trail

ⓅParking

towpath of a canal that dates from the foundry days of 150 years ago. The woods are excellent for migrant songbirds in spring; here, you can expect to find most species of flycatchers, kinglets, thrushes, vireos, warblers, tanagers, grosbeaks, and orioles that pass through New Jersey at that season. The abundance and variety are not quite as great as at Princeton—but there are no mobs of birders to contend with, either, and the open canopy makes the birding easier.

After about a quarter-mile you will pass a pond on the right which attracts migrant flycatchers. On the far side of the pond is the Nature Center. Continue along the towpath trail for another one-half mile until you approach the underpass at I-195, and turn onto a trail leading left. This trail makes a long loop through the mature deciduous woodland down to the Manasquan River, then eventually rejoins the towpath trail near the Nature Center.

Another productive trail is the nature trail that begins near the sawmill site, just below the fishing pond at Allaire Village. To reach this spot from the parking lot, walk east along the towpath past the Visitor Center, then turn right onto the path that parallels the fishing pond. You will soon come to an intersection of several paths, where the nature trail entrance is marked by a sign. This trail makes a circuit along the floodplain of the Manasquan River, where giant old American Sycamores and Silver Maples tower overhead. This is where Yellow-throated Warbler has nested.

Another good birding area at Allaire is the path around the pond at the family camping area. Drive back to Allaire Rd. and turn left. Go about 0.9 miles to a parking lot on the right, just beyond the entrance to the family camping area. The trail leads along the Mingamahone Brook, and is the best spot in the park for Prothonotary Warbler. Brisbane Lake has Ring-necked Ducks in early spring. It is located on Allaire Rd. about 0.4 miles east of the main park entrance.

Approximately one-third of Allaire State Park lies south of the Manasquan River. This part of the park lies within the Pine Barrens, and contains all the usual birds of that region. It is traversed by a hiking and horseback trail about 4 miles long (round trip), and is also crossed by an unimproved dirt road that is negotiable by most vehicles. To reach this area from the main entrance drive east on Allaire Rd. for about 1.3 miles to Hospital Rd., then turn right. Drive about 1.2 miles to a parking area, on the right, where you can take the hiking/horseback trail.

You can also walk the dirt road shown on the map; to reach it continue on foot a quarter-mile past the parking lot on Hospital Rd. to the road on the right. The dirt road is about 2 miles long and ends at Herbertsville Rd.; about 1.7 miles along it a side road on the right leads north to the Manasquan River. To return to I-195 from the Hospital Rd. parking area, continue south for about 0.5 mile to Allenwood Rd., go about 0.8 miles to Herbertsville Rd., and turn right again. Next, drive about 1.2 miles to Rt. 547 and turn right. Interstate 195 is 0.3 miles ahead.

Breeding birds at Allaire, in addition to those already mentioned, include Wood Duck; Broad-winged Hawk; Eastern Screech, Great Horned and Barred Owls; Whip-poor-will; Red-bellied Woodpecker; Eastern Phoebe; Eastern Kingbird; Purple Martin; Carolina Wren; White-eyed and Yellow-throated Vireos; Blue-winged, Yellow, Pine, Prairie, and Black-and-white Warblers; American Redstart; Louisiana Waterthrush; Rose-breasted Grosbeak; and Indigo Bunting.

There are rest rooms in the basement of the General Store near the main parking lot, and there is a snack bar at the adjacent Visitor Center. An entrance fee is charged at the main parking lot in summer.

North Shore Tour

The New Jersey coast from Point Pleasant to Long Branch is known to birders as the North Shore. It includes numerous freshwater ponds, estuaries, inlets, and oceanfront in Monmouth and northern Ocean counties. From October through March this area is excellent for loons, grebes, Northern Gannet, Great Cormorant, geese, ducks (dabblers, divers, and sea ducks), Purple Sandpiper, gulls, and, occasionally alcids.

Rarities that have been recorded along the North Shore within the past 10 years include Eared and Western Grebes, Brown Pelican, Barrow's Goldeneye, Sooty Tern, Dovekie, Thick-billed Murre, and Razorbill. Other noteworthy species that occur annually in varying numbers are Red-necked Grebe; Eurasian Wigeon; Common and King Eiders; Harlequin Duck; Little, Common Black-headed, Iceland, Lesser Black-backed, and Glaucous Gulls; and Black-legged Kittiwake.

Outlined below is a suggested tour that covers the area of interest. To bird the entire route requires the better part of a day, but you can omit parts of it to fit your schedule. In general, the area north of Shark River Inlet is less productive than that to the south. Regardless of where you come from, it is easiest to cover the coast from south to north, so the trip begins in Point Pleasant. A spotting scope is essential.

Directions

From the north, take the Garden State Parkway south to Exit 98 (Rt. 34). Follow Rt. 34 south for about four miles until it merges with Rt. 35. Continue south on Rt. 35 for abut 3.5 miles through the center of Point Pleasant. Just after the junction with Rt. 88 on the right, you will cross some railroad tracks and come to a traffic light. Turn left at this light onto Ocean Ave., go about 0.2 miles, and turn left

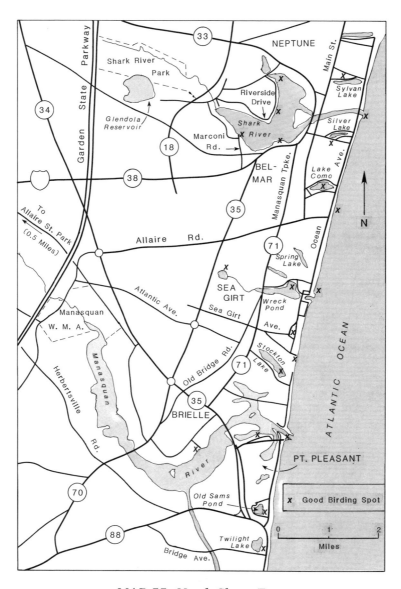

MAP 55. North Shore Tour

onto Elizabeth Ave. Lake of the Lilies (or Old Sam's Pond, as it is known to birders) is just ahead on the right.

From the west, take Interstate 195 east to its terminus at Rt. 34. Follow Rt. 34 toward Point Pleasant, proceeding as just described.

From the south, take the Garden State Parkway north to Exit 88 (Rt. 70), then follow Rt. 70 north for about 2.3 miles to the Laurelton traffic circle. Take Rt. 88 east from the circle (second right) for about 4.6 miles to Rt. 35. Bear right onto Rt. 35 south over the railroad tracks to the traffic light at Ocean Ave. Turn left onto Ocean and then left at Elizabeth as directed above.

Birding

Despite its modest size, Old Sam's Pond is the best of the shore ponds for seeing some of the diving ducks at close range. A large flock of Canvasbacks stays here as long as the water is not frozen; among them are Redhead, Greater and Lesser Scaup, Ruddy Duck, and Pied-billed Grebe. Dabbling ducks that frequent the pond are American Black Duck, Mallard, Northern Pintail, Northern Shoveler, Gadwall, and American Wigeon. An immature Snow Goose or two will sometimes join the flock of tame Mallards and domestic geese that scramble for handouts at the west side of the pond. There are usually plenty of American Coot, although they are even more abundant on some of the ponds further north.

When the water is partly frozen in winter, gulls of several species come to sit on the ice and bathe in the water. In addition to the big three (Ring-billed, Herring and Great Black-backed), Bonaparte's Gull is regular and Common Black-headed, Iceland, Lesser Black-backed, and Glaucous Gulls occur almost every year. In late fall, there will probably be lingering Laughing Gulls.

After driving around the perimeter of Old Sam's, turn right onto Washington Ave. and go one block back to Ocean Ave. Turn left at Ocean and go about 1.1 miles to Broadway; you will pass Little Silver Lake on the left, which may have Buffleheads but very little else. Turn right onto Broadway and park on either side of the short, dead-end street. Walk north along the boardwalk at the end of the street for about 100 yards to a platform overlooking Manasquan Inlet.

In late fall, migrating loons and scoters can be seen heading south off the end of the jetties that protect the inlet. East or southeasterly winds at that season can bring large numbers of gannets close to shore, particularly in foggy or rainy weather. Parasitic Jaeger is occasionally seen from shore under these conditions in October; Black-legged Kittiwake is regular in November and December. With a lot of luck you might find a Dovekie, Razorbill, or Thick-billed Murre in the inlet.

The inlet is attractive to gulls, especially Bonaparte's, from fall through spring. It is one of the most reliable places for Common Black-headed Gull, and a good spot to look for Little, Iceland, and Glaucous as well. If the weather is not too bad, you may want to walk out on the jetty. Instead of parking on Broadway, take Ocean one more block to its end and park in the lot along the seawall. Walk east along the seawall to the jetty.

The road along the seawall (Inlet Dr.) winds around and rejoins Broadway. Turn right, cross the bridge, and turn right onto Channel Dr. Check the water wherever you can get to it between the restaurants and boat docks for gulls; one or two Common Black-headed Gulls have wintered in this area for several years. When Channel rejoins Broadway go right, then make the right turn onto Rt. 35.

Cross the Manasquan River, which has lots of wintering Brant, Canvasback, and scaup, and exit right onto Rt. 71 (about one mile from Broadway). Follow Rt. 71 north for about 1.6 miles to the traffic light at Sea Girt Ave. Turn right, cross the railroad tracks, and bear right (still Sea Girt Ave.) alongside the state police training center and National Guard parade grounds. Scan the parade grounds for the occasional flocks of Horned Lark and Snow Bunting (rarely accompanied by Lapland Longspur), in addition to the omnipresent Brant, Canada Geese, and gulls.

After about a mile, the road ends at a chain-link fence; Western Grebe, Common Eider, Harlequin Duck, Little Gull, and Thick-billed Murre have been seen on the ocean here, but it is no longer accessible, so take the last left, First Ave. Go about 0.3 miles to Trenton Blvd., turn right, go to the end and scan the ocean and jetties. Next, turn around and take the first right, a dirt lane through an American Holly forest. After about 200 yards, there is a place to park on the left. This small city park has been a good place for Great Horned,

Barred, and Long-eared Owls in winter, as well as American Woodcock, Hermit Thrush, American Robin, and Cedar Waxwing.

Continue through the holly forest to the paved road, where you rejoin First Ave. Turn right at the third street, New York Blvd., and continue one block to Ocean Ave. Turn left and park on the right; scan the ocean for seabirds and the jetties for Purple Sandpiper. Drive north for about 200 yards to the dead end, then left onto Beacon Blvd. Go one block back to First Ave., turn right, then take the first left onto a dirt road, The Terrace. This road provides good views of the southeast side of Wreck Pond, one of the largest of the shore ponds and, because it is brackish, one of the last to freeze. Wreck Pond has many diving ducks, especially mergansers and Bufflehead. It is the best spot on the coast for Common Merganser.

Follow The Terrace to its end (about 0.4 miles), then go left one block back to Beacon Blvd. Go right onto Rt. 71, cross the upper end of Wreck Pond, then take the first right onto Shore Ave. This soon joins Ocean Rd., which continues for about 0.5 miles to Ocean Ave. Like all the shore ponds, Wreck Pond is especially good for gulls when it is partly or completely frozen. The two white-winged gulls and Lesser Black-backed Gull are seen here annually.

Turn left (north) onto Ocean Ave. For the next mile and a half, the ocean is too far from the road for birding. If you have time, stop at a couple of places and walk out to the boardwalk to scan the water. Just before Lake Como the road approaches the beach, and you can scan the jetties for gulls and the ocean for seabirds. Turn left immediately before the brick arches and follow the road clockwise around Lake Como. In addition to a variety of the usual dabbling and diving ducks, the lake regularly has Eurasian Wigeon.

After returning to Ocean Ave., continue north for about 1.3 miles to Shark River Inlet. Park on the right just before the drawbridge and check the inlet and the jetties. Harlequin Ducks hang out here on occasion, and the inlet has been known to harbor an alcid or two. Black-legged Kittiwakes sometimes follow the fishing boats back to the inlet; scan the flocks of gulls with a scope as the birds approach the jetties, because the Kittiwakes usually turn back before the boats enter the inlet.

Make a U-turn and head south to Fifth Ave. Turn right, then bear left along the shore of Silver Lake, which has had goodies such as Eurasian Wigeon and Lesser Black-backed Gull. (Red-crested Pochard and Mandarin Duck have been here as well, but they are escapees and you can't count them.) Turn right at Eighth Ave. and follow it through Belmar for about one-half mile to Rt. 35. Turn left onto Rt. 35 and parallel the marina for about 0.3 miles. Turn right at the far (west) end of the marina and drive out to the parking area along the bulkhead. The large body of water before you is the Shark River estuary.

Shark River is the best place for wintering waterfowl along the north coast. Large numbers of grebes, geese, ducks, and gulls—as well as a few rarities—can be found here throughout the winter. A drake Barrow's Goldeneye wintered on the estuary every year from 1970 to 1984; this bird (assuming that it was the same one all along) has probably been seen by more birders than any other duck in the history of North America. The parking lot is a good place from which to scan for the Barrow's among the many Common Goldeneyes that winter here.

Species to be expected around Shark River in winter are Pied-billed and Horned Grebes; Great Blue Heron; Mute Swan; Brant (abundant); Canada Goose; Green-winged Teal; American Black Duck; Mallard; Northern Pintail; Northern Shoveler; Gadwall; Eurasian Wigeon (one or two drakes every winter); American Wigeon (abundant); Canvasback; Redhead; Ring-necked Duck; Greater and Lesser Scaup; Common Goldeneye; Bufflehead; Hooded, Common, and Red-breasted Mergansers; and Ruddy Duck. Wintering shorebirds include Black-bellied Plover, Sanderling, Dunlin, and sometimes both yellowlegs.

After scanning the estuary from the boat launch area go back to Rt. 35 and turn right. Stop at the far end of McCreary Park (about 0.3 miles) if you haven't yet found the Barrow's Goldeneye. Continue on to the traffic light at Belmar Blvd. (0.2 miles) and turn right. Just ahead on the right is a small bridge. Stop before the bridge and check out the ducks for the drake Eurasian Wigeon that likes to hang out here. Go another 0.5 miles and take the second right, Marconi Rd. When Marconi turns left after about 0.2 miles continue straight ahead down to the water. This is the best place to search for dabbling ducks and is the prime spot for Eurasian Wigeon. Hooded and Common Mergansers also prefer this upper end of the estuary.

Shark River can also be birded from the north side. To reach it, go back up the hill to the stop sign at Marconi Rd. and turn right. Go right at the next stop sign (you're still on Marconi Rd.), and follow Marconi for about one mile to the next stop sign, just before the entrance to Rt. 18. Turn right, cross the bridge over Shark River, and take the first paved road on the right, Riverside Dr. Stay left when the road forks almost immediately, then bear right at the second crossroads (about 0.4 miles), down the hill to the water. Riverside Dr. follows the waterfront for about 1.4 miles, and offers numerous places to stop and scan.

When you reach the stop sign at Lakewood Rd. you have a big decision. If you have had enough for one day and are going south or west, a left turn will take you back to Rt. 18 south then Rt. 38 and the Garden State Parkway. If you are going north, a right turn will take you to Sylvania Ave. (about 0.4 miles), which leads west to Rt. 33 and the Parkway. If you want to continue, there are a few more spots to hit.

A right turn at Sylvania will take you back to Rt. 35, where you should take the exit for Avon and continue on Sylvania to the ocean front. The ocean and ponds north of Shark River are less productive than the area farther south. Ponds worth checking are Sylvan Pond, three blocks north of Sylvania Ave., Deal Lake on the north side of Asbury Park, and Lake Takanassee in Long Branch; all three are on Ocean Ave. When Ocean Ave. ends in Bradley Beach, go left, then take the third right turn at Main Street (Rt. 71). Follow Rt. 71 for about 2 miles to Deal Lake, then rejoin Ocean Ave. at the east end of the lake.

At Lake Takanassee, about 4 miles north of Deal Lake on Ocean Ave., a series of ponds runs inland for about a mile. The main pond is good for Canvasback and Bonaparte's Gull and has had Common Black-headed and Lesser Black-backed Gulls. The next pond inland is one of the best coastal places in the state to see Ring-necked Duck. To reach it, drive one block north to Cedar Ave., go left across the raiload tracks, and take the second left turn; go a couple of short blocks to the pond, on the right. This and the next two ponds are good for Hooded Merganser and have had Eurasian Wigeon.

Return to Cedar Ave. and turn right, toward Ocean Ave. Turn left on Ocean Ave. (which becomes Ocean Blvd.) and go about 0.4 miles to Howland Ave., on the right. This road makes a short loop along the bluff overlooking the beach and jetties. Over the years, this area has often had Harlequin Duck. When the road returns to Ocean Blvd., turn right and go one-half mile to Bath Ave. Go one block to Ocean Ave. and turn left. The jetties along Ocean are worth scanning. In about one mile you will come to the Long Branch fishing pier, a favorite roosting site for Great Cormorant in winter.

If you have stopped at every spot along this route, it is now probably too dark to see. To return to the Garden State Parkway, continue north on Ocean Ave. for about 0.5 miles to Rt. 36. Turn left and follow Rt. 36 for about 6 miles to the Parkway.

There are no public rest rooms open in winter along the North Shore route. You may want to stop at a diner for coffee or lunch and use its facilities; there are also many service stations.

Cattus Island Park

Cattus Island Park is located on the shores of Barnegat Bay, about 3 miles northeast of Toms River. Its 497 acres, managed by the Ocean County Parks and Recreation Department, include both pine-oak woodland and salt marsh. Although it is not known for any rare or unusual species, the park is a good spot to see birds native to the bays and adjacent uplands of coastal New Jersey. Since these coastal areas are rapidly diminishing because of development, Cattus Island offers a birding environment not easily found in New Jersey.

Directions

Take the Garden State Parkway to Exit 82 (Rt. 37 East). Follow Rt. 37 east toward Seaside Heights for about 4.5 miles to Spur Rt. 549 (Fischer Blvd.). Turn left, via a jughandle, onto Rt. 549 and go north about 2.1 miles to Cattus Island Blvd. Turn right and drive about 100 yards to the park entrance, on the left. Follow the entrance road for almost a mile to the parking area at the Cooper Environmental Center.

Birding

Go into the modern Nature Center, which has rest rooms, and obtain a copy of the trail map and a bird checklist. There are two main areas to the park, with two or three trails in each area. The western area consists mainly of Pine Barrens woodland, with a short section of swamp and salt marsh along a boardwalk that starts on the south side of the Nature Center. The boardwalk connects with the red trail, which leads in turn to the blue trail and the yellow trail; all three trails wander through typical Pine Barrens habitats.

MAP 56. Cattus Island Park

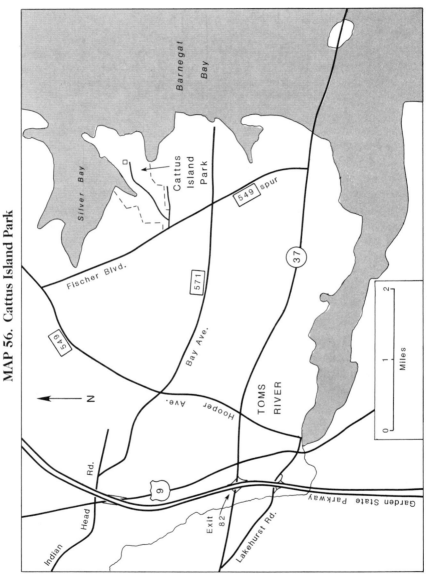

The eastern section of the park is perhaps more interesting, especially a maintenance road which runs from the north side of the Nature Center across a salt marsh to an island, then over the island and across more salt marsh to another, smaller, island. Here the road ends on a point of land that separates Silver Bay on the west from Barnegat Bay on the east. The orange trail makes a circuit of the larger island, including a field where a mansion formerly stood.

Breeding birds in the western part of Cattus Island Park include Northern Bobwhite; Whip-poor-will; Carolina Wren; Brown Thrasher; White-eyed Vireo; Blue-winged, Yellow, Pine, Prairie, and Black-and-white Warblers; and other typical Pine Barrens species.

The two islands and the salt marsh in the eastern part of the park offer a greater diversity of habitat than the westen part. Additional breeding birds here include Clapper Rail, Marsh Wren, and Sharp-tailed, Seaside, and Swamp Sparrows. In summer, various herons and egrets frequent the salt marsh, while offshore in migration and in winter there are many ducks and geese, especially diving ducks. A few species of shorebirds visit the tidal edges, mainly in fall. Numerous raptors pass through the park in migration, especially Northern Harrier and American Kestrel; Merlin and Peregrine Falcon are regular in the fall. Winter is a quiet time at Cattus Island, except for the waterfowl in Barnegat Bay. A stop at this attractive little park is easily combined with a visit to Island Beach State Park.

Island Beach State Park

Island Beach State Park contains one of the few unspoiled stretches of barrier beach on the New Jersey coast. The park is almost 10 miles long, but is only a few hundred yards wide over most of its length. It retains the native vegetation of Dune Grass, Beach Plum, Bayberry, and American Holly, and a large portion of the park is protected as a botanical preserve.

Forming as it does part of our outer coastal strip, Island Beach is an excellent place to see both migrant land- and seabirds, especially in fall. Sea watching can be very productive in October and November, when such species as Northern Gannet, Parasitic Jaeger, and Black-legged Kittiwake regularly occur, along with thousands of loons, cormorants, geese, and ducks. Land birding can be frustrating because of the severely restricted access to most of the park, but such rarities as Orange-crowned Warbler, Clay-colored Sparrow, and Lark Sparrow are seen every year. Operation Recovery, a fall bird-banding project conducted at Island Beach for almost 30 years, has resulted in the capture of many rarities, some of which have never occurred elsewhere in New Jersey.

In winter, Island Beach has wintering loons, Great Cormorant, sea ducks, gulls, Snow Bunting, Lapland Longspur (rare), and occasionally a Snowy Owl. In addition to the birds mentioned above, rare or unusual species that have occurred here in recent years (other than netted birds) include Cory's Shearwater (rare from shore), Brown Pelican, Harlequin Duck (annual), Little Gull, Lesser Black-backed Gull, and Say's Phoebe. Other vagrants have included Long-tailed Jaeger, Ivory Gull, and Bridled Tern.

Directions

Take the Garden State Parkway to Exit 82 (Rt. 37, Toms River). Go east on Rt. 37 for about 6.8 miles, crossing the bridge over Barnegat

Bay, and exit right at the sign for Island Beach State Park, Seaside Park. After about 0.7 miles and several curves, you will be headed south on N. Central Ave. Continue south for another 2 miles to the state park entrance. An entrance fee, charged year round, is higher in summer, but has reached $4.00 off-season in 1990.

Birding

Drive south along the park road, watching the roadside in fall for sparrows and the trees for perched Merlins and Peregrine Falcons. About 3.5 miles south of the tollbooth you will come to the first bathhouse, which offers indoor rest rooms from spring through fall and outdoor portable toilets in winter. Walk along the left side of the building toward the beach, where you will find a wooden platform at the edge of the dunes; the slight elevation of this platform makes it an excellent lookout for scanning the sea.

The best times for a sea watch are October and November, although winter and early spring can also be good. In fall, a good migration day can produce hundreds of Red-throated and Common Loons, Double-crested cormorant (mainly September–October), scaup, and scoters. Occasionally, mixed in with the other ducks, you will see a Common Eider, King Eider, or Harlequin Duck. Laughing Gull and Common Tern are abundant migrants at this season. If the winds are from the east, you may see dozens of Northern Gannets migrating or fishing offshore; usually they stay at least a quarter-mile off, but sometimes they come closer. In November and December you may see Black-legged Kittiwake as well. Other pelagic species that get blown close to shore on easterly winds are Parasitic Jaeger (September–October) and Cory's Shearwater (rare). In winter, there is a possibility of an alcid, but I have never been lucky enough to see one at Island Beach.

One of the best places at Island Beach for fall migrant sparrows is the maintenance area between the parking lots for the two bathhouses. From the first bathhouse, drive or walk to the south side of the parking lot, checking the edges of the lot for songbirds. Yellow-rumped Warblers are abundant, Orange-crowned Warbler is rare but regular, and many different kinds of sparrows can be expected in October and November. The maintenance area is just beyond the south end of the parking lot. Clay-colored and Lark Sparrows have been seen here, and Lincoln's and White-crowned Sparrows are regular.

Return to your car and continue driving south along the park road, still watching the road edges for feeding sparrows—I have found Clay-colored and Lark Sparrows in this way. About 4.8 miles from the bathhouse you will come to the end of the road at the last parking area. If you feel up to an invigorating hike, you can reach the south end of the park by walking along the beach for about 1.5 miles. Along the way, scan the ocean for seabirds and the dunes for Snow Bunting—and for Snowy Owl, which has occurred here in some winters.

At the south end of the peninsula, a long jetty guards the north side of Barnegat Inlet. If the tide and weather permit, it is worth hiking out this jetty as far as you can. From late fall to early spring, you will see Great Cormorants sitting on the tower at the end, and you may find Harlequin Duck, eiders, or alcids along the edges of the rocks. Purple Sandpiper is common from late fall to May and other shorebirds, such as Sanderling, Dunlin, and Ruddy Turnstone, are often present as well.

Also, from late fall to early spring, a walk inland from the jetty along the inlet may produce Horned Lark, Snow Bunting, and, occasionally, Lapland Longspur feeding in the grassy areas at the edges of the dunes. Large flocks of gulls sometimes gather at the southern end of Island Beach, so be sure to look for Iceland, Glaucous, and Lesser Black-backed Gulls. At certain times, many hundreds of Bonaparte's Gulls gather to feed in the channel of Barnegat Inlet. At such times, you have a fair chance of seeing a Little Gull or a Common Black-headed Gull among them, but the gatherings are very erratic and unpredictable.

Additional Birding Spots in North Coastal New Jersey

Cheesequake State Park

The Raritan Bay area in eastern Middlesex County is the site of this 1,000-acre state park. Cheesequake encompasses a range of habitats, including dry Pitch Pine woods, mature upland deciduous forest, freshwater marsh, salt marsh, and an Atlantic White Cedar swamp. A variety of birds visit the park, mainly during spring and fall migrations. Both Black-capped and Carolina Chickadees can be found here because the park lies within the narrow zone of overlap of these two species.

Directions

Take the Garden State Parkway to Exit 120 (Lawrence Harbor). Turn right onto Lawrence Harbor—Morristown Rd. and go about 0.2 miles to Cliffwood Ave. Turn right onto Cliffwood, drive about 0.2 miles, and turn right onto Gordon Rd. The entrance to the state park is about 0.3 miles ahead. Continue past the tollbooth (a fee is charged in the summer) to the parking area for the Nature Trail.

Hartshorne Woods

This Monmouth County park contains several hundred acres of upland deciduous forest on the highlands above Sandy Hook (see Map 53). The park has migrant songbirds in spring and fall and supports a small variety of breeding birds.

Directions

Follow the directions for Sandy Hook. About 0.8 miles past the traffic light in Atlantic Highlands, bear right at a traffic light onto Leonardville Rd., where Rt. 36 bears left. Go about 0.6 miles, then turn left onto Navesink Ave. A parking area for the park is about one-half mile ahead on the right.

Manasquan River Wildlife Management Area

Located just east of the Garden State Parkway along the Monmouth–Ocean County Line, this 726-acre WMA includes both fields and deciduous woodland, as well as some riparian habitat along the Manasquan River. This spot receives little attention from birders, so, it is difficult to assess its full potential, but it has many of the same species as nearby Allaire State Park. The location of the area is shown on Map 55.

Directions

Take the Garden State Parkway to Exit 98 (Rt. 34, Point Pleasant). Turn right onto Allenwood Rd. immediately after passing under the Parkway. The road enters the WMA in a little over one mile. Other points of access are along Ramshorn Dr., which is the second left turn off Allenwood Rd.

Shark River Park

Owned by the Monmouth County Park Commission, this park encompasses more than 1,000 acres of recreational facilities, woods, fields, and riparian habitat along the Shark River. The main entrance to the park is off Schoolhouse Rd., but there is also access along Gully Rd.

Directions

Take the Garden State Parkway to Exit 100 (Rt. 33). Go east on Rt. 33 for 0.4 miles, then turn right onto Schoolhouse Rd. The park entrance is about one-half mile on the left. Gully Rd. is about 0.4 miles east of Schoolhouse Rd. on Rt. 33.

Tatum Park

Also belonging to Monmouth County, this park contains an interesting mix of deciduous woods, thickets, and tangles in a hilly section of Middletown. It is excellent for songbirds in migration and provides sufficient food and cover to harbor good numbers of birds in winter.

Directions

Take the Garden State Parkway to Exit 114 (Holmdel). From the exit ramp, turn left if coming from the north, right if coming from the south, onto Red Hill Rd. Go about 0.3 miles to the first intersection, where Red Hill Rd. bears right. Continue on Red Hill Rd. for about 1.5 miles to the park entrance, on the left.

Manasquan River Reservoir

A new birding spot opened in 1990; this 1,100-acre recreation area includes the 740-acre reservoir. Recreation facilities are managed by the Monmouth County Park Commission, which currently provides access at two points: the main parking area and boat ramp on Windeler Road, and a small parking lot on Georgia Tavern Road, both open from 8:00 A.M. to dusk. A five-mile-long perimeter trail circles the reservoir.

Directions

From the north or the coast, take the Garden State Parkway to Exit 98 (Interstate 195). Go west on I-195 for about 7 miles to Exit 28B (Rt. 9 North). Turn immediately right at the traffic light onto Georgia Tavern Rd., go 0.3 miles and turn right onto Windeler Rd.; drive about 1.6 miles to the recreation area entrance, on the left. The second parking area is on Georgia Tavern Rd., about 1 mile beyond the turnoff for Windeler Rd.

From the west, take the New Jersey Turnpike to Exit 7 (Interstate 195), then follow I-195 east for about 21 miles to Exit 28B and proceed as just described.

Kentucky Warbler

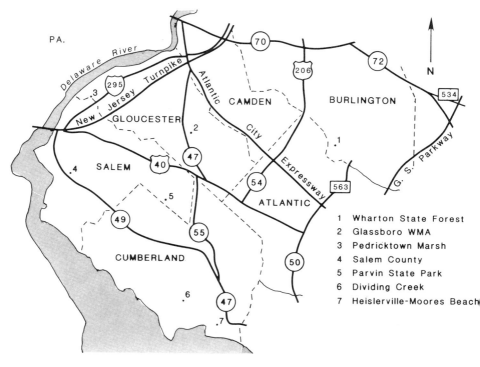

MAP 57. Southwest Region

1 Wharton State Forest
2 Glassboro WMA
3 Pedricktown Marsh
4 Salem County
5 Parvin State Park
6 Dividing Creek
7 Heislerville-Moores Beach

Southwest

Wharton State Forest

More than 100,000 acres of unspoiled wilderness invites the adventurous birder to explore this little known area of New Jersey. Wharton State Forest, in the heart of the Pine Barrens, lies mostly in southern Burlington County, with smaller sections in adjacent Atlantic and Camden counties. It is a canoeist's paradise, with numerous rivers and streams that flow gently through cedar swamps, pines, and deciduous woods toward the Atlantic Ocean. US 206 crosses the western part of the tract at Atsion and there are a few other paved roads around the perimeter, but none in the interior. In fact, no other area in New Jersey is farther from a paved road than the central part of the Wharton Tract, as it was formerly known. There are numerous sand roads, however, that connect the former iron-foundry towns of Atsion and Batsto with the ruins of Hampton Furnace, Quaker Bridge, Washington Forge, and many other places.

The Pine Barrens is better known for its interesting plants, reptiles, and amphibians (including the endangered Pine Barrens Tree Frog) than for its birds. The birdlife of Wharton State Forest is similar to that of Lebanon State Forest (covered in its own chapter). Some of the more unusual breeding birds to look and listen for are Northern Saw-whet Owl (rare in summer); Common Nighthawk; Whip-poor-will; Brown Creeper; Eastern Bluebird; Hermit Thrush; Black-throated Green, Prothonotary, Hooded, and Canada Warblers; and Summer Tanager. There is still much to be learned about the birdlife of the Pine Barrens, as was shown in 1981, when Ted Proctor discovered a large nesting population of Hermit Thrushes in Wharton State Forest.

Directions

From northern New Jersey, take the New Jersey Turnpike south to Exit 7 (Bordentown). Stay left through the tollbooth and merge onto

US 206 South. Follow this for 37 miles to US 30 in Hammonton, then turn left. Go east on US 30 for about 1.4 miles to Rt. 542 and turn left. In about 7 miles, you will come to Batsto Village Historical Site, which is also the state forest headquarters.

From the north coast, take the Garden State Parkway south to Exit 52 (New Gretna). From the exit ramp turn left onto Rt. 654, go one mile, and turn right onto US 9. Follow US 9 through New Gretna for about 1.5 miles to Rt. 542. Turn right onto Rt. 542 and go about 13 miles to Batsto.

From the south coast, take the Parkway north to Exit 50 (New Gretna). Go about one mile north on US 9 to Rt. 542. Turn left onto Rt. 542 and proceed as above.

From the Philadelphia area, take the Atlantic City Expressway south to Exit 28 (Hammonton). Follow Rt. 54 toward Hammonton for about 2 miles to Rt. 542 and turn right. Batsto is about 9 miles.

Birding

Wharton State Forest is best explored with the help of USGS topographic maps. These can usually be purchased at either Lebanon State Forest headquarters (see Map 49) or Wharton State Forest headquarters in Batsto, where a less detailed map of the forest is also available. Most of Wharton lies within the Atsion, Chatsworth, Green Bank, Hammonton, Indian Mills, Jenkins, and Medford Lakes quadrangles.

The Nature Trail at Batsto covers about 2 miles of Pine Barrens upland, where you will encounter a good sampling of the common birds. Most of the more interesting birds of the area are found along streams, in hardwood swamps, or around cedar swamps; such areas are best explored by canoe or by driving some of the sand roads with the help of topo maps. Many of the sand roads can be driven in an ordinary car, but do so with caution as you do not want to get stuck miles from the nearest telephone. It is best to inquire with the forest rangers about road conditions.

Bird species associated with Pine Barrens cedar swamps (especially Red Maple–White Cedar swamps) are Saw-whet Owl (rare); Brown Creeper; Black-and-white, Prothonotary, Black-throated Green, and Canada Warblers; and Louisiana (uncommon) and Northern (rare) Waterthrushes. The drier, open pine-oak forests are where you may find Common Nighthawk, Whip-poor-will, Eastern Bluebird, Hermit Thrush and Summer Tanager. Hermit Thrushes have been found near Quaker Bridge and about 2 miles northwest of Washington Forge. Before 1981, this species was not known to nest in New Jersey south of the northwestern highlands, although it is a regular breeder in similar pine-oak habitat on Long Island.

The Batona Trail, mentioned in the Lebanon State Forest chapter, also traverses 25 miles of varied habitat in Wharton State Forest, stretching from Evans Bridge to Batsto to Quaker Bridge to Apple Pie Hill. By exploring this and other areas of the state forest, you might locate some unusual species, such as Red Crossbill and White-winged Crossbill, both of which nested farther north in the Pine Barrens in the 1930s. Or, you might happen upon a Swainson's Warbler, which has never been proved to nest in New Jersey, though there are frequent rumors of its nesting in swamps of "the Barrens."

Glassboro Wildlife Management Area

(Glassboro Woods)

Glassboro Wildlife Management Area (or Glassboro Woods, as the area is known to birders) is a 2,337-acre tract located on the southeastern edge of Glassboro in central Gloucester County. It is an excellent place to observe the spring migration of songbirds and has an interesting variety of nesting species. Hooded Warbler is an abundant breeder, and Kentucky Warbler is perhaps more easily found here than anywhere else in New Jersey. Prothonotary Warbler, Worm-eating Warbler, and Louisiana Waterthrush are also among the 13 species of warblers that nest in the woods. Warbler flights also can be good in fall, and Connecticut Warbler has occurred then.

Most of our knowledge of the birdlife of Glassboro Woods comes from Jim Meritt, who has birded the tract for many years; the area deserves more attention from other birders, who usually bypass the woods on their way to points further south. Especially during the breeding season, some diligent searching might turn up an interesing addition to the list of nesting species.

NOTE: Glassboro Woods is managed for hunting. During the hunting season (September–December), visits should be made only on Sundays. The roads through the woods may be in bad shape in the early spring; portions of the roads have been washed away at times and there are no warning signs. By late spring the roads are usually repaired.

Directions

Although there are four entrances to the WMA, the most accessible is the western entrance off Rt. 47 at Carpenter Ave., a good dirt road that bisects the tract. To reach this entrance:

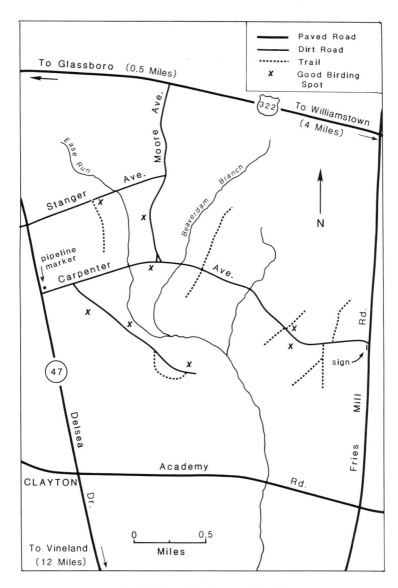

MAP 58. Glassboro WMA

From northern New Jersey, take the New Jersey Turnpike south to Exit 3 (Camden). Stay left after going through the tollbooth and merge onto Rt. 168 South (Black Horse Pike). Go about 0.9 miles to Rt. 41 and turn right. Follow Rt. 41 south for 5 miles to Rt. 47, then continue straight ahead on Rt. 47. After 5.8 miles you will pass the turnoff for US 322 East. From here it is about 1.2 miles to Stanger Ave. on the left, one of the entrances to the woods. If you continue past Stanger 0.5 miles, you will come to a dirt road on the left with a red gas pipeline marker on the corner. This is Carpenter Ave.; the Gloucester County Road Department is just beyond it on the right.

From the Philadelphia area, take Interstate 76 or 676 south to Rt. 42 (the North-South Freeway). Exit at Rt. 41 and go south for about 3.4 miles to Rt. 47, then continue as described in the preceding paragraph.

From coastal New Jersey, take the Atlantic City Expressway north to Exit 38 (Sicklerville). Turn left onto Sicklerville Rd. (Spur Rt. 536), and go about 2 miles to US 322. Turn right onto US 322 West and go 7 miles to Rt. 47 in Glassboro. Carpenter Ave. is 1.7 miles south (left) on Rt. 47.

Birding

Most of Glassboro Woods is heavily wooded, with areas of lowland deciduous swamp and oak-pine forest. A number of open patches and hedgerows are maintained for wildlife. The terrain is very flat, and the several streams that run through the tract create extensive wet areas where the swamp vegetation flourishes. Red Maple, Sweetgum, Black Gum (Tupelo), Gray Birch, and Sassafras (the latter two around the drier edges) are the dominant trees, mixed with a few Atlantic White Cedars; the understory is a dense and impenetrable tangle of Sweet Pepperbush, Mountain Laureal, blueberries, azaleas, and other shrubs. The drier areas support a more open forest consisting of either mature oaks and hickories with a Scrub Oak–Mountain Laurel understory or a mixed oak–Pitch Pine woods.

The woods are at their best during spring migration. While the flights are not as heavy as those in some of the better known areas farther north, they do produce a wide variety of warblers and other migrants. In addition, the woods have the virtue of being a quiet and little-used spot where you can bird in relative solitude. About 70 species of birds nest here, and May and early June are good times to search for them. Later in the summer, the insects are so abundant that birding is difficult. The woods do not receive much attention in the fall, particularly after the hunting season begins, but the warbler flights in late August and September can be good.

There are several passable dirt roads through parts of the WMA, and numerous trails branch off from the roads. Carpenter Ave. bisects the area from Rt. 47 on the west to Fries Mill Rd. on the east, a distance of about 2.6 miles. The road goes through all the available habitat types, so it is a good place to start your birding; the western part is especially productive.

About one-quarter mile in from Rt. 47, a road branches off from Carpenter Ave. to the right. You can take this road south for about one mile until it ends at a turnaround. On the left, the road parallels a stream through a swampy woodland; on the right are somewhat drier woods with a few clearings. At the end of the road is an open area of oaks and pines. Most of the characteristic species of the tract can be found along this road, including Ruffed Grouse; Northern Bobwhite; Yellow-billed Cuckoo; Red-bellied Woodpecker; Great Crested and Acadian (uncommon) Flycatchers; Eastern Wood Pewee; Carolina Wren; Blue-gray Gnatcatcher; Wood Thrush; Brown Thrasher; White-eyed Vireo; Blue-winged, Yellow, Pine, Prairie, Black-and-white, Kentucky, and Hooded Warblers; American Redstart; Louisiana Waterthrush; Yellow-breasted Chat (open areas); and Scarlet Tanager.

Other noteworthy species that breed on the tract are Broad-winged Hawk; Eastern Screech, Great Horned, and (probably) Barred Owls; Whip-poor-will; Ruby-throated Hummingbird; Brown Creeper (rare, not every year); Cedar Waxwing; Yellow-throated Vireo; Prothonotary (along streams) and Worm-eating (irregular) Warblers. A little additional field work in late May or early June might add Willow Flycatcher, Yellow-throated Warbler (has occurred in spring), Summer Tanager, Blue Grosbeak, or other species to the list of breeding birds.

Return to Carpenter Ave. and turn right. About 0.6 miles farther on is the junction with Moore Ave. on the left. Kentucky Warbler nests in the woods around the field on the south side of this intersection. Moore Ave. goes north for about 1.3 miles to US 322. Along the way it passes through some oak woodlands where Hooded Warbler is abundant. About 0.6 miles up Moore Ave. is the junction with Stanger Ave., which leads west out to Rt. 47. Stanger crosses a stream called Little Ease Run where Prothonotary Warbler has nested for years.

Continuing east on Carpenter Ave. from Moore Ave., you will cross another stream, Beaverdam Branch, then pass through alternating sections of dry oak-pine woods and wet deciduous swamp until you reach the eastern end of the tract at Fries Mill Rd. Along the way there are numerous side trails to be explored. The trails are mainly old roads that are no longer suitable for driving; they make for easy walking, although you may encounter some wet spots.

To return to the intersection of Rt. 47 and US 322, you can either retrace your route on Carpenter Ave. or go north on Fries Mill Rd. for 1.3 miles to US 322, then west on 322 for about 3 miles to Rt. 47.

Pedricktown Marsh

Pedricktown is famous for the annual spring gathering of Ruffs in the marshes of Oldman's Creek, just north of town. Many other shore-birds stop off here in April, including Lesser Golden-Plover, Common Snipe, Pectoral Sandpiper and both yellowlegs, but they yield center stage to the star attraction.

Directions

To reach the causeway across the marsh at Pedricktown:

From northern New Jersey, take the New Jersey Turnpike south to Exit 2 (Swedesboro). After passing through the tollbooth, turn left onto US 322 West. Go 4 miles to Interstate 295, and take I-295 southbound. Go about 1.6 miles to Exit 10 (Center Square Rd.) and turn right (west) onto Center Square Rd. (An alternative route is to take the Turnpike south to either Exit 7 or Exit 4 and cross over to I-295, then continue south to Exit 10 on I-295.) Drive one mile to the first crossroads and turn left; this is Pedricktown Rd., although the street sign may be missing. After about a mile, the road becomes a causeway across the extensive marshes of Oldman's Creek.

From the Philadelphia area, you can take either Interstate 76 or Interstate 676 to I-295, then go south to Exit 10 and proceed as above. Or, take Interstate 95 south to the US 322 exit in Chester, then follow Rt. 322 across the Barry Bridge to US 130. Turn right onto 130, go about one mile, and turn left onto High Hill Rd., just past the marshes of Raccoon Creek. Pedricktown Rd. is about 1.3 miles ahead, on the right; the marshes of Oldman's Creek are about 1.6 miles south on Pedricktown Rd.

From coastal New Jersey, take the Atlantic City Expressway to I-295, then go south for about 15 miles to Exit 10 at Center Square Rd.

MAP 59. Pedricktown Marsh

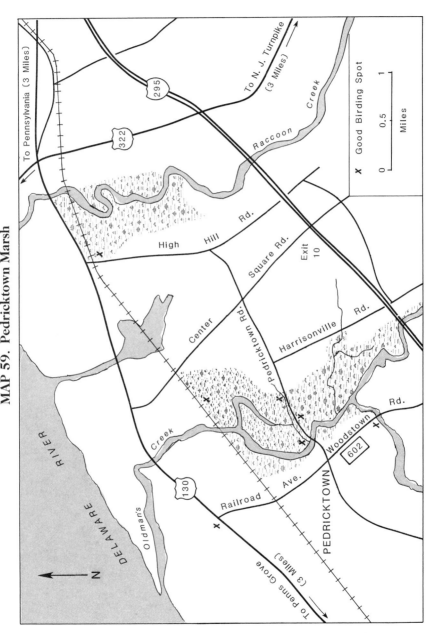

Birding

Pedricktown Rd. is a causeway across the marsh for about 0.6 miles to the bridge at Oldman's Creek, but the marshes extend for a couple of miles east and west of the road. At the monthly spring tides (at full and new moon), the road is under water. The first Ruffs, still in winter plumage, arrive as early as the middle of March, although in some years none are found before April. By the time the last ones depart at the end of April, they will be in full breeding dress, each male different from the others, with the magnificent, colorful ruffs that give them their name. As many as a dozen individuals may pass through in some seasons, including several females (Reeves), attractive birds but not as spectacular as the males. The maximum number of males present at any one time is usually three or four.

The best times to find Ruffs is usually 1–3 hours before (best) or 1–3 hours after high tide. (High tide at Pedricktown occurs about five hours later than at Sandy Hook or Cape May, and about one-half hour earlier than at Philadelphia.) At low tide, the exposed mudflats are so extensive that picking out the birds is nearly hopeless. A spotting scope is indispensable. Finding the Ruffs requires careful and frequent scanning of the mudflats. The rising tide forces the birds out of some of the more remote areas of this large system of marshes and (frequently) into the gradually dwindling spots closer to the Pedricktown causeway.

Although you can occasionally see them fly in, the Ruffs usually just appear out of nowhere on one of the mud islands. As high tide approaches, all the mud becomes submerged and the birds fly off to some other spot. They frequently return on the falling tide, then disappear for hours as the tide remains low. Seeing the Ruffs at Pedricktown is not a sure thing; you might be lucky enough to drive up and find them there, but many birders have scanned for hours and gone home disappointed. Patient, diligent scanning is the key to success.

Migrant Tundra Swans stop off at Pedricktown in February and early March and sometimes linger into April; flocks of 200–300 are common. A variety of other spring migrant waterfowl can be seen, especially Green-winged Teal, which walk around on the mud and feed on the marsh vegetation. King Rail nests in the marshes and is occasionally seen swimming in one of the channels or scurrying across an open expanse of mud. The most common breeding bird, however, is Common Moorhen, which vies with Muskrat for the title of most abundant animal on the Pedricktown marsh.

The Ruffs usually arrive with early groups of Greater Yellowlegs. By the end of March, other shorebirds have begun to arrive, especially Lesser Yellowlegs, Common Snipe, and Pectoral Sandpiper. As many as 400 Pectorals have been seen in mid-April, making Pedricktown the best place in the state to observe this species in spring. A few Lesser Golden-Plover (up to 15) appear in early April, and some of them stay to the end of the month. By the time they depart, one or two may have acquired most of the spectacular breeding plumage that we seldom see in New Jersey. Other shorebirds that occur regularly during April are Black-bellied and Semipalmated Plovers, Killdeer, Spotted and Least Sandpipers, Dunlin, and Short-billed Dowitcher.

Although shorebirds are the main attraction, Pedricktown has other things to see as well. Migrant hawks, mainly Northern Harriers, Broad-winged and Red-tailed Hawks, and American Kestrels, pass through in April. A pair of Peregrine Falcons has recently taken up residence under the nearby Commodore Barry Bridge and sometimes is seen harassing the ducks and shorebirds over the marsh. In 1984, a pair of Great Horned Owls nested in some trees on an island in the marsh; during March and April, the hen could be seen sitting on the nest with her rapidly growing chick.

Migrant swallows are a familiar sight over the marsh in April, when all the eastern species can be expected (although Cliff Swallow is uncommon). By mid-April other early migrants start to appear, and they and the local residents tune up their spring songs. The marsh and nearby woods resound with the familiar songs of Eastern Phoebe; Carolina Chickadee; Carolina and House Wrens; Gray Catbird; Northern Mockingbird; Brown Thrasher; White-eyed Vireo; Yellow Warbler; Common Yellowthroat; Rufous-sided Towhee; Chipping, Song, and Swamp Sparrows; Red-winged Blackbird; and House Finch.

After birding the marsh at Pedricktown, continue south across the bridge into town. Turn right at the first intersection (Railroad Ave.) and drive about 1.3 miles to US 130. The field diagonally across 130 to the left is frequently flooded in spring, and is an excellent spot for Common Snipe. Many of the other shorebirds seen in the Pedricktown marshes, including an occasional Ruff, can be found here also.

To reach another spot where you can get a view of the marsh at Oldman's Creek, drive north on US 130 from Railroad Ave. for about 1.4 miles to the first right turn (Center Square Rd.). Go about 0.6 miles to some railroad tracks and park on the right. Walking southwest along the railroad for several hundred yards will take you into the north corner of the marsh, about one mile from the Pedricktown Rd. causeway, which you can see to the south.

Another good shorebirding spot that receives relatively little attention is the marsh at Raccoon Creek. To reach it, go back to US 130 and turn right. Go north on 130 for about 1.6 miles to the second right turn, at High Hill Rd. Go about 100 yards on High Hill and park at the railroad tracks. The Raccoon Creek marsh extends for more than one-half miles to your left (northeast). By walking along the tracks (watch out for trains; the tracks are used occasionally) you'll get a good view of the marsh.

Most birders combine a visit to Pedricktown with a trip to some of the other interesting Salem County spots, which are covered in the Salem County Tour chapter.

To return home: US 130 North leads back to US 322 East or West (just beyond Raccoon Creek) and merges a few miles further on with I-295; US 322 West leads across the Barry Bridge to Pennsylvania; and US 322 East will take you back to the New Jersey Turnpike (about 6 miles).

Another spot where the Ruffs have been seen in recent years is where Harrisonville Rd. crosses part of the marshes of Oldman's Creek. From the north end of the Pedricktown Rd. causeway, go north for 0.3 miles to the first right turn, Harrisonville Rd. Go 0.7 miles and park on the right, just before the bridge. The Ruffs may be on either side of the bridge.

WARNING: Do not park on the Pedricktown Rd. causeway; you may get a ticket and will annoy the local residents, whose good will is important to the welfare of the marshes.

Salem County Tour

Salem County, an area long neglected by most of the state's birders, has received increasing attention in recent years not only because of the Ruffs at Pedricktown, but also because of Upland Sandpipers near Sharptown, Lesser Golden-Plovers at Pedricktown and Mannington Marsh, and the growing population of Black Vultures in the central part of the county. Birders from the more populous regions are now discovering what local residents have known for many years: There are many good birds and birding areas in Salem County. The locations described below provide a sampling of the better spots, but there are many others to be investigated. Parvin State Park, a beautiful 1,125-acre preserve in southeastern Salem County, and Pedricktown, with its Ruffs, are covered in their own chapters.

Directions

Because most birders visit Salem County during their spring treks to the marshes of Pedricktown, the directions for this tour start in the center of Pedricktown (see Map 59).

County Rt. 602 is the first intersection south of the bridge across Oldman's Creek; it is called Railroad Ave. on the west and Pedricktown-Woodstown Rd. on the east. Take Pedricktown-Woodstown Rd. east for about 4.2 miles to Auburn-Sharptown Rd. (Toward the end of this 4.2-mile stretch, you will cross the New Jersey Turnpike; Auburn-Sharptown Rd. is just beyond the Turnpike, on the right.) Go south for 1.8 miles to Featherbed Lane and turn left.

This point also can be reached directly from the New Jersey Turnpike Exit 2 (Swedesboro). Go west on US 322 for 0.8 miles to Rt. 551 (Kings Highway). Follow Rt. 551 south for 5 miles through Swedesboro (where it becomes Auburn Rd.), and continue to Auburn. Bear left in town, then take the first left turn, cross the New Jersey Turn-

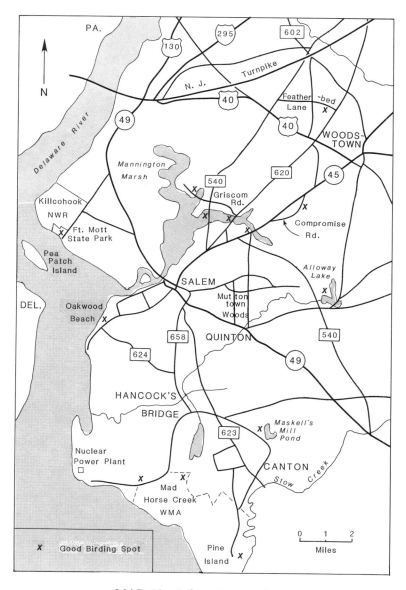

MAP 60. Salem County Tour

pike and turn immediately right onto Auburn-Sharptown Rd. Continue south 1.8 miles to Featherbed Lane and turn left.

Birding

Just over half a mile along Featherbed Lane, you will come to the crest of a hill that overlooks beautiful pastures on both sides of the road. The fields stretch for another half-mile to Swedesboro Rd. (Rt. 620). Among the birds nesting in these fields are Upland Sandpiper, Savannah and Grasshopper Sparrows, Bobolink, and Eastern Meadowlark. The "Uppies" arrive during the last part of April and can frequently be heard giving their marvelous courtship song. There are fewer than a dozen places in New Jersey where this species is known to nest, and Featherbed Lane is one of two sites in Salem County.

Huge flocks of Canada Geese feed on the pastures in spring, and the pond on the south side of the road attracts Ring-billed Gulls, Killdeer, and occasionally Ring-necked Ducks. Large numbers of Turkey Vultures usually can be seen soaring off to the east and south, and a Black Vulture or two is frequently among them. A Scissor-tailed Flycatcher was seen along Featherbed Lane in June 1982.

Continue on Featherbed Lane to Swedesboro Rd. and turn right. Go south for 1.5 miles to US 40 and turn left. Follow Rt. 40 east for about 1.6 miles (watching for Black Vulture along the way) to the traffic light on Rt. 45. Turn right and go about 2.2 miles to the left turn onto Compromise Rd. (the second left after the Vo-Tech School). Compromise Rd. makes a 2.3-mile loop, eventually rejoining Rt. 45. At least one pair of Upland Sandpipers has recently nested in the fields that stretch along the left side of the road for the first half-mile. This area has been the stronghold of the Black Vulture population in Salem County, so keep an eye to the sky and watch for birds perched on fenceposts or in trees.

When Compromise Rd. rejoins Rt. 45, turn left onto Rt. 45 and go 0.4 miles to a creek and park on the right; this is Mannington Creek and the upper reaches of Mannington Marsh. In addition to being a good area for Black Vulture, Mannington Marsh attracts many migrant waterfowl in spring and fall. Because it is tidal, there are a few good spots for shorebirds, as well. Herons and egrets from the Pea

Patch Island, Delaware, heronry (only about 8 miles away) come here to feed in the extensive marshes. Great and Little Blue Herons, Great and Snowy Egrets, Cattle Egret (in the fields), Black-crowned Night-Heron, and Glossy Ibis are common; Tricolored Heron is also seen.

The section of the marsh west of Rt. 45 to Swedesboro Rd. about a mile, is good for grebes and migrant waterfowl. Some birds, especially Canada Geese, winter at Mannington, but the greatest variety of species occurs in March and April. Pied-billed and Horned Grebes are common in spring. Large flocks of Tundra Swans (several hundred) stop off on their way north, and there are usually a few Snow Geese among the Canadas. Green-winged Teal, Northern Pintail, Northern Shoveler, Gadwall, and American Wigeon are the common migrant dabbling ducks, while Ring-necked Duck, Common Merganser, and Ruddy Duck are the common divers. The same species occur in the fall (October–November), but (except for the Canadas) usually in smaller flocks.

Continue south on Rt. 45 for another 1.2 miles, then turn right onto Gordon Rd.; follow this 0.6 miles to its end, and turn right onto Swedesboro Rd. (Rt. 620). Go one-half mile and park on the shoulder of the causeway across Mannington Creek. Here you have a view east toward Rt. 45, and west, across a big expanse of water, toward Rt. 540. This is the best vantage point for observing migrant ducks, which seem to prefer the areas within a half-mile of Swedesboro Rd.

At the far end of the causeway, turn left onto Griscom Rd. and go 1.1 miles to Rt. 540 (Pointers-Auburn Rd.). Turn left on Rt. 540; in about 0.4 miles you will reach a long causeway that crosses Mannington Marsh. The best shorebirding area is on the right toward the northern end of the causeway. Because there is no place to park here on this heavily traveled road, the safest practice is to drive to the south end of the causeway, where there is ample parking room, and walk back.

Shorebirding at Mannington Marsh is only possible when the tide is low; for several hours before and after high tide (which occurs about one hour earlier than at Philadelphia and 4 hours later than at Sandy Hook), the mudflats are underwater and the birds are elsewhere. The best month for migrants is April, before the marsh vegetation has grown too thick. If the flats are exposed, walk north along the causeway about three-quarters of the way across, and scan for

Lesser Golden-Plover on the mud where there is emerging vegetation. Check for Ruff, too—at least one is seen here every spring. As you walk back toward your car, look for roosting gulls farther out on the bare mudflats. Scan the gulls (mainly Ring-billed and Laughing) for Forster's and Caspian Terns. This is probably the best spot in New Jersey for finding Caspian Tern in spring.

Continue south on Rt. 540 to Rt. 45 (1.2 miles), bear right onto Rt. 45 and follow it into Salem to the intersection with Rt. 45 (2 miles). At this point, you can turn right for a side trip to Fort Mott State Park or turn left to continue the tour.

To reach Fort Mott, go west on Rt. 49 for about 2.8 miles, then bear left on Lighthouse Rd. Go 2.4 miles to Fort Mott Rd., and turn left toward the park; the entrance is one mile ahead on the right. This 104-acre park preserves historic Fort Mott, built near the mouth of the Delaware River to guard the approach to Philadelphia from the sea. The fort looks across the river to Pea Patch Island and New Castle County, Delaware. An historical land grant establishes the boundary of Delaware as the low tide line on the New Jersey side for a 24-mile stretch of the river starting at the Pennsylvania state line. If you wade into the water at Fort Mott, you are in Delaware.

Pea Patch Island is about a mile from the fort, and the herons and egrets that nest there can usually be seen perched in the trees or flying around. Black and Turkey Vultures frequently roost in the trees and can sometimes be seen soaring over the island.

To continue the tour from the junction of Rts. 45 and 49, go east on Rt. 49 for 0.7 miles and turn right on Magnolia St. (shown on some maps as Salem–Hancock's Bridge Rd.). Follow this road for about 4.5 miles to Hancock's Bridge, where the road ends at Alloway's Creek Neck Rd. Turn right onto this road, which continues 5.5 miles to the Salem Nuclear Generating Station. Along the way you'll pass numerous fields, some of which are often flooded in spring and attract migrant ducks and shorebirds.

The last 2 miles of the road are private, but they are open to the public and lead to a Visitor Center at the power plant. The road runs through tidal marshes near the shore of Delaware Bay. Herons, egrets, and dabbling ducks can be seen in the marshes, and Canvasback and scaup gather offshore in the spring. Large numbers of waterfowl use the marshes in the fall. A pair of Ospreys that nest on one of the electrical transmission towers near the road is an annual attraction.

The marshes to the south and east of this private section of the road are part of the 5,826-acre Mad Horse Creek Wildlife Management Area, a popular fall waterfowl hunting area. At the sharp bend in the road near the east end of the private section of the road, two dirt roads lead off into some wooded spots in the WMA. You can park off the paved road and explore these dirt roads for local resident birds and for early migrants in spring.

To visit another interesting part of the WMA, return to Hancock's Bridge and continue straight ahead on Alloway's Creek Neck Rd. Bear right at the fork (0.3 miles beyond the junction with the Salem–Hancock's Bridge Road—not shown on the map), and continue another 0.7 miles to Rt. 623, the Harmersville-Canton Road. Turn right, go 2.3 miles to Canton, then turn right onto Frog-Ocean Road. Go about one-half mile to the first left turn, which is Stow Neck Rd. This road wanders through farmland and marsh for almost 4 miles until it ends at Pine Island, where there is a boat launch and parking area.

Pine Island is a forested "island" of Pitch Pine, Loblolly Pine, oaks, and American Holly, surrounded by marshes. It has many of the resident birds typical of the "mainland" and attracts small numbers of migrant songbirds in spring. It looks like the kind of place that might attract a pioneer Brown-headed Nuthatch, if one ever strayed over from Delaware (which is one of the reasons I keep going back). So far, nothing unusual has been found, but Boat-tailed Grackle has recently moved into this area—the farthest extension of its range up the Delaware Bayshore. Good numbers of Northern Harrier and Rough-legged Hawk can be seen along Stow Neck Rd. in winter.

Some other good birding spots in Salem County, most of which can be found with the help of a good county map, are Sinnickson Landing Road and Oakwood Beach, west of Salem; Thompson's Woods along the Elfsborg–Hancock's Bridge Rd., between Amwellbury Rd. and Walnut St.; Maskell's Mill Pond near Canton, a state WMA containing a 33-acre pond; Muttontown Woods, along Clancey Rd. between Salem and Penton; Elmer Lake, on the east side of Elmer; Palatine Lake, 3 miles south of Elmer; and the many farm roads in the vicinity of Woodstown and Pole Tavern, some of which have attracted Upland Sandpiper and even Dickcissel in recent years.

To return to northern New Jersey or the Philadelphia area from Canton, follow Rt. 623 north into Salem and go left on Rt. 49, then right on Rt. 45. Turn left onto Rt. 540 after 2 miles, and follow it for almost 7 miles to the entrance to the New Jersey Turnpike. The junction with I-295 is another quarter-mile ahead.

Parvin State Park

Parvin is a beautiful, 1125-acre state park in southeastern Salem County. Is is a good birding spot in migration, especially in the spring, and has a number of interesting breeding birds. For more than 30 years, Parvin has been noted for its nesting Prothonotary Warblers, which are especially common in the swampy areas along Muddy Run. Some of the other common breeding birds are Yellow-billed Cuckoo; Red-bellied Woodpecker; Acadian Flycatcher; Wood Thrush; Black-and-white, Kentucky, and Hooded Warblers; Louisiana Waterthrush; and Scarlet Tanager. Barred Owl and Summer Tanager (uncommon) also nest here.

Directions

Follow the directions for Glassboro WMA to the junction of Rt. 47 and US 322 West in Glassboro. Go west on US 322 for one long block to Rt. 553 and turn left. Drive south on Rt. 553 for 13 miles to Centerton and turn left onto Centerton-Norma Rd. (Rt. 540). Go 1.3 miles to a gate on the right and a paved road that leads a short distance to a parking area; this spot is shown as Second Landing on the park map. If you arrive before 8 A.M., the gate probably will be locked. In that case, park along the entrance road, but do not block the gate.

Birding

Parvin is heavily wooded, except for two lakes, Parvin and Thundergust, that cover 107 acres in the eastern part of the park. Parvin Lake is by far the larger of the two, and was created as a millpond around the turn of the century by damming Muddy Run, a tributary of the Maurice River. The land around the two lakes includes a bathing beach, two campgrounds, some cabins, and a picnic site.

MAP 61. Parvin State Park

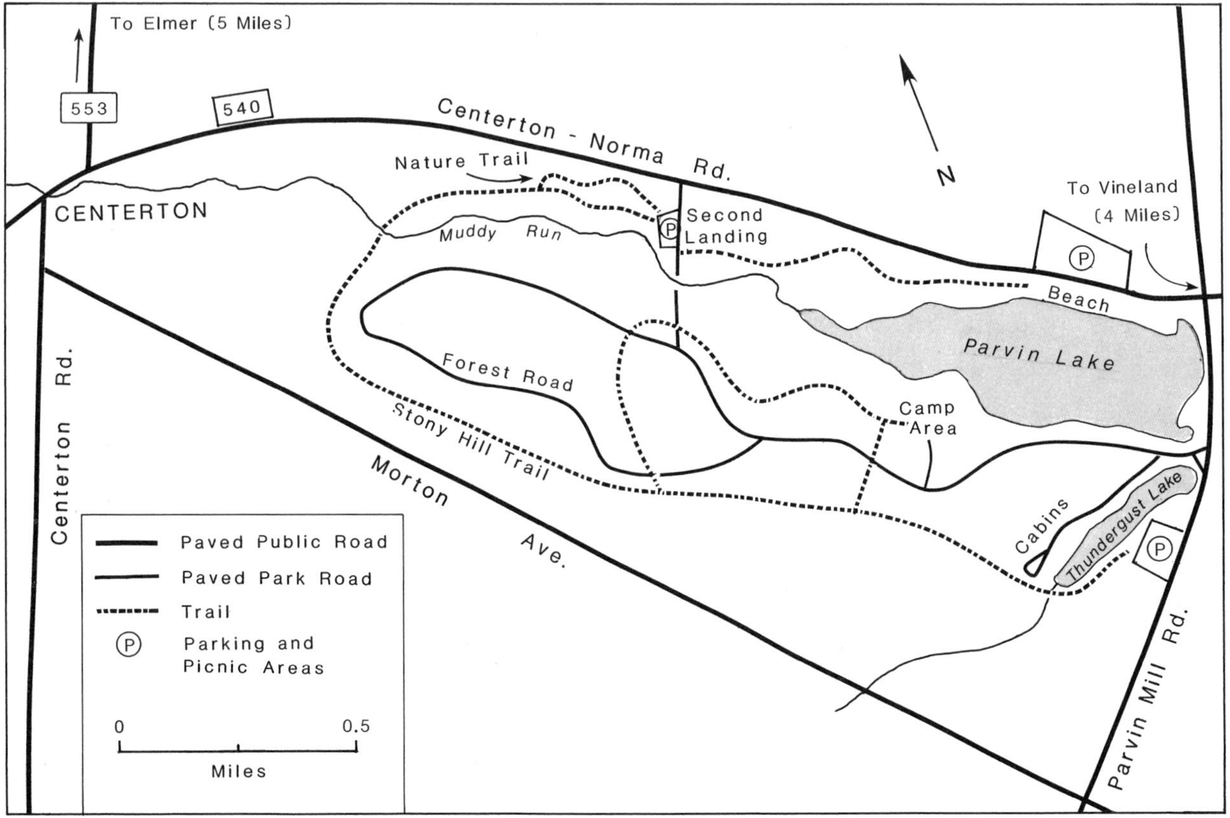

To Elmer (5 Miles)

To Vineland (4 Miles)

553

540

CENTERTON

Centerton Rd.

Centerton - Norma Rd.

Nature Trail

Muddy Run

Forest Road

Stony Hill Trail

Morton Ave.

Second Landing

Beach

Parvin Lake

Camp Area

Cabins

Thundergust Lake

Parvin Mill Rd.

N

Paved Public Road

Paved Park Road

Trail

Parking and Picnic Areas

P

Miles

0   0.5

The western part of the park, which has been designated a Natural Area, is more interesting for birds. Here the habitats range from a hardwood–cedar swamp with dense vegetation, through a transition area of oaks, American Holly, Mountain Laurel and Sassafras, to a very open oak-pine woods. Several trails and an unused paved road meander through this section of the park, offering visitors a sample of all the habitats.

From late April to early June is the best time to visit Parvin. Many migrants as well as the local breeding birds are present early in this period; later on, you will find only the breeding birds. By mid-June the foliage is dense, especially in the swampy areas, and the insects are plentiful. The fall migration in late August and September is also productive, although the thick foliage makes birding difficult.

At the Second Landing parking area there are picnic tables and some primitive toilets. A trail (the Nature Trail shown on the park map) leads down a few steps from the parking area and forks; take the left fork. You will immediately find yourself in the swamp that extends along both sides of Muddy Run for the length of the park. It is dominated by large Red Maple, Atlantic White Cedar and Black Gum trees, with a dense understory of Sweet Pepperbush, Leather-leaf, Mountain Laurel, and other shrubs. Although there are a few boardwalks, the going may get rather wet underfoot, especially in early spring.

In April and early May, a variety of migrant songbirds pause on their journey north to find food and shelter in the shrubs and trees along the trail. Some of the regular nesting birds of the swamp are Yellow-billed Cuckoo; Barred Owl; Red-bellied Woodpecker; Eastern Wood-Pewee; Acadian Flycatcher; Blue-gray Gnatcatcher (abundant); Wood Thrush; White-eyed, Yellow-throated (uncommon), and Red-eyed Vireos; Yellow, Black-and-white, Prothonotary, and Kentucky Warblers; and Louisiana Waterthrush.

After about one-quarter mile, you'll reach a trail junction. To the right, the Nature Trail returns to the parking area. The left trail parallels Muddy Run for about 0.6 miles, then crosses the stream via a wooden bridge, where a Prothonotary Warbler sings in spring. About 200 yards farther, on the left is another fork. If you are short of time, the left trail will lead you quickly to Forest Rd., a paved road, where you should turn left; continue 0.6 miles until you reach two stone markers for a trail on the left. Take this trail to a paved path, turn left, and you'll be headed back to Second Landing.

If you are not pressed for time, continue straight ahead on the trail that is marked Stony Hill Trail on the park map. The trail emerges abruptly from the swamp, passes through a transition zone, and enters an open mixed oak–Pitch Pine woodland. Breeding birds that you may encounter here (in addition to many of the species mentioned above) are Broad-winged Hawk; Northern Bobwhite; Eastern Screech-Owl; Whip-poor-will; White-breasted Nuthatch; Carolina Wren; Brown Thrasher; Cedar Waxwing; Blue-winged, Pine, Prairie, and Hooded Warblers; Ovenbird (abundant); Summer Tanager (uncommon); and Scarlet Tanager.

About a mile beyond the fork mentioned above, you will come to another junction with a trail on the left. A pair of Summer Tanagers was here in June 1984. Follow the left fork, and you soon will cross Forest Rd. and enter an open oak woods, then an oak-holly woods. After about one-third of a mile you will cross Forest Rd. again. Continue another 100 yards and turn left on the paved path which leads to the parking area at Second Landing. You can hike the long loop— starting from the parking area and including parts of the Nature Trail and the Stony Hill Trail—and return to the parking area in two to three hours, depending upon the amount of time you spend birding.

The park map shows several other trails which you may enjoy exploring if you have the time. Although Parvin State Park may not have quite the abundance and diversity of birdlife to be found in some other parts of the state, you will find few places in New Jersey that are more attractive.

Dividing Creek

Bald Eagle; Black and King Rails; Acadian Flycatcher; Sedge Wren; Northern Parula; Yellow-throated, Prothonotary, Worm-eating, Kentucky, and Hooded Warblers; Summer Tanager; Blue Grosbeak; and Orchard Oriole are just a few of the many species that have nested during the past 10 years near the village of Dividing Creek in Cumberland County. Except for Sedge Wren, all these species occur annually, and most of them are fairly common. This interesting variety of breeding birds attracts many birders from all parts of New Jersey and neighboring states.

The Cumberland County June Bird Count focuses on the Dividing Creek area and turns up 130–140 species. While the list includes numerous migrant shorebirds and summering nonbreeders, it reflects the tremendous variety of birdlife to be found here in the early summer. The following list of birding spots concentrates on the more unusual species, but in searching for them, you will encounter many of the more common birds of southern New Jersey. Nearby Heislerville WMA and Moores Beach, also excellent birding spots from spring through fall, are covered in their own chapter.

Although the Dividing Creek area is noted mainly for its breeding birds, it also has high diversity of wintering species. Large numbers of raptors feed and roost in the woods and marshes along Delaware Bay at this season, including a few Bald and Golden Eagles. Nearby Fortescue has long been famous for the spectacular concentrations of Snow Geese that gather offshore in early spring.

Directions

From northern New Jersey or the Philadelphia area, follow the directions for Glassboro Woods (p. 312) to the junction of Rt. 47 and US 322 in Glassboro. Continue another 10 miles on Rt. 47 to the intersection with US 40 near Malaga. Go west on US 40 for about

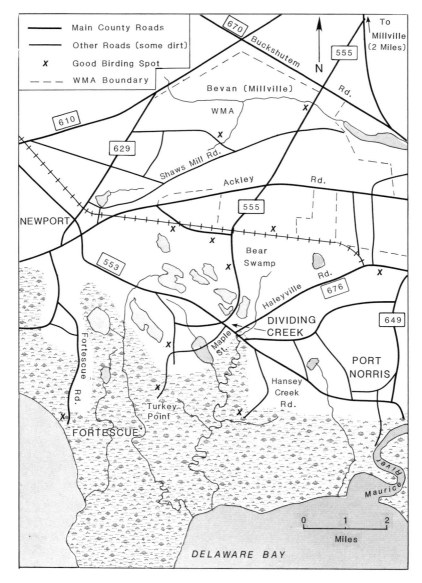

MAP 62. Dividing Creek

one mile to Rt. 55 and turn left. Follow Rt. 55 south for 11 miles to the exit for Rt. 47 South. Take Rt. 47 into Millville for about 2.3 miles to the intersection with Rt. 49 (Main St.), then turn right. Go 0.3 miles to Cedar St., the second left after the bridge across the Maurice River, and turn left; this is Rt. 555. After about 0.2 miles, stay on Rt. 555 as it veers left onto Race St. (not well marked). Bear right with Rt. 555 at another poorly marked intersection about 1.2 miles further along. Continue south on Rt. 555 for almost 2 miles until you cross Buckshutem Rd., where you will enter the Edward G. Bevan WMA. About a third of a mile beyond Buckshutem Rd., park on the right at a swampy area where Buckshutem Creek flows under the road.

From coastal New Jersey, there are several options. The shortest is to take the Garden State Parkway to Exit 44 (Pomona). Follow Rt. 575 for 8 miles through Pomona to US 40. Take US 40 west for about 7 miles, past Mays Landing, to the junction with Rt. 552, which leads to Millville. Follow Rt. 552 and Spur Rt. 552 (continue straight ahead on the spur when Rt. 552 turns right) for 16 miles to Rt. 47 in Millville. Turn left and go one-half mile to the intersection with Rt. 49 (Main St.); proceed as above.

Birding

The birding spots around Dividing Creek include several WMAs and much private land that can be birded from public roads. Observe No Trespassing signs and help make birders welcome.

The Edward G. Bevan WMA encompasses more than 12,000 acres of oak-pine forest in southern Cumberland County. Buckshutem Creek, where you have parked, is the main stream that drains the half of the WMA lying west of Rt. 555, and the associated Buckshutem Swamp offers much interesting habitat. Prothonotary Warbler and Louisiana Waterthrush often can be heard singing at this spot. A dirt trail on the north side of the stream leads into the woods for a half mile before turning away from the swamp. Here you might find Hooded Warbler, plus many more common species.

The best way to explore the WMA is with the help of a topographic map (Cedarville and Dividing Creek quadrangles) or the *Guide to Wildlife Management Areas* (see Bibliography). About 0.7 miles south of the creek, a dirt road (Shaw's Mill Rd.) goes right toward Newport. Two roads that turn right off Shaw's Mill Rd., one after 0.6 miles and another after 1.5 miles, will take you through some of the backwoods areas toward the upstream sections of Buckshutem Creek.

Continue south on Rt. 555 toward Dividing Creek. About 3.6 miles south of Buckshutem Creek you will cross some railroad tracks and come to a paved road on the right. Park on the left, opposite the paved road, and walk east over a dirt mound (away from the paved road), along the dirt road that parallels the railroad. The tracks border the northern edge of Bear Swamp and provide some of the most interesting birding in the area. Species that nest here include Yellow-billed Cuckoo; Common Nighthawk; Whip-poor-will; Ruby-throated Hummingbird; Red-bellied Woodpecker; Acadian Flycatcher; Eastern Bluebird; Wood Thrush; Yellow-throated Vireo; Yellow-throated, Pine, Prairie, Black-and-white, Kentucky, and Hooded Warblers; American Redstart; Summer Tanager (uncommon); Scarlet Tanager (abundant); and Chipping Sparrow. Although you can walk the road for almost two miles before coming to a sand mine that is private property, the first mile is the most productive.

Return to your car and drive west along the railroad tracks on the paved road toward the sand mine. After about one-third of a mile, there is a dirt road on the left. Park and walk down the dirt road, where, in 1975, the second known nesting of Summer Tanager in New Jersey in this century occurred (the first one being in 1955). Within two years, five male Summer Tanagers were found in the immediate vicinity, and from this foothold, the species spread north through most of the Pine Barrens to Middlesex County, though it is still very uncommon.

Return to your car and continue along the paved road past the sand mine, where there is a large colony of Bank Swallows; about 1.3 miles from Rt. 555 the road crosses the railroad tracks. Park on the right and walk west along the railroad for a few hundred yards. This area has nesting Barred Owl and Kentucky and Hooded Warblers, plus numerous other species. You must be content to bird from the tracks, however, as the vegetation and bugs are dense. The paved road continues through some mature deciduous woods to Ackley Rd., where a left turn will lead you toward Newport. Blue Grosbeak nests in the overgrown fields along the road.

Retrace your route back to Rt. 555 at the railroad tracks, and turn right toward Dividing Creek. Drive slowly south for the next few miles, stopping occasionally to listen for singing birds. Acadian Flycatcher and Yellow-throated, Prothonotary, Kentucky, and Hooded Warblers are regulars along this stretch of road; Worm-eating Warbler has nested here, and Northern Parula seems to be making a comeback. The *dominica* race of the Yellow-throated Warbler first established itself as a breeding subspecies in New Jersey near Dividing Creek in the 1970s. Since then, it has spread east into Cape May County, north into Atlantic County, and even to Allaire State Park, Ocean County.

The land along Rt. 555 is private, but the birds can be heard from the wide apron of the road and can usually be coaxed into view by squeaking or "pishing." About 1.5 miles south of the railroad tracks, the woods end and some borrow-pit ponds appear on both sides of the road. Osprey, Belted Kingfisher, and various swallows are often around the ponds, and a loon or two usually lingers late in spring.

After another 0.8 miles, you will come to the junction with Rt. 553 in the town of Dividing Creek. Turn left and go about 200 yards east to Maple St. on the right; the junction is very inconspicuous, so watch carefully for the hidden street sign. Turn right on Maple and drive south toward Turkey Point. After about one-half mile, you will come to a causeway that crosses two tidal pools. Spotted Sandpipers are frequently on the rocks along the causeway. A little farther on are some agricultural fields on the right, where Killdeer and Black-bellied Plover stop in migration. About 1.4 miles south of Dividing Creek, Maple St. merges into Turkey Point Rd. Continue straight ahead on Turkey Point Rd., through a deciduous woods where Chuck-will's-widow and Whip-poor-will call at night. After about 0.4 miles you will pass a wet meadow on the right, which is one of the last known (1977) nesting sites for Sedge Wren in New Jersey. That year there was also Black Rail in the marsh across the road. Both species were present in the same general area in May 1985.

A little more than one mile south of the junction with Maple St. you will come to a wooden bridge, where it is prudent to park and continue on foot. Here you are in the midst of the vast marshes of Turkey Point, which is not a point in the usual sense of the word (it is, in fact, two miles inland from Egg Island Point on Delaware Bay). Black Rail is a regular breeding bird here, and, if you come on a warm, still, *moonless* night in late May or June, you may be fortunate enough to hear several males giving their *kick-ee-doo* (or *kee-*

kee-kerr) call from the marsh. With a great deal of luck and courage, you might even get a glimpse of one by trudging out into the marsh in the direction of their calls, but beware of the numerous channels and mosquito-control ditches.

King Rail and Virginia Rail are common nesters in the marshes of Turkey Point, and Short-eared Owl probably breeds here on occasion. By day, you will see numerous herons and egrets, although they do not nest nearby. Northern Harrier is a regular breeder, with at least seven pairs around Turkey Point in 1983. New Jersey's only nesting pair of Bald Eagles live in a remote area near Dividing Creek, and are often seen hunting in the vicinity. The recent breeding success of this pair, and a reintroduction program sponsored by the Division of Fish, Game and Wildlife, build hope for an expanding eagle population along the Delaware Bayshore in the future.

Drive back toward Dividing Creek to the junction with Maple St. and turn left, following Turkey Point Rd. The next two-thirds of a mile is good for Yellow-breasted Chat, Blue Grosbeak, and Orchard Oriole. After about 1.5 miles you will rejoin Rt. 553. To reach Fortescue, which is famous for its Snow Geese in spring, continue west on Rt. 553 for about 2.6 miles to Newport, then turn left on Fortescue Rd. (Route 637). Follow this road for about 3 miles to its end at Delaware Bay in Fortescue, where the Snow Geese gather.

Another good spot for night birds is Hansey Creek Rd. From the junction of Rts. 555 and 553 in Dividing Creek, go east on Rt. 553 for about 0.9 miles to Hansey Creek Rd., the first right turn after crossing the bridge over Dividing Creek. This road runs through woods, fields, and marshes for about 2 miles to its end at the northeast corner of the 2,000-acre Egg Island–Berrytown WMA. Great Horned Owl, American Woodcock, Chuck-will's-widow, and Whip-poor-will call from the wooded areas at night, while King Rail and Virginia Rail are abundant in the marshes.

Many birders combine a trip to the Dividing Creek area with one to nearby Heislerville WMA and Moores Beach. In addition, there are numerous other good birding spots around Dividing Creek to be explored with the help of USGS topographic maps, the *Guide to Wildlife Management Areas*, and a Cumberland County map. Exploration of some out-of-the-way places could produce more good finds like the discoveries of nesting Yellow-throated Warbler and Summer Tanager during the 1970s.

Heislerville Wildlife Management Area— Moores Beach

The Heislerville Wildlife Management Area, located along the Delaware Bayshore in southeastern Cumberland County, comprises almost 4,000 acres of formerly diked salt-hay marshes, impoundments, tidal marshes, and pine-oak upland. Access to the area is from four roads; Matt's Landing, East Point, Thompsons Beach, and Moores Beach Rds. The latter three end at Delaware Bay, and each provides a little something different.

Waterbirds are the main attraction at Heislerville. A variety of herons and egrets can be found here from spring to fall, although there are no known heronries nearby. Migrant waterfowl include a good selection of puddle ducks in the ponds and large concentrations of Snow Geese (offshore). Many species of shorebirds occur in the impoundments at Heislerville and at Moores Beach, but the best show is the spectacular concentrations of Ruddy Turnstones, Red Knots, Sanderlings, and Semipalmated Sandpipers along the bayshore in late May. Numbering in the hundreds of thousands, these flocks are the biggest spring gatherings of shorebirds on the east coast of North America.

Among the rarities that have been reported from the Heislerville area are Brown Pelican, White Ibis, Greater White-fronted Goose, Black-necked Stilt, Curlew Sandpiper, Ruff, and Northern Wheatear. Noteworthy nesting birds include Least Bittern; Yellow-throated, Prothonotary and Kentucky Warblers; Blue Grosbeak; and Orchard Oriole. Sedge Wren and Henslow's Sparrow were formerly common nesters along the Bayshore through the late 1950s.

MAP 63. Heislerville-Moores Beach

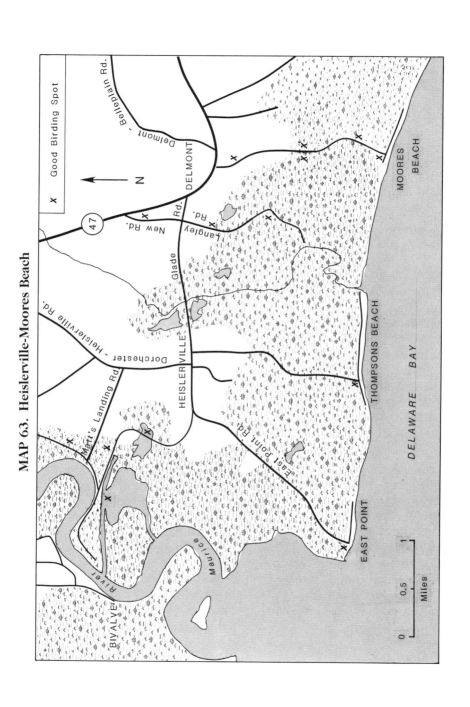

x   Good Birding Spot

N

Delmont - Belleplain Rd.

DELMONT

47

New Rd.

Langley Rd.

Dorchester - Heislerville Rd.

Glade

Matt's Landing Rd.

HEISLERVILLE

East Point Rd.

BIVALVE

Maurice River

EAST POINT

THOMPSONS BEACH

MOORES BEACH

DELAWARE BAY

0   0.5   1

Miles

Directions

To reach Moores Beach Road: From the Philadelphia area, take Interstate 76 or 676 south to Rt. 42, the North-South Freeway. Exit at Rt. 41 and go about 3.4 miles to Rt. 47, the Delsea Drive. Continue straight ahead on Rt. 47 for about 15 miles to US 40. Go right (west) on Rt. 40 for about one mile to Rt. 55. Take Rt. 55 south for 21 miles to its end at Rt. 47 in Port Elizabeth. Continue south on Rt. 47 for about 8.8 miles to Moores Beach Rd., which is the first right after Glade Rd. If you come to the Delmont-Belleplain Rd. on the left, you have come 1,000 feet too far.

From northern New Jersey, there are two options: (1) Take the New Jersey Turnpike south to Exit 3 (Runnemede). Go south (left) on Rt. 168 (Black Horse Pike) for about one mile to Rt. 41. Take Rt. 41 south for about 5 miles to Rt. 47 and continue as in the preceding paragraph. (2) Take the Garden State Parkway south to Exit 25 (Marmora). Go west into Marmora to the traffic light at Rt. 9 and turn left. Go 0.2 miles to the next traffic light and turn right. Continue straight ahead for about 0.4 miles, turn left onto Rt. 631, and follow it west for about 3.6 miles to Rt. 610. Bear left onto Rt. 610 and go 8 miles to Rt. 47. Turn right and drive west for about 8 miles to Moores Beach Rd. on the left, 1,000 feet beyond the Delmont-Belleplain Rd.

Birding

About 0.2 miles down Moores Beach Rd. is a wet area on the left that often has nesting Red-bellied Woodpecker and Prothonotary Warbler; a little farther on you might find Orchard Oriole nesting in the trees in front of the houses along the street. Approximately 0.7 miles from Rt. 47, the road emerges from the settled area into the open, with wet meadows on the left, where there are nesting Least Bitterns, and a large impoundment on the right.

The edges of the pond attract a wide variety of shorebirds in migration; Ruff is an annual visitor. Many different ducks stop here in spring and fall, and White-fronted Goose has occurred in March. Forster's Terns are common, while Black and Caspian Terns are regular migrants. Herons and egrets can also be found along the edges of the ponds, and White Ibis has appeared at least once. Continue to the end of the road at Delaware Bay (about 2 miles from Rt. 47), where the huge concentrations of shorebirds can be found, especially at low tide in late May.

Return to Rt. 47, go left for about 0.4 miles to Glade Rd., and turn left. After about 0.2 miles you will come to an intersection with Langley Rd. on the left and New Rd. on the right. New Rd. is about 0.6 miles long and leads back to Rt. 47; just before it reaches Rt. 47, there is a spot where Kentucky Warbler sometimes nests. Langley Rd. may have nesting Blue Grosbeak in the field bordering the road, and you can usually find Orchard Oriole around the two-story farmhouse about 0.4 miles down Langley Rd.

Back at Glade Rd., go another 1.4 miles and take the left turn for Thompsons Beach. This road, which is about 1.8 miles long, passes through some woodland, then through much salt marsh until it ends at Delaware Bay. The birdlife is similar to that along Moores Beach Rd. On June 1, 1981, a male Northern Wheatear spent most of the day in the rubble at the end of the road.

Upon returning to Glade Rd., go left toward East Point. After one block, you will pass the Dorchester-Heislerville Rd. on the right. Continue straight ahead on what is now called East Point Rd. In about 0.5 miles the road will bend left and a dirt road will continue straight ahead. Don't take the dirt road now, but note it for the return trip. East Point Rd. continues for another 2.4 miles to a quaint little lighthouse on Delaware Bay. Along the way it passes through some woodland and a great deal of salt marsh. On June 19, 1983, a picnic party at East Point was treated to the sight of 100 Brown Pelicans flying by, part of a big invasion of southern New Jersey. The beach at East Point is another gathering place for masses of shorebirds in late spring.

Head back toward Heislerville and turn left on the previously noted dirt road, which leads to a dike along several impoundments. After about 0.6 miles, you will reach a water control structure separating the impoundment on the right from the salt marsh on the left. This is a good area for herons and egrets, ducks, and shorebirds. If the water in the impoundment is not too deep, it is an excellent spot for shorebirds at high tide. In late May of 1977 and 1978, a Curlew Sandpiper was present for about a week. In recent years, the water has tended to be too deep for shorebirds, and there have been no rarities.

Continue along the dike and you will soon come to another impoundment that usually has a pair of Mute Swans; a feral pair of Australian Black Swans nested here one year. Forster's Terns hover over the pond in search of fish, and Black-crowned and Yellow-crowned Night-Herons can sometimes be seen roosting in the trees at the east edge of the pond. To your left is the mouth of the Maurice River. At low tide, a vast expanse of mudflats is exposed and in migration tens of thousands of shorebirds will be feeding on them. Unfortunately, most of them will be too far away to identify, even with a telescope; as the tide rises, the birds are forced closer to the dikes, so your chances are improved. (High tide at East Point occurs about one and a half hours later than the published tides for Sandy Hook and Cape May Harbor, and about four hours earlier than high tide at Philadelphia; the tides at Heislerville are a little bit later.)

The dike road ends at Matt's Landing Rd. Turn right toward Heislerville, and go about 1.5 miles to the junction with the Dorchester-Heislerville Rd. Turn left and go about 1.7 miles to the first paved road on the right. Just beyond this intersection a wet woodland on the right has nesting Kentucky Warbler. Just ahead on the right is another paved road, which leads back to Rt. 47 in about 0.4 miles.

This is the end of the tour, which can just as well be done in the reverse order if you can follow the instructions backwards. Many birders combine a trip to Heislerville with one to Dividing Creek, which is covered in a separate chapter.

Additional Birding Spots in Southwestern New Jersey

Bass River State Forest

An attractive and popular campground on Lake Absegami is one of the main features of this 17,645-acre state forest. Conveniently located off the Garden State Parkway, the forest is near the popular birding spots of Brigantine NWR and Tuckerton. Here you will find typical Pine Barrens habitats, including many cedar swamps along the Bass River and the numerous small streams that traverse the area. Birdlife is similar to that in Lebanon State Forest, Stafford Forge, and Wharton State Forest, covered in separate chapters.

Directions

From the north, take the Garden State Parkway to Exit 52 (New Gretna). Turn right (north) onto Rt. 654, go about one mile to the junction with Stage Road, and follow the signs to the state forest campground. From the south, take the Garden State Parkway to Exit 50 (New Gretna, US 9). Follow US 9 into New Gretna for a little over a mile, then turn left onto Rt. 679 toward Chatsworth. Bear right after about 1.5 miles, turning off Rt. 679, which bears left. In another half-mile, you will come to the junction with Stage Rd.; turn right and follow the signs to the State Forest campground.

Berlin Park

This small city park in Berlin, Camden County, contains an excellent stand of mature deciduous forest and is good for songbirds in migration. Basically a local birding spot, it has seldom been visited by birders from outside the area.

Directions

From Exit 4 of the New Jersey Turnpike, go south on Rt. 73 for about 10 miles to a traffic circle. Take the first right turn (Walker Ave.) out of the circle, go a few hundred yards, and then turn left onto Zulker Ave. After about 0.4 miles, you will come to the White Horse Pike. Cross over the Pike onto Rt. 689 (Berlin–Cross Keys Rd.). Go about 0.2 miles and turn left at the park entrance.

Fish House

Fish House Cove is a protected bay of the Delaware River in Pennsauken, Camden County. More than 200 species of birds have been found here, including a tremendous variety of waterfowl. Up to 25,000 Ruddy Ducks formerly wintered in the area, but oil spills have drastically reduced their numbers. Some of the land, mainly marsh and wet woods, is owned by Pennsauken Township, which maintains a boardwalk and nature trail. Most of the land, however, has been developed as private industrial parks and refineries. Be careful to observe No Trespassing signs when birding this area.

Directions

From Exit 4 of the New Jersey Turnpike, go west on Rt. 73 for 1.5 miles, then turn left onto Rt. 38. Drive about 1.5 miles to Church Rd., turn right, and follow Church Rd. (which eventually becomes Cove Rd.) for about 3.5 miles to River Rd. Access to the cove is along Cove Rd. or 36th St., which is about 1.2 miles south on River Rd.

Flood Gates

This spot, just north of the Commodore Barry Bridge in Gloucester County, has the largest concentration of wintering Ruddy Ducks in the state, but the numbers found along the Delaware River are much reduced from former times. Gulls, cormorants, and hawks are found here in winter and in migration, and in fall a variety of shorebirds occur on the mudflats at low tide. Great Cormorant has been seen here in winter. In addition to the Ruddies, various other species of waterfowl winter along the river.

Directions

From Exit 2 of the New Jersey Turnpike, go west on US 322 for 4 miles to Interstate 295. Drive north on I-295 for about 2 miles to the exit for Repaupo Rd. Take Repaupo Rd. west for about 0.6 miles to Rt. 44, where it becomes Flood Gates Rd. Continue straight ahead on Flood Gates Rd. for about 1.5 miles to the end, and park. Scan the water from the dikes; cormorants like to sit on the rock jetty to the north.

Union Lake Wildlife Management Area

One of the newest WMAs, this tract contains almost 5,000 acres of pine-oak woodland and deciduous forest, as well as Union Lake, the largest lake in southern New Jersey. It is located on the outskirts of Millville, Cumberland County. The birdlife in this WMA is similar to that in the Edward G. Bevan WMA, just south of Millville (see Dividing Creek chapter). Among the more interesting breeding species is Summer Tanager.

Directions

Take Rt. 55 to Sherman Ave. (Rt. 552), about 4 miles north of downtown Millville. Go west on Sherman for about 1.5 miles to a dirt road on the left and a sign marking the entrance to the WMA. You can follow the dirt road for a couple of miles through the tract, to the junction with Carmel Rd., just west of Millville.

Winslow Wildlife Management Area

Winslow, surely one of the least known WMAs, encompasses more than 6,000 acres along the Great Egg Harbor River in Camden and

Gloucester counties. Access is rather limited and the woods along the river are almost impenetrable, but the habitat here is very interesting. Rumors of Swainson's Warbler have emanated from farther down the Great Egg Harbor River and the setting is similar to that species' haunts in the south. This area certainly deserves further exploration during the breeding season.

Directions

Take the Atlantic City Expressway to Exit 38 (Spur Rt. 536). Follow Spur Rt. 536 south to Williamstown and Rt. 42. Go south on Rt. 42 until it merges with US 322; after about 7 miles (from Rt. 536), turn left (via a right jughandle) onto Piney Hollow Rd. Drive north for about one-half mile to the border of the WMA. The headquarters is on the left after about one mile. Other points of access to Winslow WMA are off the Williamstown-Winslow Road (Rt. 723). This is reached by turning left off Piney Hollow Rd. onto Rt. 73, just before the Atlantic City Expressway. Go about one mile on Piney Hollow Rd., then turn left onto Williamstown-Winslow Rd.

American Oystercatchers

1 Barnegat Light
2 Manahawkin WMA
3 Holgate
4 Stafford Forge WMA
5 Tuckerton Marshes
6 Brigantine NWR
7 Brigantine Island
8 Atlantic County Park

9 Tuckahoe WMA
10 Longport Sod Banks
11 Corson's Inlet
12 Jakes Landing
13 Cape May County Park
14 Stone Harbor
15 Wildwood Crest
16 Cape May

MAP 64. South Coast Region

South Coast

Barnegat Light

The town of Barnegat Light is at the north end of Long Beach Island and is separated from Island Beach State Park by Barnegat Inlet, which connects the ocean and Barnegat Bay. Although the area is completely developed, there are several excellent birding spots. Because the area is bordered by water on three sides, the birds seen here are mainly those associated with water; large numbers of migrant landbirds do pass through in fall, however. This is one of the best places in New Jersey to look for Great Cormorant, Northern Gannet, Common and King Eiders, Harlequin Duck, and Black-legged Kittiwake. You can also see here many of the other birds that migrate or winter along the coast, especially loons, geese, and ducks. Barnegat Light is worth visiting any time from October to April, with winter providing the most interesting—if also the coldest—birding.

Directions

From the intersection of Rt. 72 with the Garden State Parkway at Exit 63 (Manahawkin), go east on Rt. 72 for 7 miles, crossing the bridge to Long Beach Island. At the third (and last) traffic light after crossing the bridge turn left onto Long Beach Blvd. Follow this road north for about 8 miles and you will see the lighthouse. You are now in the town of Barnegat Light, the road name has changed to Central Ave., and you can follow the signs at the cross streets as they decrease from 30th St. Turn right onto 8th St. and park near the end of the road, observing the signs which say "No parking beyond this point."

Birding (see note, page 355)

From the end of the road, cross the dunes and bear right. This site is known among birders as "the 8th St. jetty." During the past few dec-

351

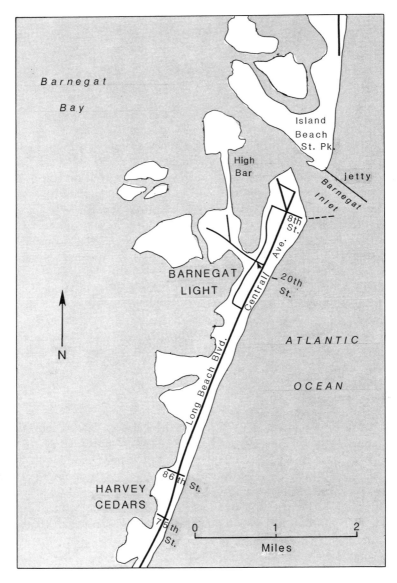

MAP 65. Barnegat Light

ades, this has been the most reliable spot in the state for Common and King Eiders and Harlequin Duck. It is also excellent for Great Cormorants, which like to gather on the tower at the end of the jetty on the north side of the inlet. Purple Sandpipers are frequent visitors to the jetty from November through March.

The area around the 8th St. jetty is a favorite wintering site for Oldsquaw and Red-breasted Merganser. Sometimes there are rafts of Greater Scaup, all three scoters, Bufflehead, and a few Common Goldeneyes. A small flock of Brant usually frequent the near end of the jetty. In late fall, especially during November, large numbers of Red-throated and Common Loons can be seen migrating just offshore. Northern Gannet is regular here at this season and, if the winds are from the east or southeast, you may see several hundred. These same winds bring Black-legged Kittiwake close to shore at this point.

Fall and early winter bring long skeins of scoters migrating south. Depending on the winds, they may fly from 100 yards to a mile or more offshore; easterly winds bring them closest. This season also brings migrant gulls from the north. Bonaparte's Gulls appear sometime in November–December, frequently by the hundreds; among them there is almost always a Little or a Common Black-headed Gull. With the arrival of the larger gulls in December, it is time to look for Glaucous, Iceland, and Lesser Black-backed Gulls, which are seen around Barnegat Inlet annually.

The 8th St. jetty has been largely destroyed by winter storms and is partly covered by a large sandbar that starts at about 10th St. and runs almost to the lighthouse; construction began in 1987 on a new jetty north of the old one. What this will mean for birders is uncertain—the new jetty may prove attractive to the same species that frequented the old one, but it will probably take a few years for the marine life around it to develop suitably.

Returning to your car, drive back to Central Ave., then jog left and quickly right onto Broadway, which leads toward the lighthouse. Just before the end of the road is the entrance to Barnegat Light State Park, which charges a fee in summer. In winter, modern rest rooms are open in the small building on your right just after you enter the park; at other seasons use the rest rooms in the bathhouses near the lighthouse. Drive to the far end of the parking lot and walk out to the base of the lighthouse.

The area around the lighthouse provides a vantage point for scanning the inlet and the Island Beach side of the inlet. A Snowy Owl occasionally winters at the inlet, so scan the north jetty and the beach cottages on Island Beach with a spotting scope. In winter, flocks of Bonaparte's Gulls frequently feed in the channel. The shrubs surrounding the parking lot provide refuge for migrant passerines in fall; Western Kingbird is seen here occasionally in fall or early winter.

Just outside the park, at the end of Broadway, a small parking area overlooks the bay side of the inlet. Here you can scan the sandbar islands for gulls and shorebirds; Gyrfalcon occasionally has been seen here, but you will be very lucky to see one. Large numbers of Brant, Red-breasted Merganser, and Oldsquaw are usually present in winter. Listen for the *owl-omelette* courtship call of the male Oldsquaw, which can be heard almost as frequently here as on the Arctic tundra where the species nests.

From the end of Broadway you can see a long spit of land that extends west into Barnegat Bay. This mile-long sandbar is known locally as "High Bar" or "the dike," and is owned partly by the state and partly by the federal government. The outermost part of the bar, which was created by dredge spoil from Barnegat Inlet, has existed long enough for shrubs and small trees to grow, and supports a heronry in summer. At the present time, the area is accessible on foot and is worth checking in winter for Snowy Owl and the ever elusive Gyrfalcon.

To reach High Bar, go south on Broadway for two short blocks, turn right on 6th Street, then left onto Bayview Ave. As you drive south on Bayview, watch the boat channels for gulls and ducks; a female Harlequin Duck once wintered with the Mallards along here. The water tower to your left is a favorite perch for Snowy Owls when they are around, and a flock of Boat-tailed Grackles usually winters here. Turn right at 20th St., right again on Arnold Blvd. (the first street you come to), then immediately right on Sunset Blvd. Follow Sunset for about one-half mile to its end, then park on the street, being careful not to block the driveways of the houses. Cross through the fence and walk north to the end. When active dredging is underway, this area is closed to the public, so read the signs.

Return to Central Ave. and head south. If you haven't seen Purple Sandpiper, check some of the jetties in Harvey Cedars and Surf

City—those between 75th St. and 87th St. in Harvey Cedars are especially reliable. As you drive south in winter, watch the pine plantings along either side of the road for crossbills. When you get back to Rt. 72, you can either turn right to go back to the Parkway or, if you want to take a long walk, continue straight ahead toward Holgate, described in its own chapter.

NOTE: The 8th St. jetty is no longer worth visiting, but the new jetty protecting the inlet has been completed and is proving to be an excellent spot for birding, especially in winter. The jetty, which is about a mile long, starts near the base of the lighthouse and parallels the jetty on the opposite side of the inlet. Harlequin Ducks are here every winter, and can usually be seen at very close range.

Manahawkin Wildlife Management Area

The Manahawkin Wildlife Management Area is a 965-acre tract of diverse habitat, including Pitch Pine and deciduous woodlands, fields, salt marsh, and several freshwater impoundments. It is best known for some unusual breeding species and for a number of rarities. The area was virtually unknown until the early 1970s, when the first rarity appeared; with increased attention many more were found, and the interesting nesting species of the area were discovered. In recent years the freshwater impoundments, which furnished most of the exciting records, have become overgrown with vegetation and have produced little of interest. As a result, the area is less frequently visited today than 10 years ago, and any occasional rarity that passes through here may escape unnoticed. Manahawkin is still a regular stop on winter trips, however, for the many Northern Harriers, Rough-legged Hawks, and Short-eared Owls that winter here.

Note: This area is managed for hunting, so visits during the hunting season (roughly October–December) should be made on Sundays. On weekdays or Saturdays, do not wander off Stafford Ave.

Directions

From the intersection of Rt. 72 and the Garden State Parkway at Exit 63 (Manahawkin), take Rt. 72 east for about 1.5 miles to Rt. 9. Go north on Rt. 9 for 0.1 miles to a traffic light at Bay Ave., then take the next right onto Stafford Ave. In about 0.3 miles you will come to a blinking red light at Parker St. Continue straight ahead for 0.6 miles to Hilliard Blvd.; just before reaching Hilliard you enter the boundary of the Manahawkin WMA.

MAP 66. Manahawkin WMA

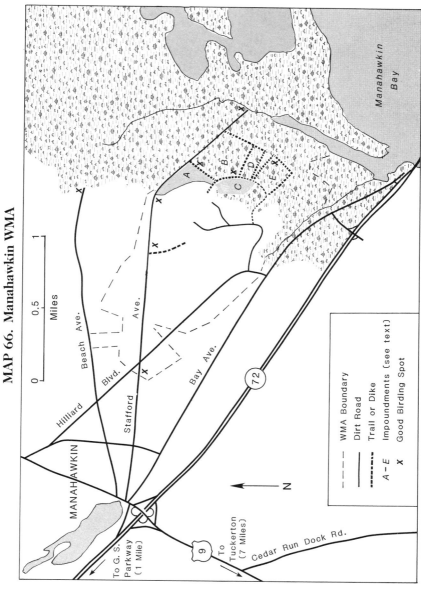

Birding

The woods along Stafford Ave. between Parker St. and Hilliard Ave. have nesting Hooded Warbler from mid-May through the summer. Stop along the road and listen for their song; singing males can frequently be coaxed into view by "pishing" or by a Screech-Owl call. The deciduous woods with Mountain Laurel is a habitat similar to that chosen by Hooded Warbler in northern New Jersey. Other species present include the usual assortment of Carolina Chickadee, Gray Catbird, Rufous-sided Towhee, and others.

Continue on Stafford Ave.; after the stop sign at Hilliard, the road passes through more woodland for about a mile, and there are several paths that lead off to the right. These paths receive little attention, but are worth exploring for migrants and for nesting species, such as Red-bellied Woodpecker, Acadian Flycatcher, Hooded Warbler, and other species typical of coastal-plain deciduous woodlands. Just before the woods give way to salt marsh, there is a wet area with dead trees on the right. This spot has nesting Prothonotary Warbler and Acadian Flycatcher and is a good place for migrant Olive-sided Flycatcher in late May and early June.

Whip-poor-will is abundant along this stretch of road and has recently been joined by smaller numbers of Chuck-will's-widow. The best way to find these species is to park along the road at dusk or before dawn and wait until they start singing. Sometimes they come out and sit on the dirt road or perch on a tree branch. In the poor light in which these birds are usually seen, field marks cannot be used to distinguish the two species. Size is the best distinction— Whip-poor-will is about the same size as an American Robin (though of different proportions), while Chuck-will's-widow is almost as big as a Rock Dove. Their songs differ mainly in the cadence, the strongest accent being on the *first* syllable for Chuck-will's-widow and on the *last* syllable for Whip-poor-will.

Just past a bend, the road emerges from the woods into an area of salt marsh on the left (which is part of Barnegat National Wildlife Refuge) and an impoundment on the right (pond A on Map 66). Scan the pond for herons, waterfowl, and (if the water is low) shorebirds. One-half mile after you leave the woods, a dike on the right separates pond A from pond B. Park here and walk out the dike. The five impoundments were originally constructed to study mosquitoes in shallow saltwater ponds. Now they are mainly fresh, and attract many species of waterfowl. In summer, the dike harbors innumerable Yellow Warblers and Common Yellowthroats, as well as Song and Swamp Sparrows, while pond B has nesting Last Bittern, Blue-winged Teal, and Mute Swan. At times, both these ponds and the ones farther on have harbored such rarities as White Ibis, Cinnamon Teal, Black-necked Stilt, and Ruff, as well as more frequent desirables such as Wilson's Phalarope and Buff-breasted Sandpiper.

After about 300 yards, you will come to a T-intersection with another dike. In front of you will be another large pond (C); to your right the dike leads into the woods, and to your left the dike leads towards two other ponds. Pond C is large, but generally very shallow. When the water is deep, you can find Wood Duck and various dabbling ducks; when it is low, there may be shorebirds. Walk left along the dike and watch for Least and American Bitterns. The last pond (E) is a favored roosting area for Black Skimmer and Forster's Tern; Black Tern is occasionally seen here in migration, mainly during late summer. The dikes that separate the impoundments on your left (the east side of the dike) were once walkable, but they have become so overgrown that now they are nearly impassable. If you should attempt to walk them you will find yourself covered with ticks. The main dike continues on to a parking lot used by hunters that is accessible from Hilliard Blvd., but you should retrace your path back to your car on Stafford Ave.

If the road is passable (and after a heavy rain it sometimes isn't) continue for another one-half mile to the end of the road at an old wooden bridge. The salt marsh on either side of the road and across the bridge has nesting Clapper Rail, Seaside Sparrow, and Sharp-tailed Sparrow. In some years there also has been breeding Black Rail, both here and in the salt marsh north of Stafford Ave., opposite pond A. During the mid-1970s there were many reports of Black Rail at Manahawkin; since then, however, Black Rail appears to have abandoned the area, although there is an occasional report of one being heard there.

To search for Black Rail, choose a warm, still, moonless night in late May or June. After 10 P.M., listen at various points along the road for the unique *kick-ee-doo* or *kee-kee-kerr* call of the male. Although the Black Rail is no bigger than a Song Sparrow, its call is very loud and carries a long way. If you should be fortunate enough to hear one, you might try to venture into the salt marsh in the direction of the call, but beware of the many deep channels and mosquito ditches. Your best chance for approaching a rail will occur if you should hear one that is beyond the wooden bridge at the end of the road, for here the ditches can be crossed or circumvented. Another good spot is beyond the small, wooded island about 100 yards north of the road, opposite the first impoundment. Note, however, that this area is in the Barnegat NWR and is closed to the public. Contact the refuge personnel at Brigantine NWR about the possibility of entering the Barnegat area. You will have to be very lucky to hear a Black Rail, let alone see one.

Henslow's Sparrow was formerly a regular breeding bird in the upper reaches of the salt marsh around Manahawkin, but disappeared before 1970. Sedge Wren also nested there and around pond B, but has not been seen regularly since about 1975. Much speculation about the reason for the decline and disappearance of these species has failed to produce a definitive answer, although ditching for mosquito control may be a factor. There have been occasional sightings of both species here since 1975, including some late enough in spring to suggest prospective nesters, but none of the birds has stayed. As with Black Rail, you will be extremely fortunate to find one.

In winter, the ponds are frozen and the woods are almost deserted. The salt marsh, however, is an excellent place for Northern Harrier, Rough-legged Hawk, and Short-eared Owl, which can be observed from many points along Stafford Ave. Harriers and Roughlegs are about all day, but the owls usually appear only at dusk (although they occasionally are seen on overcast days).

You may want to combine a winter visit to Manahawkin with a trip to Barnegat Light.

Three other places a short drive south of Manahawkin are good in winter for Northern Harrier, Rough-legged Hawk, and, especially, Short-eared Owl. (1) Take Stafford Ave. back to its end at Rt. 9. Turn left and go south for about one mile to Cedar Run Dock Rd. Turn left and follow this road for 3.0 miles to the end; the last 2 miles go through salt marsh, where the hawks and owls may be seen. (2) Return to Rt. 9, turn left, and go about 4.0 miles to Bay Ave. in Parkertown. Turn left and follow Bay for about 2.5 miles to the end; the last mile or so is salt marsh. (3) Go back to Rt. 9, turn left, and go about

0.6 miles to Dock Rd. Turn left and follow Dock Rd. about 2 miles to the end. Obviously, if you are looking for Short-eared Owl at dusk, you won't be able to try all these spots. Any of them should produce owls in season, but Dock Rd. has been the most reliable in recent years. To return to the Garden State Parkway, go north on Rt. 9 for about 5.5 miles to Rt. 72, then take Rt. 72 west for 1.4 miles to the Parkway.

Holgate

Holgate peninsula (the south end of Long Beach Island) is one of the few remaining relatively unspoiled stretches of barrier island left in New Jersey. It is roughly 2.5 miles long and constantly changing, with ocean beach, tidal mudflats on the bay side, salt marsh, and low dunes. The area above mean high tide is now a unit of Brigantine National Wildlife Refuge, and is patrolled during the summer by refuge personnel and volunteers in an effort to keep people out of the bird nesting colonies (Holgate supports some of the largest nesting colonies of Piping Plover, Common Tern, Least Tern, and Black Skimmer in the state). In addition to its interesting nesting species, Holgate is well known for the variety of gulls, terns, and shorebirds that stop here in migration.

Directions

From the intersection of Rt. 72 with the Garden State Parkway at Exit 63 (Manahawkin), go east on Rt. 72 for 7 miles, crossing the bridge to Long Beach Island. At the third (and last) traffic light after crossing the bridge, turn right onto Bay Ave., which is also called Long Beach Blvd., depending on which municipality you are in. Follow this road south for 9 miles (and a couple of dozen traffic lights) to its end. There is a parking lot at the end which charges a fee during the summer but is free at other times. You can also park along Lincoln Ave., which is one block north. Be sure to pay attention to the signs, which allow you to park on one side of the street for part of the week and the opposite side of the street for the remaining days.

Birding (see note, page 365)

Holgate is at its best from May to September. In May there are migrant shorebirds in addition to the breeding species, which are al-

362

ready actively engaged in nesting activities. July brings the first southbound shorebirds, and increased bustling about the tern colonies as parents busily feed their young. From late July through September, flocks of terns and shorebirds gather on the bay side on sandbars and mudflats. By late September the flocks have thinned somewhat, but there are still some migrant shorebirds, mainly juveniles, and this is a good time to look for godwits and other rarities.

The main birding areas at Holgate are near the south end of the peninsula, a walk of more than 2 miles from the parking lot. As you walk south along the beach in May, watch for late migrant waterfowl, loons, and Northern Gannets. During June and July, you might find a Common Loon (usually in winter plumage), Common Eider, or one of the scoters. As you proceed, you will pass two or three large Least Tern colonies. The terns nest on shell- or gravel-covered sandy areas in the dunes above the high water mark. These sites are fenced and posted in summer to keep people out of the colonies. Each Least Tern colony usually has several pairs of Piping Plovers associated with it, since the two species have similar nesting habitat requirements. Both of these birds are on New Jersey's list of endangered species.

Holgate was the last known nesting site for Wilson's Plover in New Jersey, through the late 1950s. The species has occurred further south in New Jersey four times in recent springs (three in 1983) and might someday return to breed; if so, Holgate is a likely spot.

After about two miles you will see a small cove on the bayside, with mudflats and a sandbar island that is completely covered at high tide. This is the best birding spot, but, at the present time (1985), you cannot cross over here. Instead, you must continue for about one-third of a mile to the end of the peninsula and walk up the bayside to the cove. If possible, visits should be timed to coincide with the tides—the best birding conditions are usually about halfway between low and high tides, preferably on the rising tide, although the several hours after high tide can be good also. At these times, terns and shorebirds gather on the mudflats or the sandbar island to feed or rest. (At low tide the birds are widely dispersed over the exposed mud, while at high tide the island is submerged, the mudflats limited, and the birds tend to fly off to other places. The walk down the beach is much easier on the hard-packed sand left by a falling tide than on the loose sand above the high-water mark, so the best walking conditions do not always coincide with the best birding. The tides at Beach Haven Inlet occur at approximately the same time as at Cape May and Sandy Hook, and 5.5 hours earlier than Philadelphia.

In migration, shorebirds feed on the mudflats and the summer resident Willets and American Oystercatchers gather in flocks of 50–100 after the breeding season. Dowitchers and Red Knots are abundant, and there are lesser numbers of Black-bellied Plovers, Sanderlings, and Semipalmated Sandpipers. Semipalmated Plovers are common migrants, and the local Piping Plovers feed on the mudflats as well as the ocean beaches. Wilson's Phalarope and Hudsonian and Marbled Godwits are annual visitors in small numbers.

In addition to shorebirds, the mudflats and the sandbar island are favorite gathering spots for terns, especially in the late summer. Common Terns and Black Skimmers from the nearby breeding colonies use these sites for loafing and for feeding their fledged young. Forster's Terns can usually be seen fishing in the bay and Least Terns are present until the young have fledged. Holgate is the second-best place in N.J. to find Roseate and Sandwich Terns, which probably occur annually, but are very rare. Roseate Tern was formerly an occasional breeder in Common Tern colonies in New Jersey, and may still nest every now and then. The birds that show up at Holgate appear to be nonbreeders; July is probably the best time to look, but it may take many trips before you find one. The Sandwich Terns come north from their southern nesting grounds with the flocks of Royal Terns that appear in New Jersey in mid- to late summer. Also regular visitors to Holgate are Black Tern (mid-July through August) and Caspian Tern (August–September).

From the cove, walk back to the end of the peninsula. Here you can look west across the mile-wide Beach Haven Inlet to the salt marshes of Great Bay Wildlife Management Area (covered in its own chapter under Tuckerton Marshes). To the south are the remains of Tucker Island, a sandbar favored by gulls, terns, and Double-crested Cormorants, and Little Beach Island with its dunes and heronries, inaccessible except by boat and too far from land to peruse by telescope. At the tip of Holgate there is a large mixed colony of Common Terns and Black Skimmers. The skimmer colony, with 600–700 pairs, is often the largest in the state.

Because of the lack of habitat diversity, few other species breed at Holgate. Clapper Rail is common in the salt marsh, as are Sharp-tailed and Seaside Sparrows and Boat-tailed Grackle. A few pairs of Horned Larks and Savannah Sparrows can be found in the sandy dunes. The salt marsh on the bay side was an historically famous place for nesting Black Rail; however, the entire character of Holgate has changed since the 1950s, and no one searches here for the rails anymore, although there might be a few. Laughing and Herring Gull round out the list of breeding species. Rare gulls are more easily found elsewhere, but a subadult Little Gull spent the summer at the cove in 1983. Other rarities show up on occasion, as in the summer of 1983, when up to 35 Brown Pelicans roosted on the sandbar island.

From late fall through the winter, Holgate is a rather barren place. Offshore there are rafts of scaup, scoters, and Oldsquaw, plus a few loons, but one good reason for a visit is the possibility of finding a Snowy Owl. Almost every winter one of these vagrants from the north is seen here, and occasionally one stays for several weeks. Other winter visitors to be looked for are the Ipswich race of the Savannah Sparrow, Lapland Longspur, Snow Bunting, and Short-eared Owl. On the bayside, you can find a number of wintering waterbirds, including Bufflehead, Brant, Common Goldeneye, Horned Grebe, and possibly American Bittern.

NOTE: As of 1990, most of Holgate is closed to entry (pedestrians and vehicles included) from April 1 to about August 31 (later if the refuge personnel deem it necessary) in order to protect the nesting Piping Plover and other nesting birds. This policy is likely to continue in the future. Although this has removed one of the prime late-summer birding spots from the list of places for New Jersey birders to visit, the potential benefits to the nesting species outweigh that inconvenience.

Stafford Forge Wildlife Management Area

Stafford Forge Wildlife Management Area covers 2,788 acres of ponds and pine barrens in southern Ocean County, just west of the Garden State Parkway. Four contiguous ponds, which were created by a series of dams along Westecunk Creek, are the main attraction for both birds and birders. The southernmost pond, which is the largest and shallowest, is especially attractive to Tundra Swan and Ring-necked Duck in migration. When the water level is low enough to expose the grassy areas around the shore in August and September, you may find Lesser Golden-Plover and Baird's and Buff-breasted Sandpipers, along with numerous other shorebirds.

Note: Stafford Forge is a popular hunting area from October through December; visits at that season should be confined to the paved road or should be made on Sunday.

Directions

Take the Garden State Parkway to Exit 58 (Tuckerton and Warren Grove). From the exit ramp, turn right onto Rt. 539. Go 0.3 miles and turn right onto Rt. 606 (Forge Rd.). In about 1.3 miles, you will come to the large, southernmost pond, on the left; carefully pull off on the shoulder and park. Coming east, you can also take Rts. 70 and 72 to Rt. 539, turn right, and go south for about 10 miles to Forge Rd., the last left turn before you come to the Parkway.

Birding

The large pond is the farthest downstream of the four ponds. It is frequented by Tundra Swan from late fall through early spring, as long as the water is open; flocks of 25 to 50 are not uncommon. Ring-necked Duck also frequents this pond, especially in early spring, when as many as 100 gather here. The grassy edges of the pond have

MAP 67. Stafford Forge WMA

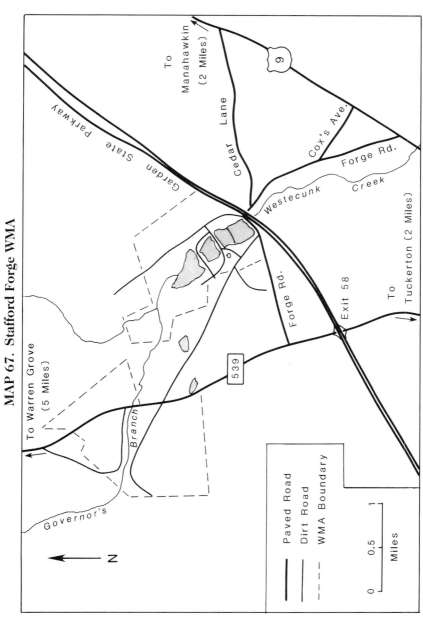

attracted modest numbers of shorebirds in some years; the best area is usually the southwestern shore of the pond (to your left as you face the pond) near the road. In addition to the rarities mentioned above, you might find Solitary, Spotted, or Pectoral Sandpipers, or Common Snipe, among other shorebirds.

To reach the other ponds, continued along Forge Rd. to the far end of the first pond and turn left at the entrance to the WMA. Follow the entrance road between two fields, where Ring-necked Pheasant and Northern Bobwhite often call from the hedgerows, and turn left on another dirt road. Go about 0.6 miles on this road, then turn left onto a dirt road; in a few hundred yards you will come to the dike road that separates the second and third ponds. Continue along the dike, scanning the water for geese and ducks and the edges of the ponds for shorebirds. Wood Duck and Canada Goose are common visitors in the fall.

At the far end of the dike you can turn either right or left on dirt roads. A right turn will lead you past a parking area to the dike that divides the third and fourth ponds. The fourth pond still has standing dead trees where Tree Swallow and Purple Martin nest in abundance. Turning right at the end of the dike between the third and fourth ponds will lead you back to the parking area noted above.

If you turn left after crossing the dike between the second and third ponds, the road will take you along the shore of the second pond, then lead away to the right into the woods. About 0.4 miles after turning left you will intersect another dirt road. Turn left, and after another 0.4 miles you will come to Forge Rd., just west of your starting point by the first pond.

Most of Stafford Forge is covered with typical Pine Barrens vegetation, and harbors birds characteristic of this habitat. Approximately half the WMA lies west of Rt. 539, along both sides of Governor's Branch. This portion and its associated cedar swamp receives virtually no attention from birders. You might find something different there.

Many birders combine a trip to Stafford Forge with a visit to Manahawkin WMA. To get to Stafford Forge from Manahawkin, take US 9 south from the intersection with Rt. 72 in Manahawkin for about 2.0 miles to the junction with Cedar Lane on the right. Turn right and go about 2 miles on Cedar Lane to its end at Forge Rd. Turn right, go under the Parkway, and the entrance to Stafford Forge is just ahead on the right.

Tuckerton Marshes

(Great Bay Wildlife Management Area)

The Tuckerton Marshes, or simply "Tuckerton," as the area is known among birders, is an extensive area of salt marsh just south of the town of Tuckerton in Ocean County. Most of the area is within the 5,000-acre Great Bay Wildlife Management Area administered by the New Jersey Division of Fish, Game and Wildlife. It is accessible by means of Great Bay Blvd., also known as Seven Bridges Road (there are only five), which traverses the marsh for 5 miles to its end at Little Egg Inlet. Tuckerton is known primarily as a shorebirding spot, but is also good for raptors, and the bushes along the road can harbor hordes of migrant songbirds after the passage of a fall cold front. American Oystercatcher is the specialty of the house and can be found here from early spring through fall. Interesting rarities, such as White-faced Ibis, Sandhill Crane, Curlew Sandpiper, and Black-throated Gray Warbler, are always a possibility.

Directions

From the north, take the Garden State Parkway south to Exit 58 (Tuckerton). Follow Rt. 539 south for three miles to the traffic light at Rt. 9. Turn right and go about 0.2 miles to a fork (opposite a large lake) where Rt. 9 continues straight ahead and Great Bay Blvd. bears off to the left. Take the left fork onto Great Bay Blvd.; after about 1.6 miles you will emerge onto the salt marsh.

From the south, take the Garden State Parkway north to Exit 50 (Rt. 9, New Gretna). Follow Rt. 9 through New Gretna for about 7 miles to Tuckerton. Just past a self-service car wash, turn right onto Gale Rd. Follow this road for about one mile until it dead-ends at Great Bay Blvd. Turn right and go about one mile to where the road emerges onto the salt marsh.

369

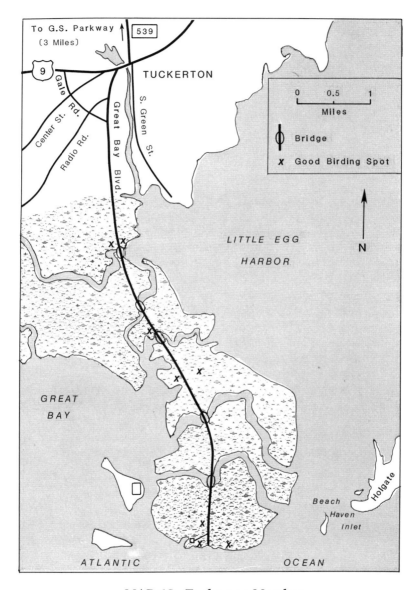

MAP 68. Tuckerton Marshes

Birding (see note, page 374)

Great Bay Blvd. continues for 5 miles across the salt marsh, crossing 5 bridges along the way. Just before the first bridge (2.5 miles from Rt. 9) there is a parking area on the left side of the road. The marsh here is a favorite stopping-off place for Whimbrel, especially in spring. In some years, they have been accompanied by an individual of one of the Eurasian races, formerly considered a separate species. They differ from our Whimbrel in having a conspicuous white wedge on the lower back, like a dowitcher. The last week of April through the second week in May is the best time to search through the flocks of Whimbrels, which may number more than 100.

As you cross the first bridge, you will see a sandy beach on either side of the road. If there are not too many cars and people around, these areas may have American Oystercatcher, Black-bellied Plover, or even Lesser Golden-Plover, and possibly Hudsonian Godwit in August and September. From late April through summer and fall, Forster's Terns fish in the channel behind the boat dock to your right. Study them carefully, and refer to your field guides, because the terns you will see at the end of the road are usually Common Terns.

The stretch of road between the first and second bridges (about 0.8 miles) is not very productive, but you should begin to see herons and egrets if your visit occurs between late April and early October. All of New Jersey's nesting herons and egrets are found at Tuckerton. Green-backed Heron is fairly common, Snowy and Great Egrets are abundant and conspicuous, Great Blue Heron only slightly less so. This is an excellent place to observe Tricolored Heron at close range, as this species seems to prefer the open marshes here to the closed ponds at Brigantine NWR that are popular with the other species. Little Blue Heron is fairly common at Tuckerton, but may be more easily seen at Brigantine (as is Cattle Egret, which prefers to feed in drier areas). Black-crowned Night-Heron is usually present, but is less active during the day and therefore somewhat less conspicuous than the others; Yellow-crowned Night-Heron, although present in small colonies just a few miles away, is seldom seen here. On the other hand, Glossy Ibis is abundant, and it is always worth checking them for a possible White-faced or White Ibis, which have occurred here.

The section of road between the second and third bridges (about 0.5 miles) is usually more interesting, particularly when the tide is high enough to force the shorebirds away from the mudflats and onto the small shallow ponds that dot the salt marsh near the road. Between the third and fourth bridges (1.3 miles) there is even more of this type of habitat, which provides the best birding until you reach the end of the road. A wide variety of shorebirds can be found here, although their numbers have declined substantially in recent years. Whether this change is temporary or permanent remains to be seen.

Spring shorebirding is mostly confined to the month of May, but the fall migration here, as elsewhere, begins in early July and runs into October. During July and August, however, early-morning birding is recommended to avoid the automobile traffic. Most of the regularly occurring coastal shorebirds can be expected here. Black-bellied and Semipalmated Plovers; American Oystercatcher; Greater and Lesser Yellowlegs; Willet (abundant); Whimbrel; Hudsonian Godwit (uncommon in fall); Ruddy Turnstone; Red Knot; Sanderling; Semipalmated, Western (mainly fall), Least, White-rumped, Pectoral, and Stilt (fall) Sandpipers; Purple Sandpiper (on the sod banks at the end of the road in winter and spring); Dunlin; Short-billed and Long-billed (mainly fall) Dowitchers; Common Snipe; and Wilson's Phalarope (uncommon in fall). Rarer species that occasionally occur are Lesser Golden-Plover, Piping Plover (at the end of the road), Marbled Godwit, Curlew Sandpiper (formerly, at the end of the road), Ruff, and Red-necked Phalarope.

Between the third and fourth bridges, watch for the Osprey nest on the left (north) side; it has been occupied for many years. The road between the fourth and fifth bridges (about one mile) is less productive and has been in terrible condition. It was patched during the fall of 1983, but time will tell how durable the repairs are. At times the road has been almost impassable without four-wheel drive. And, during monthly spring high tides, it can be under a foot of salt-water, especially if there are strong east winds. Check tides carefully. A flock of Boat-tailed Grackles frequently hangs out around the end of the road just before the fifth (and last) bridge.

When you cross the fifth bridge, you will see a long line of telephone poles going off to the right toward a former seafood processing plant on a distant island. Look for an Osprey nest atop one of the poles. The last stretch of road (0.8 miles) is lined with small shrubs, mainly bayberry. Under the right conditions, this vegetation can harbor hundreds of migrant passerines in September and October. Passage of a cold front during the day, followed by clearing skies and strong northwest winds overnight—the same conditions that bring massive flights to Cape May—forces many night-migrating song-birds out to sea or out over the coastal marshes. At dawn they struggle landward, where the bushes along Great Bay Blvd. provide welcome shelter and a chance to recover from their long flight. The marshes along both sides of the road have nesting Sharp-tailed and Seaside Sparrows, a few of which are present year-round. Clapper Rail is a common breeder, and the ponds along the roadside provide good feeding areas for herons, egrets, and shorebirds.

At the end of the road, extensive sodbanks are exposed at low tide, which occurs at about the same time as at Sandy Hook and 20 minutes later than at Barnegat Light. These are favorite feeding grounds for shorebirds, especially Black-bellied Plover (year-round), American Oystercatcher (spring through fall), Red Knot (spring, fall, occasionally in winter), and Dunlin (all winter). A wide variety of shorebirds can be found here from July through October; during the 1960s this was a favorite stopping place for Curlew Sandpiper, but none has been reported here in recent years.

Oystercatchers nest in the marsh about one-quarter mile north of the road's end, and they gather here and at nearby Holgate in large concentrations in late summer. (Holgate is the south end of Long Beach Island and is the peninsula that you see from the end of the road looking about 45 degrees to the left across Beach Haven Inlet; it is covered in its own chapter.) The sandy area to the left of the road's end sometimes has Piping Plovers, which also fly over from their nesting grounds on Holgate. They used to nest at Tuckerton as well, but disturbance by beachwalkers and recreational vehicles has driven them off. One species that continues to nest here is the Common Tern. Interestingly, this species and the oystercatcher have adapted here (and at many other sites in New Jersey) to nesting in the salt marsh, rather than in the grassy dune areas where they formerly nested, but were subject to frequent disturbance by people. A walk along the shore through the salt marsh to the north can be interesting and may turn up a few extra species of shorebirds, but waterproof boots are advised.

In winter, Tuckerton has little to offer. A few diving ducks gather in the channels and inlets; there are usually Black-bellied Plover and Dunlin, and sometimes Purple Sandpipers forage on the sod-banks at the end of the road. Rough-legged Hawk and Northern Harrier are here, and you can always hope for a Gyrfalcon or a Snowy Owl as you scan southeast across Little Egg Inlet toward Little Beach Island, where these species were seen in January 1984. More likely, you will see some of the hordes of Brant that winter in the bays of south coastal New Jersey.

Most birders try to combine a trip to Tuckerton with one to nearby Brigantine NWR, which has rest rooms.

NOTE: As of 1990, the fourth and fifth bridges are closed to vehicle traffic and it is unlikely that they will be repaired and re-opened. They are still open to foot (or bicycle) travel, however, so it is still possible to reach the end of the road by those means. The distance is about 1.8 miles.

Brigantine National Wildlife Refuge

Brigantine National Wildlife Refuge, or "Brig" as it is affectionately known to birders, is famous throughout the United States as one of the two best birding spots in New Jersey, with Cape May being the other prime area. Near Atlantic City in northeastern Atlantic County, Brig embraces more than 20,000 acres of coastal salt marsh, islands, open bays, and channels, bordered by fields, upland brush, and woodlands. Two large, fresh-brackish impoundments created by diking off about 1,600 acres of salt marsh are the main attraction for birds and therefore for birders. Although the refuge was established in 1939 primarily to aid in the protection and management of waterfowl along the Atlantic Flyway, especially Brant and Black Duck, it has become a haven for birds of many species, from grebes to songbirds. The name has recently been changed to Brigantine Division, Edwin B. Forsythe National Wildlife Refuge, but to birders it will always be Brigantine.

Brigantine is an outstanding place to observe the migration of shorebirds in spring, summer, and fall, and to see migrant and wintering ducks, geese, and swans from October through April. In winter, raptors (including Bald and Golden Eagles) are an added attraction, while the warmer seasons bring a variety of breeding herons and egrets, rails, gulls, and terns. The woods and fields attract a surprising variety of migrant songbirds in spring and fall, and a modest number of species nest in the oak-pine forest that is typical of the coastal plain at the edges of the Pine Barrens.

Because of its proximity to the coast and its combination of saltwater, freshwater and upland habitats, Brigantine attracts a wide variety of birds, including many rarities. The refuge checklist includes 270 species that occur regularly, but more than 300 species have been reported. Some of the more sought-after species that occur annually are Eurasian Wigeon, Lesser Golden-Plover, American

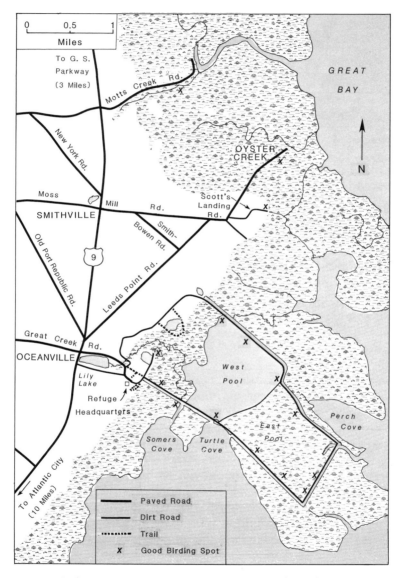

MAP 69. Brigantine National Wildlife Refuge

Avocet, Hudsonian and Marbled Godwits, Baird's and Curlew Sand-pipers, Ruff, Wilson's and Red-necked Phalaropes, Western King-bird, and Yellow-headed Blackbird. Rarities that have occurred from one to several times during the past 15 years include Eared Grebe, American White Pelican (several times in recent years), White and White-faced Ibis, Fulvous Whistling-Duck, Greater White-fronted and Ross' Geese, Gyrfalcon, Sandhill Crane, Wilson's Plover, Black-necked Stilt, Spotted Redshank, Little Stint, Black-tailed and Bar-tailed Godwits, Red Phalarope, Lesser Black-backed Gull, Snowy Owl, Fork-tailed Flycatcher, Sedge Wren, Northern Wheatear, Moun-tain Bluebird, Northern Shrike, and Clay-colored and Lark Spar-rows. Goodies such as these can occur at any season, so there is al-ways a chance of finding something unusual at Brig. After reading this paragraph, you are probably tempted to go there on your next day off and, for the uninitiated, directions follow.

Directions

From northern New Jersey, take the Garden State Parkway south to Exit 48 (US 9 South). Drive south on Rt. 9 for 6 miles to Great Creek Road in Oceanville, where there is a small sign pointing left to the refuge. Turn left, and, passing a sign that marks the entrance to the refuge, continue to a bridge that spans Doughty Creek, which forms ponds on both sides. Park at the edge of the road by the bridge.

From the Philadelphia area or southwestern New Jersey, take the Atlantic City Expressway southeast to Exit 7 (Garden State Parkway North). Drive north on the Parkway for 3 miles to the service area at Mile 41. Drive into the service area and proceed to the far (north) end, following the obscure signs for Jim Leeds Rd. The exit to Jim Leeds Rd. is a commuter access road between the service-area exit for northbound traffic and the entrance for southbound traffic. From this short access road, turn right onto Jim Leeds Rd. Go 0.4 miles and bear left at the fork onto Great Creek Rd. (Jim Leeds Rd. continues straight ahead.) Continue on Great Creek Rd. for 3.1 miles to Rt. 9; cross Rt. 9 and proceed to the bridge mentioned above.

From southern New Jersey, take the Garden State Parkway north to the service area at Mile 41, and proceed as just described.

Birding

Least Bittern and King Rail nest along the marshy edges of Doughty Creek, but you will be lucky to see either one. Wood Duck, Blue-winged Teal, Virginia Rail, and Sora are resident during the breeding season, while Pied-billed Grebe and American Coot are likely visitors at other times, if the water is not frozen.

Continue along the paved entrance road for 0.3 miles, as it turns first right and then left, until you come to the parking lot, on the left. Here there are modern rest rooms and an information booth; the headquarters is across the road on the right. Stop in the information booth to obtain a checklist and to examine the book of recent bird sightings; the location of rarities can be determined using a grid map in the booth. The list of bird sightings, sometimes referred to as "the book of lies" by those who fail to find reported rarities, is an important means of communication among the many birders who visit Brigantine; if you should find something unusual, by all means record it in the book, so that others can search for and enjoy your discovery.

The People's Trail in back of the rest rooms is worth exploring for migrant thrushes, vireos, and warblers in spring and fall; although Brigantine is not considered a prime spot for migrant songbirds, an excellent variety of passerines can be found here in May and in August—September. In summer, you will find only the limited number of breeding species that reside in this Pine Barrens fringe habitat, while in winter the local population will be increased by migrant sparrows. Tree Swallows and Purple Martins use the boxes in the field near the parking lot; Loggerhead Shrike and Western Kingbird have been found here in fall.

Most of Brigantine is accessible only by boat, but an 8-mile auto tour route is the principal attraction for birders. The tour route circles the dikes that contain two large impoundments, the West Pool and the East Pool. High tide is the best time to be on the dikes at Brig, so try to plan your trip accordingly. (Tides at Brig occur approximately one hour later than at Sandy Hook and Cape May.)

The tour starts at the parking lot; after about 200 yards, a small parking area on the right marks the beginning of the Leeds Eco-trail. A pamphlet is available at the information booth that describes this trail, which loops through a variety of habitats. The trail may provide a glimpse of Clapper Rail or Long-tailed Weasel, but is best known for the several Sedge Wrens that frequented the southeastern corner of the loop in the late fall and early winter in 1980 and 1981.

About 200 yards beyond the parking lot for the Leeds Eco-trail, the main tour route turn right onto the south dike, but the road you are on goes straight. Continue on this road, which passes a pond on the left and soon ends at the West Tower, which overlooks Gull Pond and an adjacent area of shallow ponds and marsh. There you can expect Little Blue Heron; ducks in migration (especially Hooded Merganser); occasional shorebirds in migration (Common Snipe is regular); and gulls in fall, winter, and spring (Lesser Black-backed Gull has occurred here several times). In winter, the tower provides an excellent point for scanning the marshes to the east and the tree lines to the north and west for Bald and Golden Eagles.

Retrace your path to the main tour route, and turn left onto the south dike. At low tide the channel on your right is an exposed mudflat where hundreds of peep (mainly Semipalmated Sandpipers) and yellowlegs feed in May and again from July through September. The marshes beyond the channel attract Glossy Ibis, Great Egret, and Snowy Egret, plus hordes of gulls (mostly Laughing Gulls in summer, Herring Gulls in winter). The channel on the left is part of the West Pool and is not tidal; other than a few Canada Geese, a Great Blue Heron, and some Common Moorhens, you are not likely to see much in it. The large expanse of *Phragmites* beyond the channel obscures any view of the water beyond.

After about 0.3 miles, you will come to the first mandatory birding stop, an open area in the *Phragmites* on the left about 100 yards across. This area is known to birders as the redshank pool, in honor of the Spotted Redshank that appeared here for two weeks in September 1978 and returned in September 1979. If the water is not too high, this can be a very good spot for shorebirds in migration, especially in fall. It is popular with Greater and Lesser Yellowlegs, Stilt Sandpiper, Short-billed and Long-billed Dowitchers, and (if the water is low enough to expose some grassy areas) Pectoral and Least Sandpipers. On the far side of the pool, an opening in the reeds provides a glimpse of a protected part of the West Pool where many ducks gather in spring and fall. In November–December, you may see hundreds of Hooded Mergansers and some Common Mergansers, along with thousands of American Black Ducks, Mallards, Northern Pintail, Gadwall, Green-winged Teal, Northern Shoveler, and American Wigeon.

About 0.3 miles further along the dike is a water-control structure used to regulate the water level in the West Pool. The West Pool covers about 900 acres, most of which is an open expanse of water varying in depth from a few inches to a few feet. The water is fairly fresh, as it is supplied by rainfall and by Doughty Creek, which enters the pool near the West Tower. At low tide, the outlet from the pool is a favorite feeding area for Ruddy Turnstone and sandpipers, which can often be observed at close range. The channel that leads south to Somers Cove is a feeding area for ducks, herons, and egrets (especially Great Blue Heron), while the muddy flat across the channel from the water-control outlet is a roosting spot for shorebirds and Least and Forster's Terns.

As you continue east along the dike, the *Phragmites* on the left gradually give way to the open water of the West Pool; here you can obtain an unobstructed view across to the north dike, about one mile away. Tens of thousands of ducks, geese, and swans rest and feed here in migration. One or two Eurasian Wigeon are seen annually, mixed in with American Wigeon, and the Eurasian race of the Green-winged Teal has been found on occasion.

Large flocks of Canada and Snow Geese visit the refuge in October–November and February–March, and most of them can usually be found on the West Pool, or feeding in the marshes outside the dikes. One or two Greater White-fronted Geese have occurred with the Canadas several times during the past 15 years. A Ross' Goose that appeared with a flock of Snow Geese in January 1971 was the first New Jersey record. In October 1982, another Ross' Goose was found in the West Pool with Snow Geese, and was seen around the refuge for several weeks. Since then, what is presumably the same bird has returned annually to Brigantine with Snow Geese, and is often found around the west pool. Tundra Swan is another migrant that prefers the West Pool; November and February are the best times to look for this elegant species (as many as 1,000 have been seen), but a few are present in midwinter if the water is not frozen, and some linger into March. The introduced Mute Swan is now a common permanent resident in both the West Pool and the East Pool; its numbers are augmented by migrants in winter.

About one mile from the start of the south dike you will come to the South Observation Tower. From here you may view the West Pool to the north and Turtle Cove and the surrounding marshes to the south. Climb the tower and scope the West Pool for waterfowl, gulls, terns, and shorebirds. American White Pelican has become an annual visitor to Brigantine in recent years, and one or two birds can often be seen floating in the middle of the west pool. To the northeast you will see a tower with a box on top of it. This is the home of the resident pair of Peregrine Falcons, an endangered species that has been reintroduced into New Jersey by the Cornell University Peregrine Fund project. The birds that inhabit the tower were hatched in captivity and raised in "hacking towers" such as this one. Upon reaching adulthood, the birds returned and established residence in the towers provided for them. One or both of the birds can usually be seen sitting on one of the crossbeams of the tower.

Scan south from the observation tower across Turtle Cove. Double-crested Cormorants can be seen at any season sitting on poles far out in the bay. In fall, winter and spring, the cove is a good spot for Horned Grebe and for various diving ducks such as Canvasback, scaup, Common Goldeneye, Bufflehead, and Red-breasted Merganser. Eared Grebe has been reported from this spot a couple of times. Large flocks of Brant, one of the species for which the refuge was created, winter on the bay to the south and feed on the marshes along the south dike. The Brant population has fluctuated widely in this century owing to such factors as loss of their principal winter food (eelgrass) and severe weather conditions in the high Arctic. Approximately three-quarters of the western Atlantic Brant population winters in New Jersey, many of them in the bays and inlets around Brigantine.

Just beyond the South Tower on the left is the cross dike, which is open only to photographers with permits to use the blinds. On the right is the shore of Turtle Cove, where Ruddy Turnstones, Sanderlings, and Semipalmated Sandpipers swarm to feed on horseshoe crab eggs in late May. At the west end of the cove is an old boathouse where Barn Swallow nests. This is one of several spots along the tour route where Northern Wheatear has occurred in fall.

The cross dike marks the beginning of the East Pool, which presents an entirely different aspect from the West Pool. Unlike the latter, the 700-acre East Pool has much more land than water; it is also more saline, being fed only by rainwater and by saltwater from a water-control gate near the north end of the east dike. The many islands, covered with *Phragmites* and shrubs, provide nesting habitat for Canada Geese and a variety of ducks, including Green-winged Teal (a rare breeder), American Black Duck, Mallard, Blue-winged Teal, Northern Shoveler, Gadwall, and Ruddy Duck (a rare breeder). This area also is a favorite feeding ground for herons and egrets from nearby colonies. From April to October, look for American Bittern (rare), Great Blue Heron (also in winter), Great, Snowy, and Cattle Egrets, Little Blue and Tricolored Herons, Black-crowned and Yellow-crowned (uncommon) Night-Herons, and Glossy Ibis. White Ibis (always immatures) has occurred numerous times, and three of the four New Jersey records of White-faced Ibis are from the East Pool. Among the other breeding species are Forster's Tern (abundant), Gull-billed Tern, Marsh Wren, Yellow Warbler, Common Yellow-throat, Swamp and Song Sparrows, and Red-winged Blackbird (watch for Yellow-headed Blackbirds among the flocks of Red-wings in late summer). Black Skimmers from nearby nesting colonies roost on the islands in the pool, and Boat-tailed Grackles and Fish Crows (abundant) feed along its edges. The marshes outside the dikes are full of nesting Clapper Rail, Sharp-tailed Sparrow, and Seaside Sparrow.

Except for a couple of spots around the West Pool, the East Pool has been the place where shorebirds have congregated in recent years. Although the numbers and variety of shorebirds can be staggering, they tend to remain rather far from the dike, so a spotting scope is essential. Among the regularly occurring species are Black-bellied and Semipalmated Plovers, Lesser Golden-Plover (rare), Piping Plover (rare away from outer beaches), American Oyster-catcher, American Avocet (uncommon in late summer–fall), Greater and Lesser Yellowlegs, Willet (common breeder), Spotted Sandpiper, Upland Sandpiper (rare in late summer), Whimbrel (mainly in the grassy marshes outside the dikes), Hudsonian and Marbled Godwits (both uncommon), Ruddy Turnstone, Red Knot, Semipalmated Sandpiper (abundant), Western Sandpiper (mainly in fall), Least Sandpiper, White-rumped Sandpiper, Baird's Sandpiper (rare, fall only), Pectoral Sandpiper, Dunlin, Curlew Sandpiper (rare), Stilt Sandpiper (fall), Buff-breasted Sandpiper (rare), Ruff (rare), Short-billed Dowitcher, Long-billed Dowitcher (mainly in fall), Wilson's Phalarope, and Red-necked Phalarope (uncommon).

About 1.5 miles from the South Tower, you will come to the southeast corner of the East Pool, where the road turns left. Several hundred yards to the east of this corner is a mudflat known as "Godwit Flats." A Black-tailed Godwit and a Bar-tailed Godwit, both extreme rarities, were present at Brigantine during the summer of 1971, and were frequently seen on the Godwit Flats. Although the flats are easily accessible only by boat, some observers waded the channels and trudged across the salt marsh to glimpse these birds. Marbled and Hudsonian Godwits were also present during that summer, and a few lucky birders were able to see all four of the world's godwits in one day, an achievement that may never have been equaled anywhere else.

As you drive north along the east dike, stop frequently to check out the ducks and shorebirds. Least Terns that nest on nearby barrier islands frequently fish in the impoundment along with the many resident Forster's Terns. The terns fishing in the channel outside the dike are usually Common Terns from the colonies in the salt marshes to the east. In winter, Snowy Owls occasionally have been seen sitting on the dikes around the East Pool, and the east dike was a favorite hangout of several Gyrfalcons during the winter of 1971–72.

After 0.7 miles, you will come to the northeast corner of the East Pool, where you turn left onto the north dike. The bay to your north, known as Perch Cove, has many migrant and wintering Brant, bay ducks, and mergansers. There are many good spots for ducks and shorebirds along the north dike, so stop wherever you find concentrations of birds. In about 1.1 miles, the north end of the cross dike comes in from the left, and the road makes a dogleg right. The area on your left—the northeast corner of the West Pool—has been the best single shorebird spot at Brig over the past 10 years. Unfortunately, the water in the West Pool is kept too high for shorebirds much of the time, but when the level is down or a strong northeast wind blows the water out of this corner, the pool attracts masses of shorebirds, including many rarities.

As you head west along the north dike, there are few places where you can get a glimpse of the water through the *Phragmites* on the left. To your right is a vast expanse of salt marsh, where Ospreys perch on poles in summer and Rough-legged Hawks hunt in winter; Northern Harriers are common all over the refuge at most times of the year. After about a mile, you will see the first of several small islands in the West Pool, where Double-crested Cormorants, gulls, and terns roost. These islands are especially favored by Gull-billed and Caspian Terns in late summer.

You will soon come to the end of the north dike, where you should be sure to scan the tree line to the north for roosting Bald Eagle in winter. These magnificent birds also like to sit on the ice or on islands in the West Pool, where they frequently find dead birds to feed on. At the end of the dike, 1.4 miles from the cross dike, the auto tour road climbs a small hill overlooking a borrow pit on the right, where much of the material used to build the dikes came from. The water level in this pit fluctuates wildly, but when it is very low (but not dry) in late summer and fall, it attracts species such as Black-necked Stilt, Baird's Sandpiper, and Buff-breasted Sandpiper. Sedge Wren has been found in the thick undergrowth on the back side of this pond.

The field on your left has nesting Eastern Meadowlark and (usually) Grasshopper Sparrow. In late fall it is a favorite feeding ground for Canada Goose and Snow Goose (plus Ross's Goose in 1983), and Northern Shrike has occurred in winter along its eastern edge. At the southeast end of the field is an old hacking tower that was used in the mid-1970s for the first Peregrine Falcons introduced at Brigantine. In recent years, however, it has been the home of a pair of Barn Owls, which can sometimes be seen roosting in a corner of the box. The road turns left at the western edge of the field, the spot where New Jersey's only Mountain Bluebird spent part of an afternoon in November 1982.

About 0.6 miles from the end of the west dike, you will cross a small stream, where a Belted Kingfisher often feeds, and come to a parking area on the left, where a gate marks the entrance to a trail. The trail is good for migrant songbirds, and has nesting Northern Bobwhite, White-eyed Vireo, Yellow Warbler, Common Yellowthroat, and Swamp Sparrow, among others. The path leads to the Experimental Pool, a spot that was good for grassland-loving shorebirds during the mid-1970s, but which has had very little since. A Fork-tailed Flycatcher was seen near the beginning of the trail in September 1974, and a Fulvous Whistling-Duck was found in August 1982, the only occurrence at Brig since a flock of 17 visited the refuge in 1974.

After passing by another field, where Canada Geese feed, the tour road enters the woods. Here you will find the expected permanent residents and summer visitors for this oak–pitch pine type habitat, including American Woodcock. Chuck-will's-widow and Whip-poor-will nest in these woods; however, because you are not supposed to be in the refuge after dark, you might plan on searching for these species along nearby Leeds Point Rd. and Scott's Landing Rd.

The tour road ends 1.6 miles from the end of the west dike, just after you cross another bridge over Doughty Creek, where the dirt road joins Great Creek Rd. You can park on the left just before the stop sign and explore some of the trails that lead along the creek and through the woods. To return to the parking lot at the headquarters, turn left and drive about 0.2 miles; if you have seen anything of interest, record it in the book at the information booth. To rejoin US 9, turn right and go 0.6 miles back to the first stop sign.

Leeds Point and Scott's Landing Roads

These roads are excellent in summer for Chuck-will's-widow and Whip-poor-will, and in winter for eagles and other raptors. From the intersection of Great Creek Rd. and US 9, go north on Rt. 9 for 0.1 miles, and bear right onto Leeds Point Rd. Follow this for about 2 miles to a stop sign and turn right. The second road on the right, after about 0.2 miles, is Scott's Landing Rd., which leads down to the edge of the salt marsh. The woods along this road are home to the two nightjars from late April through the summer. At the landing, you can scan the tree line and marshes for raptors.

From the stop sign mentioned above, Leeds Point Rd. ends in about 1.5 miles at the village of Oyster Creek, where there is a favorite local seafood restaurant. The first half-mile or so passes through woods where the nightjars are common. The road then enters a large open expanse of salt marsh, where Bald Eagle and Golden Eagle are regular winter visitors, along with Rough-legged Hawk and numerous Northern Harriers.

It is easy to spend four to six hours at Brig if the birding is good. Particularly in shorebird season, a second trip around the dikes may yield a very different array of species.

Brigantine Island

Much of this 6-mile-long barrier-beach island has been destroyed by housing developments; however, the northern 2.5 miles, almost 700 acres in total, has been preserved as the North Brigantine Natural Area, one of the few remaining unspoiled examples of this type of landform in New Jersey. It lies to the east of Brigantine National Wildlife Refuge, part of which is just across the inlet at the north end of the island. The Natural Area is also a good place for seeking a number of interesting birds, especially in winter.

Among the species that frequent Brigantine Island and its offshore waters from fall to spring are loons, grebes, sea ducks, falcons (including Merlin, Peregrine, and [rarely] Gyrfalcon), shorebirds, terns and gulls (including Black-legged Kittiwake), Snowy Owl (rare, but regular in winter), Savannah (Ipswich) Sparrow, Lapland Longspur (rare in winter), and Snow Bunting. A winter walk along the beach to the north end of the island can be an invigorating, and sometimes unusually rewarding, experience.

Directions

From the north, take the Garden State Parkway south to Exit 40 (US 30, Absecon). Follow US 30 east for about 9 miles into Atlantic City and take the exit for the town of Brigantine (also marked Farley State Marina); this exit, a jughandle turn at Illinois, will put you on Huron. Take Huron east for about one-half mile to the traffic light at Brigantine Blvd. and turn left. Follow Brigantine Blvd. past the huge Harrah's Casino and across Absecon Inlet to Brigantine Island, where the road becomes Brigantine Ave. Continue north for almost 4 miles to the end of the road and park at Brigantine Castle.

From the Philadelphia area, take the Atlantic City Expressway to its terminus in Atlantic City and turn left at Arctic, the first street after Baltic (where you cannot turn left). Go 9 blocks (about 0.7 miles) to South Carolina, and turn left. After one-half mile, at the

US 30 traffic circle, take the exit onto Brigantine Blvd. Continue straight ahead as described above.

From the south, take the Garden State Parkway north to the Atlantic City Expressway. Follow the Expressway into Atlantic City and proceed as above.

Birding

Birding at North Brigantine Natural Area is rather straightforward—you walk north along the beach for 2.5 miles to the end of the island at Brigantine Inlet, and then walk back. Along the way, you scan the ocean for loons, grebes, Northern Gannet, scaup, scoters, and gulls (especially Black-legged Kittiwake, which often comes close inshore in late fall and early winter). You also keep an eye on the dunes for Snowy Owl in winter; at least one is seen here almost every year. Flocks of Snow Buntings fly along the beach, but usually land in the dunes to feed; one or two Lapland Longspurs are often among them.

In fall, many Merlins and Peregrines migrate along the barrier beach. A few of them winter in the area and can be seen hunting along the beach or perched on posts. During the winter of 1983–84, a Gyrfalcon was occasionally seen on Little Beach Island off the north end of Brigantine Island.

Another winter bird at Brigantine Island is the Ipswich race of the Savannah Sparrow. Although no longer regarded as a distinct species, this large, pale subspecies is nevertheless a rare and interesting part of our coastal avifauna.

A trip to Brigantine Island can be combined with a visit to the more famous Brigantine National Wildlife Refuge.

Atlantic County Park

Atlantic County Park at Estelle Manor is essentially unknown to most birders. Its 1,672 acres include a diverse selection of habitats along South River and Stephens Creek, where the two streams flow into the Great Egg Harbor River about 4 miles south of Mays Landing. The park was formerly a game farm, and the land was acquired by Atlantic County in 1974. It includes Pine Barrens uplands, ponds, cedar swamps, hardwood swamps, fields, streams, freshwater marshlands, and about 250 acres of developed recreational parkland.

As at Tuckahoe WMA, just a few miles south, the diversity of habitats at Atlantic County Park attracts a wide variety of migrants, Pine Barrens residents, and coastal birds. Among the breeding birds are Wood Duck, Marsh Wren, Acadian Flycatcher, and Yellow-throated and Prothonotary Warblers. Ospreys, and Great Blue Herons from nearby colonies, fish along the streams in summer. The swamps along South River, in the northern part of the park, are the kinds of places where something interesting might be found nesting. Explore them and find out.

Directions

From northern New Jersey, take the New Jersey Turnpike south to Exit 3 (Runnemede, Rt. 168). Follow Rt. 168 south for 3 miles to Rt. 42, then go south on Rt. 42 (which soon becomes the Atlantic City Expressway) for 33 miles to Exit 17 (Rt. 50). Take Rt. 50 south for about 6 miles to Mays Landing, where Rt. 50 joins US 40 for one-half mile. When Rts. 40 and 50 diverge, turn left onto Rt. 50, toward Cape May, and continue 3.7 miles further to the Atlantic County Park entrance, on the left. If you arrive before the gate is opened (7:30 A.M. weekdays, 9:00 A.M. weekends), turn left into the dirt road just beyond the entrance, and park in the space provided.

From the Philadelphia area, take the Atlantic City Expressway as described above.

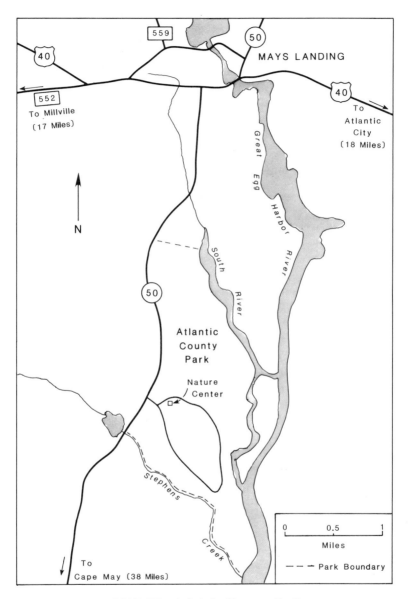

MAP 70. Atlantic County Park

From the New Jersey shore, take the Garden State Parkway to Exit 7 (Atlantic City Expressway). Go north on the Expressway for 5 miles to Exit 12 (US 40), then take Rt. 40 for 6 miles into Mays Landing and the junction with Rt. 50. Proceed as described above. From Cape May, the entrance to the park is about 7.5 miles north of the Tuckahoe River bridge on Rt. 50.

Birding

Drive in the entrance road for 0.1 miles to the modern new Nature Center. The center has rest rooms, maps, and information. Three miles of well-marked trails and ten miles of unmarked trails provide access to all parts of the park.

A 1.5-mile Nature Trail begins at the center and covers many of the habitats available at Atlantic County Park; you can hike the trail in a leisurely one and a half hours.

A one-way, 2.2-mile paved road also departs from the Nature Center, looping through the southern portion of the park. There are many places to stop along the way and explore the adjacent woods and trails. One especially good area to visit is the trail to the observation deck at Stephens Creek; this is part of the nature trail, but can also be reached by driving 0.8 miles along the loop road, where you can park on the right. Along this trail in summer I have found Great Blue Heron, Osprey, Belted Kingfisher, Acadian Flycatcher, Blue-gray Gnatcatcher, Yellow-throated Warbler, American Redstart, and many other species. Another good point of access to Stephens Creek is the floating dock at the large picnic area, about 0.3 miles farther along the loop.

The best way to explore the more secluded northern portion of the park, which includes about three-quarters of the acreage, is to park at the Nature Center and hike the many trails that crisscross the area. Most of these trails are abandoned railroad beds that date from the days when the area was a game farm. Also remaining from these former times are the numbered markers on many of the trees. The trail map available at the Nature Center shows the locations of many of these numbers, and makes it easy to find your way around.

Other birds that nest at Atlantic County Park or visit the area in summer include Green-backed Heron; American Black Duck; Turkey Vulture; Broad-winged and Red-tailed Hawks; Ruffed Grouse (rare); Northern Bobwhite; American Woodcock; Laughing Gull; Yellow-billed Cuckoo; Great Horned Owl; Whip-poor-will; Chimney Swift; Red-bellied Woodpecker; Eastern Phoebe; Eastern Kingbird; Purple Martin; Tree Swallow; Wood Thrush; White-eyed Vireo; Blue-winged, Yellow, Pine, and Prairie Warblers; and Scarlet Tanager.

Many other species occur in migration (especially in fall) and in winter—even Bald Eagle has been seen soaring overhead at the latter season. If you should find any unusual birds while exploring Atlantic County Park, be sure to report them to Cathy Smith, a birder-naturalist at the Nature Center.

Tuckahoe

(McNamara Wildlife Management Area)

The Lester G. McNamara Wildlife Management Area (formerly known as Tuckahoe–Corbin City WMA and still "Tuckahoe" to birders) encompasses almost 12,500 acres of salt marsh; freshwater rivers, marshes, and impoundments; and Pine Barrens woodland in Atlantic and Cape May counties. This diversity of habitat attracts a wide variety of birds. In addition to the typical birds of the Pine Barrens, you will find herons, egrets, ducks, geese, swans, shorebirds, gulls, terns, and wintering raptors, including Bald and Golden Eagles.

Among the more noteworthy breeding birds at Tuckahoe are Northern Harrier; Ruffed Grouse (rare); Black Rail; Acadian Flycatcher; and Yellow-throated, Prothonotary, and Hooded Warblers. Rare or unusual species that have occurred include Wood Stork, Fulvous Whistling-Duck, Purple Gallinule, Ruff, and Curlew and Buff-breasted Sandpipers. Because it is not as productive or as famous as such nearby hot spots as Brigantine and Cape May, and because it is a little off the beaten path, Tuckahoe is not heavily birded. The long list of interesting species that summer, winter, or just visit here, suggests that additional attention from birders would be amply rewarded.

Note: As a WMA, Tuckahoe is heavily used by hunters from October through December (except on Sundays, when no hunting is allowed). You can still drive the roads at that season, but it is best to stay in your car.

Directions

Take the Garden State Parkway to Exit 25 (Ocean City and Marmora). From the exit ramp, turn west (right if coming from the

MAP 71. Tuckahoe (McNamara WMA)

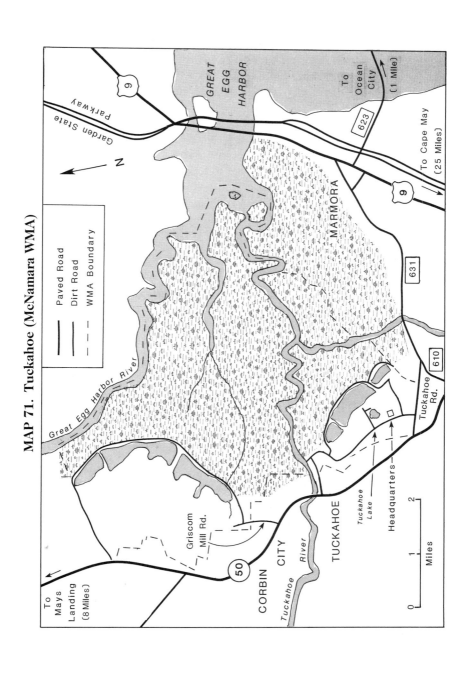

north, left if coming from the south) onto Rt. 623 toward Marmora. Go 0.2 miles to the traffic light at Rt. 9 and turn left. Drive another 0.2 miles to another traffic light at Rt. 631 and turn right, following the sign for Tuckahoe and Camden. After 0.5 miles, at a stop sign, follow Rt. 631 left and drive about 4.5 miles to the entrance to McNamara WMA, on the right.

From the Philadelphia area, you can follow the same directions, or take the Atlantic City Expressway to Exit 17 (Rt. 50). Take Rt. 50 south through Mays Landing for 18 miles to the town of Tuckahoe. Continue about 2 miles on Rt. 50, turn left onto Rt. 631, and drive about 0.3 miles to the entrance to the McNamara WMA.

Birding (see note, page 396)

Drive along the entrance road (where in summer you will find Pine and Prairie Warblers and other common birds of the Pine Barrens) for 0.2 miles to a dirt road on the right; turn onto this road, which leads to the freshwater impoundments. For about a mile, the road passes through pine-oak woodlands where you may find a variety of migrants in spring and fall, and the usual breeding birds in summer. Winter is usually unproductive, although kinglets, Red-breasted Nuthatch, and even Red Crossbill are possibilities.

The road emerges from the woods at a small impoundment on the right that is especially good for herons, waterfowl, and rails. This is where Fulvous Whistling-Duck (a flock of 17) and Purple Gallinule have been found. The road continues along the dikes for almost 2 miles, past a large impoundment and then a smaller one, both on the left. On the right are the salt marshes of Tuckahoe River and Cedar Swamp Creek, which feed into Great Egg Harbor Bay at the east end of the WMA.

Many herons and egrets from the nearby coastal colonies feed in the impoundments from spring through fall, and Least Bittern and Green-backed Heron nest. Migratory waterfowl include all the dabbling ducks, and an occasional diver. Ony Wood Duck, Blue-winged Teal, and possibly American Black Duck remain to nest. Large flocks of Canada Geese can be found most of the year, and Snow Geese drop in occasionally in the fall. Tundra Swan is a regular migrant, mainly on the Corbin City tract (discussed shortly), in late fall and winter.

Several species of rails nest in the impoundments and in the adjacent salt marsh. Among these, the most unusual is Black Rail, which has been found nearby in modest numbers during the past few years. (Interestingly, the first nest of Black Rail in New Jersey was found in 1844 at Beesley's Point, site of the power plant visible just a couple of miles east of Tuckahoe.) Most of the Black Rails found here recently have been on private property, but some have been heard from the dikes at Tuckahoe. Be aware that the WMA is officially closed at night, so obtain permission at the headquarters before venturing onto the dikes after dark.

Raptors are usually conspicuous at Tuckahoe. In summer, you will find nesting Turkey Vulture, Osprey and Northern Harrier, while in winter you can expect harrier, Red-tailed and Rough-legged Hawks, and possibly Bald and Golden Eagles. The impoundments attract many migrant shorebirds, especially in late summer when the water is low. You can expect such common species as Black-bellied and Semipalmated Plovers; Greater and Lesser Yellowlegs; Solitary, Spotted, Semipalmated, Least, and Pectoral Sandpipers; Short-billed Dowitcher; Common Snipe; and American Woodcock; but you never know when a rarity might appear.

Shortly after the road leaves the dikes, it intersects the main road through the WMA. Here you can turn left and drive through a pine-oak woodland with occasional wet areas, where Acadian Flycatcher and Yellow-throated Warbler nest. After 1.2 miles, turn left onto a road that leads toward Tuckahoe Lake. In about one-quarter mile, you will come to a short road on the right that leads about 100 yards to Tuckahoe Lake. Prothonotary Warbler nests around the lake, and Common Nighthawk has been seen here in summer.

Retrace your route to the main road, and turn right. After about 1.6 miles, you will come to a fork, leading, on the right, to a boat landing on the Tuckahoe River; this area should be checked for raptors, especially in winter. Continuing on the main road, you will come to pavement in about 0.4 miles, and then to Rt. 50 after another 0.3 miles. Turn right onto Rt. 50, where you will immediately cross the bridge over the Tuckahoe River.

To reach the Corbin City portion of the McNamara WMA, go north from the bridge for 0.9 miles to Griscom Mill Rd., where there is an old schoolhouse and a sign for the John S. Hembold Education Center. Turn right onto Griscom Mill Rd., which becomes dirt after 0.3 miles. After about 2 miles, you will come to the first of three large impoundments.

For several miles, the road follows the dikes of the impoundments, which are excellent for wintering raptors and for many of the migratory species as well. Then the road passes through some Pine Barrens woodland that has nesting Ruffed Grouse, Red-bellied Woodpecker, Brown Creeper, Yellow-throated Vireo, and Hooded Warbler. After having traversed almost 7 miles of dikes and woods, the road rejoins Rt. 50 about 3.6 miles north of Griscom Mill Rd. A small sign marks this north entrance to the WMA, which is just opposite the Holiday Haven Campground. Since the birdlife of the McNamara WMA has not been thoroughly surveyed, further investigation by birders may reveal that this area has even more of interest.

NOTE: The road along the dikes of the impoundments at the Tuckahoe portion of McNamara WMA is closed to automobiles as of 1990. You can drive to the edge of the impoundments from either direction, park, and walk the dikes; the length of the closed section is about 1.5 miles. The road along the dikes at Corbin City is still open to vehicles.

Longport Sod Banks

The Longport Sod Banks, located along the causeway between Longport and Ocean City, is a mile-long tidal flat of sand, grass, and mussel beds on Great Egg Harbor Inlet. This area is excellent for shorebirds at almost any season, although there are usually more people than birds in summer. In addition to the many expected shorebirds, Longport is especially known for the Bar-tailed Godwit that appeared here during May in seven of the eleven years from 1972 to 1982. Many gulls, terns, diving ducks, and other seabirds can be seen near the bridge to Ocean City or around the jetties in the town of Longport.

Directions

From the north, take the Garden State Parkway south to Exit 30. Follow Rt. 52 southeast for one mile, crossing Rt. 9, to the Somers Point traffic circle. Go three-quarters of the way around the circle, then follow the sign toward Pleasantville onto Shore Rd. north. Go one mile to the first traffic light, then turn right onto Maryland Ave. (Rt. 152). Follow this road for just over two miles across the salt marsh and a couple of bridges to the intersection of Rt. 152 and the road to Ocean City at The Dunes restaurant on the right.

From the south, take the Garden State Parkway north to Exit 29. Make the first right turn onto Somers Point–Mays Landing Rd., and follow it for one-half mile to the Somers Point traffic circle. Go halfway around the circle, exit onto Shore Rd., and proceed as described above.

Birding

As you cross the salt marsh on Maryland Ave., watch for Boat-tailed Grackles perched on the many pilings and billboards. Keep an eye

MAP 72. Longport Sod Banks

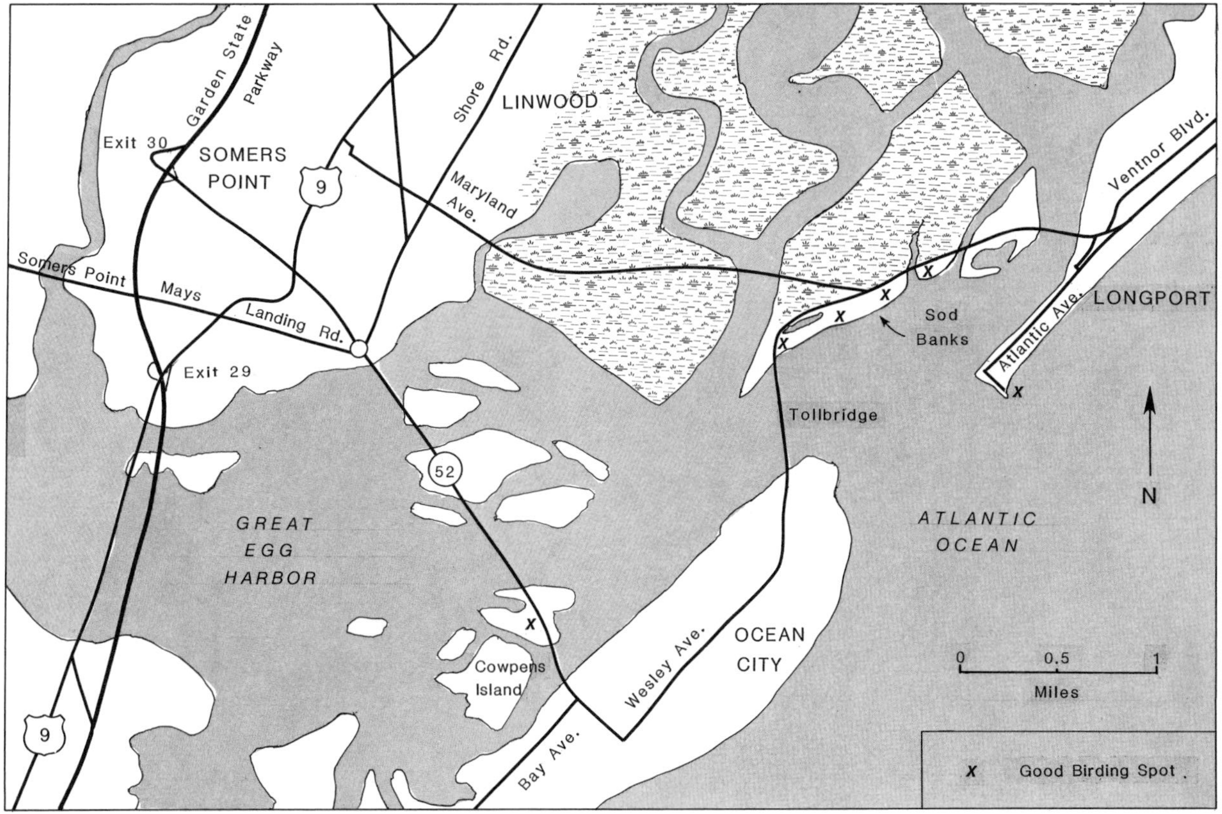

Garden State Parkway

Exit 30

SOMERS POINT

Shore Rd.

LINWOOD

Maryland Ave.

Ventnor Blvd.

LONGPORT

Atlantic Ave.

X

Sod Banks

X

X

X

Tollbridge

N

ATLANTIC OCEAN

Somers Point

Mays

Landing Rd.

Exit 29

9

52

GREAT EGG HARBOR

X

Cowpens Island

Wesley Ave.

Bay Ave.

OCEAN CITY

9

0   0.5   1

Miles

X   Good Birding Spot

out for shorebirds in numerous tidal ponds along the way, but be careful about stopping, as the road is heavily traveled. Find a wide shoulder and pull well off the road.

After the stop sign for Ocean City Blvd., continue straight ahead and immediately look for a place to park on the right shoulder. There is a beach-buggy trail leading to the beach, and the best place to park is just beyond it. Walk down to the beach and scan the sod banks in both directions—they are favored feeding grounds for a wide variety of shorebirds. The banks are under water for several hours before and after high tide, so it is best to plan your visit accordingly; a visit on a falling tide is usually the most productive. (High tide occurs here about 15 minutes later than at Sandy Hook or Cape May and about 35 minutes later than Barnegat Light.)

The sod banks are worth visiting at any season, although May and July–September will have the greatest variety. During July and August, there will also be many people, however, especially in the afternoon. In spite of the constant foot and off-road-vehicle traffic, a few pairs of Piping Plover still try to nest on the gravel- or shell-covered sand above the high-water mark. Migrant shorebirds are the main attraction, including some rarities. The area for a quarter-mile in either direction from the intersection of Maryland Ave. and Ocean City Blvd. is where the Bar-tailed Godwit appeared. This bird was found in the spring of 1972, and was seen for periods of a few days to two weeks each May up through 1979, with the exception of 1976. In May 1982, what was presumably the same bird reappeared at Longport, but it has not been seen since. Curlew Sandpiper is found in some years, usually during May.

Most of the regular migrant shorebirds can be found at Longport, including Black-bellied and Semipalmated Plovers, Lesser Golden-Plover (rare), American Oystercatcher, Greater and Lesser Yellowlegs, Willet (nests in the marsh nearby), Spotted Sandpiper, Whimbrel, Hudsonian and Marbled Godwits (both occasional in fall), Ruddy Turnstone (very common), Red Knot (abundant at times), Sanderling, Semipalmated Sandpiper, Western Sandpiper (mainly fall), Least and White-rumped Sandpipers, Baird's Sandpiper (rare in fall), Pectoral Sandpiper, Purple Sandpiper (late fall through spring), Dunlin (common fall–spring), Stilt Sandpiper (fall), Short-billed Dowitcher, and Long-billed Dowitcher (mainly fall). The best shorebirding is usually in the half-mile stretch centered at the beach-buggy road where you park and cross over to the beach.

From late fall to early spring, a variety of loons, grebes, and waterfowl may be seen just offshore. Red-throated and Common Loons are regular, as is Horned Grebe. Large flocks of Brant winter in the inlet, while the common ducks are Oldsquaw, Greater Scaup, and Red-breasted Merganser. Lesser numbers of Bufflehead, Common Goldeneye, Canvasback, and all three scoters are present, and any of the other bay or sea ducks are possible, including both eiders and Harlequin Duck.

After you have walked the beach in both directions and exhausted the birding possibilities here, return to your car, turn around, and head south toward Ocean City. Just before the bridge (about one-half mile) is a parking area on the right that will hold half a dozen cars. From here you can search the bay to the west for diving ducks and Great Cormorant in winter or Double-crested Cormorant in summer. Cross the road and scan the inlet for waterfowl and gulls. The mudflats here are not as attractive to shorebirds as the ones up the beach to the north, but may have Sanderling and Dunlin in season.

About 100 yards north of the bridge, between the road and the beach, there is a long, narrow pond in the dunes that is a favored roosting place for many shorebirds, gulls, terns, and skimmers, especially when the tide is high. A Wilson's Plover appeared here for two days in spring 1983. It is a good place to observe shorebirds at fairly close range, and they often seek refuge here when the beach is overrun with people.

In winter, the jetties at the south end of Longport are worth checking. To reach them, continue east on Ocean City Blvd. across the bridge into Longport, then bear right onto 27th Ave. Go two blocks to Atlantic Ave. and turn right. Follow Atlantic to the end (about 0.9 miles), turn left onto 11th Ave., and drive one long block to the end. Take notice of the No Parking signs here and do not stray far from your car, although the police are not too active here in winter. The jetties at the end of 11th Ave. and off the end of Atlantic Ave. are good for Purple Sandpiper, while the waters around the jetties may harbor scoters, eiders, Harlequin Duck, or even alcids.

In summer, the road from Somers Point to Ocean City is good for herons, egrets, and terns. To reach this area, return to the Somers Point traffic circle and go three-quarters of the way around it to Rt. 52 toward Ocean City. Just before the last bridge along the causeway to Ocean City, park at the information building on the right to observe the heronry on Cowpen's Island, just to the southwest.

Since this chapter was written, the bridge and road along Rt. 152 have undergone major construction that has further diminished the value of the birding areas at the sod banks. For now, the best place to park is at the bridge to Ocean City; from there you can walk north along the beach.

Corson's Inlet

From Ocean City south to Cape May, a stretch of salt marsh and tidal bays borders the coast, separating mainland New Jersey from the barrier beaches of Cape May County. Four inlets cross the barrier beaches, linking the salt-marsh islands and bays to the Atlantic Ocean. These inlets provide a variety of feeding, breeding, and roosting habitats for many species of birds. A visit at any season can be rewarding, but in summer you will have to contend with thousands of beachgoers at the popular summer resorts along this strip.

At Corson's Inlet, the northernmost of the four inlets, 341 acres of salt marsh and coastal dunes have been preserved as Corson's Inlet State Park. Here you can find a wide variety of loons, grebes, cormorants, and diving ducks from late fall through spring; a good selection of shorebirds in spring and fall; and an abundance of herons, egrets, gulls, and terns from spring through the fall.

Directions

Take the Garden State Parkway to Exit 25 (Ocean City and Marmora). From the exit ramp, turn east (left if coming from the north, right if coming from the south) onto Rt. 623 toward Ocean City. Go 2 miles to West Ave. (second light after the bridge), and turn right (south) onto West Ave. (Rt. 619). Drive 2.1 miles to the traffic light at 55th St. Following Rt. 619, turn right onto 55th St., which soon becomes Ocean Dr., and go 0.9 miles to a parking lot on the left with a sign for Corson's Inlet State Park.

Birding

The wet, marshy area on the left, just before the parking lot, is a favorite feeding area for herons and egrets from the nearby colonies, and for shorebirds in migration. From the parking lot, walk across the dunes toward the ocean. On the dunes, you may find Horned

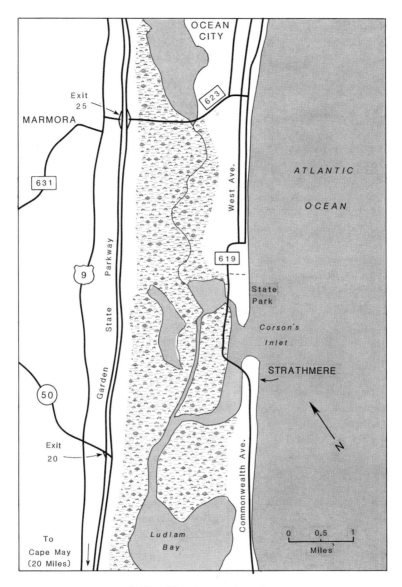

MAP 73. Corson's Inlet

Lark, Snow Bunting (winter), and several species of sparrows, including the Ipswich race of the Savannah Sparrow (winter).

In and around the inlet, from October through April, you will find a variety of waterbirds, including Red-throated and Common Loons; Horned Grebe; Double-crested Cormorant (all year); Brant; American Black Duck; Canvasback; Redhead (rare); Greater Scaup; Lesser Scaup (uncommon in winter); Oldsquaw; Black, Surf, and White-winged Scoters; Common Goldeneye; Bufflehead; and Red-breasted Merganser. American Coot, Common Merganser, Ruddy Duck, and various puddle ducks are also present at times. Rarely, a Red-necked Grebe or an eider is seen.

Starting in spring, the salt marshes around Corson's Inlet attract many herons, egrets, and Whimbrel (in migration), plus breeding Clapper Rail, Willet, American Oystercatcher, Laughing Gull, Common and Forster's Terns, and Sharp-tailed and Seaside Sparrows. On the beaches there are Black Skimmer, Least Tern, and Piping Plover, three species which have become endangered in New Jersey, primarily because of loss of breeding habitat to beachgoers.

The mudflats around the inlet attract many migrant shorebirds, including Black-bellied and Semipalmated Plovers; Willet; Ruddy Turnstone; Red Knot; Sanderling; Semipalmated, Western, and Least Sandpipers; Dunlin; and Short-billed Dowitcher. In late summer and fall, large flocks of Forster's and Royal Terns gather on the sandbars to roost; at these times, there are frequently a few Caspian Terns among them, and, rarely, a Sandwich Tern.

From the parking lot at the state park continue south along Ocean Dr. across an island that is part of the state park. You can pull off and park along the side of the road (carefully—this is a busy road) and scan for birds. Piping Plover nest above the high-tide line along this stretch of island. After about a mile you will come to the tollbridge across Corson's Inlet. Stop just before and just after the bridge to scan the water and the mudflats for birds.

Townsend's Inlet

The next inlet south is Townsend's Inlet, which can be reached by continuing south on Ocean Drive through Strathmere and Sea Isle City for almost 7 miles. The sandbars that form on either side of this inlet sometimes attract immense concentrations of shorebirds and terns in fall.

Jakes Landing Road and Reeds Beach

Two quite different but worthwhile birding spots in southwestern Cape May County are Jakes Landing Rd. and Reeds Beach.

Jakes Landing Rd. is the main access road for the Dennis Creek Wildlife Management Area, and is one of the premier places in New Jersey to observe wintering raptors, especially Bald Eagle, Northern Harrier, Rough-legged Hawk, Golden Eagle, and Short-eared Owl. In spring and summer Yellow-throated Warbler nests in the pine woods along the road, and Virginia, Clapper, and King Rails in the marsh at the end of the road.

Reeds Beach is a shorebird spot, especially in late May and early June, when tens of thousands of Ruddy Turnstones, Red Knots, Sanderlings, and Semipalmated Sandpipers gather to feed on horseshoe crab eggs. This is the time to look for rarities such as Curlew Sandpiper, a regular visitor, and Little Stint (one New Jersey record). Many other species of shorebirds can also be found here in spring and from late July through September.

Directions

Follow the directions in the Tuckahoe chapter to Marmora. After turning left at the stop sign onto Rt. 631, go 3.5 miles and bear left onto Rt. 610. Continue almost 8 miles to Rt. 47, in Dennisville. Turn right onto Rt. 47 and drive 1.4 miles to Jakes Landing Rd., on the left (the first left turn after turning onto Rt. 47).

Birding

Jakes Landing Rd. is only about 1.4 miles long. The first mile passes through a section of Belleplain State Forest, most of which is open deciduous woods, where you will find many of the common upland

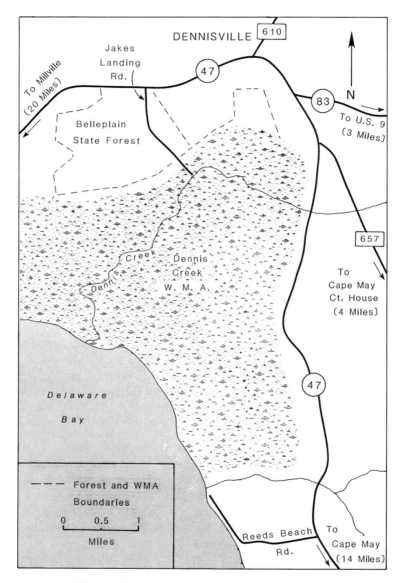

MAP 74. Jakes Landing Road and Reeds Beach

species of the Delaware Bayshore. The last quarter-mile of this section has several pine and spruce plantings; the mature pines are where the Yellow-throated Warblers nest.

Continue to the parking lot at the end of the road. This is where you will hear, and perhaps see, the several species of rails in summer. In winter, Northern Harriers and Rough-legged Hawks are always in evidence, and there are usually several Bald Eagles and Golden Eagles in the area. A little time and patience will often be rewarded by views of these magnificent raptors.

To reach Reeds Beach, return to Rt. 47 and turn right. Drive a little more than 8 miles on Rt. 47 to Reeds Beach Rd. (Rt. 655), on the right. (Despite the long drive, this will be only the second right turn after leaving Jakes Landing.) Follow Reeds Beach Rd. for one mile to its end, then turn right and take Beach Ave. about three-quarters of a mile to its end at Bidwell Creek. Although there are often large groups of shorebirds anywhere along this road, the area around the creek outlet is usually the most reliable place to see them. Late May and early June is the best time to bird Reeds Beach, but shorebirds, as well as flocks of Forster's Terns, also are present in late summer.

Do not stop, pause, or park anywhere along Reeds Beach Rd. before the parking lot at the jetty. If you walk back along the road, don't trespass. The residents here are extremely hostile to birders and further aggravation of the situation is unwarranted. A very good alternative is Hands Ave. Ext., which is the next major road south on Rt. 47, about one-half mile south of Reeds Beach Rd. Drive to the boat launch area at the end, which provides good views of the same birds that are found at Reeds Beach.

Cape May County Park

This attractive little park in southern Cape May County is best known for its small, but reliable, colony of Red-headed Woodpeckers. During the 1970s, this was virtually the only spot in New Jersey where one could go and be reasonably confident of finding this species. With the discovery of nesting populations at several spots in the Pine Barrens and a slight increase in the northern part of the state, the park is no longer unique. The Red-headed Woodpeckers are still easier to find here than elsewhere, however. Among the other nesting species are Eastern Bluebird and Pine Warbler.

Directions

Take the Garden State Parkway south to the traffic light at Mile 11. Turn right and go one block to Rt. 9. The entrance to the park is straight ahead across Rt. 9.

Birding

From the entrance to the park, continue straight ahead alongside the playing fields for about 0.3 miles, until the road bends right at the zoo. Park on the right at the stone wall, where there are some steps up to the group picnic area. Red-headed Woodpeckers inhabit the open woods around the picnic area and the playgrounds further in. Walk north (away from the zoo) through the woods listening for their characteristic call and watching for the flashes of black and white as they fly from tree to tree. The call of the Red-headed is similar to, but harsher than, that of the more common Red-bellied Woodpecker, which is also present in the park.

After about 200 yards, you will come to a dirt road along the northern edge of the park; on the other side of the road is a golf course. The area along this short stretch of road on either side is

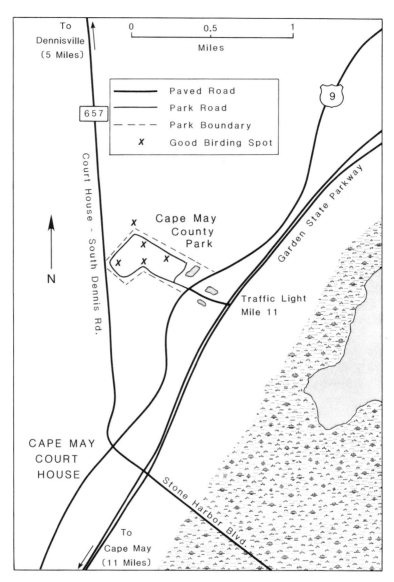

MAP 75. Cape May County Park

good for the woodpeckers, Northern Flicker, Eastern Bluebird, Pine Warbler, and Chipping Sparrow. On the north side, the open fairways with scattered trees are especially popular with bluebirds. Scan for them from the edge, however, and do not venture out onto the golf course. Pine Warblers usually arrive at the end of March, and in April and May they are easy to locate by their distinctive trilled song.

To complete a visit to the park, I usually continue walking along the dirt road for a short distance west, where it turns left. The road then passes through a pine-oak woodland for about 0.2 miles, turns left, then left again, returning to the zoo area where your car is parked. Common resident species in the park include Downy Woodpecker, Blue Jay, American Crow, Carolina Chickadee, Tufted Titmouse, White-breasted Nuthatch, Carolina Wren, American Robin, Northern Mockingbird, Northern Cardinal, and Song Sparrow. Other, less common, nesting species include House Wren, Blue-gray Gnatcatcher, Gray Catbird, Brown Thrasher and Rufous-sided Towhee.

There are modern rest rooms in the large building at the west end of the playing fields.

Birders frequently combine a stop at the Cape May County Park with a visit to nearby Stone Harbor (covered in its own chapter). It's also easy to stop at the park on a trip to or from Cape May.

Stone Harbor

Stone Harbor is famous for its heronry, a 21-acre oasis in a sea of residential development. It is the most accessible heronry in New Jersey and one of the biggest on the Atlantic Coast north of Florida. There are other birds to see at Stone Harbor besides those at the heronry, however. The causeway leading from the Garden State Parkway into town is excellent for shorebirds in fall. Stone Harbor Point, at the south end of town, is noted for shorebirds, gulls, and terns in fall, and for Short-eared Owls in winter.

Nummy Island, between Stone Harbor and North Wildwood, is the best place of all for terns, skimmers, and shorebirds, especially American Oystercatcher, Hudsonian Godwit, and Marbled Godwit. Neighboring Ring Island has the largest Laughing Gull colony in New Jersey—upwards of 10,000 pairs.

The Stone Harbor area can provide good birding at any time of the year, but the most productive months are May and August–October. In August, you will have to contend with the swarms of summer beachgoers.

Directions

Take the Garden State Parkway south to the traffic light at Mile 10, the well-marked exit for Stone Harbor. Turn left (east) onto the Stone Harbor Causeway.

Birding

From the traffic light at the Parkway, go about 2.1 miles until you cross the bridge. Pull well off the road and park, then walk across the road to the north side, watching out for the heavy traffic. The mud flats here attract many shorebirds in migration, especially in fall. Common species are Black-bellied and Semipalmated Plovers; Greater

411

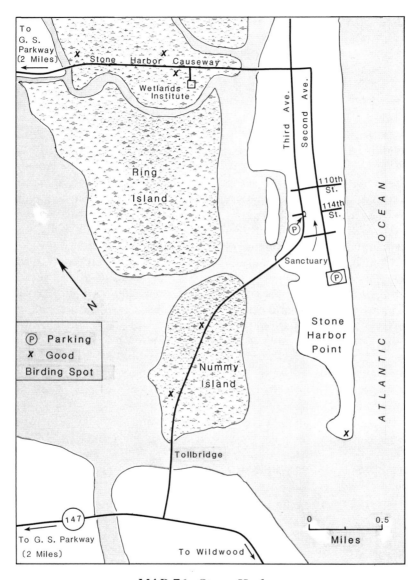

To
G. S.
Parkway
(2 Miles)

X Stone Harbor Causeway

X

Wetlands
Institute

Third Ave.

Second Ave.

Ring
Island

110th
St.

114th
St.

Ⓟ

Sanctuary

OCEAN

Ⓟ

Stone
Harbor
Point

Ⓟ Parking
X Good
Birding Spot

X

Nummy
Island

X

ATLANTIC

X

Tollbridge

147

To G. S. Parkway
(2 Miles)

To Wildwood

0   0.5

Miles

MAP 76. Stone Harbor

and Lesser Yellowlegs; Willet; Semipalmated, Western (mainly fall), Least, Pectoral, and Stilt (mainly fall) Sandpipers; Dunlin; and Short-billed and Long-billed (fall) Dowitchers.

Continue along the causeway for another 0.4 miles and park on the right opposite a large shallow pond on the left. Along the way you will probably see many Forster's Terns fishing in the nearby channel; Laughing Gulls are everywhere from April to October. The pond on the north side of the road is another good feeding and roosting area for shorebirds; in addition to the common species, White-rumped Sandpiper is regular here. The salt marsh on the south side of the road is a favorite area of Red Knot, Whimbrel, and many herons and egrets.

Just ahead on the right is the Wetlands Institute, a private, non-profit organization, which offers exhibits and information about the ecology of coastal New Jersey. The ponds around the Institute have their share of shorebirds, and a pair of Ospreys usually nests in the "backyard."

Continue along the causeway, across the bridge over the intra-coastal waterway, for about 0.8 miles to the first traffic light in Stone Harbor. Turn right onto Third Ave. and go about one mile to the Stone Harbor Bird Sanctuary, on the left. The parking lot and main viewing area are opposite 114th St., about halfway down the long block containing the sanctuary.

Established in 1947, Stone Harbor Sanctuary is a dense tangle of shrubs and small trees, remnants of the typical vegetation that for-merly covered much of New Jersey's barrier beaches. It currently supports the largest heronry in New Jersey; although numbers fluc-tuate, there are usually about 2,000 pairs of breeding birds.

The sanctuary's many birds include all the herons and egrets that nest in the state except Great Blue Heron and the two bitterns. Great and Snowy Egrets, Black-crowned Night-Heron, and Glossy Ibis are the most abundant species, followed by smaller numbers of Cattle Egret, Little Blue and Tricolored Herons, and Yellow-crowned Night-Heron. Green-backed Heron, not normally a colonial nester, is occasionally present. Most of the species arrive in April and stay until October or November. In late summer and fall the numbers are at a peak, as the population of adults has been augmented by many immatures. Early morning and evening are the best times; a spec-tacular show can be seen from the parking lot at dusk, watching the return of hundreds of "day" birds from the marshes to roost and the departure of the night-herons for an evening of hunting.

The birds must be viewed from outside the fence that surrounds the sanctuary and a walk around the perimeter looking for migrant songbirds can be productive in May and September–October. Sparrows sometimes feed in the grassy area near the parking lot; one year a Clay-colored Sparrow and a Lincoln's Sparrow entertained hundreds of birders as they fed together for an entire afternoon in early October. Late summer and fall are also the times to search through the herons for the occasional White Ibis, a rarity that has appeared here several times in the past 10 years.

In order to see Yellow-crowned Night-Heron, you must walk or drive around to the east side of the sanctuary along Second Ave. The main nesting group of about 25 pairs—the largest colony in the state—can usually be seen through the thick undergrowth at the intersection of 115th St. and Second Ave.

Continue south on Second Ave. to its end at the parking lot for Stone Harbor Point. Waves and currents have changed the point dramatically in recent years, so it is difficult to predict its condition or the birds that might be there. Over the years, however, it has been a good spot in fall for Piping Plover (formerly nested), a variety of other shorebirds, Caspian Tern, and large flocks of Royal Terns, in addition to local breeders such as Least, Common, and Forster's Terns. To reach the point, walk south from the parking lot for about a mile. In late fall and winter, you may see Short-eared Owls hunting over the scrubby dunes at dusk.

To reach Nummy Island, go back north on Second Ave. to 117th St., turn left, and go one block to Third Ave. Turn left onto Third Ave. and follow it southwest across the bridge for about 0.5 miles to Nummy Island. The large island to the right is Ring Island, which has the enormous colony of Laughing Gulls. Although there may be birds anywhere along the 1.2-mile stretch of road that traverses the Nummy Island salt marsh, two areas are usually the most productive. The first of these is about one-half mile beyond the bridge, where there are several ponds on both sides of the road (watch for Boat-tailed Grackles in the shrubby growth along the way).

The ponds on the right (northwest) side of the road are best. In addition to many of the herons and egrets from the sanctuary, there is usually a wide variety of shorebirds here. All the regularly occurring shorebirds mentioned above can be expected, plus American Oystercatcher and Ruddy Turnstone. Additional possibilities include Lesser Golden-Plover (rare), Hudsonian and Marbled Godwits, and Wilson's and Red-necked Phalaropes. Among the birds that nest on Nummy Island are Osprey (on an artificial platform); Clapper Rail; Willet; Laughing, Herring, and Great Black-backed Gulls; Common Tern; and Sharp-tailed and Seaside Sparrows.

Continue southwest for about 0.4 miles, to just before the road bends left. The ponds on the right frequently have American Oystercatcher and are favored by godwits. A variety of other shorebirds, gulls, and terns can be expected. Just ahead about 0.2 miles is the bridge to North Wildwood Rd. Stop just before the bridge and scope the sandbar on the opposite side of the channel—a favorite roost site for Black Skimmer, American Oystercatcher, shorebirds, gulls, and terns. High tide is the best time to visit Nummy Island, while a low or falling tide is better at Stone Harbor Point. (The tides at Hereford Inlet occur at about the same time as those at Sandy Hook and Cape May Harbor.)

Cross the tollbridge and go about 0.3 miles to North Wildwood Rd. (Rt. 147). To return to the Garden State Parkway northbound, turn right and go about 2.5 miles to the entrance. To go south on the Parkway, you will have to continue another 0.3 miles to Rt. 9, turn left, and go about 2.6 miles south to Rt. 47, then left again and 0.4 miles east to the Parkway entrance.

Wildwood Crest
(Cape May Coast Guard Jetty)

The jetties at Cold Spring (Cape May) Inlet that protect the entrance to Cape May Harbor have surpassed the 8th St. jetty at Barnegat Light in some recent winters as the place to find eiders, Harlequin Duck, and alcids. Only the north jetty is accessible to the public, from the town of Wildwood Crest, but it provides a good view of the inlet and both jetties, except for the south side of the south jetty. Some of the species seen here are Northern Gannet (regular close to shore), Great Cormorant (regular in winter), Common and King Eiders, Harlequin Duck, Purple Sandpiper (regular November to May), Little Gull, Black-legged Kittiwake, and Thick-billed Murre.

Directions

Take the Garden State Parkway south to its end, and continue another 0.3 miles to the first traffic light. Turn left toward Wildwood Crest, and follow Ocean Drive for about 2.5 miles to a marshy pond on the right.

Birding

The pond is a good spot for shorebirds at any season. In winter, you might find Black-bellied and Semipalmated Plovers, Greater and Lesser Yellowlegs, Western and Least Sandpipers, Dunlin, Long-billed Dowitcher, and even a few lingering herons and egrets.

Continue on Ocean Drive another 0.7 miles to the traffic light at Jefferson Ave. and turn right. Go one-quarter mile to Atlantic Ave. and turn right. Park along the road or in the lot of one of the motels that is closed for the winter, then walk down to the beach. The jetty is visible about 1.5 miles south along the wide beach. Walk toward the jetty, stopping occasionally to scan the ocean for loons, grebes, gannets, ducks, gulls, and alcids. Along the way, you should encounter Ruddy Turnstone, Sanderling, and Dunlin feeding at the edge of the water.

After about 0.3 miles, you will come to a fence that marks the boundary of the U.S. Coast Guard Electronics Station. Go around the end of the fence or over the stile and continue along the beach (as long as you stay on the beach, you are not trespassing). When you get to the jetty, walk out to the end (about 500 yards); be very careful not to slip on the rocks, which are especially treacherous when wet or icy. The best time to visit the jetty is when the tide is at least half-way out. (The tide times at the jetty are only a few minutes different from those published for Cape May Harbor and Sandy Hook, and are about 6.5 hours earlier than the tides at Philadelphia.) **Do not attempt to walk on the jetty if there is a strong north or east wind, as the pounding surf and spray make the rocks extremely dangerous.**

As you walk out the north jetty, scan both sides of it and the edges of the south jetty for ducks (especially eiders and Harlequins, which tend to remain near the rocks) and Purple Sandpipers, which feed on the rocks just above the water line. The Thick-billed Murre that stayed here for two weeks in December 1982 also swam close to the jetty. Great Cormorants, on the other hand, sit on the rocks or on the light towers.

From the end of the jetty, scan for loons, grebes, and gannets, and check the passing gulls for kittiwakes and rarities. In addtion to being a good place in winter, the jetty also is ideal for a seawatch in spring or fall, when you might see something really unusual.

Cape May

To the birders of New Jersey and the Northeast, Cape May is a mecca. In the fall, we are drawn by the thousands to witness a spectacle that is unsurpassed in eastern North America and has few equals elsewhere in the world—the migration of thousands of hawks, shorebirds, flycatchers, thrushes, vireos, warblers, sparrows, and other songbirds heading south for the winter. Although fall is the best season in Cape May, winter is outstanding, spring is superb, and summer is rich in rarities. Even on a dull day, Cape May is better than most other birding spots in the state.

At this writing, the Cape May County bird list is approaching 400, and most of the species on the list have been seen on Cape Island. Cape Island is what birders are referring to when they talk about Cape May; it is a triangular wedge of about six square miles at the extreme southern tip of the state, separated from the rest of New Jersey by the Intracoastal Waterway canal. Cape Island contains several municipalities, including Cape May city, West Cape May, Cape May Point, and part of Lower Township. There are numerous good birding areas around the Island, and each will be covered separately.

In addition to seeing swarms of hawks, falcons, and songbirds, it is the hope of seeing a rarity that brings many birders to Cape May. The list of rarities that have occurred here is far too long to list here and includes many first records for New Jersey. In 1984 alone, there were sightings of 30 species of rare or accidental occurrence: Brown Pelican, Anhinga, White Ibis, Greater White-fronted Goose, Common Eider, King Eider, American Swallow-tailed Kite, Mississippi Kite, Swainson's Hawk, Golden Eagle, Sandhill Crane, Marbled Godwit, Baird's Sandpiper, Wilson's Phalarope, Black-headed Gull, Sandwich Tern, Roseate Tern, Arctic Tern, Common Ground-Dove, Western Kingbird, Scissor-tailed Flycatcher, Fork-tailed Flycatcher, Sedge Wren, Loggerhead Shrike, Orange-crowned Warbler, Townsend's Warbler, Dickcissel, Clay-colored Sparrow, Lark Sparrow, and Brewer's Blackbird.

MAP 77. Cape May

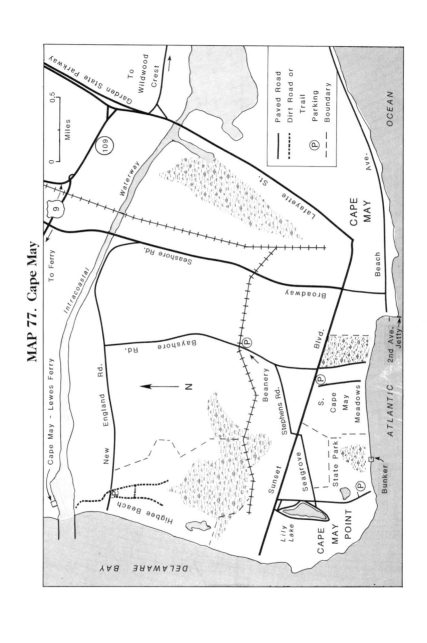

If you have never been to Cape May before and are visiting in September or early October, I recommend that you start at Higbee Beach at dawn. Later in the day you can explore the other areas. Directions for all birding spots are given from Cape May Point State Park, the location of Cape Island's most conspicuous landmark— the Cape May Point Lighthouse.

Directions

To reach Cape May Point State Park from anywhere else in New Jersey, take the Garden State Parkway south to its end. Turn right onto Rt. 109, following the signs for the Lewes–Cape May Ferry. Go 0.6 miles and take the jughandle turn for the ferry at the junction with Rt. 9. Follow Rt. 9 (Ferry Rd.) for one-half mile to the traffic light at Seashore Rd. (Rt. 526), and turn left. Take Seashore Rd. (the name changes to Broadway in West Cape May) across the bridge over the canal (from which you can see the lighthouse to the south) for about 2.4 miles to the traffic light at Sunset Blvd. Turn right onto Sunset, and go 1.7 miles to Lighthouse Ave. on the left (along the way, you will pass the South Cape May Meadows, a good birding spot which we shall mention later). Turn left onto Lighthouse Ave., and drive 0.7 miles to the state park entrance, on the left just before the lighthouse. Drive into the state park, and park in the large paved lot.

An alternate route, which takes you into picturesque but congested Cape May city, is to continue straight ahead on Rt. 109 at the end of the Parkway. This road becomes Lafayette St. after you cross the bridge over the canal. After about 2 miles, bear right onto Perry St. at the stop sign where Lafayette ends. In about 0.4 miles, you will come to the traffic light at Broadway and Sunset. Continue straight ahead on Sunset for 1.7 miles to Lighthouse Ave.

Birding

Cape May Point State Park

The state park occupies about 300 acres of land at the southern tip of New Jersey. It has been the site of a lighthouse since 1823, when the first one was constructed about one-third mile south of the present lighthouse. The rising sea level (which is continuing today) necessitated moving the lighthouse twice, the last time in 1859, to the present site. The land around the lighthouse served as a coastal defense base and radio relay station until 1963, when it was given to the State of New Jersey. Most of the buildings around the park date from the military period. The headquarters building, which has a nature museum and modern rest rooms, is on the west side of the parking lot, not far from the lighthouse.

Cape May Point State Park is the site of a hawk watch, conducted by New Jersey Audubon Society's Cape May Bird Observatory, where comprehensive tallies have been kept every year since 1976. The hawk-watching platform is located on the east side of the parking lot and is usually crowded with people in September and October. It is manned by an official counter every day from late August through November, weather permitting, and is a "must" stop on any visit to Cape May in fall. In addition to being an excellent spot to observe the migration of raptors, it is also the place to find out what rare birds might be in town and to meet old friends.

Most of the hawks that migrate through Cape May are accipiters and falcons that spend their summers in the forests and tundra of the northeastern United States and Canada. On their fall migration, many species reach the Atlantic Coast, which they then follow southwestward. For the falcons, the coastal route is the principal one, and they are uncommon inland, but for the Sharp-shinned and Cooper's Hawks, their abundance along the coast depends very much on the passage of cold fronts with strong northwest winds. When they reach Cape May, many individuals are apparently intimidated by the 14 miles of open water between the Point and Cape Henlopen, Delaware. Instead of crossing, as the falcons and Ospreys do, they turn and head north and then west along the Delaware Bay-shore toward Philadelphia.

The hawk flight at Cape May begins in late August, with the appearance of the first Ospreys and a few Bald Eagles; it peaks in late September and early October with the big flights of accipiters and falcons, and dwindles in November, when Red-tailed Hawks and the occasional Golden Eagle and Goshawk pass through. The numbers of hawks in a good season can be staggering; 1981 was the record year, with almost 89,000 hawks passing the Point. Sharp-shinned

Hawks dominate the tally every year, with a record 61,167 in 1984 (including 7,000 on October 4). However, Cooper's Hawks, which are scarce at most other hawkwatches, can be almost common at Cape May. A record 2,679 were counted in 1985. Clearly, Cape May is the place to learn to distinguish Sharp-shinned from Cooper's.

Even more than the accipiter flight, the migration of falcons at Cape May excites the hawk-watcher. American Kestrel is abundant, although this species has shown a disturbing decline in the past few years. Almost 22,000 were recorded in 1981, but in 1983 there were fewer than 7,000, the smallest count ever. The rarer falcons, Merlin and Peregrine, are what birders come to see, however, and Cape May Point is the place to see them. In late September and early October, these two are hard to miss, especially on days with easterly or southerly winds. The largest Merlin flight was in 1985, with 2,869, and daily tallies of more than 100 are routine. Peregrine Falcons have shown a remarkable resurgence in the past few years, and the seasonal total regularly exceeds 300 birds (480 in 1984). Daily counts of 25 or more are unremarkable, but the 72 Peregrines that passed the hawk watch on October 9, 1983, provided a thrilling day for dozens of birders (including me).

Ospreys are also a big attraction at Cape May Point, with as many as 3,018 seen in a season, mainly in September and October. Other regular migrants include Turkey Vulture (all fall), Northern Harrier (September–November), Red-shouldered Hawk (October–November), Broad-winged Hawk (September–October), Red-tailed Hawk (October–November), and Rough-legged Hawk (November). Rarities that show up annually are Black Vulture, Mississippi Kite (more often seen in spring), and Swainson's Hawk (maximum of 7 in 1981).

There are many things to see other than raptors at the state park. Walk toward the beach from the hawk-watching platform and you will pass a small pond on the right that has harbored Baird's Sandpiper and Sedge Wren in the fall. A little further along is a much larger pond on the left, known to birders as Bunker Pond. This is a favorite feeding and roosting site for herons and egrets, ducks, gulls, terns, and shorebirds, including Baird's Sandpiper. Least Bittern nests in the reeds around the pond and may be seen flying about, especially in spring.

Continuing on to the beach, you will see the "bunker," a large concrete structure that served during World War II as a magazine for four antiaircraft guns mounted just offshore from it. The bunker is being rapidly undermined by the sea, but it still provides an excellent vantage point for scanning the water for loons, ducks, gulls, and terns. In late fall and winter, you may see Northern Gannet, Common Eider, King Eider, jaegers, or even an alcid, if you are very lucky. A walk along the dunes toward Cape May city should produce Palm Warbler and Savannah Sparrow in October.

Return to the parking lot of the state park. The bushes around the edges of the large open area can be very good for migrant songbirds in fall. New Jersey's first Chestnut-collared Longspur was found feeding on the grassy area in June 1980, and other ground-feeding birds such as sparrows frequent the edges of the parking lot. Purple Martins nest in the martin houses around the headquarters from late April through the summer. A sight rivaling the big Sharp-shin flights is the enormous flocks of Tree Swallows, numbering in the tens of thousands, that sometimes gather on the wires around the state park from late August to early October.

A network of nature trails begins on the east side of the parking lot, just north of the hawk-watching platform. To the left of the hawk watch, as you face it from the parking lot, is a picnic pavilion; and to the left of the pavilion is the entrance marker to the trails. A map showing the trails can be obtained at the headquarters. The main trail makes a loop, with one side spur, through the dense shrubs and trees, and provides access to Lighthouse Pond at two points. The trails can be good for migrants in spring and fall. In summer, White-eyed Vireo and Yellow-breasted Chat are common along the trails. Blue-winged Teal and Least Bittern nest around the pond, and a Purple Gallinule spent several weeks here in the summers of 1981, 1982, and 1985. Least Terns hover over the pond searching for minnows from May through August. This is the kind of spot where a rarity might show up, so it is always worth checking.

Lily Lake

Drive out of the park and turn right onto Lighthouse Ave. Drive 0.5 miles, past Seagrove Ave. on the right, and bear left onto Lake Dr. Park immediately on the right, at the sign for the Cape May Bird Observatory; Lily Lake is across the street on your left. The observatory, a unit of New Jersey Audubon Society, is located in the white house in the woods on the right, and is a good place to visit to find out what birds are in town. The staff conducts field trips and birding workshops, operates the hawk watch, and runs a small bookstore. The woods along Lighthouse Ave., and along Seagrove Ave. are excellent for migrant songbirds in spring and fall. You can easily spend an hour or two walking the roads near the observatory on a good flight day in the fall, watching for thrushes, vireos, warblers, and sparrows. A favorite route is a walk around Lily Lake, scanning the bushes for migrant songbirds and the water for migrant ducks. Watch the wires around the north end of the lake for Western Kingbird in the fall; this seems to be a favorite spot for flycatchers—two Scissor-tailed Flycatchers were here in June 1984.

Lily Lake is a surprisingly good spot for migrant waterfowl and for feeding herons, egrets, Belted Kingfisher, and Spotted and Solitary Sandpiper. Redhead and Ring-necked Duck are regular in fall, and Eurasian Wigeon is seen almost every year. Rarities that have shown up at the lake include White-faced Ibis, Wood Stork, Fulvous Whistling-Duck, Sandhill Crane, Swallow-tailed Kite (seen soaring over the lake in spring on several occasions), and Northern Shrike.

Sunset Beach

From the state park, take Lighthouse Ave. back to Sunset Blvd. and turn left. Go one-half mile, past an abandoned magnesite plant (soon to be removed and replaced with condominiums), to the end of the road and park. Offshore is the wreck of a concrete ship, built during World War I, but decommissioned soon after. It served as a restaurant for a short time, but has long since deteriorated. From October through May it provides a roosting place for Purple Sandpipers, especially at high tide.

Sunset Beach is a good spot to scan for Red-throated Loon and for passing gulls and terns including Roseate Tern in May. Forster's and Royal Terns like to roost on some pilings down the beach to your right, and have occasionally been joined by Sandwich Tern. Jaegers, Black-legged Kittiwakes, even storm-petrels, shearwaters, and alcids have been seen from this spot after strong southeast winds.

South Cape May Meadows (see note, page 430)

From the state park, take Lighthouse Ave. back to Sunset Blvd. and turn right. Go about 0.9 miles to a parking area on the right. The

South Cape May Meadows is a large, wet pasture, which along with some adjacent marsh on the east side of the meadows, was acquired by The Nature Conservancy in 1982. Covering a little more than 180 acres, the area is bounded on the south by some low dunes that (usually) protect it from the Atlantic Ocean. The pasture is periodically flooded by sea water, and also has numerous ponds that collect rainwater.

"The meadows," as it is known to birders, is an outstanding spot for migrant shorebirds; for migrant or summering herons, egrets, and terns; for migrant or wintering gulls; and even for migrant songbirds. To explore it, walk out the dirt road that bisects the pasture as far as the dunes, scanning the fields and ponds along the way. From the dunes, you can scope the water offshore for loons, grebes, and ducks from fall through spring. To return to your car, you can either retrace your steps, or walk along the beach toward Cape May city for a couple of hundred yards, then bear left along the sand fence to a path that runs along the east side of the meadows back to Sunset Blvd. This path is often the better one in the early morning, because the sun is behind you. When walking through the meadows, do not stray from the two main paths.

Piping Plover and Least Tern nest on the sandy overwash near the ocean; in recent years, the tern colony has attracted Arctic, Roseate, and Sandwich Terns for brief visits.

Spring shorebird migration brings many plovers and sandpipers to the meadows, but it is mainly the fall migration (early July–October) that attracts the greatest numbers and variety. Semipalmated Plover; Killdeer; Greater and Lesser Yellowlegs; Semipalmated, Least, and Pectoral Sandpipers; and Short-billed Dowitcher are the most common species, but virtually all of New Jersey's shorebirds can be found during the course of a season. The meadows is an especially good place to see Stilt Sandpiper and Long-billed Dowitcher. Such rare or uncommon species as Lesser Golden-Plover; Upland Sandpiper; Hudsonian Godwit; White-rumped, Baird's, and Buff-breasted Sandpipers; and Wilson's Phalarope occur every fall, and often can be viewed at very close range. Other rarities that don't show up every year include Black-necked Stilt, American Avocet, Curlew Sandpiper, Ruff, and Red-necked and Red Phalaropes.

The meadows is the best place in New Jersey to see migrant Loggerhead Shrike in August (usually only one or two a year), while a little later in the year you might find a Lark Sparrow or an Orange-crowned Warbler. One of the highlights of the fall season is watching the numerous Merlins and Peregrines chasing shorebirds around the meadows.

Throughout the year, the meadows is a gathering place for gulls. In summer, they will be mostly Laughing Gulls; the rest of the year, you'll find Herring, Ring-billed, Great Black-backed, and sometimes Bonaparte's. Every year there are rarities, however. Iceland and Glaucous Gulls are now regular in winter, while Lesser Black-backed Gulls are becoming more commonplace. Little and Common Black-headed Gulls are occasionally seen with Bonaparte's in the spring, while Franklin's Gull has occurred at least twice in late summer.

The South Cape May Meadows is worth a stop anytime you are in Cape May, but especially in late summer and fall. Rarities that have appeared here in recent years, in addition to those already mentioned, are Brown Pelican (along the beach), Wood Stork, Wilson's Plover, Fork-tailed Flycatcher, and Sedge Wren.

The Beanery (see note, page 430)

From the state park, take Lighthouse Ave. back to Sunset Blvd. and turn right. Drive one mile to the junction with Bayshore Rd. and turn left (this is just past the parking lot for South Cape May Meadows). Continue 0.4 miles on Bayshore Rd. to a lima-bean processing plant (the beanery) on the left. Most of the year, you can park on the left side of the road, beyond the machinery. *In late August, September, and October, however, do not park on the left (west) side of the road, as the machinery is in use.* You can park on the right opposite the bean machines, or you can continue north for another hundred yards to a railroad track and park on the side of the road north of the track. Do not block access to the field on the right just before the tracks, as it is sometimes used by trucks.

From Bayshore Rd., walk west along the abandoned railroad tracks. The weeds on your left and the wet woods on your right are good for migrants in fall. Soon you will come to a cornfield on the right. The field edge is excellent for Ruby-throated Hummingbird (September), Connecticut Warbler (September–early October), and Orange-crowned Warbler (October). Yellow-headed Blackbird has occurred several times among the Red-wings in the cornfield, and Red-headed Woodpeckers like the dead trees around the edges in the fall. Be alert to the possibilities at this spot; all the regular migrant songbirds can be expected here, and any rarity might occur.

Continue along the railroad tracks, which lead behind the bean machines. In fall, the big patch of ragweed and other weeds on your left is a favorite spot for migrant Mourning, Connecticut, and Orange-crowned Warblers, and for a variety of sparrows. Lincoln's and White-crowned Sparrows are regular here, and Clay-colored has been found. Blue Grosbeaks and Indigo Buntings are also attracted to the weed seeds. There is often a wet area between the machinery and the weeds where Solitary Sandpipers like to feed and where a Purple Gallinule was found one spring.

A couple of hundred yards farther along the railroad tracks, you will enter a wet woodland that is excellent for migrants in spring and fall. You can continue along the tracks for more than a mile, passing through woods and along fields, and eventually emerging into Pond Creek Marsh, a vast area of reeds, where you can see hawks migrating overhead. In fall, the woods along the way are good for Olive-sided Flycatcher, thrushes, vireos, warblers, and sparrows.

The area around the beanery is the best spot to look for Mississippi Kites in late May and early June. Several immatures (up to about 7) show up in Cape May every spring. One of the best spots to search for them is from the top of the gray mound of magnesite tailings just south of the bean machines. Variously known as Moon Mountain or Sutton's Pile (after Clay Sutton, a local raptor enthusiast), it provides a good panorama of the surrounding sky; I have seen as many as four Mississippi Kites in the air at one time in early June from this vantage point.

To get to the magnesite pile, you must go through a gate, which you should be careful to close behind you to prevent farm animals within from wandering. All the land around the beanery is private property, so be careful not to abuse the privilege of using it. Birders are tolerated by the courtesy of the landowners, Les and Ernie Rea.

Higbee Beach

From the state park, follow the directions for the beanery, but continue north along Bayshore Rd. for 1.2 miles past the railroad tracks to the stop sign at New England Rd. Scan the wires around this intersection for Western Kingbird in October and November; the field on the southeast corner of this intersection attracted a Fork-tailed Flycatcher for three days in May 1984. Turn left onto New England Rd. and drive 1.2 miles to the end of the road at the parking lot for Higbee Beach.

Higbee Beach Wildlife Management Area is a 416-acre preserve that was acquired by the New Jersey Division of Fish, Game and Wildlife in the early 1980s, in recognition of its importance to migratory birds. It is the best place in Cape May for migrant songbirds, and is excellent for raptors as well. The combination of upland deciduous woods, weedy fields, beach, dunes (including the highest in New Jersey), and a well-developed low forest of American Holly, Eastern Red Cedar, Pitch Pine and Beach Plum behind the dunes, provides a diversity of habitat that attracts and holds the hordes of migrants at Cape May in the fall.

To be at Higbee Beach at dawn on the morning of a major fallout of migrants in late August, September, or October is an experience never to be forgotten. This usually happens only once or twice a year, when the right combination of cold front, clear skies and northwest winds combine to push a wave of songbirds down from the north. As day is breaking, many of these birds find themselves over the Cape May Peninsula or out over the ocean. Turning toward land and the protection offered by the woods at Higbee Beach, the birds swarm through the trees by the thousands. At such times, one can only stand in awe as the birds pass by, and hope to identify one in ten. As the sun rises higher, the passage slows down and it is easier to identify the many species present.

Even on days when there is only a minor flight of migrants, Higbee Beach can provide exciting birding. Many raptors roost in the trees at night, especially Osprey, Sharp-shinned Hawk, Cooper's Hawk, Peregrine Falcon, and Merlin, and in the morning they sit in the trees or fly about overhead. Northern Flickers are everywhere, flying from tree to tree and screaming in distress when pursued by a Sharpie. In late September and October, every tree plays host to Yellow-bellied Sapsuckers.

But it is mainly the songbirds that provide the excitement at Higbee Beach. All the migrant passerines that occur in New Jersey can be expected here in fall. Thirty species of warblers have been tallied in a single day, plus all the vireos and thrushes and most of the flycatchers. Sparrows arrive a bit later, and any species is likely to occur. Some of the more sought-after migrants found at Higbee are Olive-sided Flycatcher (regular in late August), Yellow-bellied Flycatcher (fairly common), Western Kingbird (rare), Gray-cheeked Thrush (regular in late September–early October), Philadelphia Vireo (fairly common), Orange-crowned Warbler (regular in October), Connecticut Warbler (almost daily in September), Mourning Warbler, Dickcissel, Clay-colored Sparrow (annual), Lark Sparrow (annual), and Henslow's Sparrow (very rare). Rarities that have occurred here in recent years are Anhinga, Magnificent Frigatebird, American Swallow-tailed Kite, Mississippi Kite, Common Ground-Dove, Townsend's Warbler, and Swainson's Warbler.

Higbee Beach is not noted for its diversity of breeding birds, but it does have good populations of Chuck-will's-widow, Carolina Wren, White-eyed Vireo, Yellow-breasted Chat, and Blue Grosbeak. In late fall and winter, there are many American Woodcock and numerous sparrows, plus a few year-round residents such as Carolina Chickadee, Tufted Titmouse, and Northern Cardinal.

The best birding at Higbee Beach is along the trails and dirt roads that radiate from the parking area. At the entrance to the parking area, a road on the right leads down to the Cape May Canal. This road can be driven, but it is better to walk it, as the birding is excellent. After several hundred yards, the road emerges into some *Phragmites*. Here there is a spoil dike of dredgings from the canal. Climb up on the dike and walk right to where you approach the woods. This spot provides an excellent vantage point for seeing birds moving through the woods, as you are high enough for them to be at eye level.

Also at the entrance to the parking lot, another dirt road, blocked by a cable, goes left along a hedgerow separating two fields. You can walk this road for several hundred yards into an open area where there is a pond built for Tiger Salamanders; the birding is excellent along the way. Another trail parallels this road; it starts at the southwest corner of the parking lot and follows the edge of the woods along one of the fields. It continues into some woods, and then follows the edges of two more fields. At the far end of the third field the trail diverges into two paths that lead into the woods; if you have the time, they are worth exploring and will eventually lead you to the beach, where you can turn right and walk back (north) toward the parking area. Another well-traveled trail is the one that leads from the parking lot straight down to the beach. This trail is only about two hundred yards long, but the first section of it is excellent for migrants.

A new parking lot on New England Rd., about one-half mile west of Bayshore Rd., provides access to the fields and trails of the recently acquired Hidden Valley Ranch section of Higbee Beach. Please close all gates behind you and stay out of the horse corral areas.

Cape May City

Cape May city offers birding only along the oceanfront, but the Second Ave. jetty is the best local spot for Purple Sandpiper, Red-throated Loon, Great Cormorant, Northern Gannet, and various other seabirds. To reach the jetty from the state park, take Lighthouse Ave. back to Sunset Blvd. and turn right. Follow Sunset 1.7 miles back to the traffic light at Broadway and turn right. Go 0.4 miles to the junction with Beach Ave., turn right, then go 0.2 miles to the end of the road and park on the left.

The jetty is the last jetty in town, and protects the cove that stretches between Cape May city and Cape May Point. From the edge of the jetty, scan the ocean and the cove. In addition to the species mentioned above, Common Eider and King Eider are often seen here from late fall to early spring, usually with a flock of Black Scoters. The pilings to the right are a favorite roosting spot for Great Cormorant, and the beach around the old sewer outfall (just beyond the pilings) is a good spot for Ruddy Turnstone, Dunlin, and Sanderling. There are many other jetties northward along Beach Ave., but they seldom have much to offer. Royal Terns are common on the beaches in late summer, and Bonaparte's Gulls are offshore from fall through spring.

If you have the time and the energy in winter, a trip to the Coast Guard Jetty at Wildwood Crest (covered in a separate chapter) may produce Harlequin Duck, Common Eider, or even an alcid.

Additional Birding Spots in South Coastal New Jersey

Beaver Swamp

The Beaver Swamp Wildlife Management Area is a little known but very birdy expanse of swamps, dense deciduous forests, creeks, and small ponds between Swainton and South Dennis in Cape May County. Among the more interesting birds that nest on this 2,700-acre tract are Acadian Flycatcher, Yellow-throated and Prothonotary Warblers, and Summer Tanager. Use the *Guide to Wildlife Management Areas* (see Bibliography) to find the several points of access from US 9, Rt. 83 and, Rt. 657 (Cape May Court House–S. Dennis Rd.). Several dirt roads enter the area, but the dense vegetation and the many swamps and streams make the going rough. One place I have birded is along the railroad tracks off Rt. 657, 3 miles north of the intersection with US 9 in Cape May Court House; walk north along the tracks to find all the species mentioned above.

Directions

To reach the intersection of US 9 and Rt. 657 in Cape May Court House, take the Garden State Parkway south to the traffic light at Mile 10, Stone Harbor Blvd. (Rt. 657). Turn right onto Rt. 657 and go 0.3 miles to the traffic light at US 9.

Belleplain State Forest

This somewhat fragmented state forest contains more than 11,000 acres in Cape May and Cumberland counties. It consists of pine-oak woods, mixed deciduous forest, and Atlantic White Cedar swamps, with several lakes and ponds. Birdlife is similar to that of Dividing Creek, although visits by birders are so infrequent that Belleplain's potential has not been completely assessed. There is a campground at Lake Nummy.

Directions

To reach Lake Nummy, follow the directions for Jakes Landing Road to Rt. 610. Follow Rt. 610 south for about 4.5 miles to Rt. 550 and turn right. Take Rt. 550 west through Woodbine for almost 5 miles to Henkensifkin Rd. and turn left. Go about 0.6 miles to the first crossroad (second right turn), Meisle Rd., and turn right. Lake Nummy is on your right and the state forest headquarters is one-half mile ahead on the left. You can obtain a map by mail from the headquarters at Box 450, Woodbine, NJ 08270.

Pelagic Trips

Boat trips out into the Atlantic Ocean offer the only opportunity to see some of the seabirds that rarely or never come close to shore at our latitudes. And, for species that do occur more regularly within sight of land, boat trips offer the best opportunity for observing these birds closely and in large numbers. Pelagic birding is the last frontier for bird explorers in North America, and continually produces surprises and sometime new records. The oceans are large and interconnected and seabirds wander widely. No other type of birding activity can match pelagic trips for the possibility of the sudden appearance of an extreme rarity, nor can any activity match the endless, inescapable hours of boredom that can haunt an unsuccessful trip across an empty sea. The rewards can be spectacular, however, as in October 1984, when a chartered pelagic trip out of Barnegat Light, New Jersey, found a Buller's Shearwater—a species never before recorded in the Atlantic Ocean.

Opportunities to go on organized pelagic trips out of New Jersey are, unfortunately, few. The only regularly scheduled trip is run jointly by the Delaware Valley Ornithological Club and the Urner Ornithological Club. It is run on the last Saturday in May, when the clubs charter the Miss Barnegat Light, which sails from the town of Barnegat Light near Barnegat Inlet at the north end of Long Beach Island. The same boat has occasionally been chartered at other seasons for all-day pelagic trips druing the course of the year, especially in winter. The best way to stay informed about organized pelagic trips is to call the rare bird alerts (RBAs) regularly; when a trip is planned it will be advertised on the RBAs. When you hear of a trip, respond promptly if you want to go; because of the intense interest among birders and the limited number of trips, these chartered trips usually sell out fast.

There are other ways to see pelagic birds, however. You can always make a pelagic trip on your own, especially if you are already familiar with some of the species you are likely to see. Innumerable party fishing boats depart regularly during most of the year from ports

Wilson's Storm-Petrels

along the New Jersey coast, such as Atlantic Highlands, Belmar, Point Pleasant, Barnegat Light, Atlantic City, and Cape May. Most of the boats do not go far offshore, but many of them go 30 to 40 miles out, which is far enough to see some of the pelagic species. A few boats make scheduled trips farther offshore, including some to the Hudson Canyon (about 90 miles out) for tuna and tilefish. "The Canyon," as it is known to birders and fishermen alike, is the destination of most of the chartered pelagic trips out of Barnegat Light, because it is the beginning of the deeper water and is the place where the largest numbers of seabirds are found off the New Jersey coast. Many (but not all) of the captains who sail to the Hudson Canyon are willing to take birders along, usually at a substantial discount from the price the fishermen are paying; the only requirement is that you stay out of the way. If you are interested in such a trip, watch the Philadelphia, Newark, or New York City newspapers for ads for trips to the Hudson Canyon, then call the captain to see if he will take you along as a nonfishing rider for a reasonable fee ($40–$50 for a 24-hour trip); the worst he can say is no.

If you go on the chartered pelagic trip at the end of May, you can expect to see Cory's Shearwater (a few), Greater Shearwater (many), Sooty Shearwater (many), Wilson's Storm-Petrel (very many), Red-necked Phalarope (usually a few), Pomarine Jaeger, and South Polar Skua (one or two most years). Other species often seen at the season are Northern Fulmar, Manx Shearwater (annual in recent years), Leach's Storm-Petrel, Northern Gannet (stragglers), Red Phalarope, Parasitic Jaeger, Long-tailed Jaeger, and Arctic Tern. A pelagic trip in summer or early fall should produce larger numbers of Cory's Shearwaters. All New Jersey records of Audubon's Shearwater are from July and August, and there are a few summer records of White-faced Storm-Petrel and Band-rumped Storm-Petrel, mostly from beyond 100 miles offshore. Sabine's Gull is a possibility in September and October.

From late fall to early spring, different species of seabirds can be expected. Northern Fulmar is a rare, but regular, visitor at this season. Northern Gannet is common, as is Black-legged Kittiwake. The few records of Great Skua for New Jersey have been on pelagic trips from November to March. Winter is also the season to look for alcids, which can be frustratingly difficult to identify because they dive at the approach of a boat, or speed away on whirring wings.

Dovekie and Razorbill are the most frequently encountered species, but Thick-billed Murre and Atlantic Puffin are possible. The murre is more apt to be seen along the shore, but even there it is rare.

In addition to the birding opportunities, pelagic trips also offer the chance to see marine mammals. Fin Whale, Pilot Whale, Common Dolphin, and Bottle-nosed Dolphin are the species most frequently encountered off New Jersey, but Minke Whale, Right Whale, and Risso's Dolphin (Grampus) have been seen. Thre are many other possibilities in North Atlantic waters, especially from late spring to late fall.

Another option for birders who want to see seabirds is to take a pelagic trip from one of the nearby states. Probably the most convenient are the trips run out of Ocean City, Maryland. These are scheduled throughout the year and are presently being run by Ron Naveen, whose current address is 2378 Rt. 97, Cooksville, MD 21723. Also, there are occasional trips from Montauk, Long Island, by the Federation of New York State Bird Clubs. These trips, which are irregularly scheduled, are advertised on the New York Rare Bird Alert—(212) 832-6523. Farther afield are the many whale-watching and bird-watching trips run from Cape Cod, Massachusetts, by the Brookline Bird Club, Massachusetts Audubon Society, Manomet Bird Observatory, and other organizations.

Be sure to take along plenty of warm clothing on a pelagic trip, preferably with a waterproof outer layer. The long hours of wind and wet can chill you to the bone. It is always colder than you think it will be, especially in late spring, when the warm temperatures on land can deceive you; the ocean warms up much more slowly than does the land. If you are at all prone to motion sickness, be sure to take something to help ward off seasickness—nothing can be more agonizing than a 24-hour pelagic trip during which you are seasick for 23 hours. In addition to the pills or ear patches used to prevent motion sickness, many birders take along a generous supply of pretzels, crackers, or similar dry munchies and keep nibbling on them constantly. Sometimes it even works.

Hawk-Watching

Fall hawk-watching is becoming increasingly popular, and some of the best sites in the country are in or near New Jersey. Cape May is nationally famous for enormous numbers of accipiters and falcons during fall migration, while nearby Hawk Mountain in Pennsylvania is equally famous for its large flights of buteos, numerous eagles, and many other species. Several lesser-known places in northern New Jersey are part of the same migratory flyway as Hawk Mountain; however, these places usually get smaller numbers of birds. A few other hawk-watching sites in neighboring parts of New York and Pennsylvania are also frequented by New Jersey birders.

Except for the coastal locations, all the hawk-watching sites are associated with mountain ridges. In fall, many species of raptors follow the ridges, which generate updrafts that assist the birds' flight as they work their way south. The best conditions for a big hawk flight usually occur a day or two after the passage of a cold front, which is followed by strong northwesterly winds. However, good flights are possible whenever there is a northerly wind. Large Broad-winged Hawk movements have been observed on southerly winds, but the bigger buteos and eagles generally appear only when the wind has a northerly component.

The fall migration begins in late August, and largest numbers of Osprey, Bald Eagle, Broad-winged Hawk, and American Kestrel occur in September. Late September and early October are the peak times for Merlin and Peregrine Falcon, which migrate mainly along the coast. October is the prime month for Sharp-shinned and Cooper's Hawks, while late October and early November bring most of the bigger raptors, such as Northern Goshawk; Red-shouldered, Red-tailed, and Rough-legged Hawks, and Golden Eagle. Turkey Vulture, many of which are nonmigratory, and Northern Harrier occur throughout the season. Rarities such as Swainson's Hawk and Gyrfalcon occur annually but unpredictably at one hawk-watching site or another, so there is always the unexpected to anticipate.

437

Sharp-shinned Hawk

Hawk-watching is the most sociable of birding activities; hours of staring at the horizon, often with long periods between hawks, are enlivened by discussions of birds, birders, birding locations, field guides, knotty identification problems, and the fortunes or misfortunes of the local pro football teams. Most of the sites mentioned below are manned on a fairly regular basis (especially on weekends) by dedicated hawk-watchers, so there is usually someone to talk to and to help in identifying the hawks. Trying to identify a distant raptor can be a frustrating experience for the beginner, so it helps to go to a site where knowledgeable raptor enthusiasts can provide assistance.

If you are going to one of the mountain ridge sites, be sure to dress warmly—it is always much colder than you think it will be. On the best days in October aand November you may be standing outside for hours in 30- or 40-degree temperatures with a 20-mile-per-hour northwest wind. Running around the hawk-watch for exercise might warm you up a bit, but the other hawk-watchers won't appreciate the distraction. A thermos of hot cocoa or other libation can help sustain a chilly birder on a cold, windy day.

Spring hawk-watching is a generally neglected activity, although the Cape May Bird Observatory has run a hawk watch at Sandy Hook since 1979 and several of the ridge sites have been monitored occasionally. April is the biggest month; Sharp-shins and Kestrels predominate along the coast, while Broad-wing is the main species along the ridges.

The 12 sites listed below are separated according to state; the first nine are in New Jersey.

Raccoon Ridge, Warren County (Northwest)

The best of the northern New Jersey hawk-watching sites, this is also the most difficult to reach. Take Interstate 80 west to Exit 12 (Rt. 521, Blairstown). Follow Rt. 521 north for 5 miles to Rt. 94 and turn left. Go about 3.8 miles to Walnut Valley Rd. and turn right (there is a Dairy Queen on the left just before the turn and a sign on the left directing you to turn right for the Yards Creek Pumped Storage Power Plant). Drive 2.6 miles on Walnut Valley Rd. to the entrance to the Yards Creek Power Plant. Stop at the gate and tell the guard that you are going hawk-watching. Continue on the road, staying right at the first fork, left at the second fork, and right at the third fork (0.4 miles from the gate), following the signs for the Boy Scout Camp. After 1.1 miles (from the entrance), you will enter the camp and see a parking area on the right; park here after checking with the ranger at the house ahead on the left. Just ahead on the left, an old road starts up the mountain. Hike up this road for about three-quarters of a mile (staying right when it forks just past an old stone house) until it intersects with the Appalachian Trail at the top of the ridge. Turn left onto the Appalachian Trail. The first lookout is a short distance up the trail, but the main one is an exposed outcropping of rocks about one-quarter mile southwest along the trail. Although the distance from the parking lot to the main lookout is only about a mile, the elevation gain is 700 feet (to 1,560 at the lookout). The strenuous hike takes 25–30 minutes.

The view from Raccoon Ridge is breathtaking. Looking down to the northwest, you will see the Delaware River, only a mile away as the Raven flies, but over 1,200 feet below. To the northeast you can see High Point, 30 miles away, and to the west, Camelback Mountain in the Poconos, only 15 miles distant. At Raccoon Ridge, the Kittatinny Mountains have narrowed to a single, steep ridge, and so all the hawks migrating along the chain are concentrated at this point; consequently, the number and variety of raptors at Raccoon are always better than at Sunrise Mountain, 22 miles to the northeast. This is the best place in northern New Jersey during the fall migration to see Osprey, Bald Eagle, Northern Goshawk, Golden Eagle, and Common Raven. Raven is one of New Jersey's rarest birds, but it is seen here several times each fall; as with Goshawk and Golden Eagle, late October and early November are best for seeing Common Raven.

Scotts Mountain, Warren County (Northwest)

Take Interstate 78 west to Rt. 519, just east of Phillipsburg. Take Rt. 519 north for about 2.7 miles to Fox Farm Rd. and turn right; the hawk-watch site is on the left, on Fox Farm Rd., about 1.5 miles from where you turn. Park near the tower on the left; the hawk flight is visible from the edge of the road. All the regular fall migrants are seen here, although not usually in as large numbers as at Raccoon Ridge or Sunrise Mountain. On September 14, 1983, however, the biggest hawk flight recorded in New Jersey in recent years occurred at Scotts Mountain. The tally of 18,500 Broad-winged Hawks, 31 Ospreys, 18 Northern Harriers, and 7 Bald Eagles shows that even the lesser-known spots can produce exciting results. The lookout is not regularly manned.

Sunrise Mountain, Sussex County (Northwest)

Follow the directions for Stokes State Forest (in that chapter) to Culvers Gap. Turn right at the sign for Sunrise Mountain onto Rt. 636 (Upper North Shore Rd.), go 0.2 miles, then turn left onto Sunrise Mountain Rd. Drive about 4 miles on this road, then bear right when the road forks at the sign for Sunrise Mountain. This road ends at a parking lot after another three-quarters of a mile. Walk up the Appalachian Trail south (to your right as you enter the parking lot) for 200 yards to a covered pavilion on top of Sunrise Mountain. The best viewing is from the open area on the south side of the pavilion. This is the most popular hawk watch in northern New Jersey and is the second best, after Raccoon Ridge. All the usual species are seen here, including Northern Goshawk and Golden Eagle; even Common Raven is seen on occasion. Winter finches, including Purple Finch, Red and White-winged Crossbills, Pine Siskin, and Evening Grosbeak often pass by later in the season. Boreal Chickadee has occurred at the hawk watch several times, and a Townsend's Solitaire made it a regular stop during its stay on Sunrise Mountain in November, 1980. There are primitive toilets at the parking lot.

High Point State Park, Sussex County (Northwest)

Follow the directions for the Monument Trail in the chapter on High Point State Park. The Raccoon Ridge Bird Observatory operates hawk watches at three sites within the park. One of these is at the Nature Center, which is worth visiting only if there is a northwest wind. Unlike the other hawk-watching sites mentioned in this chapter, the Nature Center is readily accessible to birders with physical limitations, including those in wheelchairs. The observation area looks west from the porch of the Nature Center and a reasonably good view can be had from inside in inclement weather. Species seen here are the same as at Sunrise Mountain, but the numbers are smaller. Another site in the park is the paved walkway at the base of the monument at High Point. The walkway provides a commanding view in all directions and can be worthwhile on northeasterly winds. Unlike the Nature Center, this site is not always manned. The third site is a wooden platform a half-mile south of the monument; inquire at the Nature Center for directions. There are rest rooms at the Nature Center and at the monument.

Bearfort Mountain, Passaic County (Northwest)

Take Rt. 23 northwest from Interstate 80 for about 17 miles to the exit for Rt. 513 (Union Valley Rd., West Milford). Go north on Union Valley Rd. for about 4.5 miles to Stephens Rd., on the left. Take Stephens Rd. for 0.7 miles to a parking area on the left (marked P8) on the ridge of Bearfort Mountain; the road is very rough, so proceed with caution. The Fire Tower Trail leads south (to your left as you drive up the mountain) for 0.5 miles to the fire tower. The hawk-watch site is an exposed outcropping of rocks on the west side of the trail opposite the fire tower. Unlike most of the other sites, this spot is seldom visited by hawk-watchers in the fall. Gyrfalcon and Common Raven have been seen here, but in general it is not one of the better spots.

Skyline Drive, Passaic County (Northeast)

This lookout is located on Ramapo Mountain in Ramapo Mountain State Forest. Take the Garden State Parkway to Exit 160 (Fair Lawn). Turn left at the end of the ramp onto Paramus Rd., then go about one-half mile to the exit for Rts. 4 and 208 (Fair Lawn and Hawthorne); this will put you on Rt. 4. After about 0.3 miles, bear right onto Rt. 208 toward Oakland. Follow Rt. 208 for about 11 miles to its end in Oakland, where it becomes West Oakland Ave. Go about one-half mile and turn right onto Skyline Dr., following the signs for Ringwood Manor. Go about 2.4 miles to where a pipeline right-of-way begins on both sides of the road. You can park on the right at the entrance to the pipeline right-of-way or continue a short distance along Skyline Dr. and park on the side of the road just before a sign that reads "Borough of Ringwood Helping Hands." Parking is difficult, so be careful. Cross to the west side of the road and take the Blue Dot Trail for a few hundred yards to the lookout. All the regular migrants can be seen at this site, especially Broad-winged Hawks.

Montclair, Essex County (Northeast)

Take the Garden State Parkway to Exit 151 (Watchung Avenue, Montclair). Drive west on Watchung Ave. for about 2.1 miles to its end at Upper Mountain Rd., then turn right. Continue north for about 0.7 miles to Bradford Ave. and turn left. Go about 0.1 miles on Bradford and take the second right turn, Edgecliff Rd. Follow Edgecliff for about 0.3 miles to a parking area on the right. The trail to the hawk lookout is on the north side of the street and leads to a former quarry, which is the hawk watch. Montclair gets most of the regular migrants, but is best known for its Broad-wing flight, the peak year being 1974, with 23,899. Northern Goshawk and Golden Eagle are rare. This watch has been manned regularly in fall for about 27 years. The watch used to be on the south side of the road and may relocate there again.

Sandy Hook, Monmouth County (North Coast)

Follow the directions in the chapter on Sandy Hook. The official hawk watch is located on a knoll just east of the lighthouse (park in Lot N), but anywhere on the peninsula is good, especially along the beach. This is primarily a spring (especially April) hawk-watching site; Sharp-shins and Kestrels make up the bulk of the flight, but Merlin and Peregrine are regular, as are most of the other migrant raptors except eagles. A Swallow-tailed Kite appeared in 1983 and 1984.

Cape May, Cape May County (South Coast)

This is *the* place to see hawks along the coast in the fall. The hawk watch is described in detail in the section on Cape May.

Mount Peter, Orange County, New York

Take the Garden State Parkway and the New York Thruway to Exit 15 (Suffern, Rt. 17). Continue north on Rt. 17 for about 9 miles to Rts. 210 and 17A, then turn left. Go about 8 miles on this road until you reach Greenwood Lake, where Rt. 210 branches to the left. Follow Route 17A north for about 2 miles to the Valley View Restaurant, on the right. Park in the restaurant parking lot and walk about

200 feet to the crest of the ridge behind the lot; this is the hawk-watch site. Birds are much the same as at Montclair and Skyline Drive.

Bake Oven Knob, Lehigh County, Pennsylvania

Take Interstate 78 and US 22 west through Allentown to Rt. 309. Go north on Rt. 309 for about 16 miles to the intersection with County Road 39056 (2 miles past the Rt. 143 junction). Turn right onto Rt. 39056, go 2.1 miles, then turn left onto an unmarked road. When this road bends right, you should continue straight ahead on unpaved Bake Oven Rd. Follow Bake Oven Rd. up a steep hill to a parking lot. Walk north (right) along the Appalachian Trail to the two lookouts, one about a third of a mile from the parking lot and the second about one-half mile from the lot. The birds here are basically the same ones seen at Hawk Mountain, which is 15 miles southwest along the same ridge, but there are far fewer people. The watch is regularly manned in the fall.

Hawk Mountain, Berks County, Pennsylvania

Take Interstate 78 west to Allentown. Continue on I-78 (US 22) for 18 miles from the intersection with the Northeast Extension of the Pennsylvania Turnpike to Exit 11 (Rt. 143). Go north on Rt. 143 for about 3 miles, turn left toward Eckville at the sign for Hawk Mountain Sanctuary, and drive about 7 miles to the sanctuary. This is the most famous of all the hawk watches and the most heavily visited. The sanctuary is open all year (a small fee is charged on the trail to the lookout) and the watch is manned in spring and fall. The South Lookout is only 200 yards from the entrance, but the North Lookout (the better one) is about 0.7 miles along a rocky, winding trail. The Broad-wing flight in September can be spectacular, while mid-October boasts the greatest variety of species. Falcons are scarce, but excellent numbers of all the other regular migrants are recorded each year, including numerous Bald Eagles, Northern Goshawks, and Golden Eagles. Swainson's Hawk and Gyrfalcon have occurred. Every birder should make at least one fall pilgrimage to Hawk Mountain. Once you've done so, however, the crowds (almost 50,000 visitors each year) will probably make you want to do your hawk-watching elsewhere.

Nature Clubs and
Audubon Chapters

The largest and most active natural-history society in the state is the New Jersey Audubon Society, which operates five sanctuaries and sponsors many field trips and educational programs. In addition, the sanctuaries are a good source of information about other nature activities or clubs in your area. Addresses for the sanctuaries are:

Cape May Bird Observatory
707 E. Lake Dr.
Cape May Point, NJ 08212
(609) 884-2736

Lorrimer Nature Center (NJAS Headquarters)
790 Ewing Ave.
Franklin Lakes, NJ 07417
(201) 891-2185

Owl Haven
Englishtown-Freehold Rd.
Tennent, NJ 07763
(201) 780-7007

Rancocas Nature Center
Rancocas Rd.
Mt. Holly, NJ 08060
(609) 261-2495

Scherman-Hoffman Sanctuaries
Box 693, Hardscrabble Rd.
Bernardsville, NJ 07924
(201) 766-5787

There are presently eight chapters of the National Audubon Society active in New Jersey. For the names and addresses of the current membership chairman and officers, contact the National Audubon Society, 950 Third Avenue, New York, NY 10022 (212) 832-3200. The chapters and the locus of their activities are:

Atlantic Audubon (Atlantic City area)

Bergen County Audubon (Ridgewood)

Highlands Audubon (Ringwood)

Jersey Shore Audubon (Toms River)

Monmouth Audubon (Monmouth County)

Morris Highlands Audubon (Denville)

Summit Nature Club (Summit area)

Washington Crossing Audubon (Pennington, W. Mercer County)

Some of the other bird and nature clubs around the state are:

Audubon Wildlife Society
Audubon, NJ (contact Rancocas Nature Center for information)

Burlington County Natural Science Club
Marlton, NJ (contact Rancocas Nature Center for information)

Gloucester County Nature Club
Box 63
Winona, NJ 08090

Hunterdon Nature Club
c/o Hunterdon County Park Headquarters
Rt. 31
Lebanon, NJ 08833

Salem County Bird Club
c/o Dr. Jerry Haag
RD 3, Box 452
Elmer, NJ 08313

Sussex County Bird Club
c/o Jim Zamos
136 Woodside Ave.
Newton, NJ 07860

Trenton Naturalists
c/o Mrs. Helen Huber
1020 Buckingham Way
Morrisville, PA 19067

Sea Ducks

Bibliography

Akers, James F. *All Year Birding in Southern New Jersey*. Pomona, NJ: Stockton State College, 1981.

American Birds. Published bimonthly by the National Audubon Society, 950 Third Avenue, New York, NY 10022.

Birding. Published bimonthly by the American Birding Association, Box 4335, Austin, TX 78765.

Boyle, William J., Jr. *New Jersey Field Trip Guide*. Summit, NJ: Summit Nature Club, 1979.

Brady, Alan, W. Ronald Logan, John C. Miller, George B. Reynard, and Robert H. Sehl. *A Field List of the Birds of the Delaware Valley Region*. Philadelphia: Delaware Valley Ornithological Club, 1972.

Bull, John. *Birds of the New York Area*. New York: Harper & Row, 1964.

Cassinia. Published annually by the Delaware Valley Ornithological Club, Academy of Natural Sciences, 19th and the Parkway, Philadelphia, PA 19103.

Dann, Kevin. *25 Walks in New Jersey*. New Brunswick, NJ: Rutgers University Press, 1982.

Drennan, Susan R. *When to Find Birds in New York State*. Syracuse, NY: Syracuse University Press, 1981.

Fables, David G., Jr. *Annotated List of New Jersey Birds*. Newark, NJ: Urner Ornithological Club, 1955.

Geffen, Alice. *A Birdwatcher's Guide to the Eastern United States*. Woodbury, NJ: Barrow's Educational Series, 1978.

Harding, John J., and Justin J. Harding. *Birding the Delaware Valley*. Philadelphia: Temple University Press, 1980.

Heintzelman, Donald S. *Autumn Hawk Flights: The Migrations in Eastern North America*. New Brunswick, NJ: Rutgers University Press, 1975.

———. *A Guide to Eastern Hawk Watching*. University Park, PA: Pennsylvania State University Press, 1976.

Lawrence, Susannah. *The Audubon Society Field Guide to the Natural Places of the Mid-Atlantic States: Coastal*. New York: The Hilltown Press, 1984.

Leck, Charles F. *The Birds of New Jersey: Their Habits and Habitats*. New Brunswick, NJ: Rutgers University Press, 1975.

————. *The Status and Distribution of New Jersey's Birds*. New Brunswick, NJ: Rutgers University Press, 1984.

Records of New Jersey Birds. Published quarterly by the New Jersey Audubon Society, 790 Ewing Avenue, Franklin Lakes, NJ 07417.

Perrone, Steve, ed. *Guide to Wildlife Management Areas*. Trenton: Division of Fish, Game and Wildlife, N.J. Dept. of Environmental Protection, Box CN400, Trenton, NJ 08625.

Pettingill, Olin S. *A Guide to Bird Finding: East of the Mississippi*. 2d ed. New York: Oxford University Press, 1977.

Stone, Witmer. *Bird Studies at Old Cape May*. 1937. Reprint. New York: Dover Publications, 1965.

Annotated Checklist
of New Jersey's Birds

This list provides a capsule summary of when and where you are likely to find the birds that regularly occur in New Jersey. It includes about 360 species that can be expected to occur during a five-year period, with an emphasis on recent trends in the state's birdlife. You can obtain additional information about each species by consulting the index and referring to the individual chapters noted in the list. Most of the species in the list occur every year; a few show up much less often. At the end of the main list is a compilation of those rarities that are called "vagrants" in birding jargon—birds that have occurred in New Jersey at least once in the past 25 years, but not frequently enough to warrant inclusion on the main list.

The format of the list is a modified version of that used by John and Justin Harding in *Birding the Delaware Valley*. Each entry includes a summary statement of the seasonal pattern of occurrence of each species in New Jersey, its general habitat preference, and its abundance in that habitat. Judgments on the abundance of individual species are somewhat subjective and use descriptive terms such as *common* and *uncommon* that are difficult to quantify. Nevertheless, these terms are widely used, and despite their imprecision, most birders understand what they mean. The number of individuals of a particular species that are present in a given habitat does not necessarily reflect the ease of finding and seeing it, however. Sora is far more common than Great Blue Heron at Troy Meadows, but you can guess which one you're most likely to see. I have used the following terms:

Abundant   Occurs in large numbers in its preferred habitat

Common   Always or almost always present, and usually numerous, in its preferred habitat at the appropriate season

451

Fairly common   Usually present, but sometimes only one or a few individuals, in its preferred habitat at the appropriate season

Uncommon   Occasionally present in its preferred habitat at the appropriate season, but not to be expected

Rare   Of infrequent occurrence (not necessarily annual) or only a few individuals present each year even in the preferred habitat

The second part of each entry suggests some of the places that you are most likely to encounter a particular species and an estimate of the likelihood of seeing it at that spot. This reflects not only the abundance of the species, but how easy it is to locate or see. Using Sora as an example again, this species is fairly common at Trenton Marsh, but you will be very lucky to see one (you have a better chance of hearing it). For the more common species and those that occur in a variety of habitats, the sites suggested represent only a sampling of the places that you can expect to find them. Other places within the species' range that provide similar habitat may be just as likely to produce the bird. I have tried to select sites covering a wide geographical range, while still choosing those where a species is most likely to occur. So, if you live near Eagle Rock Reservation, don't think you have to go to Jockey Hollow or Princeton to see a Scarlet Tanager. For the less common, rare, or local species, the sites suggested are those that have proven most reliable for birders over the past 10 years.

The number of asterisks next to each location corresponds to the probability of your finding the bird at that site during a field trip of several hours and reasonable weather conditions. Obviously if you only spend a few minutes at a spot or if it is pouring rain, your chances are greatly diminished. On the other hand, if you spend an entire day, your chances of finding even uncommon and rare species improve greatly. The ratings, which I have borrowed from Jim Lane's series of state "Birder's Guides," are as follows:

****   *Hard to miss*—your chances are virtually 100 percent.

***   *Should see*—unless the fates conspire against you. This may depend very much on the conditions. If you hit a big wave of migrant warblers at Princeton in May or of migrant sparrows at Island Beach in October, many uncommon or even rare species might be seen. On the other hand, if you bird Cape May in September after several days of southerly winds, even an American Redstart can be hard to find.

**   *May see*—these are species that require more effort or more luck at that particular site, but are frequently present at the proper season. This includes birds that are uncommon or for which limited habitat exists at that location; it also includes species that, although common, may be hard to see, like rails and some sparrows.

*   *Lucky to find*—the species probably occurs every year at that location, but is generally rare or uncommon anywhere in New Jersey. You will probably have to make many trips at the appropriate season before you see the bird.

†   *How lucky can you get*—these are rare birds that cannot be expected to show up at that particular site or even in New Jersey every year. The location mentioned is, however, one of the few places where the species has occurred.

The names used for each species and the order in which they are listed follow the American Ornithologists' Union *Check-List of North American Birds* (Sixth Edition, 1983). In the list, "Brigantine" refers to Brigantine National Wildlife Refuge, not Brigantine Island; designations such as "State Park" and "WMA" have been omitted from the location names—all names should be understood to refer to the specific locations discussed in the text (e.g., "Lebanon" refers to Lebanon State Forest, not the town of Lebanon).

The Checklist

Red-throated Loon Common migrant along the coast, uncommon inland, mainly November and March–April; uncommon in winter. ****Cape May; ***Barnegat Light, Holgate, Island Beach, Longport; **Sandy Hook, Round Valley.

Common Loon Common migrant along the coast, October–November and March–May; uncommon inland and along the coast in winter. ***Barnegat, Cape May, Holgate, Island Beach; **North Shore, Sandy Hook, Round Valley.

Pied-billed Grebe Fairly common to common migrant, mainly on fresh or brackish ponds and lakes; rare breeder at a few locations; uncommon in winter. ****Kearny Marsh (in summer); **Brigantine, Cape May, North Shore, Trenton Marsh.

Horned Grebe Common migrant and fairly common winter resident, mainly along the coast; has declined substantially in recent years. ****Shark River (North Shore); ***Barnegat Light, Brigantine, Cape May, Sandy Hook; **Liberty State Park, Round Valley.

Red-necked Grebe Uncommon winter and early spring visitor. Numbers vary widely from year to year, peaking in early spring. Anywhere along the coast, especially *Sandy Hook; also *Assunpink, Liberty State Park, Round Valley.

Eared Grebe Rare along the coast in winter; in most years there are no reports.

Northern Fulmar Uncommon and irregular far offshore. **Pelagic Trips.

Cory's Shearwater Fairly common far offshore, mainly in late summer, early fall; a few in spring. Occasionally seen from shore on southeast winds in September. ***Pelagic Trips; *Island Beach, North Shore.

Greater Shearwater Common far offshore in spring and summer. ****Pelagic Trips.

Sooty Shearwater Common far offshore in spring and summer, occasionally closer to land. ****Pelagic Trips.

Manx Shearwater Uncommon far offshore spring through fall. *Pelagic Trips.

Audubon's Shearwater Very rare far offshore in summer, usually in blue-water eddies of the Gulf Stream but occasionally closer to land. †Pelagic Trips.

Wilson's Storm-Petrel   Abundant far offshore in spring and summer; occasionally even within sight of land. ****Pelagic Trips.
Leach's Storm-Petrel   Rare to uncommon far offshore. *Pelagic Trips.
Northern Gannet   Common offshore from October through April; fairly common along the coast in October–November; uncommon in winter and spring. ***Barnegat Light, Island Beach, Wildwood Crest; **Cape May, North Shore.
American White Pelican   Rare visitor from the west; has occurred annually in recent years. Almost all records are from †Brigantine and †Cape May.
Brown Pelican   Rare visitor from the south; like its cousin, has occurred with increasing frequency in recent years (sometimes in large flocks) mostly in June and early July. †Cape May, Holgate, Stone Harbor.
Great Cormorant   An uncommon, but increasing, winter visitor (November–April) along the coast. ***Barnegat Light, Island Beach; **Long Branch (North Shore), Sandy Hook, Wildwood Crest.
Double-crested Cormorant   Abundant migrant along the coast, especially in autumn; uncommon inland. Fairly common on coastal bays in summer, uncommon in winter. ****Brigantine, **Liberty State Park; *Assunpink, Round Valley.
American Bittern   Uncommon and difficult-to-observe transient in fresh and brackish marshes; rare in summer and in winter. More often heard than seen. **Brigantine, Cape May, Trenton Marsh; *Troy Meadows.
Least Bittern   Fairly common but secretive summer resident of fresh and brackish marshes. Numbers appear to be declining. April–September: ***Cape May, Kearny Marsh; **Brigantine, Trenton, Troy Meadows.
Great Blue Heron   Common transient; fairly common in winter; uncommon breeder in summer. Present in fresh- and saltwater marshes. ****Brigantine, Tuckerton; ***Cape May, Great Meadows (see Jenny Jump State Forest), Great Swamp, Stone Harbor, Troy Meadows; many other locations.
Great Egret   Fairly common along the coast from Barnegat Light south to Cape May, and in the Delaware Bayshore and Salem County marshes; uncommon at inland lakes and reservoirs, mainly in late summer. Biggest numbers April–October, but a few in winter.

****Brigantine, Cape May, Stone Harbor, Tuckerton; ***Manning-
ton Marsh (Salem County); in late summer, **Assunpink, Mercer
County Park, Hackensack Meadowlands, Lincoln Park, Spruce Run.

Snow Egret   As Great Egret, but much more common along the
coast, much less common inland.

Little Blue Heron   Fairly common, April–October, in coastal
marshes and heronries from Barnegat Light south; a few in winter.
Rare inland in late summer. ****Brigantine, Stone Harbor, Tuckerton, ***Cape May; **Corson's Inlet.

Tricolored Heron   Same distribution as Little Blue Heron, but
less common; much rarer in winter.

Cattle Egret   Fairly common, early April–October, in coastal
marshes from Brigantine south to Cape May; also in farm fields and
pastures in Cape May, Cumberland, and Salem counties. ****Stone
Harbor; ***Brigantine, Cape May (Beanery, New England Rd., S.
Cape May Meadows), and along the Garden State Parkway from Mile
10 south.

Green-backed Heron   Common breeding bird throughout the
state in freshwater marshes and wooded swamps, April–October.
****Assunpink, Great Swamp, Manahawkin, Troy Meadows, Whites-
bog, Whittingham.

Black-crowned Night-Heron   Fairly common, mainly April–
November, along the coast from Island Beach south; uncommon inland, mainly in late summer; uncommon in winter. ****Stone Harbor; ***Brigantine, Cape May, Kearny (nests), Tuckerton; **Hackensack Meadowlands.

Yellow-crowned Night-Heron   Uncommon and local breeder
along the southeast coast. April–October. ***Stone Harbor Sanctuary; *Brigantine.

White Ibis   Rare visitor from the south, usually young birds in
late summer. Could be anywhere along the coast or even inland;
most records are from †Brigantine, Cape May, Manahawkin, and
Tuckerton.

Glossy Ibis   Common along the coast, from Barnegat to Cape May
and up the Delaware Bayshore to Salem County, April–October. Rare
to uncommon inland in April and again in late summer. ****Brigantine, Cape May, Manahawkin, Stone Harbor, Tuckerton.

Fulvous Whistling-Duck   Another rare visitor from the south;
the only records since 1974, when the species occurred at numerous locations, are from †Brigantine and Cape May.

Tundra Swan   A fairly common transient and uncommon winter resident, mainly along the coast and Delaware Bay, but increasing in cranberry bogs in the Pine Barrens. Peak abundance is November– mid-December and mid-February–March. ***Brigantine, Mannington Marsh (Salem County), Stafford Forge, Whitesbog; **Barnegat Bay (various sites), Pedricktown.

Mute Swan   Fairly common and increasing permanent resident of lakes, bays, and impoundments throughout the state; large flocks winter along the coast. ****Brigantine; ***Cape May; **Manahawkin, Culvers Lake.

Greater White-fronted Goose   Rare visitor (usually Greenland race), occurring with migrant or wintering flocks of Canada Geese. Most records are from †Brigantine, but the species has occurred at scattered inland locations.

Snow Goose   Abundant migrant along the coast and the Delaware Bayshore especially in spring; uncommon in winter. Uncommon inland, usually stragglers with flocks of Canada Geese. October– November and March–April. ****Brigantine, Fortescue (Dividing Creek); ***Cape May, Mannington Marsh (Salem County). Increasing numbers of the blue morph are occurring among the white Snows.

Brant   Common winter resident of coastal bays and estuaries from Sandy Hook to Cape May; uncommon along the Hudson River. November–April. ****Barnegat Light (bay side), Brigantine, Longport, Sandy Hook (bay side), Shark River (North Shore), Tuckerton.

Canada Goose   Abundant migrant and winter resident, common summer resident throughout the state; present on any body of water, corporate lawns, parks, cornfields, and marshes. ****Brigantine; virtually anywhere in New Jersey.

Wood Duck   Common summer resident of swamps and wet woodlands throughout the state; rare in winter. Late March–October: ****Great Swamp; ***Trenton Marsh, Troy Meadows, Whittingham; **Black River, Brigantine.

Green-winged Teal   Common migrant and uncommon winter resident in fresh and brackish marshes throughout the state; uncommon summer resident at a few locations. October–November and March–April: ****Brigantine; ***Kearny Marsh, Manahawkin, Mannington Marsh (Salem County), Pedricktown, Tuckahoe. Single males of the Eurasian race (Common Teal) are occasionally reported, mainly from Brigantine.

American Black Duck   Abundant migrant and common winter resident of coastal bays, estuaries, and marshes; fairly common inland in migration. Formerly a common summer resident, but breeding population much reduced. September–April: ****Brigantine, Longport, Manahawkin, Shark River (North Shore), Sandy Hook, Tuckerton; ***Liberty State Park.

Mallard   Common at all seasons on virtually any body of fresh or brackish water. ****Brigantine, Liberty State Park, Mannington Marsh (Salem County), Point View Reservoir, Spruce Run, Tuckahoe.

Northern Pintail   Common migrant and fairly common winter resident of fresh and brackish marshes and impoundments. Mainly October–November and March–April: ****Brigantine; ***Kearny Marsh, Manahawkin, Mannington Marsh (Salem County), Tuckahoe; **Assunpink, Shark River (North Shore), Troy Meadows.

Blue-winged Teal   Common migrant and fairly common summer resident at fresh and brackish marshes; rare in winter. Late March–November: ****Brigantine; ***Cape May, Kearny Marsh, Manahawkin, Mannington Marsh (Salem County), Tuckahoe; **Trenton Marsh.

Northern Shoveler   A fairly common migrant and uncommon winter resident of fresh and brackish marshes and impoundments; rare breeder at Brigantine. Look for it at the times and places suggested for Northern Pintail.

Gadwall   As Northern Shoveler, but more common in summer at Brigantine and in the Hackensack Meadowlands. Seems to be increasing.

Eurasian Wigeon   Rare visitor, occurring with flocks of American Wigeon; has appeared annually in recent years. *Brigantine, Shark River (North Shore), and Spruce Run.

American Wigeon   Common migrant and uncommon winter resident of fresh and brackish water; extremely rare breeder. ****Brigantine, Cape May, Liberty State Park, Shark River (North Shore), Spruce Run, Tuckahoe; ***Mannington Marsh (Salem County).

Canvasback   Fairly common migrant and winter resident on coastal bays, estuaries, and freshwater ponds; fairly common migrant on inland lakes and reservoirs. November–April: ****North Shore; ***Sandy Hook, Barnegat Light; **Brigantine, Longport, South Amboy, Stone Harbor.

Redhead   An uncommon migrant and uncommon to rare winter resident, usually occurring with flocks of Canvasback or scaup.

**Old Sam's Pond (North Shore); *Barnegat Light, Sandy Hook, or South Amboy; in spring: the outlet pond at **Spruce Run.

Ring-necked Duck A common migrant and uncommon winter resident on certain freshwater ponds, lakes, and reservoirs. November, and March–April: ***Assunpink, Mannington Marsh (Salem County), Point View Reservoir, Stafford Forge, Whitesbog; **Squibb Pond, Trenton Marsh.

Greater Scaup Common winter resident of coastal bays, estuaries, and open ocean from the Hudson River to Cape May and up the Delaware River to Gloucester County; uncommon inland. Late November–March; ****Barnegat Light, Holgate, Liberty State Park, Longport, North Shore, Sandy Hook, Stone Harbor, Tuckerton.

Lesser Scaup Common migrant and fairly common winter resident on ponds, lakes, reservoirs, bays, and estuaries; less common on open ocean. ***Lake Parsippany, Mannington Marsh (Salem County), North Shore, Point View Reservoir; **Assunpink, Brigantine, Squibb Pond, many other spots.

Common Eider Rare winter visitor along the coast, late November–March. Usually in ones or twos, rarely in flocks of a dozen or more. *Barnegat Light, Cape May, Wildwood Crest, Holgate, Island Beach, North Shore.

King Eider Rare winter visitor along the coast at the same times and places as Common Eider. Formerly the more "common" of the two, it is now less frequently encountered than the Common Eider.

Harlequin Duck Rare winter visitor along the coast, November–March. Almost all records in recent years are from *Barnegat Light and Wildwood Crest, with a few from the North Shore (especially Long Branch) and Sandy Hook.

Oldsquaw Common winter resident of bays, estuaries, and oceanfront from Sandy Hook to Cape May; rare inland in migration. ****Barnegat Light, Corson's Inlet, Longport, Stone Harbor, Tuckerton; ***North Shore, Sandy Hook.

Black Scoter Common migrant and fairly common winter resident along the coast from Sandy Hook to Cape May; uncommon inland in migration. October–November: ****Barnegat Light, Cape May, Holgate, Island Beach; ***Corson's Inlet, Longport, North Shore, Sandy Hook, Stone Harbor, Tuckerton. Recorded annually inland at **Culver's Lake (Stokes State Forest) and other lakes and reservoirs.

Surf Scoter As for Black Scoter, except less common and rarely recorded inland.

White-winged Scoter   Similar to Black Scoter in abundance and times and places of occurrence, except seldom reported inland.

Common Goldeneye   A common winter resident of fresh and salt water, especially along the coast. November–April: ****Barnegat Light, Shark River (North Shore); ***Brigantine, Corson's Inlet, Island Beach, Longport, Sandy Hook; or anywhere along the **Delaware River. Occurs at many places inland in migration.

Bufflehead   Common winter resident of fresh and salt water (one of the most conspicuous ducks of coastal ponds and bays). Regular migrant at many inland lakes and reservoirs. November–April: ****Barnegat Light, Cape May, Island Beach, Liberty State Park, North Shore, Sandy Hook, Stone Harbor.

Hooded Merganser   Fairly common migrant and uncommon winter resident of fresh and brackish water; a very rare breeding bird in wooded swamps mainly in northwestern New Jersey. ***Brigantine (in November); **Cape May, North Shore, Tuckahoe, *Assunpink.

Common Merganser   Fairly common migrant and winter resident on fresh water; extremely rare breeder along the upper Delaware River basin. Gathers in large flocks in November and March at favored locations: ***Assunpink, Lake Parsippany, Lincoln Park, Point View Reservoir, Wreck Pond (North Shore); **Brigantine, Mannington Marsh (Salem County), Spruce Run.

Red-breasted Merganser   Common migrant and winter resident along the coast from Sandy Hook to Cape May; extremely rare breeder along the coast and uncommon migrant inland. November–April: ****Barnegat Light, Cape May, Holgate, Island Beach, Longport, North Shore, Sandy Hook; ***Brigantine.

Ruddy Duck   Fairly common winter resident on lakes, ponds, bays, and estuaries; numbers much reduced in past 20 years. A rare, local breeder in summer, mainly at **Kearny Marsh. October–April: ***Brigantine, Liberty State Park, North Shore (especially Old Sam's Pond); **Squibb Pond; many inland locations during migration. Recent winter concentrations have been at ***Flood Gates and at Fish House on the Delaware River.

Black Vulture   An uncommon, but increasing, permanent resident of rural areas in Salem County in the southwest and Hunterdon County and surrounding areas in the northern and western parts of the state. Check the winter roost of Turkey Vultures at **Frenchtown (see Bull's Island), or explore **Salem County in spring. Black

Vultures also appear in winter Turkey Vulture roosts at Bernardsville, Somerset County; Lambertville and Mountainville, Hunterdon County; and near Princeton, Mercer County.

Turkey Vulture Common permanent resident of farmland and forests throughout the state; uncommon along the coast. Some withdraw from northern counties in midwinter. Easily found soaring anywhere except in the urban areas of the northeast. Very common in Burlington, Hunterdon, and Salem counties.

Osprey Fairly common summer resident, late March–August, along the coast from Sandy Hook to Cape May and up the Delaware Bayshore to Salem County. Nests at ****Salem County (road to nuclear plant); ***Island Beach, Manahawkin, Sandy Hook, Stone Harbor, Tuckerton. Fairly common fall migrant at inland hawk watches, common at ****Cape May in September–October.

American Swallow-tailed Kite A rare, but annual, spring visitor. Has occurred April–June in many different locations, but mainly at †Cape May and †Sandy Hook.

Mississippi Kite A rare, but annual, spring visitor; extremely rare in fall. Most records are from *Cape May during the last week of May or the first week of June.

Bald Eagle An uncommon migrant and winter resident; extremely rare breeder. A few pass the hawk watches in the fall, mainly in September. *Cape May, Raccoon Ridge, Montclair, Sunrise Mountain. Small numbers winter at *Brigantine, the Delaware Bayshore (see Jakes Landing or Dividing Creek), and along the upper Delaware River in Sussex County.

Northern Harrier Common migrant and fairly common winter resident in marshes (especially salt marsh) and farmlands: ****Brigantine, Cape May, Dividing Creek, Hackensack Meadowlands, Jakes Landing, Manahawkin, Salem County. Uncommon breeder in southern salt marshes; rare breeder elsewhere (Hackensack Meadowlands, Raritan Estuary, etc.). September–November: any hawk watch, especially ****Cape May.

Sharp-shinned Hawk Very common fall migrant along the mountain ridges and the coast; fairly common spring migrant at ***Sandy Hook. Uncommon winter resident; rare breeder in northwestern New Jersey and, possibly, in the Pine Barrens. Mid-September–early November: ****Cape May, Montclair, Raccoon Ridge, Sunrise Mountain.

Cooper's Hawk   Fairly common fall migrant along the mountain ridges and, especially, in October–early November, at ****Cape May; also at Raccoon Ridge; ***Sunrise Mountain; **Montclair. Uncommon spring migrant at ***Sandy Hook. Uncommon winter resident; rare breeder in northwestern New Jersey; formerly more common and widespread.

Northern Goshawk   Uncommon fall migrant, mainly along the mountain ridges, but also at *Cape May. Rare winter resident in the northern counties; rare, but increasing, breeder in the northwest. October–November: **Raccoon Ridge, Sunrise Mountain; *High Point.

Red-shouldered Hawk   Fairly common fall migrant along the mountain ridges and the coast, mainly in October. Rare winter resident; uncommon and declining summer resident, now largely confined to the northern counties. In fall: ***Cape May, Raccoon Ridge, Sunrise Mountain; **High Point, Montclair.

Broad-winged Hawk   Common fall migrant throughout the state, but especially along the mountain ridges in mid-September. Fairly common summer resident of deciduous woodlands, more common in the northwest. In fall: ****Montclair, High Point, Raccoon Ridge, Sunrise Mountain; ***Cape May.

Swainson's Hawk   A rare fall visitor from the west; most records are of immature birds at *Cape May in September and October.

Red-tailed Hawk   Common migrant and winter resident; biggest flights are along the mountain ridges in October and November. Fairly common summer resident throughout the state. In fall: ****High Point, Montclair, Raccoon Ridge, Sunrise Mountain; ***Cape May.

Rough-legged Hawk   Fairly common winter resident of marshes and farmland, especially near the coast; numbers vary from year to year. ***Hackensack Meadowlands, Manahawkin; **Brigantine, Jakes Landing, Dividing Creek, Troy Meadows.

Golden Eagle   Rare fall migrant along the mountain ridges; rare migrant and winter resident near the south coast. Late October–November: **Raccoon Ridge; *Cape May, Sunrise Mountain; in winter: *Brigantine, Jakes Landing, Dividing Creek.

American Kestrel   Very common migrant, especially along the coast, in spring and fall; common winter resident throughout the state. Fairly common, but declining, summer resident throughout except for central Pine Barrens. In spring: ****Sandy Hook; in fall: ****Cape May; ***Raccoon Ridge, Sunrise Mountain.

Merlin   Fairly common fall migrant along the coast, uncommon in spring. Rare fall migrant inland and rare winter resident along the coast. Mid-September–mid-October: ****Cape May; ***Island Beach; **Brigantine, Sandy Hook.

Peregrine Falcon   Uncommon, but increasing, fall migrant along the coast, rare in winter. The small, introduced breeding population is largely nonmigratory. Mid-September–October: ***Cape May (where daily counts of 20-plus are not unusual) and **Island Beach. Introduced birds are easily seen at ***Brigantine and Moores Beach.

Gyrfalcon   A rare winter visitor from the far north, exclusively along the coast, sometimes lingering for months; there are several records for †Brigantine. Extremely rare late fall migrant along the mountain ridges; in most years none are reported.

Ring-necked Pheasant   Introduced species that has become a fairly common permanent resident of fields, farmlands, and hedgerows throughout the state; numbers are augmented annually by released stock. Most easily found at wildlife management areas: ***Assunpink, Black River, Colliers Mills; **Clinton (see Spruce Run), Rancocas, Whittingham.

Ruffed Grouse   Uncommon permanent resident of deciduous woodlands throughout the state, most common in the northwest. Often heard drumming in April and May, but most easily seen in June and July when hens have their broods. **Black River, High Point, Jockey Hollow, Pequannock Watershed, Stokes, Wawayanda; *Assunpink, Lebanon.

Wild Turkey   Successfully reintroduced over much of the state. Fairly common and rapidly increasing, especially in the northwest. Shy and often difficult to observe. **Allamuchy Mountains, Stokes, Worthington; will soon be appearing in many other places.

Northern Bobwhite   A fairly common permanent resident in the southern half of the state; numbers maintained by restocking in many areas: ***Assunpink, Dividing Creek, Glassboro Woods; **Brigantine, Cape May, Colliers Mills, Rancocas.

Black Rail   Rare summer resident of southern salt marshes; difficult to hear, even harder to see. Recent records are from *Dividing Creek, Tuckahoe, Brigantine, Manahawkin.

Clapper Rail   Fairly common summer resident of southern salt marshes; rare in winter. ***Brigantine; **Manahawkin, Stone Harbor, Tuckerton; also at **Jakes Landing and Dividing Creek.

King Rail   Uncommon summer resident of fresh and brackish marshes along the Delaware Bayshore and in the interior; difficult to observe. **Dividing Creek, Salem County; *Pedricktown, Princeton (Rogers Refuge), Trenton Marsh, Troy Meadows. Watch out for Clappers in the brackish areas.

Virginia Rail Fairly common migrant and summer resident in fresh and brackish marshes; rare in winter. Most easily observed in spring, when they readily respond to tape recordings of their call. ***Dividing Creek, Troy Meadows; **Princeton (Rogers Refuge), Trenton Marsh; *Brigantine, Cape May, Manahawkin.

Sora Fairly common migrant and summer resident of freshwater marshes, mainly in the northern half of the state; very difficult to observe. **Troy Meadows; *Brigantine, Great Swamp, Manahawkin, Princeton (Rogers Refuge), Trenton Marsh.

Purple Gallinule Very rare, but annual, visitor from the south. Can show up anywhere, although most frequent at †Cape May.

Common Moorhen Fairly common summer resident of freshwater marshes; rare in winter. Late April–September: ****Kearny Marsh; ***Brigantine, Manahawkin, Trenton Marsh; **Cape May, Mannington Marsh (Salem County).

American Coot Common migrant and fairly common winter resident on ponds, lakes, reservoirs, bays, and estuaries throughout the state; uncommon and local in summer. October–May: ****Brigantine, Cape May, Kearny Marsh (also in summer), Mannington Marsh (Salem County), North Shore, Spruce Run, Tuckahoe.

Sandhill Crane Rare visitor, usually in early spring or late fall, but has occurred in summer and in winter. Reports from widely scattered locations.

Black-bellied Plover Common migrant and uncommon winter resident, mainly on mudflats along the coast; uncommon inland. May, and August–November: ****Brigantine, Holgate, Longport, Stone Harbor; ***Barnegat Light, Cape May, Island Beach, Liberty State Park, North Shore, Tuckerton.

Lesser Golden-Plover A rare spring migrant in the Delaware Valley and an uncommon fall migrant at sod farms and coastal mudflats. April: **Mannington Marsh (Salem County), Pedricktown; mid-August–early October: **Cape May, Dutch Neck–New Sharon Sod Farms, Mercer Sod Farm; *Brigantine.

Semipalmated Plover Common migrant at impoundments and tidal mudflats, less common at inland reservoirs; rare in winter.

May, and late July–October: ****Brigantine, Cape May, Holgate, Longport, Stone Harbor, Tuckerton; ***Barnegat Light, Hackensack Meadowlands, Pedricktown.

Piping Plover   Uncommon, and decreasing, spring and summer resident of beaches from Island Beach to Cape May. ***Holgate, Island Beach, Longport, Stone Harbor; **Brigantine Island, Cape May.

Killdeer   Common migrant on sod farms, fields, wet meadows, and mudflats; uncommon in winter. Fairly common breeder on fields, gravel areas, and the rooftops of schools and shopping centers. August–October: ****Cape May; ***Dutch Neck–New Sharon Sod Farms, Lincoln Park, Mercer Sod Farm, Spruce Run; **Brigantine.

American Oystercatcher   Fairly common and increasing resident, mainly March–October, of salt marshes and mudflats from Island Beach to Cape May; a few attempt to overwinter. Late summer: ****Holgate, Stone Harbor, Tuckerton; ***Brigantine, Corson's Inlet, Island Beach; **Cape May.

Black-necked Stilt   Rare spring and summer visitor on impoundments, wet meadows, and tidal marshes. Has occurred at many locations, but most often at *Brigantine. Nests as close as Little Creek, Delaware.

American Avocet   Uncommon migrant, mainly in late summer and fall, at fresh or brackish ponds and impoundments; rare in spring. August–October: **Brigantine.

Greater Yellowlegs   Common migrant April–May and mid-July–October; rare in winter, mainly in southern New Jersey. Found in wet meadows, tidal mudflats, and along the edges of ponds, impoundments, and reservoirs; more common along the coast. ****Brigantine, Cape May, Hackensack Meadowlands, Mannington Marsh (Salem County), Pedricktown, Stone Harbor, Tuckerton; ***Lincoln Park, Spruce Run, Tuckahoe.

Lesser Yellowlegs   Similar to Greater Yellowlegs, with which is it usually found.

Solitary Sandpiper   Fairly common, but solitary, migrant along freshwater ponds, marshes, streams, and rivers. Late April–early May, and mid-August–September: ***Black River, Great Swamp, Trenton Marsh; **Cape May, Hackensack Meadowlands, Lincoln Park, Stokes; *Assunpink, Spruce Run.

Willet   Common and conspicuous summer resident of southern salt marshes; rare migrant in the north, and extremely rare migrant inland. April–October: ****Brigantine, Holgate, Stone Harbor, Tuckerton; ***Cape May, Dividing Creek, Island Beach, Manahawkin.

Spotted Sandpiper Common migrant and fairly common summer resident of fresh and brackish water. May, and July–September: ***Assunpink, Brigantine, Hackensack Meadowlands, Lincoln Park, Sandy Hook, Spruce Run, Trenton Marsh; **Cape May, Great Swamp, Squibb Pond.

Upland Sandpiper An uncommon migrant on fields, meadows, and sod farms, mainly in late summer; rare and local spring migrant and summer breeder—numbers of both residents and migrants have declined in the past decade. August–early September: ***Mercer Sod Farm; **Cape May, Dutch Neck–New Sharon Sod Farms; *Brigantine. Breeding birds can still be found at **Sharptown (Salem County) and at Beekman Lane.

Whimbrel Fairly common migrant in salt marshes. Early April–mid-May and mid-July–September: at ****Tuckerton; ***Brigantine, Cape May, Corson's Inlet, Longport, Manahawkin, Stone Harbor.

Hudsonian Godwit Uncommon fall migrant at ponds, impoundments, and mudflats, mainly along the coast. August–October: *Brigantine, Hackensack Meadowlands, Holgate, Stone Harbor, Tuckerton.

Marbled Godwit Rare fall migrant along the coast: *Brigantine, Holgate, Stone Harbor, Tuckerton.

Ruddy Turnstone Common migrant and uncommon winter resident along the outer beaches (especially at jetties), the Delaware Bayshore, and tidal mudflats. Abundant in late May and early June along the ****Delaware Bayshore (Moores Beach and Reeds Beach). May, and August–October: ****Brigantine, Cape May, Holgate, Longport, Stone Harbor, Tuckerton.

Red Knot Fairly common migrant, especially in late spring, and rare winter resident along the coast. Common in late May along the ****Delaware Bayshore (Moores Beach and Reeds Beach); ***Brigantine, Holgate, Longport, Stone Harbor, Tuckerton.

Sanderling Common migrant and fairly common winter resident along the outer beaches and on tidal mudflats. Abundant along the ****Delaware Bayshore in late May (Moores Beach and Reeds Beach); ***Barnegat Light, Brigantine, Brigantine Island, Holgate, Island Beach, Stone Harbor.

Semipalmated Sandpiper   Common migrant in spring and fall at impoundments and tidal mudflats, but especially near the coast. Abundant along the ****Delaware Bayshore in late May (Moores Beach and Reeds Beach); May, and July–October: ****Brigantine, Cape May, Holgate, Longport, Stone Harbor, Tuckerton; ***Assunpink, Hackensack Meadowlands, Lincoln Park, Mannington Marsh (Salem County), Pedricktown, Spruce Run, Tuckahoe.

Western Sandpiper   Fairly common migrant (mainly in fall), and rare winter resident along the coast. August–October: ***Brigantine, Cape May, Holgate, Longport, Stone Harbor, Tuckerton; **Hackensack Meadowlands.

Least Sandpiper   Common migrant and rare winter resident at reservoirs, impoundments and tidal mudflats, especially near the coast. Occurs at the same places as Semipalmated Sandpiper.

White-rumped Sandpiper   Uncommon migrant, mainly along the coast, at reservoirs, impoundments, and tidal mudflats. **Brigantine, Cape May, Hackensack Meadowlands, Stone Harbor, Tuckerton; *Assunpink, Longport, Spruce Run.

Baird's Sandpiper   Rare fall migrant at sod farms, reservoirs, impoundments and wet meadows, most often near the coast. Late August–October: *Brigantine, Cape May, Hackensack Meadowlands, Assunpink, Dutch Neck–New Sharon Sod Farms, Spruce Run.

Pectoral Sandpiper   Fairly common migrant on grassy mudflats, both inland and along the coast. Biggest concentrations are in April at ****Pedricktown; April and early May, and July–October: ***Brigantine, Cape May, Hackensack Meadowlands, Lincoln Park, Manahawkin, Mannington Marsh (Salem County), Stone Harbor, Tuckerton; **Assunpink, Spruce Run.

Purple Sandpiper   Common winter resident on rocky jetties along the coast, some lingering to the end of May. November–April: anywhere along the coast especially ***Barnegat Light, Cape May, Island Beach, Longport; **Brigantine Island, Corson's Inlet, North Shore, Sandy Hook.

Dunlin   Very common migrant in spring and fall, fairly common winter resident on coastal mudflats and impoundments; uncommon inland. Late September–early May: ****Brigantine, Holgate, Longport, Stone Harbor, Tuckerton; ***Cape May, Corson's Inlet, Hackensack Meadowlands, Island Beach, Sandy Hook.

Curlew Sandpiper   Rare visitor in spring and fall on coastal mudflats. May, and mid-July–September: *Brigantine, Cape May, Heislerville–Moores Beach, Longport, Tuckerton.

Stilt Sandpiper   Rare spring migrant and fairly common fall migrant at shallow ponds, impoundments, and tidal pools, mainly along the coast. Early May, or mid-July–October: ***Brigantine, Cape May, Hackensack Meadowlands, Manahawkin, Moores Beach, Stone Harbor, Tuckerton, Tuckahoe.

Buff-breasted Sandpiper   Uncommon fall migrant on sod farms and grassy mudflats. August–September: **Cape May, Mercer Sod Farm; *Brigantine, Dutch Neck–New Sharon Sod Farms, Spruce Run.

Ruff   Rare, but regular, migrant in spring and fall on tidal mudflats and impoundments, mainly near the coast. Mid-March–April: ***Pedricktown (where as many as eight have appeared in a season, including five at one time). May and July–October: *Brigantine, Cape May, Hackensack Meadowlands, Longport, Moores Beach, Manahawkin, Stone Harbor.

Short-billed Dowitcher   Common spring migrant and very common fall migrant on coastal mudflats. May, and mid-July–September: ****Brigantine, Hackensack Meadowlands, Holgate, Longport, Stone Harbor, Tuckerton; ***Cape May, Manahawkin, Mannington Marsh (Salem County), Moores Beach, Pedricktown.

Long-billed Dowitcher   Fairly common fall migrant at mudflats and impoundments, mainly along the coast; rare in spring and in winter (when it is the only dowitcher likely to be seen). September–November: ***Brigantine, Cape May; **Hackensack Meadowlands, Manahawkin, Moores Beach, Stone Harbor, Tuckerton, Tuckahoe.

Common Snipe   Fairly common migrant and uncommon winter resident in freshwater marshes, wet meadows, and impoundments; a rare breeder in the north. September–early May: ***Mannington Marsh (Salem County), Pedricktown; **Assunpink, Brigantine, Cape May, Great Swamp, Manahawkin, Moores Beach, Trenton Marsh, Tuckahoe.

American Woodcock   Fairly common migrant and summer resident in wet woodlands; rare in winter. Solitary, retiring, and difficult to observe except during the evening courtship flight in spring or when flushed by surprise. Easiest to see at ***Higbee Beach (Cape May) in October. Otherwise, visit a nesting area for the courtship flight in March–April: **Assunpink, Black River, Glassboro Woods,

Great Swamp, Rancocas, Trenton Marsh, Troy Meadows, Waterloo, Whittingham.

Wilson's Phalarope Rare, but increasing, migrant in spring and fall at fresh or brackish ponds and impoundments, mainly along the coast. May, and mid-July–September: **Brigantine, Cape May, Hackensack Meadowlands; *Holgate, Moores Beach, Stone Harbor, Tuckerton.

Red-necked Phalarope Fairly common migrant in spring and fall, well offshore; rare at ponds and impoundments inland and along the coast. April–May and August–October: **Pelagic Trips; *Brigantine, Cape May, Hackensack Meadowlands, Manahawkin, Moores Beach, Tuckerton.

Red Phalarope Fairly common migrant in spring and fall, far offshore; rarely found inland. April–May and September–November: **Pelagic Trips; †Brigantine, Cape May, Culvers Lake (Stokes State Forest), Lake Musconetcong, Spruce Run.

Pomarine Jaeger Fairly common migrant in spring and fall, far offshore; rare on inland lakes and reservoirs. ***See Pelagic Trips.

Parasitic Jaeger Fairly common migrant offshore in spring and fall; uncommon along the coast in fall. See ***Pelagic Trips; September–October: *Barnegat Light, Cape May, Island Beach, North Shore.

Long-tailed Jaeger Rare migrant in spring and fall, far offshore. *Pelagic Trips.

Great Skua Rare far offshore in winter. *Pelagic Trips.

South Polar Skua Rare in spring and summer, far offshore. *Pelagic Trips.

Laughing Gull Common to abundant summer resident along the coast; fairly common inland in the southern counties, although it does not nest there; rare in winter. Noisy, conspicuous, and hard to miss anywhere along the coast in summer.

Little Gull Uncommon transient along the coast in spring and late fall; rare in winter and in summer (usually immature birds). May: **Caven Cove (Liberty State Park); *Barnegat Light, Cape May, South Amboy.

Common Black-headed Gull Rare winter resident at bays, estuaries, and inlets along the coast. November–April: **Hackensack Meadowlands, Caven Cove (Liberty State Park); *Cape May, Manasquan Inlet (North Shore), South Amboy.

Bonaparte's Gull Common migrant and fairly common winter resident along the coast usually in small flocks; uncommon inland in migration. Late October–early May: ****Barnegat Light, Cape May, Island Beach; ***Brigantine Island, Corson's Inlet, Holgate, Liberty State Park, Sandy Hook, South Amboy, Stone Harbor.

Ring-billed Gull Common migrant and fairly common winter resident at garbage dumps and on fresh and salt water. Large flocks gather on inland farm fields in April. Some nonbreeders remain through the summer. Hard to miss from August through May.

Herring Gull Common permanent resident, abundant in winter at garbage dumps and along the coast. Occurs in the same places as Ring-billed, but less likely to be found on small ponds or plowed fields. Hard to miss at any season, especially along the coast.

Iceland Gull Uncommon winter visitor from the far north at garbage dumps, and at lakes, estuaries, and beaches along the coast; rare on inland lakes and reservoirs. Look for it from November to April at ***Hackensack Meadowlands; **North Shore; *Barnegat Light, Cape May, Island Beach, Johnson Park, Liberty State Park, Sandy Hook, South Amboy.

Lesser Black-backed Gull Rare, but increasing, visitor; most common in winter, but occurs, usually in the company of Herring Gulls, September–May: **Hackensack Meadowlands, Johnson Park; *Barnegat Light, Cape May, North Shore, and wherever gulls gather.

Glaucous Gull Uncommon winter visitor (mostly immatures) from the far north. Look for it at the same times and places as Iceland Gull, which tends to be more common than Glaucous.

Great Black-backed Gull Common permanent resident along the coast, most abundant in winter; uncommon, but increasing, inland from fall through spring. ****Hackensack Meadowlands, or anywhere along the coast.

Black-legged Kittiwake Fairly common winter visitor offshore, uncommon along the coast, especially on southeast winds from November through March. Most often seen from shore in November at **Barnegat Light, Island Beach, Manasquan Inlet (North Shore), and Wildwood Crest.

Gull-billed Tern Uncommon and very local summer resident of salt marshes. Most easily found May–August at ***Brigantine, where there is a nesting colony; also at *Cape May, Longport, Manahawkin, Stone Harbor. In August, some feed at **Whitesbog.

Caspian Tern   Uncommon migrant, mainly in late summer and fall, and very rare summer resident. Most common at inlets and impoundments along the coast August–October, but occasionally encountered on inland lakes and reservoirs: **Brigantine, Corson's Inlet, Holgate, Stone Harbor; *Assunpink, Barnegat Light, Cape May; in April: *Mannington Marsh (Salem County).

Royal Tern   Fairly common late summer and fall visitor along the coast, rare in spring and early summer. Sometimes occurs in large flocks at coastal inlets. August–October: ***Cape May, Corson's Inlet, Stone Harbor; **Barnegat Light, Island Beach, Longport.

Sandwich Tern   Rare visitor from the south, usually occuring with flocks of Royal Terns in July and August. May–September: *Cape May, Holgate, or anywhere Royals gather.

Roseate Tern   Rare migrant and very rare summer resident (no recent breeding records) with Common Terns along the coast. All recent records are from *Cape May and Holgate.

Common Tern   Common migrant and summer resident along the coast, nesting on beaches and in salt marsh. Late April–October: ****Barnegat Light, Cape May, Corson's Inlet, Holgate, Island Beach, Sandy Hook, Stone Harbor, Tuckerton; ***Brigantine.

Arctic Tern   Rare migrant far offshore; occasionally seen with Common Terns along the coast. See *Pelagic Trips; May–August: *Cape May, Holgate.

Forster's Tern   Fairly common migrant and locally fairly common summer resident at salt marshes; rare inland in migration and along the coast in winter. April–November: ****Brigantine, Cape May, Heislerville–Moores Beach, Manahawkin, Stone Harbor, Tuckerton; ***Corson's Inlet.

Least Tern   Fairly common migrant and summer resident at beaches and inlets along the coast; numbers are declining. Easily seen near the large southern nesting colonies; much less common in the north. From May to early September, ****Brigantine, Cape May, Corson's Inlet, Holgate, Stone Harbor; ***Hackensack Meadowlands, Island Beach, Manahawkin, and Sandy Hook.

Black Tern   Rare spring migrant and uncommon late summer migrant at marshes, ponds, impoundments, bays, and inlets, mainly along the coast. July–September: **Brigantine, Cape May, Holgate, Manahawkin, Moores Beach, South Amboy; *Kearny Marsh, Liberty State Park; in spring: *Cape May and South Amboy; has occurred at many places, both inland and along the coast, but is unpredictable.

Black Skimmer   Locally fairly common, but declining, summer resident along the coast, often associated with colonies of Common Terns. May–October: ****Corson's Inlet, Holgate, Stone Harbor; ***Barnegat Light, Brigantine, Cape May, Island Beach, Manahawkin, Tuckerton; **Sandy Hook.

Dovekie   Irregularly fairly common winter visitor well offshore (10–30 miles); rare along the coast. See **Pelagic Trips; in winter, especially November–December: coast and inlets from Shark River to Cape May.

Thick-billed Murre   Rare winter visitor along the coast, at inlets and jetties from Shark River to Cape May.

Razorbill   Rare winter visitor well offshore and at inlets and jetties along the coast from Shark River to Cape May. See *Pelagic Trips.

Atlantic Puffin   Very rare winter visitor far offshore. See †Pelagic Trips.

Rock Dove   Common to abundant permanent resident, especially in urban areas. Hard to miss in a day's birding anywhere in New Jersey.

Mourning Dove   Common resident of fields, farmlands, and suburban areas from spring through fall; common in winter. Hard to miss at parks, reservations and WMAs anywhere in the state.

Black-billed Cuckoo   Uncommon migrant and summer resident in thickets and deciduous woodlands, mainly north of the coastal plain; numbers fluctuate widely. In May: **Assunpink, Bull's Island, Princeton, Trenton Marsh; in summer: **Black River, High Point, Pequannock Watershed, Stokes, Wawayanda; in August–September: **Cape May.

Yellow-billed Cuckoo   Fairly common migrant and summer resident in thickets and deciduous woodlands; numbers fluctuate widely. Occurs in the same places as Black-billed Cuckoo, but is also a fairly common breeder at **Lebanon State Forest and elsewhere in the Pine Barrens; at **Dividing Creek, and elsewhere along the Delaware Bayshore.

Common Barn-Owl   Fairly common permanent resident of farmlands throughout the state, but almost wholly nocturnal and difficult to see. There is a small movement of migrants through Cape May in the fall, when the bird can be seen flying around the lighthouse at Cape May Point during the night. For the past few years, a pair has inhabited a disused Peregrine Falcon hack-box at *Brigantine, where they can sometimes be seen during the day.

Eastern Screech-Owl Fairly common, but highly nocturnal, permanent resident of woodlands. Readily responds to tape recordings of its call, especially August–winter. Most often seen in winter or spring sunning itself in the opening of a tree hole or a Wood Duck box.

Great Horned Owl Common permanent resident in woodlands; nocturnal, but often seen flying away when flushed from a roost or nest. Nests in old Red-tailed Hawk nests or those of other species, occasionally in conspicuous sites where they can be observed at leisure during the day, as at *Great Swamp, Pedricktown, and Sandy Hook in recent years.

Snowy Owl Rare winter visitor from the far north, occurring in widely fluctuating numbers that reflect prey populations in arctic Canada. Most reports are from the outer beaches: *Barnegat Light, Brigantine Island, Holgate, Island Beach, Sandy Hook.

Barred Owl Uncommon permanent resident of wooded swamps in northern and far southern New Jersey, and of deciduous woodlands in the Highlands and the Kittatinny Mountains; generally absent from the Pine Barrens and rare in the central part of the state. Most common at **Great Swamp; *Black River, Dividing Creek, High Point, Pequannock Watershed, Stokes, Wawayanda.

Long-eared Owl Uncommon winter visitor and rare summer resident, mainly in conifers; more common in the north. Wholly nocturnal, this species is seldom seen unless found roosting in winter. At present, there are no publicly accessible reliable sites.

Short-eared Owl Uncommon migrant and winter resident, mainly in coastal marshes; very rare breeder in salt marshes. Also occurs over inland farm fields in winter, but your best chance to see one is at **Manahawkin, *Brigantine, or *Liberty State Park in winter at dusk.

Northern Saw-whet Owl Uncommon winter resident throughout the state; rare breeder in the Pine Barrens and uncommon fall migrant at Cape May. Most often found roosting in small conifers during the winter: **Princeton, Stony Brook–Millstone Reserve; *Troy Meadows.

Common Nighthawk Common migrant throughout the state, especially in fall; uncommon summer resident in the Pine Barrens and the northeastern and central urban areas. In May and in late

August–early September, flocks of several hundred may often be seen at dusk anywhere in the state, including **Brigantine, Cape May, Great Swamp, Hackensack Meadowlands, Lincoln Park, Princeton, Trenton Marsh, Troy Meadows. In summer (at dusk): **Dividing Creek, Lebanon, Wharton.

Chuck-will's-widow   Local and uncommon summer (April–September) resident of deciduous woods and pinelands near the southern coast. Easily heard, but much more difficult to see, at dawn or dusk May–July at ***Brigantine, Cape May, Dividing Creek, Moores Beach; **Manahawkin.

Whip-poor-will   Fairly common summer (April–September) resident of deciduous woodlands and the Pine Barrens throughout the southern part of the state; rare in the mountains of the northwest. Nocturnal and difficult to glimpse, but easily heard at dawn and dusk at ****Brigantine, Colliers Mills, Dividing Creek, Lebanon, Manahawkin, and Wharton.

Chimney Swift   Common summer resident around towns and cities. Easily seen in migration and in summer anywhere in the state, including ***Bull's Island, Cape May, Great Swamp, Lincoln Park, Parvin, Princeton, Stokes.

Ruby-throated Hummingbird   Fairly common migrant and uncommon summer resident. Most easily found in May or August–September at ***Cape May, Princeton, Stokes; **Assunpink, Bull's Island, Great Swamp, Lincoln Park, Old Troy Park, Parvin, Waterloo, and many other sites.

Belted Kingfisher   Common migrant, fairly common summer resident, and uncommon winter resident, always near water. ***Brigantine, Bull's Island, Cape May, Dividing Creek, Lincoln Park, Manahawkin; **Waterloo.

Red-headed Woodpecker   Uncommon migrant, mainly along the coast in fall; rare winter resident and rare, but increasing, summer resident. In September–October, **Cape May and *Island Beach are the most reliable spots for migrants. Breeding colonies are located at ***Cape May County Park, Lebanon; **Great Swamp, Stokes.

Red-bellied Woodpecker   Fairly common permanent resident of deciduous woodlands throughout the state, but uncommon in the Pine Barrens; increasing in the north. ****Dividing Creek, Great Swamp, Parvin; ***Allaire, Assunpink, Bull's Island, Cape May, Glassboro Woods, Princeton, Rancocas, Stokes, Trenton Marsh, Whittingham.

Yellow-bellied Sapsucker   Fairly common migrant in April and, especially, in late September–November; uncommon in winter. The highest numbers occur along the coast in October. In spring: **Bull's Island, Princeton, Sandy Hook, Trenton Marsh; in fall: ***Cape May, Island Beach, Sandy Hook, many inland sites.

Downy Woodpecker   Common permanent resident of woodlands and suburban areas.

Hairy Woodpecker   Fairly common permanent resident of woodlands throughout. Numbers seem to have declined in recent years.

Northern Flicker   Common permanent resident in woodlands; abundant migrant along the coast in fall. Commonly feeds on the ground in open, short-grass areas. The passage of thousands of flickers at Cape May in late September–early October is spectacular.

Pileated Woodpecker   Uncommon permanent resident of mature woodlands in the northern part of the state. ***Jockey Hollow; **Black River, Great Swamp, Pequannock Watershed, Scherman-Hoffman, Stokes, Waterloo, Wawayanda, Whittingham.

Olive-sided Flycatcher   Uncommon migrant in late May–early June and late August–September; usually perches in the tops of dead trees, often near water. **Allamuchy Mountain, Cape May (in fall), Great Swamp, High Point, Manahawkin, Princeton, Stokes, Trenton Marsh, Waterloo.

Eastern Wood-Pewee   Common migrant and summer resident in woodlands throughout. Mid-May–September.

Yellow-bellied Flycatcher   Uncommon woodland migrant in late May and, especially, in August–September. Regular spots for this species include **Cape May (fall), Old Troy Park, Princeton, Princeton Avenue Woods, Sandy Hook.

Acadian Flycatcher   Fairly common summer resident of deciduous woodlands in the southern part of the state and of hemlock glens in the northwest; increasing in the north. Generally absent from the Pine Barrens. Mid-May–September: ***Bull's Island, Dividing Creek, Stokes; **Glassboro Woods, High Point, Parvin, Pequannock Watershed, Wawayanda; regular fall migrant at Cape May, but difficult to identify.

Alder Flycatcher   Uncommon migrant in late May–early June and August–September; rare and local summer resident in the north. Nonsinging birds are virtually indistinguishable from Willow Flycatcher. Recent breeding locations include ***Black River; **Great Swamp, High Point; *Pequannock Watershed, Troy Meadows.

Willow Flycatcher   Common summer resident of shrubby fields, freshwater marshes, and marsh edges, mid-May–September. Common migrant, but virtually indistinguishable from Alder Flycatcher when not singing. During the breeding season: ****Assunpink, Black River, Great Swamp, High Point, Stokes, Troy Meadows; ***Cape May, Lebanon, Manahawkin, Princeton, Stony Brook-Millstone Reserve, many other places.

Least Flycatcher   Uncommon summer resident, mainly in the north; fairly common migrant throughout, especially along the coast, mainly in the fall. Has declined as a breeding bird in recent years. Present in open deciduous woodlands, usually near water; most easily identified by its call during the nesting season. May–early September: **Black River, High Point, Pequannock Watershed, Stokes, Wawayanda, Worthington; *Great Swamp, Jockey Hollow, Princeton.

Eastern Phoebe   Commom migrant throughout the state; fairly common summer resident, especially in the north; rare in winter. Usually found near water, often nesting under bridges. Late March–early October: ***Assunpink, Bull's Island, Cape May, Great Swamp, High Point, Princeton, Stokes, Waterloo, Wawayanda.

Great Crested Flycatcher   Common migrant and summer resident in deciduous woodlands and Pine Barrens.

Western Kingbird   Rare, but regular (about 5 to 10 each year), fall visitor; mainly along the coast; a few records in spring. Late August–December: **Cape May; *Assunpink, Barnegat Light, Brigantine, Island Beach, and Sandy Hook.

Eastern Kingbird   Common migrant and common summer resident of farmlands, open woodlands, hedgerows, and marsh edges. Large flocks gather at ****Cape May in late August–early September. May–September: widespread including ***Assunpink, Brigantine, Great Swamp, High Point, Parvin, Pedricktown, Princeton, Troy Meadows, Wawayanda.

Scissor-tailed Flycatcher   Rare, but annual, visitor from the southwestern United States; most records are along the coast in May and June. †Cape May and †Sandy Hook are the two most likely spots.

Horned Lark   Fairly common migrant and winter resident on grassy fields, plowed fields, or ocean dunes; uncommon summer resident in the same habitats. October–May: ***Alpha and similar farmland throughout the state; **Brigantine Island, Cape May, Holgate, Island Beach, Mercer Sod Farm, Sandy Hook; *Barnegat Light.

Purple Martin   Fairly common resident April–early September in open, rural, and suburban situations; usually nests in "martin houses" provided by parks and homeowners. Most common in the south, uncommon in the northeast. ****Brigantine, Cape May, Princeton; ***Assunpink, Great Swamp, Paulins Kill Lake (near Whittingham), Pedricktown, Squibb Pond (in migration), Trenton Marsh (in migration), Tuckerton (in August), many other places.

Tree Swallow   Common migrant in April–May, abundant migrant in August–October, especially along the coast; rare in winter along the coast. A fairly common summer resident in marshes, wooded swamps, and beaver swamps, and in nest boxes near water. The flocks of thousands that gather in September are a "must see" spectacle at ****Cape May, Corson's Inlet, Island Beach, Sandy Hook, Tuckerton; common breeder at ****Brigantine, Great Swamp, Princeton; ***Stokes.

Northern Rough-winged Swallow   Fairly common migrant and summer resident; nests under bridges, around lakes, and along streams and rivers. April–August: ***Bull's Island, Cape May, Pedricktown, Paulins Kill Lake (near Whittingham), Princeton, Trenton Marsh; **Squibb Pond.

Bank Swallow   Common migrant and fairly common, but local, summer resident. Mid-April–mid-May and August–early September: at ***Cape May, Pedricktown, Princeton, Trenton Marsh; **Assunpink, Squibb Pond, Tuckerton. Longstanding nesting colonies are near ***Bull's Island, Dividing Creek, and Paulins Kill Lake (near Whittingham).

Cliff Swallow   An uncommon migrant throughout the state; a rare and local (but increasing) summer resident, mainly along the Delaware River valley. Look for it April–early May and August–September among flocks of other swallows at **Cape May, Pedricktown, Squibb Pond, Trenton Marsh; *Assunpink, Great Swamp, Lincoln Park and Tuckerton. Fortunately, the breeding colonies at ****Bull's Island and Lambertville (see Bull's Island) are very accessible.

Barn Swallow   A common migrant and a common summer resident in open areas, such as farmland, parks, marshes (fresh or salt), swamps, or ponds. Anywhere in the state April–September: ****Assunpink, Brigantine, Bull's Island, Cape May, Parvin, Rancocas, Trenton Marsh, Tuckerton, Waterloo.

Blue Jay   Common permanent resident in woodlands and suburbs. Hard to miss in a day's birding at any location in New Jersey that has trees. Large flights of fall migrants pass through ****Cape May.

American Crow Common permanent resident in farmland, woodlands, and suburbs. Hard to miss in a day's birding anywhere in New Jersey.

Fish Crow Fairly common permanent resident, especially at fresh- and saltwater ponds and marshes along the coast and along the larger rivers and their tributaries. Uncommon (but increasing) inland away from the river systems; numbers somewhat reduced in winter. Most easily found (when calling) along the coast: ****Barnegat Light, Brigantine, Holgate, Sandy Hook, Stone Harbor, Tuckerton; ***Cape May.

Common Raven Rare fall migrant along the mountain ridges of Sussex and Warren counties. Likely to be seen only by spending a great deal of time in October–November at *Raccoon Ridge or Sunrise Mountain.

Black-capped Chickadee Fairly common permanent resident of woodlands and suburbs north and west of a line running roughly from South Amboy to Lambertville; numbers augmented by visitors from the north in winter, especially in flight years, when this species occurs well south of its normal range in the state.

Carolina Chickadee Common permanent resident of woodlands, shrubby fields, and suburbs south and east of the line from South Amboy to Lambertville.

Boreal Chickadee Rare, irregular winter visitor. Usually occurs in northern conifer groves, but has been found in such diverse places as Liberty State Park, Princeton, Toms River, and Westfield. Best bets are High Point, Pequannock Watershed, Stokes, and Wawayanda.

Tufted Titmouse Common permanent resident in deciduous woodlands, Pine Barrens, and suburbs. Hard to miss in a day's birding anywhere in New Jersey that includes appropriate habitat.

Red-breasted Nuthatch Irregularly common migrant and winter resident, usually in coniferous woodlands or at suburban suet feeders. Rare summer resident of coniferous woods (usually Norway Spruce plantings) in the Pequannock Watershed, but has nested at Princeton and as far south as Dividing Creek. Can occur anywhere in the state, but most easily found at **Cape May in September–October.

White-breasted Nuthatch Fairly common permanent resident in deciduous woodlands, Pine Barrens, and suburbs; uncommon along the coast, including Camp May. Usually seen in a day's birding in appropriate habitat anywhere else in the state: ****Allaire, Assunpink, Glassboro Woods, Great Swamp, Lebanon, Parvin, Pequannock Watershed, Princeton, Stokes, Waterloo.

Brown Creeper Common migrant and uncommon winter resident in woodlands; uncommon summer resident in mature, deciduous woodlands and hardwood swamps, but most frequent in the north. Quiet and not easily found, but can often be detected by its high, thin call and song. April and October or in winter: ***Cape May, Jockey Hollow, Princeton, Sandy Hook, Stokes, Waterloo, and many other places; breeding birds occur in ***High Point, Pequannock Watershed, Wawayanda, Worthington, and **Great Swamp.

Carolina Wren Fairly common permanent resident of thickets, hedgerows, and shrubby deciduous woodlands in the southern two-thirds of the state; uncommon in the northern third. Easy to hear, somewhat more difficult to see, at ****Cape May; ***Assunpink, Bull's Island, Dividing Creek, Glassboro Woods, Parvin, Princeton, Rancocas, Sandy Hook, Trenton Marsh.

House Wren Common migrant and common summer resident of woodlands, thickets, shrubby fields, and suburbs. Present mid-April–early October; hard to miss in a day's birding anywhere in New Jersey.

Winter Wren Uncommon (and apparently declining) migrant (April and October–November) and winter resident in wet woodlands, shrubby fields, and hedgerows throughout the state. Rare and local summer resident in the mountains of northwestern New Jersey. In migration: **Cape May, Great Swamp, Jockey Hollow, Lincoln Park, Princeton, Sandy Hook, Scherman-Hoffman, Trenton Marsh. Breeding birds have been found at *Allamuchy Mountain, Jenny Jump, Pequannock Watershed.

Sedge Wren Rare migrant in wet meadows and marshes; formerly an uncommon breeding bird, but now nearly extirpated. Recent records are in October and November at *Brigantine, Cape May, Lincoln Park; in May at Dividing Creek; in summer at Manahawkin.

Marsh Wren Common summer resident of cattail, *Spartina*, and *Phragmites* marshes throughout the state; rare in winter. ****Troy Meadows; ***Allendale Celery Farm, Brigantine, Cape May, Great Swamp, Heislerville, Kearny Marsh, Princeton, Trenton Marsh.

Golden-crowned Kinglet Common migrant and fairly common

winter resident, especially in partially or wholly coniferous woodlands or plantings. Rare and local summer resident in Norway Spruce plantings in the northwest. Easily found in March–April and October–November anywhere in the state: ***Brigantine, Cape May, Dividing Creek, Great Swamp, Jockey Hollow, Princeton, Ringwood, Sandy Hook, Trenton Marsh. Recent breeding records are from **Pequannock Watershed; *Stokes, Worthington.

Ruby-crowned Kinglet   Common migrant and uncommon winter resident in woodlands and thickets. Less partial to conifers than is Golden-crowned Kinglet and less likely to be found in winter. Peak migration times are April and October, when it can be found anywhere in the state, especially along the coast in October.

Blue-gray Gnatcatcher   Common summer resident in deciduous woodlands throughout; very rare in winter.

Northern Wheatear   Rare visitor (about one per year) along the coast, almost exclusively in September–October and usually at Brigantine or Cape May.

Eastern Bluebird   Fairly common summer resident in widely scattered locations; uncommon in winter. Late March–October: ****Colliers Mills, Great Swamp; ***Cape May County Park, Stony Brook–Millstone Reserve; **Cape May, Dividing Creek, Lebanon, Worthington.

Veery   Common migrant and common summer resident in deciduous woodlands; very common summer resident in the north. May–early October at ****Great Swamp, High Point, Jockey Hollow, Pequannock Watershed, Stokes, Wawayanda; ***Cape May (in migration), many other places.

Gray-cheeked Thrush   Uncommon spring and fall migrant in deciduous woodlands. Mid-May, and mid-September–mid-October: **Cape May, Princeton, Princeton Avenue Woods, Sandy Hook; *Bull's Island, Great Swamp, Scherman-Hoffman, Stokes, Waterloo.

Swainson's Thrush   Common migrant in spring and fall in deciduous woodlands. May, and September–October: ***Bull's Island, Cape May, Great Swamp, Princeton, Sandy Hook, Scherman-Hoffman, Stokes, Trenton Marsh, Waterloo, many other places.

Hermit Thrush   Fairly common migrant and uncommon winter resident in thickets and woodlands; uncommon and local summer resident in the Pine Barrens, and in hemlock glens and on dry ridgetops in the northwest. Migrates earlier in spring (April) and later in fall (October–November) than Swainson's Thrush and is found at the same places, but is less common.

Wood Thrush Common summer resident in deciduous woodlands, easily located by its beautiful song. May–early October: ****Allaire, Dividing Creek, Glassboro Woods, Great Swamp, Jockey Hollow, Pequannock Watershed, Princeton, Stokes, Waterloo; ***Cape May, many other places.

American Robin Common migrant and summer resident in open woodlands, edges, and suburbs; fairly common winter resident, mainly along the coast and in southern New Jersey. A common and familiar bird, easily found at parks and on corporate and suburban lawns anywhere in the state.

Varied Thrush Rare, but annual, visitor from the west. Usually at feeders, but has also occurred in orchards. Records are from all parts of the state.

Gray Catbird Common summer resident of dense thickets in deciduous woodlands and suburbs; rare in winter. Late April–October, found in appropriate habitat anywhere in the state.

Northern Mockingbird Common permanent resident of shrubby fields, thickets, hedgerows, and suburbs. ***Brigantine, Cape May, Island Beach, Lord Stirling Park, Mercer County Park, Pedricktown, Sandy Hook, Stony Brook–Millstone Reserve, Troy Meadows, many other places.

Brown Thrasher Fairly common summer resident of shrubby fields, hedgerows, thickets, semirural, but especially the thick undergrowth in the Pine Barrens, of which it is one of the characteristic birds; rare in winter. April–October: ****Lebanon, Wharton, and many other places.

Water Pipit Fairly common migrant on plowed fields, wet meadows, sod farms, and ocean dunes; rare in winter. Look for it, or listen for its flight call, in October–November and April at **Alpha, Cape May, Hackensack Meadowlands, Holgate, Island Beach, Lincoln Park, Mercer Sod Farm, Pedricktown, Sandy Hook, and on plowed fields throughout the state.

Cedar Waxwing Common migrant at woodland edges, hedgerows, holly woods, and orchards; fairly common, but erratic, in winter. Uncommon and erratic summer resident in open, shrubby areas, especially in the northwest. Found at ****Cape May in fall, but otherwise unpredictable; may occur anywhere there are good berry crops: most **WMAs, Island Beach, Ringwood, Sandy Hook, many other places.

Northern Shrike Rare winter visitor; prefers shrubby fields and hedgerows. Numbers vary from one or two to several each winter. Has occurred at many locations throughout the state, but most often in Sussex County, especially Flatbrook-Roy WMA near Stokes State Forest.

Loggerhead Shrike Rare migrant and rare winter resident. March records are from numerous inland locations, August–September ones, mainly from Cape May. Has occurred at many places in winter, especially **Rosedale Park, where one is present December–March in most years.

European Starling Abundant permanent resident throughout the state in almost every habitat. Hard to miss in a day's birding anywhere in New Jersey.

White-eyed Vireo Fairly common summer resident in dense undergrowth, thickets, and shrubby fields through most of the state; uncommon in the higher elevations of the north and west. April–October: ****Assunpink, Brigantine, Cape May, Dividing Creek, Glassboro Woods, Great Swamp, Parvin, Sandy Hook; ***Bull's Island, Princeton, Rancocas.

Solitary Vireo Fairly common migrant in woodlands throughout the state; uncommon and local summer resident in hemlock glens in the northwest. April–early May and late September–October: ***Cape May, Princeton, Princeton Avenue Woods, Sandy Hook, Trenton Marsh, Waterloo; **Great Swamp, Jockey Hollow, Scherman-Hoffman. Breeding locations include *High Point, Pequannock Watershed, Stokes, Wawayanda.

Yellow-throated Vireo Common summer resident in tall deciduous trees, usually near water; absent from the Pine Barrens. May–September: ****Bull's Island, Great Swamp, Princeton, Whittingham; ***Allaire, Assunpink, High Point, Stokes, Troy Meadows, Waterloo; **Parvin; common migrant at Cape May in fall.

Warbling Vireo Fairly common summer resident in mature deciduous trees along lakes, rivers, and streams, mainly in the northern half of the state. May–September: ***Assunpink, Bull's Island, Princeton, Waterloo; **Great Swamp, Rancocas, Scherman-Hoffman, Troy Meadows.

Philadelphia Vireo Uncommon August–September migrant in

second-growth deciduous woodlands, most common along the coast. ***Cape May, Sandy Hook; **Eagle Rock, Lincoln Park, Princeton, Princeton Avenue Woods, Trenton Marsh, Waterloo, *Brigantine.

Red-eyed Vireo Common summer resident in woodlands throughout.

Blue-winged Warbler Fairly common summer resident in shrubby fields, woodland edges, and hedgerows. Early May–early September at many locations throughout the state: ****Assunpink, Cape May, Dividing Creek, Great Swamp, Stokes, Stony Brook–Millstone Reserve, Waterloo; ***Glassboro Woods, Lebanon, Parvin, Princeton.

Golden-winged Warbler Uncommon migrant; uncommon, local, and declining summer resident in shrubby fields in the northwest. Not often seen in migration, but best spots are *Princeton in May and Cape May in August–early September. Current breeding sites are at ***Shades of Death Rd. (Jenny Jump State Forest); **High Point, Pequannock Watershed, Stokes, Wawayanda; *Waterloo.

Tennessee Warbler Common migrant in tall deciduous trees. May and late August–September: ***Bull's Island, Cape May (mainly fall), High Point, Jockey Hollow, Princeton, Scherman-Hoffman, Stokes, Wawayanda, many other places.

Orange-crowned Warbler Rare fall migrant in thickets and shrubby fields, especially along the coast; rare in winter and very rare in spring. Late September–November: **Cape May, Sandy Hook; *Island Beach, Lincoln Park, Princeton Avenue Woods, and in appropriate habitat elsewhere.

Nashville Warbler Uncommon migrant in shrubby deciduous woodlands; rare and local summer resident in bogs or in scrubby, open woods in the northwest. May and September–early October: ***Cape May, Princeton, Sandy Hook, Trenton Marsh; **Bull's Island, Great Swamp, Scherman-Hoffman, Waterloo, and elsewhere. Recent nesting records are from **High Point; *Stokes, Worthington.

Northern Parula Common migrant in deciduous woodlands; uncommon, but increasing, summer resident in the Delaware Valley. May and late August–early October: ****Allaire, Bull's Island, Cape May, Princeton, Trenton Marsh, Waterloo, many other places. Recent nesting locations are **Bull's Island, Dividing Creek, Shades of Death Rd. (Jenny Jump State Forest), and Worthington.

Yellow Warbler Common summer resident in marshes, swamps,

and shrubby fields throughout the state. Early May–early September: ****Assunpink, Brigantine, Cape May, Great Swamp, Pedricktown, Princeton, Trenton Marsh, Troy Meadows, Whittingham, many other places.

Chestnut-sided Warbler Fairly common migrant in deciduous woodlands; fairly common summer resident in scrubby second-growth deciduous woodlands in the north. May and August–September: ***Allaire, Cape May, Princeton, Sandy Hook, Scherman-Hoffman, Trenton Marsh, Waterloo, many other places. In the breeding season: ****Black River, Pequannock Watershed, Wawayanda; ***High Point, Stokes, Worthington.

Magnolia Warbler Common migrant in woodlands; very rare and local summer resident in the northwest. May and late August–September: ****Cape May, Princeton, Sandy Hook; ***Trenton Marsh, and other spots for migrants.

Cape May Warbler Fairly common fall, uncommon spring migrant in deciduous and coniferous woodlands. September–mid-October: ***Cape May (of all places) and Sandy Hook. In May: ***Cape May, Princeton, Scherman-Hoffman, Trenton Marsh, Waterloo, and other spots for migrants.

Black-throated Blue Warbler Fairly common migrant in deciduous woodlands (prefers the understory); rare and local summer resident in the northwest in deciduous woods with dense Mountain Laurel understory. May and late August–early October: ***Cape May, Princeton, Sandy Hook, and other spots for migrants; in summer: **Pequannock Watershed; *Stokes, Wawayanda.

Yellow-rumped Warbler Abundant migrant in shrubby fields, woodlands, and coastal thickets; fairly common in winter, mainly along the coast; very rare summer resident in the northwest. April and October–November: anywhere in New Jersey, especially ****Brigantine, Cape May, Island Beach, and Sandy Hook.

Black-throated Green Warbler Common migrant in deciduous and coniferous woodlands; uncommon summer resident of hemlock glens in the northwest; local summer resident of cedar swamps in the Pine Barrens. May and late August–early October: ***Cape May, Princeton, Sandy Hook, and other spots for migrants; during the breeding season: ***Pequannock Watershed, Stokes, Wawayanda; **High Point; *Lebanon, Wharton.

Blackburnian Warbler Fairly common migrant in deciduous

woodlands; uncommon and local summer resident in hemlock glens in the northwest. May and late August–early October: ***Cape May, Princeton, Sandy Hook, and other spots for migrants; during the breeding season: **High Point, Pequannock Watershed, Stokes, and Wawayanda.

Yellow-throated Warbler   Uncommon and local summer resident of tall pines along the Delaware Bayshore (*dominica* subspecies) and sycamores along the upper Delaware River (*albilora* subspecies). Late April–August: ***Bull's Island, Dividing Creek; **Jake's Landing.

Pine Warbler   Fairly common migrant in mixed deciduous-coniferous woodlands; very common summer resident in the Pine Barrens; uncommon summer resident of pines in the northwest. Late March–October: ****Dividing Creek, Glassboro Woods, Lebanon, Wharton, Whitesbog; ***Brigantine, Cape May County Park, Parvin, Tuckahoe.

Prairie Warbler   Uncommon migrant in overgrown fields; fairly common summer resident in overgrown fields (especially those with Red Cedars) in the northwest and very common summer resident in the Pine Barrens. Regular in late April–early May and September at the usual migrant spots; during the breeding season: ****Glassboro Woods, Lebanon, Wharton, Whitesbog; ***Brigantine, Cape May, Dividing Creek, Tuckahoe.

Palm Warbler   Fairly common migrant in shrubby woodlands, overgrown fields, and ocean dunes; rare in winter along the coast. April and (especially) mid-September–October: ***Cape May, Great Swamp, Island Beach, Lincoln Park, Sandy Hook, Trenton Marsh, Troy Meadows, many other places.

Bay-breasted Warbler   Fairly common migrant in deciduous woodlands. May and September–early October: ***Cape May, Princeton, Sandy Hook, other spots for migrants.

Blackpoll Warbler   Common migrant in woodlands. Mid-May–early June and September–mid-October: ****Cape May, Princeton, Sandy Hook, other spots for migrants.

Cerulean Warbler   Uncommon summer resident of mature deciduous woodlands in the north. May–early September: ***Bull's Island, Jenny Jump, Waterloo; **Pequannock Watershed, Princeton (migrant), Scherman-Hoffman, Stokes, and Worthington; hard to find in fall migration.

Black-and-white Warbler   Common migrant and fairly common summer resident in deciduous and mixed woodlands. Late April–May and mid-August–early October: ****Cape May, Princeton, Sandy Hook, other spots for migrants; during the breeding season: ***Bull's Island, Dividing Creek, Great Swamp, Lebanon, Princeton, Rancocas, Stokes, many other places.

American Redstart Very common migrant and fairly common summer resident in deciduous woodlands. May, and late August–early October: ****Cape May, Princeton, Sandy Hook, other spots for migrants; during the breeding season: ****Bull's Island, High Point, Jockey Hollow, Lebanon, Princeton, Stokes, Wawayanda, many other places.

Prothonotary Warbler Uncommon summer resident at scattered locations; generally absent from the Pine Barrens. May–August: ****Parvin; ***Dividing Creek, Glassboro Woods, Moores Beach; **Bull's Island, Lord Stirling Park, Manahawkin, Princeton; *Whittingham.

Worm-eating Warbler Uncommon summer resident on dry, deciduous slopes in the north; occasionally in wet woodlands in Cumberland County. Uncommon migrant in May at **Princeton and other migrant spots, and in August–early September at **Cape May. During the breeding season: ***Jenny Jump, Worthington; **Pequannock Watershed, Scherman-Hoffman, Stokes, Waterloo.

Ovenbird Common summer resident of woodlands throughout the state; abundant in the northwest. Late April–early October: any woodland in the state.

Northern Waterthrush Fairly common migrant in wet woodlands and along streams; local, but fairly common, summer resident in the north. During migration: ***Cape May, Princeton, Sandy Hook, and other spots for migrants; during the breeding season: ***High Point, Pequannock Watershed, Stokes, Wawayanda. Fall migrants occur August–October.

Louisiana Waterthrush Fairly common summer resident along streams. Early April–August: ***Allaire, Bull's Island, Dividing Creek, High Point, Jockey Hollow, Parvin, Pequannock Watershed, Scherman-Hoffman, Stokes, Wawayanda, many other places. Early migrant in fall.

Kentucky Warbler Uncommon summer resident in the dense undergrowth of deciduous woodlands, mainly in the southern part of the state. May–early September: ***Glassboro Woods; **Dividing

Creek, Heislerville-Moores Beach, Parvin, Princeton; *Assunpink, Jockey Hollow, Scherman-Hoffman. Difficult to find in fall.

Connecticut Warbler Uncommon late August–early October migrant in hedgerows and shrubby woodland edges. **Cape May, Lincoln Park, Princeton, Princeton Avenue Woods, Sandy Hook; *Glassboro Woods.

Mourning Warbler Uncommon migrant in thickets, hedgerows, and shrubby woodland edges. Most often detected in late May–early June by its loud song, but is probably more common in August–mid-September. **Cape May (in fall), Eagle Rock, Lincoln Park, Princeton, Princeton Avenue Woods, Sandy Hook, Scherman-Hoffman.

Common Yellowthroat Common to abundant summer resident in marshes, swamps, brushy fields, and thickets; rare in winter along the coast. April–October: ****Assunpink, Brigantine, Cape May, Great Swamp, Kearny Marsh, Princeton, Stokes, Trenton Marsh, Troy Meadows, Whittingham, dozens of other places.

Hooded Warbler Locally fairly common summer resident of open deciduous woodlands, usually with Mountain Laurel understory; not often seen in migration. Can be quite common, May–mid-September, in its preferred habitat, though it is more often heard than seen. ****Glassboro Woods, Pequannock Watershed; ***Allaire, Dividing Creek, High Point, Parvin, Stokes, Wawayanda; **Assunpink, Black River, Jockey Hollow, Manahawkin.

Wilson's Warbler Uncommon migrant in thickets, hedgerows, and shrubby woodland edges; most common in fall. Mid-May–early June and mid-August–early October: **Black River, Cape May, Lincoln Park, Old Troy Park, Princeton, Princeton Avenue Woods, Sandy Hook, Scherman-Hoffman, Troy Meadows, many other spots.

Canada Warbler Fairly common migrant in deciduous woodlands and shrubby woodland edges; locally fairly common summer resident in the northwest, frequent in association with Hooded Warbler; rare summer resident in the Pine Barrens. Look for it at all the usual spots for migrants especially ***Cape May and Princeton, in May and mid-August–September; during the breeding season: ****Black River; ***High Point, Pequannock Watershed, Stokes, Wawayanda; *Wharton.

Yellow-breasted Chat Locally fairly common summer resident in overgrown fields, thickets, and hedgerows, mainly in the south;

rare in winter. May–September: ****Higbee Beach (Cape May); ***Dividing Creek, Moores Beach; **Mercer County Park, Sandy Hook, Stony Brook–Millstone Reserve; *Great Swamp, Rancocas, Troy Meadows.

Summer Tanager Uncommon and very local summer resident in oak-pine woods, mainly in the south; numbers appear to be slowly increasing. Rare migrant in spring north of breeding range. Late April–early October: **Dividing Creek, Lebanon; *Parvin.

Scarlet Tanager Common migrant and summer resident in deciduous woodlands and Pine Barrens. Found in appropriate habitat anywhere in New Jersey, May–early October.

Western Tanager Rare visitor from the west. Occurs annually in New Jersey, usually in fall or early winter, and often at feeders. Several records from *Cape May.

Northern Cardinal Common permanent resident in open woodlands, shrubby fields, thickets, and suburbs. Hard to miss in a day's birding anywhere in New Jersey that includes the appropriate habitat.

Rose-breasted Grosbeak Common migrant in deciduous woodlands; fairly common summer resident in the northern half of the state. May and late August–early October: ****Cape May, Princeton, Sandy Hook, and other spots for migrants; in summer, ***Bull's Island, High Point, Jockey Hollow, Pequannock Watershed, Stokes, Wawayanda, many other places.

Black-headed Grosbeak Rare visitor from the west in September–November, occasionally at feeders in winter.

Blue Grosbeak Uncommon, but increasing, summer resident of hedgerows, shrubby fields, and farm roads from the vicinity of the Raritan River south. Late April–early October: ***Assunpink, Higbee Beach (Camp May); **Dividing Creek, Mercer County Park, Moores Beach, Rancocas. One or two pairs have nested at the **Hackensack Meadowlands for more than 10 years.

Indigo Bunting Common summer resident in hedgerows, overgrown fields, and woodland edges. May–October: ***Assunpink, Black River, Bull's Island, Cape May, Dividing Creek, Mercer County Park, Rancocas, Stokes, Troy Meadows, Whittingham, many other places.

Dickcissel Rare migrant along the coast in fall, and rare winter visitor at feeders. Very rare and local summer resident (not occurring every year) in farm fields. Reliably found only at **Cape May in September–November, rarely at *Island Beach and Sandy Hook. Listen for its distinctive flight call overhead.

Rufous-sided Towhee   Common summer resident in thickets, shrubby woodland edges, and pine-oak woodlands; rare in winter. One of the commonest birds of the Pine Barrens. April–October: ****Assunpink, Cape May, Dividing Creek, Glassboro Woods, Great Swamp, Lebanon, Lincoln Park, Rancocas, Troy Meadows, Wharton, many other places.

American Tree Sparrow   Fairly common winter resident in fields, thickets, and brushy woodland edges, decreasing in abundance from north to south. Late October–early April: ****Great Swamp, Hackensack Meadowlands, Lincoln Park, Mercer County Park, Sandy Hook, Stony Brook–Millstone Reserve, Troy Meadows, Waterloo; ***Assunpink, many other places.

Chipping Sparrow   Common summer resident of lawns, fields, woodland edges, and even dense coniferous woodlands; rare in winter in the south. April–October: ****Brigantine, Bull's Island; ***Assunpink, Cape May, Dividing Creek, Eagle Rock, Princeton, Sandy Hook, Stokes, Wawayanda, and many other places.

Clay-colored Sparrow   Rare visitor from the west, mainly along the coast, and almost exclusively in fall. Late September–early November: *Cape May, Island Beach, Sandy Hook, Lincoln Park.

Field Sparrow   Fairly common migrant and summer resident in shrubby fields and hedgerows; uncommon in winter. At any season, but especially April–October; ***Assunpink, Cape May, Glassboro Woods, Great Swamp, Lincoln Park, Mercer County Park, Sandy Hook, Stony Brook–Millstone Reserve, Troy Meadows, Waterloo, Whittingham, many other places.

Vesper Sparrow   Uncommon migrant, especially in fall; uncommon and local summer resident of farmlands in north-central New Jersey; rare winter resident in the south. **Alpha; *Cape May (fall), Island Beach, Lincoln Park, Mercer County Park, Sandy Hook (fall).

Lark Sparrow   Rare visitor from the west, mostly in fall, and mainly along the coast. Late August–November: *Brigantine, Cape May, Island Beach, Sandy Hook.

Savannah Sparrow   Common migrant and uncommon winter resident in fields, marshes, and dunes, especially near the coast. Uncommon and very local summer resident of farmlands at widely scattered locations. September–April: ****Brigantine, Cape May, Holgate, Island Beach, Sandy Hook, Stone Harbor, Tuckerton, Hackensack Meadowlands, Mercer County Park, Troy Meadows. Some current nesting locations are **Alpha, Beekman Lane, and Featherbed Lane (Salem County). The "Ipswich" subspecies winters in small numbers in dunes along the coast.

Grasshopper Sparrow   Uncommon summer resident in weedy fields and grassy meadows at scattered locations. Some current breeding sites are ***Assunpink; **Alpha, Beekman Lane, Featherbed Lane (Salem County), Mercer County Park; *Brigantine. Rare in migration.

Henslow's Sparrow   Very rare migrant in weedy fields; formerly nested at the edges of salt marsh along the coast and in weedy fields in the interior. Recent records are from Cape May, Lincoln Park, Mercer County Park, and Stony Brook–Millstone Reserve (the latest site of attempted nesting).

Sharp-tailed Sparrow   Fairly common summer resident in salt marsh; rare in winter. Most easily seen by walking through marshgrass or "pishing" at ***Brigantine, Conaskonk Point, Holgate, Manahawkin, Stone Harbor, Tuckerton.

Seaside Sparrow   Common summer resident of salt marsh; uncommon in winter. Generally in the same places as Sharp-tailed Sparrow, but often perches in small shrubs along the edges of the marsh. ****Holgate; ***Brigantine, Dividing Creek, Manahawkin, Stone Harbor, Tuckerton.

Fox Sparrow   Fairly common migrant and uncommon winter resident in thickets, shrubby fields, and wet woodlands. Late October–November and March–mid-April: ***Cape May, Great Swamp, Hackensack Meadowlands, Lincoln Park, Princeton, Sandy Hook, Scherman-Hoffman, Troy Meadows, Whittingham, many other places.

Song Sparrow   Common permanent resident in fields, thickets, marshes, swamps, suburbs, and woodland edges; very common in migration and in winter. One of the most widely distributed birds in the state, and hard to miss in appropriate habitat.

Lincoln's Sparrow   Uncommon migrant in shrubby fields, thickets, and woodland edges; most often seen in fall. May, and mid-September–October: **Cape May, Great Swamp, Hackensack Meadowlands, Island Beach, Lincoln Park, Mercer County Park, Princeton, Sandy Hook, Troy Meadows, Tuckerton.

Swamp Sparrow Common migrant and uncommon winter resident in shrubby fields, marshes, swamps, and wet woodlands; fairly common summer resident in marshes. ***Cape May, Great Swamp, Hackensack Meadowlands, Kearny Marsh, Lincoln Park, Princeton, Trenton Marsh, Troy Meadows, Whittingham; **Brigantine, Moores Beach, and Sandy Hook.

White-throated Sparrow Common winter resident of shrubby fields, thickets, woodlands, and suburbs; very rare breeder in the northwest. October–April: almost anywhere in the state.

White-crowned Sparrow Uncommon migrant and uncommon winter resident in shrubby fields, thickets, hedgerows, and coastal dunes. Most common in October and April–mid-May: **Alpha, Cape May, Hackensack Meadowlands, Island Beach, Liberty State Park, Lincoln Park, Mercer County Park, Sandy Hook, Troy Meadows, rural Gloucester and Salem counties.

Dark-eyed Junco Common winter resident in shrubby fields, woodlands, and suburbs; very rare and local breeder in the northwest. Hard to miss in a day's birding October–April anywhere in New Jersey. Search for it in summer along the Kittatinny Ridge.

Lapland Longspur Uncommon and irregular winter resident on plowed fields and coastal dunes, usually in the company of Horned Larks or Snow Buntings. November–March: *Alpha, Barnegat Light, Cape May, Holgate, Island Beach, Sandy Hook, Liberty State Park.

Snow Bunting Fairly common winter resident on plowed fields and, especially, on beaches and dunes; usually in flocks. November–March (sometimes April) at ***Brigantine Island, Holgate, Island Beach, Sandy Hook; **Alpha, Barnegat Light, Cape May, Caven Pier (see Liberty State Park), Round Valley, Wildwood Crest.

Bobolink Common migrant in fields, marshes, and woodland edges; uncommon summer resident of fields and farmlands, mainly in the west-central part of the state. Widespread in May, hard to miss in mid-July–October, especially along the coast. In fall: ****Cape May; ***Brigantine, Hackensack Meadowlands, Island Beach, Lincoln Park, Sandy Hook, and elsewhere; in spring and early summer: ***Alpha, Beekman Lane, Featherbed Lane (Salem County), Stony Brook–Millstone Reserve; **Assunpink, Great Swamp, Mercer County Park.

Red-winged Blackbird Common migrant and summer resident in marshes, swamps, wet meadows, and farmlands; fairly common in winter. Hard to miss, in appropriate habitat, anywhere in New Jersey.

Eastern Meadowlark   Fairly common, but declining, summer resident of grassy fields and meadows in rural areas; uncommon in winter. March–October: ***Alpha, Assunpink, Beekman Lane, Great Swamp, Mercer County Park, Rancocas, Salem County, Stony Brook–Millstone Reserve, Whittingham; and **Brigantine.

Yellow-headed Blackbird   Rare, but annual, visitor from the west; usually in marshes or fields with flocks of other blackbirds. Has occurred in every month, but most often August–December. *Brigantine, Cape May, Kearny Marsh, Troy Meadows, and wherever blackbirds gather.

Rusty Blackbird   Fairly common migrant and uncommon winter resident in wet woodlands and swamps. Late October–November and April: ***Allaire, Great Swamp, Princeton, Scherman-Hoffman, Troy Meadows, Whittingham; **Assunpink, and Cape May.

Boat-tailed Grackle   Locally fairly common, and increasing, permanent resident of southern salt marshes. Present range extends from Cape May to Sandy Hook and up the Delaware Bayshore to Salem County. ***Barnegat Light, Brigantine Island, Corson's Inlet, Holgate, Longport, Stone Harbor; **Cape May, Island Beach, Mad Horse Creek (Salem County).

Common Grackle   Common to abundant migrant and summer resident in farmlands, deciduous woodlands, swamps, and suburbs throughout; fairly common in winter, especially in the south. Often occurs in flocks numbering in the tens of thousands from late fall to early spring. Hard to miss, March–November, in a day's birding anywhere in New Jersey; December–February, more common in the south.

Brown-headed Cowbird   Common migrant and uncommon winter resident in pastures, farmland, and suburbs; more common in the south in winter. Fairly common summer resident in open deciduous woodlands and suburbs. Often occurs in large flocks with other blackbirds from fall to spring, frequenting pastures or feedlots.

Orchard Oriole   Fairly common summer resident along the wooded edges of fields, farmland, or streams; widely, but irregularly, distributed. Scarce in the northeast. May–July (it is one of the earliest fall migrants): ***Assunpink, Dividing Creek, Moores Beach; **Bull's Island, Mercer County Park, Princeton.

Northern Oriole   Common migrant throughout the state; common summer resident in open deciduous woodlands, woodland edges, and suburbs in the north; rare in winter at feeders. May, and August–September: ****Cape May (fall), Princeton, Sandy Hook, and other spots for migrants; in summer, ***Bull's Island, Eagle Rock, Great Swamp, High Point, Jockey Hollow, Stokes, Wawayanda, many other places.

Pine Grosbeak   Very uncommon and irregular winter visitor to the northern part of the state; numbers vary widely. Prefers coniferous woods, but is also found in deciduous woods and along freshly salted roads. *High Point, Pequannock Watershed, Ringwood, Stokes, Wawayanda, and Worthington.

Purple Finch   Common migrant and irregularly fairly common winter resident in orchards, woodland edges, and suburbs; uncommon and local summer resident in mixed woodlands and conifer plantings in the northwest. April–May or September–November: ***Cape May, Princeton, Sandy Hook, or other spots for migrants; regular winter visitor to feeders; in summer: **Pequannock Watershed, Wawayanda; *High Point, Stokes, Worthington.

House Finch   Common permanent resident in shrubby woodland edges, coastal dunes and woodlands, and suburbs. ****Barnegat Light, Cape May, Island Beach, Sandy Hook, Stone Harbor, and at fields and feeders anywhere in New Jersey.

Red Crossbill   Irregularly fairly common winter visitor in conifers throughout the state, but absent most years; more frequent in the north. November–March in flight years: *Barnegat Light, Cape May, High Point, Pequannock Watershed, Ringwood, Sandy Hook, Stokes, Wawayanda, Worthington, and anywhere in the Pine Barrens, where there are old nesting records.

White-winged Crossbill   Irregular and uncommon winter visitor in hemlock glens and spruce plantings, mainly in the north. In flight years: *High Point, Pequannock Watershed, Ringwood, Stokes, Wawayanda, and Worthington.

Common Redpoll   Irregularly fairly common winter visitor at overgrown fields (especially those with birches), hedgerows, and suburban feeders, mainly in the north. Numbers fluctuate widely.

Pine Siskin   Irregularly common migrant and winter resident in coniferous and swampy (with Sweet Gums) woodlands, and at suburban feeders; more common in the north. Numbers fluctuate widely. Has nested. In most winters: ** High Point, Pequannock Watershed, Wawayanda, and conifer plantings and feeders in many places.

American Goldfinch Common permanent resident in weedy fields and hedgerows; visit feeders in winter. During most of the year in appropriate habitat: ****Assunpink, Cape May, Great Swamp, Hackensack Meadowlands, Lincoln Park, Mercer County Park, Sandy Hook, Troy Meadows, Waterloo, many other places.

Evening Grosbeak Fairly common migrant, especially along the mountain ridges, and irregularly fairly common winter visitor at feeders and in deciduous woodlands; most common in the north. In fall: ***Raccoon Ridge and Sunrise Mountain; in flight years in winter: **High Point, Pequannock Watershed, Stokes, Wawayanda, Worthington, and feeders and woodlots throughout New Jersey.

House Sparrow Common permanent resident in cities, suburbs, and farmlands throughout the state. Hard to miss in a day's birding in appropriate habitat anywhere in New Jersey.

Vagrants

The following list is of extreme rarities that have been seen from one to a few times in New Jersey during the past 25 years. A number of other species have been reported, but these sightings lack sufficient documentation for inclusion here.

Pacific Loon	Cinnamon Teal
Western Grebe	Tufted Duck
Buller's Shearwater	Barrow's Goldeneye
Black-capped Petrel	Eurasian Kestrel
White-faced Storm-Petrel	Yellow Rail
White-tailed Tropicbird	Wilson's Plover
Red-billed Tropicbird	Spotted Redshank
Brown Booby	Black-tailed Godwit
Anhinga	Bar-tailed Godwit
Magnificent Frigatebird	Little Stint
White-faced Ibis	Franklin's Gull
Wood Stork	Thayer's Gull
Ross' Goose	Sabine's Gull

Bridled Tern
Sooty Tern
Brown Noddy
Common Murre
Black Guillemot
Band-tailed Pigeon
White-winged Dove
Common Ground-Dove
Boreal Owl
Black-backed Woodpecker
Say's Phoebe
Ash-throated Flycatcher
Great Kiskadee
Fork-tailed Flycatcher
Bewick's Wren
Mountain Bluebird
Townsend's Solitaire
Bohemian Waxwing

Bell's Vireo
Virginia's Warbler
Black-throated Gray Warbler
Townsend's Warbler
Swainson's Warbler
Painted Bunting
Green-tailed Towhee
Cassin's Sparrow
Black-throated Sparrow
Lark Bunting
Le Conte's Sparrow
Golden-crowned Sparrow
Harris' Sparrow
Chestnut-collared Longspur
Western Meadowlark
Brewer's Blackbird
Brambling
Hoary Redpoll

Additions to the above list since 1985 are:

Barnacle Goose
Mongolian Plover
Ivory Gull
Large-billed Tern
White-winged Tern

Index

Bold type indicates a chapter, subheading or separate entry.

504 · Index